LAND AND BOOK:
LITERATURE AND LAND TENURE
IN ANGLO-SAXON ENGLAND

SCOTT THOMPSON SMITH

Land and Book:

Literature and Land Tenure in Anglo-Saxon England

UNIVERSITY OF TORONTO PRESS
Toronto Buffalo London

© University of Toronto Press 2012
Toronto Buffalo London
www.utppublishing.com
Printed in Canada

ISBN 978-1-4426-4486-1

Printed on acid-free, 100% post-consumer recycled paper with vegetable-based inks.

Library and Archives Canada Cataloguing in Publication

Smith, Scott Thompson
Land and book: literature and land tenure in Anglo-Saxon England /
Scott Thompson Smith.

(Toronto Anglo-Saxon series)
Includes bibliographical references and index.
ISBN 978-1-4426-4486-1

1. Land tenure in literature. 2. Land tenure – England – History – To 1500.
3. Land tenure – Law and legislation – England – History. 4. English literature
– Old English, ca. 450-1100 – History and criticism. 5. Latin literature, Medieval
and modern – England – History and criticism. I. Title. II. Series: Toronto
Anglo-Saxon series.

PR179.L35S65 2012   829'093553   C2012-903934-9

University of Toronto Press gratefully acknowledges the financial assistance of the
Centre for Medieval Studies, University of Toronto, in the publication of this book.

University of Toronto Press acknowledges the financial assistance to its publishing program of the Canada Council for the Arts and the Ontario Arts Council.

University of Toronto Press acknowledges the financial support of the Government
of Canada through the Canada Book Fund for its publishing activities.

To Dad, in loving memory

Contents

Acknowledgments

Many individuals have kindly lent their support toward the completion of this book. I am grateful for all the invaluable guidance and assistance which I have received over the years from so many mentors, colleagues, friends, and family. Any mistakes or missteps which remain are entirely my own.

This project began at the University of Notre Dame, an excellent place (with an amazing library) for work in medieval studies. I am deeply indebted to Michael Lapidge and Katherine O'Brien O'Keeffe for their expert guidance and steady encouragement both then and now – they have set a professional standard to which I will always aspire and for which I will always be grateful. I am truly fortunate to have had such mentors. Thanks are also due to Thomas Hall, Maura Nolan, Thomas F.X. Noble, and Drew Jones for their assistance early in the project. I am grateful as well for the camaraderie of a number of colleagues at Notre Dame, namely Matt Brown, Julie Bruneau, Rebecca Davis, Shannon Gayk, Misty Schieberle, Paul Patterson, Jonathan Davis-Secord, Jacqueline Stodnick, Kathleen Tonry, Renée Trilling, Miranda Wilcox, and Corey Zwikstra.

I am also thankful for the support I have received from my colleagues at the Pennsylvania State University. Robin Schulze and Mark Morrisson provided steady encouragement as my department chairs, while medievalist colleagues Robert Edwards, Caroline Eckhardt, and Benjamin Hudson have been ready supporters and advisors. I am also thankful to Richard Page for his guidance as my faculty mentor. These several individuals, and a great many others like them, have made Penn State a wonderful place to begin my career. I should also express my appreciation to the College of the Liberal Arts for granting me a one-semester teaching release which allowed the time and focus to complete the manuscript.

Many colleagues, both at Penn State and elsewhere, have read and commented upon parts of this book at various stages: Julianne Bruneau, Jonathan Eburne, Robert Edwards, Charlotte Eubanks, Shannon Gayk, Debra Hawhee, Thomas Hall, Kit Hume, Drew Jones, Michael Lapidge, Garrett Sullivan, Renée Trilling, and Michael Van Dussen. I am grateful to all these readers for their many productive suggestions and questions. In addition, Rosamond Faith, Susan Kelly, and Simon Keynes graciously responded to various research queries, while Nicholas Brooks, Stephanie Clark, Susan Kelly, David Pelteret, and Samantha Zacher kindly shared forthcoming work. Drew Jones, Michael Lapidge, and Stephen Wheeler also offered their expertise on matters of Latin translation at various stages. The final product has greatly benefited from the generous contributions of all these scholars.

At the University of Toronto Press, I wish to thank editors Suzanne Rancourt and Barbara Porter for their help in guiding this book toward publication. I am also grateful to the anonymous readers for their many insightful comments and valuable suggestions, all of which have benefited this book a great deal. Finally, Katherine MacIvor has provided welcome assistance in copyediting and formatting the book for publication. UTP has proven a model of professionalism and efficiency throughout the review and production process and I feel fortunate indeed to have them as a publisher for this book.

I am also grateful to my family for the many ways in which they have given moral support over the years. My parents and siblings especially have always welcomed and encouraged my interests, no matter how idiosyncratic they might have seemed. Finally, I owe a very special thanks to my wife Emily and our young sons Wren and Erik for their steadfast love and patience. The three of you have inspired and fortified me throughout the long process of writing this book in immeasurable ways.

Part of chapter 4 appeared in an earlier form as 'Marking Boundaries: Charters and the Anglo-Saxon Chronicle' in *Reading the Anglo-Saxon Chronicle: Language, Literature, History*, published by Brepols in 2010. It appears here with the permission of Brepols Publishers.

Abbreviations

ANS	*Anglo-Norman Studies*
ASE	*Anglo-Saxon England*
ASPR	Anglo-Saxon Poetic Records
BCS	Birch, *Cartularium Saxonicum*
BL	British Library
BT	Bosworth and Toller, *An Anglo-Saxon Dictionary*
BTa	Campbell, *An Anglo-Saxon Dictionary, Enlarged Addenda and Corrigenda*
BTs	Toller, *An Anglo-Saxon Dictionary, Supplement*
CCSL	Corpus Christianorum, Series Latina
CSASE	Cambridge Studies in Anglo-Saxon England
DMLBS	*Dictionary of Medieval Latin from British Sources*
DOE	*Dictionary of Old English*
EETS	Early English Text Society
EHD I	Whitelock, *English Historical Documents*
EHD II	Douglas and Greenaway, *English Historical Documents*
EHR	*English Historical Review*
Gneuss	Gneuss, *Handlist of Anglo-Saxon Manuscripts*
JEGP	*Journal of English and Germanic Philology*
JMH	*Journal of Medieval History*
MÆ	*Medium Ævum*
MGH	Monumenta Germaniae Historica
MP	*Modern Philology*
MS	manuscript
MS	*Mediaeval Studies*
N&Q	*Notes and Queries*
OE	Old English

OMT	Oxford Medieval Texts
PASE	Prosopography of Anglo-Saxon England
PBA	*Proceedings of the British Academy*
PL	Patrologia Latina
RES	*Review of English Studies*
S	Sawyer, *Anglo-Saxon Charters*
s.a.	*sub anno*, under the year
SEHD	*Select English Historical Documents*
TRHS	*Transactions of the Royal Historical Society*

LAND AND BOOK:
LITERATURE AND LAND TENURE
IN ANGLO-SAXON ENGLAND

Introduction: The Terms of Possession

The barbarian, for all his materialism, is an idealist. He is, like the child, a master in the art of make-believe. He sees things not as they are, but as they might conveniently be. Every householder has a hide; every hide has 120 acres of arable; every hide is worth one pound a year; every householder has a team; every team is of eight oxen; every team is worth one pound. If all this be not so, then it ought to be so and must be deemed to be so. Then by a Procrustean process he packs the complex and irregular facts into his scheme.

– Frederic W. Maitland, *Domesday Book and Beyond*

In effect, English law invented an entire intellectual apparatus of artificial constructs in order to explain various forms of entitlement to land.

– Kevin Gray and Susan Francis Gray, *Elements of Land Law*

In *The Old English Boethius*, the speaker Mind (*mod*) at one point offers a brief meditation, absent in the source text, on those necessary tools and resources which a king requires to wield and maintain political power (*anweald*) effectively:

Þæt bið þonne cyninges andweorc and his tol mid to ricsianne þæt he hæbbe his land fulmannod. He sceal habban gebedmen and fyrdmen and weorcmen. Hwæt þu wast þætte butan þisum tolum nan cyning his cræft ne mæg cyðan. Þæt is eac his andweorc þæt he habban sceal to þam tolum þam þrim geferscipum biwiste. Þæt is þonne heora biwist: land to bugianne and gifta and wæpnu and mete and ealo and claþas, and gehwæt þæs ðe þa þre geferscipas behofiað. Ne mæg he butan þisum þas tol gehealdan, ne buton þisum tolum nan þara þinga wyrcan þe him beboden is to wyrcenne.[1]

[This then will be the king's materials and tools with which to rule so that he may have his land fully manned. He must have praying men, soldiering men, and working men. You know that without these tools no king may show his ability. This is also his material that he must have as provision for his tools, the three classes of men. This, then, is their provision: land to live on, gifts, weapons, food, ale, clothing, and anything else the three orders require. Without these things he cannot maintain the tools, and without the tools he cannot achieve any of the things which he needs to achieve.]

This passage is perhaps best known as an early reference to the social theory of the three estates,[2] but it also notably designates land as the first provision (*biwist*) necessary for the support of those three groups. In this schematic of power and administration, land stands as the originary and essential base from which all else proceeds, be it food, raw materials, or men. The author of this observation, long thought to be King Alfred, seems to have spoken from experience.[3] Land was indeed a vital component of political power and administration in Anglo-Saxon England, the sine qua non resource for all levels of society. Assessment of land by hides, for example, broadly determined taxation, military service, fortification work, and other obligations and services due to the king.[4] Additionally, the division of the kingdom into territorial units known as hundreds provided a basis for the administration of local courts and the maintenance of public order.[5] Political power

---

1 Godden and Irvine, *The Old English Boethius*, 1:277. Unless otherwise noted, all translations are my own.
2 See Powell, 'The "Three Orders" of Society in Anglo-Saxon England.'
3 Malcolm Godden has recently reopened debate over Alfred's authorship of the several vernacular translations traditionally attributed to him ('Did King Alfred Write Anything?'). See also Godden, 'Alfredian Project and its Aftermath.' While this is not the occasion to engage this issue, it should be noted that the above observation about the first place of land among the necessary provisions of governance does not stand or fall upon Alfred's authorship. For an overview of the authorial issue as it is treated in the most recent edition of *The Old English Boethius*, see Jones, review of *The Old English Boethius* by Godden and Irvine.
4 See Maitland, *Domesday Book and Beyond*, 357–520; Abels, 'Bookland and Fyrd Service in Late Saxon England'; Loyn, *Governance of Anglo-Saxon England*; Campbell, 'Some Agents and Agencies of the Late Anglo-Saxon State'; and Faith, *English Peasantry*, 89–152.
5 See Loyn, 'The Hundred in England'; Barlow, *Feudal Kingdom of England*, 33–43; and Reynolds, *Later Anglo-Saxon England*, 75–81.

in Anglo-Saxon England functioned through the control of land and through the matrix of social relationships and obligations which were formed and maintained through its distribution and management.

At the local level, land provided its holders with wealth and status. Two late legal texts suggest that the possession of land (rather than wealth or blood) even determined social class: if a *ceorl* possessed at least five hides of land, he could enjoy the rights of a thegn.[6] If he did not meet that requirement, however, he was a *ceorl*, regardless of any goods or distinction he might otherwise possess: 'And þeah he geþeo, þæt he hæbbe helm ꝺ byrnan ꝺ golde fæted sweord, gif he þæt land nafað, he byð ceorl swa þeah'[7] (And though he may prosper so that he possesses a helm and a mail-coat and a gold-plated sword, if he doesn't have the land, he is still a *ceorl*). This 'five-hide rule' has been read as a nostalgic 'lament for the fact that the thegnage was becoming more of a closed and landed elite, less of a ministerial class, and that upward mobility by means of service was no longer possible.'[8] By the end of the Anglo-Saxon period, the finite resource of land had apparently become the crucial factor in achieving social distinction and prosperity.[9] At the same time, early law-codes indicate that the association between land and status was already in place long before the end of the tenth century. Ine's laws, for example, contain early evidence of land-based status in several provisions regarding both noblemen (*gesiðcund*) and Welshmen (*wealh*).[10] A Welshman who possesses five hides commands a wergild of 600 shillings, for

---

6 *Geþyncðo* 1–2; *Norðleoda laga* 9–12. See Liebermann, *Gesetze*, 1:456–61; *EHD* I, 468–70; and Wormald, *Making of English Law*, 391–4. The term *ceorl* indicates a broad category of men below the status of thegn who are 'best described as non-noble free men, who might, by the favour of their lords, advance their fortunes and acquire thegnly status' (Williams, 'Bell-house and a Burh-geat,' 226).

7 Liebermann, Gesetze, 1:460 (*Norðleoda laga*, ch. 10).

8 Faith, *English Peasantry*, 127. See also Whitelock, *Beginnings of English Society*, 85–6. Some scholars have questioned the accuracy of these provisions in describing the realities of social status. Richard Abels, for example, has suggested that the term thegn in the provisions may indicate a position of royal service rather than a noble rank (*Lordship and Military Obligation*, 141–2). Still, the designation of landholding as a requisite for thegnly status in both texts demonstrates a clear ideological association between property and status.

9 See Chadwick, *Studies on Anglo-Saxon Institutions*, 87–102; Loyn, 'Gesiths and Thegns in Anglo-Saxon England'; Charles-Edwards, 'Kinship, Status and the Origins of the Hide'; and Faith, *English Peasantry*, 155–9. Some freemen claimed thegnly status on the basis of holdings much smaller than five hides. See Stafford, *East Midlands in the Early Middle Ages*, 156–7.

10 See Ine 24.2, 32, 45, and 51.

example, while one who owns a single hide commands only 120 shillings.[11] In Anglo-Saxon England, land determined one's value in both life and death.

Beyond its material and practical worth, land also assumed a powerful emotive and conceptual value as property. Patrick Geary has argued, for example, that property functioned in early medieval Europe as a 'symbolic language through which people discussed, negotiated, affirmed, and delimited the boundaries of family.'[12] In this sense, land-as-property provided not only a material source of wealth and status, but also a means for articulating and maintaining identity over time. As property, land uniquely carries a complex set of associative meanings, obligations, and attachments that transcend the mere provision of material asset. According to one recent assessment, 'The law of property incorporates a series of critical value judgements, reflecting the cultural norms, the social ethics and the political economy prevalent in any given community. It is inevitable that property law should serve in this way as a vehicle for ideology, for "property" has commonly been the epithet used to identify that which people most greatly value.'[13] In this view, property constitutes a conceptual locus around which clusters an array of cultural mores, ideals, and anxieties. The written precepts and social practices of land tenure in this way form a discourse, an ideological field which encompasses a range of normative meanings and procedures as well as potentially troubling elements of disruption and contradiction.

Tenurial discourse offered the Anglo-Saxons a diffuse and flexible field for engaging key cultural issues such as political dominion, salvation, sanctity, status, and obligations both social and spiritual. I adopt the term tenurial discourse to signify broadly the vocabulary, tropes, and practices which constitute the cultural field of landholding in Anglo-Saxon England; this discourse includes both the procedural language (legal and tenurial terminology) and social practices (the demonstration and protection of possession, the problems of dispute and forfeiture, and so on) of property. This book considers different modes of writing in both Old English and Latin which engage, appropriate, or represent tenurial discourse and issues creatively across genres – that is, it is primarily interested in the resonance and referential power of a shared discourse. The language and tropes of property inform a wide range of textual genres and functions in Anglo-Saxon England, including the legal (charters), the literary (Old English poetry), the ecclesiastical (hagiography, homilies), and the historical (the

---

11 Ine 24.2 and 32 (Liebermann, *Gesetze*, 1:100 and 102).
12 Geary, 'Land, Language and Memory,' 171.
13 Gray and Francis Gray, *Elements of Land Law*, 88.

Anglo-Saxon Chronicle). While such disciplinary and generic categories can obscure the broad commitment to property issues in Anglo-Saxon texts, this book demonstrates that tenurial writing could be many things at once: legal, literary, ecclesiastical, historical, practical, and imaginative. It should be said that this book does not claim to be a comprehensive study of land tenure or a full survey of the written instruments for conveying land in Anglo-Saxon England; it instead considers how the apparatus of land tenure yielded a discursive field which fostered textual innovation and rhetorical display across a wide range of texts and genres in both Latin and Old English.[14] Consequently, this study is driven by a fusion of literary, historical, and legal interests. Tenurial discourse provided a ready medium for religious and intellectual reflection, for exhortation, for literary performance, and for endorsement and documentation. In other words, land tenure constituted not only a procedural system, but also a literary and philosophical mode.

The Anglo-Saxons used a number of written instruments in both Latin and English for recording the possession, use, and transmission of property.[15] The Anglo-Saxons clearly recognized the enduring value of the written word in recording and protecting landed interests over time, and they were eager to develop and exploit the use of documents toward that end. Most of our knowledge about the actual practices of land tenure in Anglo-Saxon England has come from the descriptive evidence of charters, a broad class of documents which includes royal diplomas, leases, wills, writs, dispute narratives, estate memoranda, and other records.[16] At the

14 The book favours those legal texts – the Latin diploma and the vernacular dispute narrative – which have received limited attention in literary studies. Consequently, it minimizes the discussion of vernacular law-codes and wills since these texts have received more extensive discussion elsewhere.

15 For Anglo-Saxon land tenure in general, see Stenton, *Anglo-Saxon England*, 301–18; John, *Land Tenure in Early England*; Wormald, 'Bede and the Conversion of England'; Williams, 'How Land was Held Before and After the Norman Conquest'; Reynolds, *Fiefs and Vassals*, 323–42; Williams, 'Land Tenure'; Blair, *Church in Anglo-Saxon Society*, 84–108, 251–61, and 397–401; Oosthuizen, 'Sokemen and Freemen'; Baxter, *Earls of Mercia*, 125–51; and Tinti, *Sustaining Belief*, 75–224.

16 Alistair Campbell commented that, 'The word "charter" (German *Urkunde*) is one used recklessly in Old English studies to describe documents of the most varied nature: royal grants, private agreements, wills, records of proceedings of councils, &c' (*Old English Grammar*, 5–6). For charters in general, see Stenton, *Latin Charters*, 31–65; John, *Land Tenure in Early England*, 1–63; Wormald, 'Bede and the Conversion of England'; Keynes, *Diplomas*; Kelly, 'Anglo-Saxon Lay Society,' 39–51; Keynes, 'Royal Government and the Written Word,' 244–57; and Keynes, 'Anglo-Saxon Charters: Lost

same time, the landholding and inheritance practices of the peasantry, the non-aristocratic majority of Anglo-Saxon society, have left meagre trace in the written record. As Dorothy Whitelock has reminded us, 'A great amount of customary law, such, for example, as that relating to inheritance and other family matters, was probably never put into writing at all, being too well known and too fixed to require written statement.'[17] While the extant documentary evidence accordingly offers only a partial view, this book attends specifically to how land becomes property through the operations of written discourse. Land in writing becomes not only an object of proprietary interests, but a cultural idea which bears an array of associations and values both practical and theoretical.

Within the Old English vocabulary of property, three terms have received sustained attention in modern scholarship: *bocland*, *folcland*, and *lænland*. These three categories of landholding are not comprehensive,[18] but they do represent common modes of tenure in Anglo-Saxon England and thus they merit some preliminary discussion. King Edward the Elder's (r. 899–924) first law-code divides property into two general categories when it assigns penalties for anyone who interferes with someone's rights 'oððe on boclande oððe on folclande'[19] (either in bookland or folkland). Stephen Baxter has summarized these two tenurial categories as follows: 'Bookland was simply land vested by a royal diploma, and folkland was any (and all) land that was not bookland. The fundamental characteristics of bookland were that it was alienable (i.e. its holder had freedom of disposition), and was held in perpetuity (i.e. grants of bookland were in theory non-revocable). It was thus possible to distinguish between inherited land to which kin could automatically lay claim, and bookland which they could not.'[20] Bookland provided special privileges and was

---

and Found.' The standard reference for Anglo-Saxon charters remains Sawyer, *Anglo-Saxon Charters* (hereafter abbreviated as S). A revised version of Sawyer is currently available at www.esawyer.org.uk/.

17 *EHD* I, 362. See also Faith, 'Peasant Families and Inheritance Customs in Medieval England'; Jones, 'Nucleal Settlement and its Tenurial Relationships'; Wormald, '*Lex Scripta* and *Verbum Regis*,' 11; and Faith, *English Peasantry*.

18 See chapter 3 below. Cf. Reynolds, *Fiefs and Vassals*, 324–5.

19 1 Edward 2 and 2.1 (Liebermann, *Gesetze*, 1:140). See also Wormald, *Making of English Law*, 286–90.

20 Baxter, *Earls of Mercia*, 145. See also Reynolds, *Fiefs and Vassals*, 331. In Patrick Wormald's assessment, 'What one inherited from one's kin could not be alienated from one's kin; but what one acquired in any other way could be distributed at one's pleasure … The value of a charter, as its main formulaic elements show, was that it bestowed

distinguished by its written instrument, the Latin royal diploma; folkland, a notoriously general and thinly attested term, by contrast, was land *not* held by charter. Paul Vinogradoff influentially defined folkland as 'land held under the old restrictive common law, the law which keeps land in families, as contrasted with land which is held under a book, under a *privilegium*, modelled on Roman precedents, expressed in Latin words, armed with ecclesiastical sanctions, and making for free alienation and individualism.'[21] Another key distinction was, as Stenton emphasized, that 'bookland, unlike folkland, was land exempt from the heaviest of public burdens.'[22] The practice of holding land by diploma, then, introduced by the church in the seventh century, constituted a tenurial innovation which fused property, privilege, freedom, and textuality. Bookland provided a more secure and enduring form of possession, which was achieved through and guaranteed in writing.

In sum, bookland, which Pollock memorably described as 'a clerkly and exotic institution,'[23] granted land in perpetual possession with the freedom of alienation, the ability to bequeath the property outside of the family group.[24] The grant itself was represented by a Latin diploma which served

---

perpetual right, but was also proof of acquisition rather than inheritance, and hence of a beneficiary's right to select its destination' ('Bede and the Conversion of England,' 156). For bookland, see Brunner, *Zur Rechtsgeschichte der römischen und germanischen Urkunde*, 151–208; Jolliffe, 'English Book-Right'; Kennedy, 'Disputes about *Bocland*'; Rumble, 'Old English *Boc-land* as an Anglo-Saxon Estate-Name'; Reynolds, 'Bookland, Folkland and Fiefs'; and Wood, *Proprietary Church in the Medieval West*, 152–60.

21 Vinogradoff, 'Folkland,' 11. Pollock and Maitland endorsed Vinogradoff's arguments, defining folkland as 'land held without written title under customary law' (*History of English Law*, 1:62). The term has nonetheless occasioned long-running debate. See Liebermann, *Gesetze*, 2:403, s.v. 'folcland'; John, *Orbis Britanniae*, 64–127; Reynolds, 'Bookland, Folkland and Fiefs'; Loyn and Insley, 'Folkland'; Jurasinski, *Ancient Privileges*, 49–77; and Baxter, *Earls of Mercia*, 147–8.

22 Stenton, *Anglo-Saxon England*, 310.

23 Pollock, 'Anglo-Saxon Law,' 269. Pollock also observed, 'The truth is that we know very little about any form of Anglo-Saxon land-holding save book-land, which is a foreign excrescence on ancient Germanic usages' (ibid., 270). Both comments made their way into the first edition of Pollock and Maitland's *History of English Law* (1895), but the description of bookland as 'a foreign excrescence' was excised from the second edition (1898).

24 This form of possession, with its intimations of absolute ownership and control over time, resembles the later category of the estate in fee simple, 'an estate that is potentially infinite in duration by reason of its transferability and general inheritability' (Bergin and Haskell, *Preface to Estates in Land*, 23). See also Hargreaves, *Principles of Land Law*, 55–8. A distinction between folkland and bookland might also be seen in

as an evidentiary title to the property. The documentary promise of a permanent right importantly suggested an absolute ownership which was impervious to challenge and change.²⁵ Bookland was originally used by ecclesiastics to protect church endowments from later challenges by disgruntled kindred who sought the return of their family lands – the freedom of alienation accordingly was a crucial element of bookland because it separated the land from the claims of kin.²⁶ The act of documentation transformed land into property which was theoretically free from its history. The conveyance of bookland imagined land as if it had been made anew, unencumbered by past claims or interests.

Not surprisingly, the granting of land by diploma was soon appropriated for secular use, for bookland offered families a powerful means of managing their landed resources strategically over time.²⁷ Eric John observed that bookland provided aristocratic families with 'a stability and continuity they cannot have had before. Whatever else their books did for them, they gave the magnates the power to choose their heirs.'²⁸ A number of extant wills clearly show such estate planning in action. The will of the widow Wynflæd, which survives in an eleventh-century single-sheet manuscript, for example, specifies the exact bequeathal of her property, including a booked estate which is to go to her daughter Æðelflæd: 'Ꝓ þæt land æt Ebbelesburnan ꝥ þa boc on éce yrfe to ateonne swa hyre leofosð sy ꝥ hio [an h]yre þara manna ꝥ þæs yrfes ꝥ ealles þæs þe þær þenne on bið butan þæt man scel for hyre saulle þærof don ægþer ge an mannon ge an yrfe' (and the estate at Ebbesborne and the title-deed as a perpetual in-

---

Honoré's observation that, 'the alienable, heritable and indefeasible fee simple was evolved from the inalienable and intransmissible tenancy in fee, subject to onerous incidents of tenure' ('Ownership,' 142).

25 The notion of absolute ownership, which had been present in Roman law, entered the legal traditions of the early Germanic kingdoms through vulgar Roman law. See Levy, *West Roman Vulgar Law*; and John, *Land Tenure in Early England*, 1–23. Levy showed how the distinction between *dominium* and *possessio* which had been active in classical Roman law, i.e., the difference between 'the essentially total right of control and the limited rights others might have in the thing,' did not survive in Roman vulgar law, the practices of which deeply informed the property law of the Germanic kingdoms (*West Roman Vulgar Law*, 34, 61–72, and 84–96). See also Hargreaves, *Principles of Land Law*, 42–5.

26 Faith, *English Peasantry*, 159–61.

27 See Lowe, 'Nature and Effect of the Anglo-Saxon Vernacular Will.' For an insightful analysis of inheritance and property strategy in King Alfred's will, see Wormald, 'On þa wæpnedhealfe.'

28 John, *Orbis Britanniae*, 69.

heritance to dispose of as she pleases; and she [Wynflæd] grants to her the men and the stock and all that is on the estate except what shall be given from it both in men and stock for the sake of her soul).[29] This provision shows the key elements of bookland – the evidentiary document (*þa boc*), eternal possession (*on ece yrfe*), and freedom of alienation – but it also clarifies that in such grants the land typically came already provided with men and resources. The recipient of bookland importantly received with the property those jurisdictional dues and profits, rents, renders, and customary services (collectively known by the formulaic phrase 'sake and soke') owed by those who lived on the land. In this sense, even booked land in reality came with an established history of use, a matrix of customs, expectations, and obligations which accompanied the property. Even with its many proprietary privileges and its assurance of lasting possession, then, bookland – like all holdings of land – carried the trace of past activity and interests and was consequently subject to the pressures of history and, by extension, the potential for contest and loss.

In addition to folkland and bookland, there was land held by lease, also known as *lænland* (loanland).[30] Leases survive from the late eighth century and become common in the vernacular from the ninth century.[31] *Lænland* was a precarious form of tenure which was defined by its limited terms of possession and transmissibility. A lease 'loaned' land for a specified number of lifetimes, typically three, with the stipulation that the land would return to the grantor – who maintained ownership throughout the term of the lease – following the death of the grantee(s). A leasehold provided the temporary use of property with the essential requirement that the land would revert to its actual owner. In a Worcester charter dated to

---

29 S 1539. Whitelock, *Anglo-Saxon Wills*, no. 3 at pp. 10 and 11. Abbreviations expanded. See also Kelly, *Shaftesbury*, 56; and Wareham, 'Transformation of Kinship and the Family in Late Anglo-Saxon England,' 381–3. For Anglo-Saxon wills and inheritance, see also Sheehan, *The Will in Medieval England*; Crick, 'Women, Posthumous Benefaction, and Family Strategy'; Drout, *How Tradition Works*, 125–66; and Tollerton, *Wills and Will-Making in Anglo-Saxon England*.

30 This term appears less frequently in the extant corpus than the scholarship would suggest. Some attestations include S 1334, 1347, 1350, 1367 (all Worcester leases), and S 1504 (the will of Ealdorman Æthelwold, dated to 946/7).

31 The earliest leases include a Peterborough lease dated sometime between 789 and 796 (S 1412) and a Worcester lease dated sometime between 718 and 745 (S 1254). Both are written in Latin. See Kelly, *Peterborough*, no. 7 at pp. 202–5. For leases in general, see also King, 'St Oswald's Tenants'; Baxter, *Earls of Mercia*, 125–51 and 208–9; and Tinti, *Sustaining Belief*.

904, for example, Bishop Werferth leases a single hide of land to his reeve Wulfsige for three lives (i.e., Wulfsige and two of his designated heirs) under the condition that the land is to go back to Worcester 'butan elcon wiðercwide'[32] (without any contention). Such defensive language was a pragmatic but not always effective precaution. Tenants were often reluctant to surrender land which had been attached to their family for generations, and failure to recover leased lands could significantly diminish a church's endowment over time.[33]

Among these three modes of tenure, bookland, distinguished by its written instrument and its superior powers, was clearly the most desirable form of possession.[34] Bookland offered benefits and privileges which were absent in other forms of landholding and its possession also increasingly came to indicate status.[35] At the same time, however, bookland carried a set of limitations and obligations which tempered its promise of eternal possession and its intimation of absolute ownership. King Alfred's lawcode states that a man who has inherited bookland cannot alienate that property from his family if there be document or witness that such a course had been prohibited 'by those men who acquired it in the beginning and

---

32 S 1281. Robertson, *Anglo-Saxon Charters*, no. 18 at p. 34. The document survives as an original single-sheet, the lower part of a chirograph.

33 See Baxter, 'Archbishop Wulfstan and the Administration of God's Property,' 175–6. Baxter estimates that Worcester lost nearly a fourth of its endowment between 1016 and the 1090s to recalcitrant tenants of *lænland*. The difficult retrieval of leased property constituted 'one of the most serious tenurial problems encountered by the church of Worcester during the course of the eleventh century' (ibid., 176). See also Tinti, *Sustaining Belief*, 165–8 and 222–3. Leases could go wrong in other ways as well. Bath lost its Tidenham estate, nearly a quarter of its landed endowment, after the property had been leased to Archbishop Stigand sometime between 1061 and 1065 and then lost when all his lands were forfeited to King William in 1070. The land was never recovered. See Kelly, *Bath and Wells*, 26–7, 101, and 146.

34 In a way which Anglo-Saxon texts do not, modern legal vocabulary typically distinguishes between ownership and possession: 'possession is a mere fact, independent either of other facts or of legal rules, whereas ownership, whatever its origin, is generally regarded as the creation of law' (Hargreaves, *Principles of Land Law*, 19). See also Krier, *Property*, 17. For a useful survey of the several rights and incidents attendant upon ownership, see Honoré, 'Ownership.' Honoré generally defines ownership as 'those legal rights, duties and other incidents which apply, in ordinary case, to the person who has the greatest interest in a thing admitted by a mature legal system' (ibid., 107). Because Anglo-Saxon diplomas typically use the noun *possessio* and the verb *possidere*, this book generally uses 'possession' and 'possess' to indicate the legal rights and obligations of ownership.

35 Reynolds, *Fiefs and Vassals*, 333.

by those who gave it to him.'[36] This limitation significantly curtails one of bookland's crucial benefits, the ability to separate property from previous interests.[37] More significantly, even though Eric John rightly observed that the acquisition of 'book-right' achieved a transition from 'precarious to permanent tenure,'[38] the security of bookland still remained contingent on a range of social obligations, pressures, and circumstances. Estates could be forfeited to the king, for example, in penalty of certain major crimes.[39] Moreover, there is abundant evidence that challengers often disputed the provisions of bookland in order to resume control of contested property.[40] The frequency of such disputes in the surviving written record shows that those provisions forbidding trespass against diplomatic terms were not always successful insurance.

In addition, despite its freedom from most public obligations, bookland did maintain obligations to the state in the form of the three common burdens: military service, bridge maintenance, and fortress work.[41] And by the end of the Anglo-Saxon period, a pre-mortem payment known as the 'heriot' (normally paid in arms or money as determined by rank) was due to one's lord, typically the king, in order to ensure the distribution of inheritance as stipulated by written will, including the bequeathal of bookland.[42] In one historian's succinct assessment, 'The heriot was a key to inheritance, failure to pay it resulted in loss.'[43] Bookland consequently offered what Richard Abels has described as 'a privileged but still dependent form of

---

36 *EHD* I, 415. Alfred 41 (Liebermann, *Gesetze*, 1:74).
37 This provision resembles an early form of the fee tail, which was later designed to keep land in the family. See Pollock and Maitland, *History of English Law*, 2:17–19; Hargreaves, *Principles of Land Law*, 59–64; Krier, *Property*, 85–6; and Keynes and Lapidge, *Alfred the Great*, 309n24.
38 John, *Land Tenure in Early England*, 39.
39 The relevant law-codes are Alfred 4 and 4.2, V Æthelred 28, II Cnut 13.1, and II Cnut 77 and 77.1 (Liebermann, *Gesetze*, 1:50, 244, 316, and 364). See also II Edmund 1.3, II Edmund 6, and Hundred Ordinance 3.1 (Liebermann, *Gesetze*, 1:188 and 192). See also Keynes, 'Crime and Punishment,' 77n66; Wormald, *Making of English Law*, 149n106 and 306–7; and Baxter, *Earls of Mercia*, 140 and 147n90.
40 See Kennedy, 'Disputes about *Bocland*'; and Wormald, 'Handlist.'
41 See Brooks, 'Development of Military Obligations'; Dempsey, 'Legal Terminology in Anglo-Saxon England'; and Abels, *Lordship and Military Obligation*.
42 Abels, 'Heriot.' See also II Cnut 71 (Liebermann, *Gesetze*, 1:356–8); Liebermann, *Gesetze*, 2:500–2, s.v. 'Heergewäte'; Brooks, 'Arms, Status and Warfare in Late-Saxon England'; and Reynolds, *Fiefs and Vassals*, 336.
43 Stafford, *Unification and Conquest*, 160.

tenure' in which land was 'held directly of the king.'[44] Even the promise of eternal possession vested in an authoritative and lasting document, then, was constrained by tenurial limitations and the worrying potential for dispute or forfeiture.

All three modes of tenure outlined above faced the problem of the loss or diversion of property in some significant way. All landholding was vulnerable to the demands and claims of historical pressure and social obligations. In this sense, there was a significant gap between tenurial rhetoric and social practice, between expectation and experience. Legal scholars Gray and Francis Gray usefully distinguish between two common views of property, the 'absolutist' view, or 'the passionate and instinctive belief that ownership is sacrosanct, oppositional, irreducible and inviolable,' and 'a more "relativist" perception that entitlements of property are constantly defined and redefined by competing user rights, by social contexts, and by requirements of reasonableness and community-directed obligation.'[45] This distinction neatly locates the difference between traditional conceptions of property (the ideal) and the actual experience of social and legal practice (the real).[46] Despite the ambitious rhetoric of bookland, there was no absolute possession in Anglo-Saxon England. All forms of landholding were limited, or 'relativist,' to some degree: *folcland* remained attached to family interests and expectations (although through alienation it could be lost to the kin entirely); *lænland* was held for a set term with the stipulation that the property would revert to the owner (though from the owner's perspective, it also carried the danger of a tenant later resisting that reversion); and *bocland*, which over time offered the holder the greatest degree of control, still carried obligations to the state and was subject to confiscation and redistribution if those conditions were not met. As Maitland dryly observed, 'To wish for an ownership of land that shall not be subject to royal rights is to wish for the state of nature.'[47] Lay and church endowments alike were vulnerable to dispute and deprivation throughout the

---

44 Abels, 'Bookland and Fyrd Service in Late Saxon England,' 3 and 5.
45 Gray and Francis Gray, *Elements of Land Law*, 86.
46 See also Honoré, 'Ownership,' 144–5. Honoré observes, '"Absolute" is perhaps the most ambiguous word met in discussions of ownership. Sometimes it is used to deny the "temporary" (intransmissible or determinate) character of an interest, sometimes to deny its defeasible character (liable to be divested by another, liable to escheat or forfeiture), sometimes to emphasize its exemption from social control' (ibid., 144). As we shall see, Anglo-Saxon tenurial discourse was deeply concerned with such problems of impermanence and loss.
47 Pollock and Maitland, *History of English Law*, 2:3.

Anglo-Saxon period. The idea of absolute possession inherent in bookland belies the evidence that the possession of land in Anglo-Saxon England was always to some extent a precarious enterprise.

Many tenurial texts accordingly work to inscribe claims on land while concurrently registering some concern over the stability and longevity of such claims. Nicholas Howe has argued that for the Anglo-Saxons, any 'story of place had always to deal with the intertwined acts of possession and dispossession, both as historical fact and as future possibility.'[48] Howe's comment appears within his evocative discussion of the physical traces of past possession in the landscape of early Anglo-Saxon England (such as earthworks, graves, and Roman ruins) and the ways in which 'the Anglo-Saxons viewed landscape through the material accumulation of the past.'[49] As a human possession, I argue, land-as-property over time likewise carries a residue of past claims and use, its own 'intertwined acts of possession and dispossession.' Land never comes free of the past. This notion of an abiding historical presence, in conjunction with the felt pressure of competing claims (past, present, and future), engenders a strain in many tenurial texts between the insistence on secure and enduring possession and the anticipation of change and reversal.

This conceptual dissonance frequently generated compensatory innovation and elaboration in tenurial writing. Legal texts increasingly employ literary language and conceits, especially in and after the 930s, even as other textual genres employ tenurial vocabulary and practices in other literary and ideological contexts. Emily Steiner has argued that 'medieval writers borrowed, and sometimes even distorted, the textual apparatus of the law to invent a *documentary poetics*, by which I mean the ways in which legal documents – both their external material forms and their internal rhetorical modes – call attention simultaneously to poetic form and cultural practice.'[50] Steiner's analysis pertains specifically to late medieval England, but this book demonstrates that a productive collaboration between law and literature was already in place in England by the tenth century. *Land and Book* aims to expand the field of Anglo-Saxon literature by considering texts hitherto undervalued or ignored as non-literary.[51] The

48 Howe, 'Landscape of Anglo-Saxon England,' 93.
49 Ibid., 95.
50 Steiner, *Documentary Culture*, 17.
51 The term 'literary' can be an elusive one. For the purposes of this study, I understand 'literary language' to be that which 'shows the language being tested to the full, being used by individuals who think seriously about the right choice and use of language and

book consequently examines a range of cross-disciplinary texts concerned with land, including those generally delimited as 'legal writing' or 'documents of practice': Latin diplomas, vernacular dispute records, law-codes, leases, and memoranda on estate management. Many of these texts employ prominent elements of narrativity, literary display, and/or rhetorical craft. In other words, they are not merely formulaic or functional documents, but stylistically ambitious texts that merit and reward serious literary analysis within a specific field of cultural activity – the possession of land and its representation in writing.

This book furthermore attends to the social pressures and expectations that produced writing in Anglo-Saxon England at specific historical moments, particularly in the tenth century, which was a time of increased tenurial activity. The tenth century witnessed what several historians have called a 'land market,' in which a large number of estates were granted, sold, transferred, exchanged, bequeathed, or divided into smaller holdings.[52] The late ninth and tenth centuries saw significant developments in, and concerns over, land tenure and the written word. The law-codes of Alfred and Edward, for example, made specific provisions about bookland and folkland; the vernacular boundary clause had become a standard component in royal diplomas by the early tenth century; written statements in English were frequently produced as evidence in property disputes; vernacular wills date from the mid-ninth century onwards; and the prose Anglo-Saxon Chronicle introduced vernacular verse in the tenth century which prominently celebrates dynastic continuity and territorial control. These various innovations indicate that land tenure had become an increasingly important matter which enabled and required new modes of writing. Consequently, this book primarily considers literary and legal texts which were composed or circulated during the tenth century, a time during which tenurial discourse acquired a strong resonance across a wide range of cultural productions.

---

are prepared to employ the full range of possibilities and even to invent, or to break the boundaries of ordinary discourse. Thus an account of literary language is inevitably both a description of its general characteristics and an exploration of the ways in which individual writers have gone beyond them' (Godden, 'Literary Language,' 490–1).

52 See Stafford, *Unification and Conquest*, 155–6; Williams, 'Bell-house and a Burh-geat,' 233; Reynolds, *Fiefs and Vassals*, 331; Faith, *English Peasantry*, 154–5; Reynolds, *Later Anglo-Saxon England*, 123–34; Keynes, 'Edgar, *rex admirabilis*,' 36–7; and Tinti, *Sustaining Belief*, 153–5.

The book is divided into two parts. The first section considers modes of signification and style in legal texts and the second analyses the influence of tenurial language and tropes in other, primarily non-legal, writings. The first two chapters provide formal readings of two classes of legal document, the Latin diploma and the vernacular dispute narrative, complemented by considerations of their theoretical implications for landholding and tenurial discourse. The three following chapters examine the ideological or exemplary function of tenurial discourse across a range of vernacular texts, including law-codes, homilies, philosophy, the Anglo-Saxon Chronicle, and Old English poetry. As a whole, these five chapters demonstrate the conceptual energy and stylistic range of tenurial discourse as well as its broad circulation across genre and language.

Chapter 1 examines the Latin diploma, the major written instrument for land tenure in Anglo-Saxon England from the late sixth through the eleventh century. The single-sheet diploma represents the original grant of bookland in a material text which provides a tactile-visual sign of possession. The authority of the original document theoretically lasted for all time – the diploma would be delivered to the new owner whenever the land changed hands – and as a material text it aspired to defy time and changeability. The grant was most often framed in an economy of salvation (the earthly gift of land secures an eternal place in heaven) underwritten by royal and divine support. The diploma's solemn authority was further bolstered at times by ceremonial performance: sods of earth might be placed on the gospels, or diplomas on a church altar. This performative element was eventually transferred from public ritual to verbal display within the text itself. These moments of literary ornamentation, however, also frequently amplify concepts of instability and loss, introducing troubling contradictions within a solemn text dedicated to affirming eternal possession and the immutability of the grant. The instinct for innovation and showmanship in Anglo-Saxon diplomas accordingly can unsettle the declarations of permanence and stability invested in bookland.

Latin diplomas imagine ambitious terms and conditions to ensure the possession and transmission of land over time, but such expectations frequently were complicated or frustrated in social practice. The large number of property disputes in the Anglo-Saxon period generated a class of vernacular document featuring a compact narrative which demonstrated rights of possession for one party in a dispute. Such documents typically advance a simple ethical basis to justify changes of possession: those who lost property only did so due to transparent and legitimate reasons. Chapter 2 considers how these texts employ narrative arguments which compete against other potential claims to possession. In contrast to the royal diploma, which promises eternal possession and imagines land as existing outside time, the vernacular charter account strategically arranges the evidence of past conflict and dispossession within an authoritative narrative which turns the contingencies of human activity to its own favour. Despite their clear narrativity, these texts have been largely neglected by literature scholars.[53] Chapter 2 provides an overview of this understudied genre followed by an extended analysis of one remarkable text (S 1447) written sometime between 968 and 988. This particular charter juxtaposes its local story of a tangled and prolonged dispute with recent contentions in dynastic succession, thereby aligning its claims with the movement of royal politics. In addition to its topical strategies, S 1447 also employs a hybrid of literary and legal diction as well as fictive techniques such as direct speech and dramatic scenes in order to amplify its truth claims through rhetorical and narrative ornamentation. Defying reductive categorization as a 'legal' or 'literary' text, S 1447 shows how the social challenges of land tenure generated innovative writing in Anglo-Saxon England.

The next three chapters consider the lexical and conceptual 'translation' of tenurial discourse and concerns across a range of textual genres and productions.[54] By the middle of the ninth century the Anglo-Saxons had developed a number of textual modes in the vernacular for regulating the possession and transmission of land. The Latin vocabulary of land tenure was also translated into the vernacular, and while some of these translations were direct calques from the Latin (such as Old English *ece yrfe* for Latin *aeterna hereditas*), other vernacular terminology semantically enriched established tenurial concepts. The compounds *bocland* (bookland) and *lænland* (loanland), for example, represent common forms of Anglo-Saxon landholding (eternal possession and temporary lease), but their internal

---

53 Notable exceptions include Lees and Overing, *Double Agents*, 68–77; Rabin, 'Old English *Forespeca*'; Smith, 'Of Kings and Cattle Thieves'; Rabin, 'Anglo-Saxon Women Before the Law'; Rabin, 'Female Advocacy and Royal Protection in Tenth-Century England'; and Rabin, 'Testimony and Authority in Old English Law.' A number of historians have also considered vernacular dispute narratives in productive or suggestive ways, including Stenton, *Latin Charters*, 43–4; Kennedy, 'Disputes about *Bocland*'; Wormald, 'Charters, Law and the Settlement of Disputes'; Keynes, 'The Fonthill Letter'; Kennedy, 'Law and Litigation in the *Libellus Æthelwoldi episcopi*'; and Brooks, 'The Fonthill Letter, Ealdorman Ordlaf and Anglo-Saxon Law in Practice.'
54 For an analogous discussion of how legal language and customs can inflect the production of non-legal texts, see Cubitt, '"As the Lawbook Teaches": Reeves, Lawbooks and Urban Life in the Anonymous Old English Legend of the Seven Sleepers.'

lexical links also enable a theoretical mode for thinking about land, writing, time, and salvation. Chapter 3 analyses several texts that theorize land tenure in such ways. First, the chapter considers two texts that employ metaphors drawn from tenancy and estate management. The preface to the law-code known as 'IV Edgar' builds an analogy between tenant duties and Christian observance in order to explain the ravages of a recent plague and to call upon the English people to honour their dues to God. The deity becomes a figural landlord who justly punishes the default of his tenants. The prose preface to the Old English translation of Augustine's *Soliloquies* builds a more complex metaphor for salvation by conflating ideals of tenancy, service, labour, and learning. Whereas Edgar's law-code employs tenurial metaphors toward admonition and justification, the prose preface imagines land tenure as a productive system which offers transformative rewards for an earthly life of dedication. Finally, the vernacular homily Vercelli X employs innovative metaphors of land tenure and inheritance as an organizing device in its compilation of materials drawn from various Latin sources. The homilist works with two main tenurial conceits: legal documentation as a means for controlling the distribution of goods over time, and the metaphor of salvation as an originary charter written by Christ (the *frumgewrit*). Even as the homily uses a mythic document to represent the promise of salvation, however, it also presents the efficacy of written instruments for controlling land over time as a vain fiction. Vercelli X thus rehearses the same uneasiness evident in other tenurial writing over the stability and value of the possession of land. This chapter as a whole demonstrates the extra-legal circulation of tenurial discourse and its versatility for pedagogical and persuasive writing in Anglo-Saxon England.

The final two chapters of *Land and Book* examine the ways in which historical and poetic texts can exhibit discursive, lexical, and situational elements which resonate powerfully with proprietal issues and tenurial discourse. Chapter 4 reads the Anglo-Saxon Chronicle as a hybrid text which incorporates prose annals, poetry, and royal genealogy into a sustained proclamation of dynastic authority over an increasing amount of territory. The Chronicle annals for the years 900–46 record the expanding boundaries of West Saxon political authority (*anweald*) by employing two techniques common to contemporary diplomas: the textual mapping of land boundaries and the use of literary display. The chapter first focuses on two discrete sets of annals in Chronicle manuscripts A and B: the annals dedicated to Edward the Elder (s.a. 912–20AB) and those annals known as 'the Mercian Register,' mainly dedicated to Æthelflæd, 'Lady of the Mercians' (s.a. 896–924B). Each set of annals carefully records the territorial movements of dynastic figures as they expand the bounds of the realm over time, primarily through the systematic construction of fortresses in contested border areas. As the Chronicle textually maps the kingdom's expanding borders over the years, its language and syntax parallel that found in vernacular boundary clauses as it inscribes its temporal record of political and territorial power. After its annals for Edward and Æthelflæd, the Chronicle dramatically introduces two poems (s.a. 937 and 942) which celebrate the dynastic control of territory in heroic verse. Just prior to the composition of these poems, a draftsman known as 'Æthelstan A' produced an influential series of royal diplomas distinguished by their conspicuously learned Latin and their ambitious nomenclature for designating royal power. These documents render land matters in a self-consciously literary language. The vivid vocabulary and images in these texts anticipate the introduction of the specialized diction and tropes of vernacular poetry to the prose environment of the Anglo-Saxon Chronicle. These discursive parallels clarify the Chronicle's ideological interest in updating dynastic claims on land and people over time.

The final chapter considers the presence of legal language and tenurial themes in Old English poetry which deals with a heroic or legendary past. The two Exeter Book poems examined in this chapter, *Guthlac A* and *Deor*, both feature prominent tropes of property, especially the idea that the possession of land determines status and identity. In each text the act of possession or dispossession represents a transformative experience for a central character in both religious and secular contexts. *Guthlac A* stages property dispute – figured as a territorial contest between saint and demons in an abstracted space – as a proving ground for sanctity. The text features a significant amount of legal vocabulary which accentuates its figural cultivation of property dispute as an exemplum for salvation, but *Guthlac A* notably sanitizes the threat of dispute by assigning it a decisive end through the miraculous intervention of supernatural arbitration. The poem imagines land cleansed by dispute as a regenerated 'estate' – the saint enjoys his earthly holding entirely free from competing claims to possession. This tenurial fantasy prefigures the reward of a seat in God's eternal kingdom, laying bare the metaphorical associations between landholding and salvation. While property dispute seems a transformative experience in *Guthlac A* in the most positive sense, the action of the poem also demonstrates that land can be claimed and held only through the displacement of competing interests. In this way, the text maintains a negative counterpoint in its celebratory account of a saintly hero who wins his way to an eternal home. This unsettling aspect of dispossession, only half acknowledged in

Guthlac A, finds full expression in *Deor*, a poem which directly confronts those negative conditions which are typically suppressed, if only partially, in other tenurial texts. In this poem, the gift of land and the social status which it represents – signified as *landriht*, a word with distinct poetic and legal senses – are undone through the shock of unforeseen reversal. *Deor* situates the loss of land and identity as the final item in its grim catalogue of legendary misfortune, thereby dramatizing the dark antithesis of eternal possession: the total loss of place and identity.

These chapters together demonstrate how land-as-property becomes a fraught commodity through the operations of discourse. Tenurial writing in Anglo-Saxon England affirms and amplifies the value of property even as it returns again and again to the problem of dispute and the potential for loss. Royal diplomas, for example, celebrate the permanence of writing even as they insistently look ahead to possible challenges to their provisions – a defensive function which inflects the demonstrative function with apprehension. This double expectation of permanence and loss, I argue, sustained a multivalent and cross-generic discourse which often carried the unsettling elements of its own contradiction. In this aggregate textual field, land acquires a conflicting value as a resource that is at once secure and vulnerable, permanent and temporary, of inestimable but elusive worth. This conceptual tension is nowhere more evident and extreme than in the Latin diplomas of the tenth century, a time when rhetorical and compositional innovations in those texts both served to amplify the majesty of the document and to unsettle the integrity of its grand guarantees.

1 The Most Solemn Instrument

It was the most solemn form of record that human wit could devise. Drafted by unskilful hands it might become obscure but it was always impressive.
— F.M. Stenton, *The Latin Charters of the Anglo-Saxon Period*

Anglo-Saxon charters say both less and more than they mean.
— Patrick Wormald, 'Bede and the Conversion of England: The Charter Evidence'

The royal diploma was the primary written instrument for recording the conveyance and possession of land in Anglo-Saxon England.[1] The Latin diploma had been established in England by the last quarter of the seventh century,[2] and aside from a gap in production between 910 and 924,

---

1 See Stenton, *Latin Charters*, 31–65; John, *Land Tenure in Early England*, 1–63; Chaplais, 'Origin and Authenticity'; Bruckner, 'Zur Diplomatik der älteren angelsächsischen Urkunde'; *EHD* I, 369–89; Keynes, *Diplomas*, 1–39; Wormald, 'Bede and the Conversion of England'; Edwards, *Charters of the Early West Saxon Kingdom*; Kelly, 'Anglo-Saxon Lay Society,' 39–47; Brooks, 'Anglo-Saxon Charters'; and Keynes, 'Anglo-Saxon Charters: Lost and Found.' For diplomatics in general, see Boyle, 'Diplomatics'; and Bedos-Rezak, 'Diplomatic Sources and Medieval Documentary Practices.'
2 Augustine and Archbishop Theodore have both been credited with introducing the charter to England. See Levison, *England and the Continent*, 226–33; Chaplais, 'Who Introduced Charters into England?'; Wormald, 'Bede and the Conversion of England,' 147–53; and Kelly, *St Augustine's*, lxxiii–lxxvi.

it remained in regular use well into the eleventh century.[3] Approximately one thousand Latin diplomas survive from the Anglo-Saxon period with about 150 surviving as original or contemporary single-sheets.[4] Diplomas seem originally to have been written in monastic scriptoria, but a royal writing office had been established by the early tenth century and continued to be in use into the eleventh century.[5] These documents have been long recognized for their value in gleaning various historical data,[6] but several scholars have argued more recently that diplomas were also used as vehicles for ideological statement in addition to their practical function. Royal titles in the documents, for example, have long been considered as evidence for the political ambitions of kingship.[7] Furthermore, Pauline Stafford has made the case that the charters of King Æthelred II (r. 978–1016) generally 'debate and justify action and

---

3 For the 'hiatus' in the early tenth century, see Dumville, 'Æthelstan, First King of England,' 151–3; and Keynes, 'Edward, King of the Anglo-Saxons,' 55–6. It has been suggested that the utility of the vernacular writ gradually superseded the Latin diploma in the first half of the eleventh century, but this hypothesis is far from certain. See Chaplais, 'The Anglo-Saxon Chancery: From the Diploma to the Writ'; and Keynes, *Diplomas*, 140–5.

4 Royal diplomas survive nearly exclusively in ecclesiastical archives of limited geographical concentration. See Keynes, 'England, 700–900,' 19–21. The great majority of diplomas furthermore have been preserved in cartulary copies with many having been altered or manipulated in some way. Difficult questions of authenticity can accordingly complicate the study of the documents. See Scharer, *Die angelsächsische Königsurkunde*; *EHD* I, 369–75; and Keynes, *Diplomas*, 1–13.

5 A longstanding debate over the production of diplomas lies behind this generalization. For representative views, see Drögereit, 'Gab es eine angelsächsische Königskanzlei?'; Chaplais, 'Origin and Authenticity'; Keynes, *Diplomas*, 14–83; Brooks, *Early History of the Church of Canterbury*, 168–72; Chaplais, 'The Royal Anglo-Saxon "Chancery" of the Tenth Century Revisited'; Dumville, 'English Square Minuscule Script: The Mid-Century Phases,' 156–64; Keynes, 'The "Dunstan B" Charters'; Insley, 'Charters and Episcopal Scriptoria in the Anglo-Saxon South-West'; Thompson, *Anglo-Saxon Royal Diplomas*, 8–18; and Foot, *Æthelstan*, 70–3 and 82–9. The question of whether (or when) charters were produced by a royal writing office or by local ecclesiastical scriptoria has significant implications for our understanding of both the functioning of the Anglo-Saxon state and the formation and circulation of diplomatic conventions. As I mainly consider diplomas from the tenth century, a period with strong evidence for centralized production, issues of local currents in diplomatic and government are largely beyond the scope of this book. See also the salutary remarks in Keynes, 'Re-Reading King Æthelred the Unready,' 82–7.

6 Dorothy Whitelock gives a useful overview of 'the historical interest of charters' (*EHD* I, 381–2). See also Bedos-Rezak, 'Diplomatic Sources and Medieval Documentary Practices.'

7 See John, *Orbis Britanniae*, 1–63.

define good kingship within a set of values and ideals which allow examination of the common political discourse of late tenth-century England.'[8] Following Stafford, Charles Insley has claimed that 'the language and formulation of Anglo-Saxon charters had a pedagogical and ideological function in the tenth century, to create and sustain a political and religious agenda.'[9] In this view, Anglo-Saxon diplomas are sophisticated texts capable of simultaneously working toward several ideological and practical purposes. This chapter accordingly considers royal diplomas as an active force in shaping both tenurial discourse and the conceptual freight which circulated with it in Anglo-Saxon England: the cultural connection between land and writing, problems of temporality and continuity, the value of literary display, and resilient anxieties over dispute and loss.

The diploma delivered bookland, a form of tenure that was, in theory, eternal and largely unencumbered by worldly burdens. Diplomas were intended to provide long-term possession of land and to protect the owner against future challenges to ownership through a formal and abiding textual monument. These documents assumed authority in multiple ways: solemn content, a distinct manuscript layout, evidentiary status, compounded endorsements (sacred and royal), and elements of display (textual and ritual). In short, royal diplomas were items of power invested with the enduring security of the written word. The authority of the official muniment was frequently bolstered by forms of supplemental display such as extra-textual public ceremony and intra-textual literary performance. While ceremonial display seems to have been more common in the early period, literary ambitions become more consistently pronounced in the diplomas of the tenth century – over time, the imperative of display was sublimated within the text itself. Rhetorical amplification and ornament enhanced the general solemnity of the document, but such embellishment could also produce moments of tensions or ambivalence over the theoretical value and security of bookland. After a preliminary overview of Anglo-Saxon diplomas, this chapter examines how the various components of these documents can create a multivocal text which evades monologic coherence or even enables competing views about land-as-property. The Latin diploma's several parts work in combination, but not always in undisturbed concert.

---

8 Stafford, 'Political Ideas,' 73.
9 Insley, 'Where Did All the Charters Go?' 118.

Land in Writing

The diploma is composed of a regular series of distinct formal elements with some variation across the period.[10] The text usually begins with a pictorial element, often a cross or Chi-Rho, followed by a verbal invocation of divine support. The proem then offers a meditation on some theme such as the endurance of writing or the transience of earthly things.[11] The disposition, usually written in the voice of the king, next names the grantor and grantee and states the location and size of the estate. The sanction offers a blessing and/or anathema in support of the documentary provisions. Other components typically include the boundary clause, witness list, exemption clause, dating clause, endorsement, and subscription clause. These various formulaic components all combine to represent the grant in an enduring and authoritative document. Sarah Foot has argued that the royal diploma's 'single, comprehensive pattern' effectively provides a narrative of conveyance: 'The plot of a charter is the giving of the land; the narrative voice is that of the donor, usually a king.'[12] The various discrete elements of the document thus collaborate to enable a larger discursive and evidentiary function. The royal diploma recreates the immediate presence of the originary grant in a formal document: the issuing authorities endure in the first-person voice of the king and the list of witnesses,[13] while the boundary clause embodies the land itself within the document (particularly in vernacular clauses with their detailed perambulations around the property borders). These acts of textual presence aspire to exist outside of time: the eternal authority of God, the living voice of the king, the landscape features of the bounds, the

---

10 See Thompson, *Anglo-Saxon Royal Diplomas*, 27–54. Michael Lapidge has succinctly described the royal diploma as 'tripartite' in structure: 'it consists in (1) a proem or exordium in which God's omnipotence and the universal order is proclaimed (or some such statement); (2) the verbal disposition in which the donation is specified (in the tenth century this disposition is usually accompanied by an explanation in English of the boundary clauses); (3) the anathema, a curse on anyone who might dare to alter the terms of the charter. A list of witnesses, usually the king and the principal lay and ecclesiastical ministers of the realm, is appended' ('Hermeneutic Style,' 137).

11 By the 930s, Latin proems had generally become more expansive and elaborate, frequently employing the hermeneutic style. From the reign of Æthelstan, 'The proem is henceforth written in an intentionally ostentatious and pompous style, no doubt to convey an impression of the majesty of the royal donor and the importance of his donation' (Lapidge, 'Hermeneutic Style,' 137–8).

12 Foot, 'Reading Anglo-Saxon Charters,' 49 and 53.

13 Beginning in the 930s, the subscriptions of the witnesses also appear with the first-person pronoun *ego*. See Thompson, *Anglo-Saxon Royal Diplomas*, 42–9.

political authority of the witnesses, and the possession and privileges provided over the land are all memorialized in the document. The diploma fixes land and possession within a material text which symbolizes the conjunction of land and writing and whose form and language defy the changeability of human history.

After the diploma had been delivered to the grantee it acted as a kind of title-deed which provided evidence of possession.[14] An individual or institution could produce the diploma many decades (or even centuries) after the date of the original grant in order to demonstrate the right of possession. The original diploma would likewise be handed over to a new owner in cases of sale, exchange, or forfeiture.[15] The lasting authority of the diploma depended in part on its singularity – multiple copies could generate competing claims of possession and were consequently avoided. As an originary and evidentiary text, the document preserved the timeless authority of the original grant in writing. 'The value of a diploma as a title-deed,' Susan Kelly has observed, 'resided less in the information which it contained than in its function as a potent symbol of ownership.'[16] The diploma provided a powerful material sign of possession, a written representation of land and proprietary right which was, in theory, eternal.

The Latin diploma had been introduced in England to record and to protect the privileges and lands of the church. The general form, constitutive elements, and formulae in these early documents were based on Italian models,[17] and the earliest originals are written in Uncial script, a hand used primarily for religious texts.[18] From its beginnings, the Anglo-Saxon diploma consequently assumed a religiosity that would endure even in documents produced for entirely secular conveyances.[19] Diplomas typically

---

14 The evidentiary value of these documents appears through the many recorded cases in which landowners sought to replace lost or damaged diplomas (see Keynes, *Diplomas*, 32n53) and in which diplomas were forged or stolen (see Wormald, '*Lex Scripta* and *Verbum Regis*,' 24n112).

15 'In the context of Anglo-Saxon land law it was the possession of the diploma itself that established ownership of the land to which it referred or right to the privileges which it created. Thus, when an estate changed hands the diploma was transferred together with the land to the new owner; indeed, the act of transferring the diploma could apparently effect the change of ownership' (Keynes, *Diplomas*, 33). See also Brunner, *Zur Rechtsgeschichte der römischen und germanischen Urkunde*, 166–74.

16 Kelly, 'Anglo-Saxon Lay Society,' 44.

17 Levison, *England and the Continent*, 226–33; Chaplais, 'Origin and Authenticity,' 29–31; and Chaplais, 'Some Early Anglo-Saxon Diplomas,' 66ff.

18 See Lowe, *English Uncial*; and Prescott, 'The Developing State: Manuscripts,' 44.

19 See Keynes, *Diplomas*, 28–34; and Brooks, 'Anglo-Saxon Charters,' 182.

situate the grant as property within an economy of salvation in which the grantor gives up earthly treasures in exchange for heavenly rewards, casting off the temporary for the eternal. A diploma issued by King Æthelred of Wessex in 869 or 870 contains a typical example of the motif: 'Omnia que uidentur temporalia sunt et que non uidentur eterna sunt; iccirco terrenis et caducis eterna et iugiter mansura mercanda sunt'[20] (All things which are seen are temporary and those which are not seen are eternal; therefore the eternal and that which endures without end ought to be bought with earthly and transitory things). Moreover, diplomas often cite biblical verses in the proem and anathema, investing tenurial discourse with a pronounced and enduring sacral element.[21] The enterprise of landholding, the act of conveyance, and the maintenance of the documentary provisions consequently all became figuratively charged as matters of salvation and damnation.

Unlike continental documents, Anglo-Saxon diplomas carried no outer signs of authenticity such as seals, the attestation of notary or scribe, or autograph signatures. Pierre Chaplais consequently argued that the Anglo-Saxon diploma achieved its 'authenticity' through its pronounced religious character and always 'remained essentially an ecclesiastical instrument, at least in form if not always in purpose.'[22] Diplomas conventionally begin with pictorial and textual invocations of divine support, for example, while the named witnesses were corroborated by the sign of the cross, not by autograph signature or mark. Moreover, while continental charters threatened secular penalties and monetary fines, Anglo-Saxon diplomas warn off trespassers with threats of excommunication and eternal

---

20 S 334. Kelly, *Shaftesbury*, no. 5 at p. 22. See also Keynes, 'West Saxon Charters,' 1123–31; and Edwards, *Charters of the Early West Saxon Kingdom*, 309. The statement is based in part on 2 Cor. 4:18 (see also Matt. 6:19–20, 1 Tim. 6:7, and 1 Tim. 6:17–19). The same idea of exchange appears in the poem *An Exhortation to Christian Living*, lines 35–7a: 'Ceapa þe mid æhtum eces leohtes, / þy læs þu forweorðe, þænne þu hyra geweald nafast / to syllanne' (Dobbie, *Minor Poems*, 68) [Buy eternal light for yourself with possessions lest you be destroyed when you lack the power to give them].

21 Common biblical citations include Luke 6:38 ('Give and it will be given to you'), Eccl. 1:2, Job 1:21, Matt. 19:29, and Matt. 25:41 (in the anathema). For a discussion of how 'ecclesiastical property exists within a scheme of ideology' shaped by biblical and patristic writings, see Ganz, 'The Ideology of Sharing.' For church property in general, see Wood, *Proprietary Church in the Medieval West*.

22 Chaplais, 'Origin and Authenticity,' 33. For Chaplais, the early use of Uncial script represented a key aspect of this ecclesiastical authentication: 'In the eyes of a seventh-century scribe uncials may have represented a superior kind of script, possibly even a sacred script, reserved for writings of unquestionable authenticity' (ibid., 34).

damnation.[23] In many ways, then, the Anglo-Saxon diploma presents itself as a sacred text. In Patrick Wormald's summation, 'They have the "smell" of ecclesiastical documents, written, as some of the earliest are, in the sumptuous uncial script of holy books, on precious and carefully cut vellum; sanctioned as they are by the penalties of the next world rather than this, and by the use of the cross not as a witness's mark, but as a solemn symbol defying perjury or contradiction; motivated as many are by concern for the spiritual welfare of donor, beneficiary and others.'[24] The royal diploma consequently frames earthly business in unearthly terms, casting the possession of land in the rhetoric of salvation and eternal time. Since Anglo-Saxon diplomas carried no official marks of authentication, they demanded from their users a degree of faith in the sacrosanct nature of the written document and its lasting authority.[25] In this way, the Anglo-Saxon diploma was more than a functional instrument for recording conveyance and possession; it also contained a theoretical mode which enabled and sustained certain beliefs about land-as-property.

Eternal Possession

The Latin diploma granted bookland, a form of perpetual tenure which carried the freedom of alienation (i.e., the power to bequeath the property to any desired party). This disposition allowed land to be separated from family groups and subsequently transferred to the church. This powerful mode of tenure was prominently couched in the language of perpetuity: typical phrases include *aeternam possessionem*, *aeternam hereditatem*, *in sempiterno possidenda*, *perpetua hereditas*, and later, in the vernacular, *ece yrfe*.[26] Paul Brand has observed that declarations of perpetual possession

---

23 Levison, *England and the Continent*, 228; and Chaplais, 'Origin and Authenticity,' 33. For Frankish charters in general, see Ganz and Goffart, 'Charters Earlier than 800 from French Collections'; McKitterick, *Carolingians and the Written Word*, 77–134; and Rio, *Legal Practice and the Written Word*.

24 Wormald, 'Bede and the Conversion of England,' 142.

25 Charters were sometimes stored with royal treasures and relics (Keynes, *Diplomas*, 148–9). King Eadred reportedly entrusted to Dunstan 'all the best of his goods, namely many title-deeds and also the ancient treasures of preceding kings,' for example (*EHD* I, 900); several memoranda and wills also mention multiple copies, one of which has been committed to the king's *haligdom* (see S 939, 981, 1478, and 1521). Tenurial documents were clearly precious objects.

26 A grant of eternal possession appears in the oldest diploma (S 8) to survive as an original single-sheet. In this charter, dated to 679, Hlothere, king of Kent, grants an

were primarily interested 'in controlling the past, in cutting off claims based on the history of the property prior to their making, rather than in controlling the future.'[27] Through its power of alienation, bookland separated the property from previous obligations and cleansed it of old burdens. The diploma traditionally acted as a defensive instrument, 'an insurance against forgetfulness and treachery' which protected the recipient against the potential claims of lingering interests previously attached to the land.[28] The idea of perpetual possession essentially denies history while remaining acutely aware of historical pressure. By making timeless claims for land in a sacred environment, the Anglo-Saxon diploma attempted to fix possession and to refuse changeability, and these affirmations of permanence were driven in part by resilient fears of imminent conflict and reversal.

In addition to their sacral veneer, royal diplomas began to incorporate rhetorical flourishes in order to amplify their general solemnity. These stylized elements maintained the conventional religious character of the Latin diploma, even after bookland (and its written instrument) had been appropriated for secular use. One diploma which survives as an original single-sheet, for example, records a grant of land from King Offa to his *minister* Dudda in 779. Despite its secular context, the document retains the traditional ecclesiastical accoutrements of the diploma. The proem expounds briefly on the theme of worldly transience and then advocates the exchange of earthly goods for heavenly gain: 'Regnanti in perpetuum domino nostro Jhesu Christo . Universa quippe quæ hic in præsentia visibus humanis corporaliter contemplantur nihil esse nisi vana et caduca transitoriaque ex sacrorum voluminum testimoniis certissimi verum patet . Et tamen cum istis æternaliter sine fine mansura alta polorum regna et jugiter florentis paradisi amoenitas mercari a fidelibus viris queunt'[29] (With our Lord Jesus Christ reigning forever, all things that are here physically present to human sight are certainly considered as nothing but empty and fallen and transitory. This truth is well known from the surest

---

unspecified amount of land to Abbot Beorhtwald: 'Teneas possedeas tu posterique tui inperpetuum defendant a nullo contradicitur' (Brooks and Kelly, *Christ Church, Canterbury*, no. 2). 'May you hold and possess it, and your successors maintain it for ever. May it not be contradicted by anyone' (*EHD* I, 483). See also Chaplais, 'Some Early Anglo-Saxon Diplomas,' 65–78; for Kentish diplomatic, see Kelly, *St Augustine's*, lxxi–xcvi.

27 Brand, '*In perpetuum*: The Rhetoric and Reality of Attempts to Control the Future,' 103.

28 Chaplais, 'Origin and Authenticity,' 31.

29 S 114. *BCS*, vol. 1, no. 230 at p. 320.

testimony of sacred books. And yet with such things the lofty kingdoms of the heavens, enduring without end, and the delights of paradise continually blooming can be bought eternally by faithful men). Dorothy Whitelock cited this particular document as a forerunner of 'a striving after a more inflated style' in later Anglo-Saxon diplomas.[30] Such embellishment would make for a more impressive document, but in this case the content of the proem troubles the authority of the diploma as an evidentiary text. The statement that all visible things of the world are unreliable and impermanent is a commonplace sentiment,[31] but its claim about the diminished value of earthly things extends, perhaps ironically, to the diploma itself. Because the diploma acts as a material sign of possession, something to be held in hand and examined by eye, it falls within the category of the *vana et caduca*, those things which are visible within a transitory world. Moreover, the proem reserves the ideal of permanence to the deferred space of the heavenly – the language of the eternal clusters exclusively in a promise of a salvation which is envisioned through figures of territory and land. The proem thus diminishes the value of the material text, and by extension, its assurances of enduring possession in a failing world. The conveyed estate itself consequently assumes a reduced value as a temporary asset, something to be exchanged for more desirable and durable goods to be held elsewhere. The proem amplifies the solemnity of the document, but its stylistic ambitions quietly trouble the promised terms of possession, generating a paradoxical effect which would become much more pronounced in later diplomas.

Supplemental Display

While ornamental content could generate dissonance within the whole diplomatic text, Anglo-Saxon diplomas attempted at times to suppress such tensions through various forms of performative display. As we have seen, the diploma bolstered the authority and longevity of its claims through a solemn veneer which was itself a hybrid of royal and ecclesiastical

---

30 *EHD* I, 377. Whitelock notes that 'this tendency steadily increases until one reaches the absurdly elaborate and florid style of Athelstan's charters' (ibid.). See pp. 37–46 and 176–80 below for a discussion of the style of King Æthelstan's diplomas.

31 Mercian diplomas of the ninth century and earlier often contain literary elements, with worldly transience being a favourite theme in the proem. S 197, dated 844 for 848, stands as one prominent example (Kelly, *Peterborough*, no. 8 at pp. 206–15). See also Kelly, *Selsey*, 44.

sanctions. While it carried no official marks of verification, the diploma invoked the presence of secular and spiritual powers abiding within the text itself. In short, the royal diploma aspired to authentication through awe. This element of display within the diplomatic text was augmented at times by public ceremonies of conveyance or confirmation. In Maitland's words, 'One could not be too careful; one could not have too many ceremonies.'[32] References to such performative rituals are more frequent in early documents and relatively rare after the eighth century.[33] In these ceremonies sods from the land would be placed on an altar or gospel book, or charters presented at the altar. The practice of placing earth on the gospels is recorded in an early grant dated sometime between 670 and 676. In this document, Coenred gives thirty hides to one Bectun, abbot at an unidentified minster: 'Nam earundem supradictarum cespites pro ampliori firmitate euuangelium superposui, ita ut ab hac die tenendi, habendi, p[o]ssidendi in omnibus liberam et firmam habeat potestatem'[34] (Now I have placed for more complete security sods of the above-mentioned lands on the gospels, so that from this day he may have in all things free and secure power of holding, having, possessing).[35] The ceremonial element visually enacts the sacred endorsement which attends the grant as well as the enduring union of land and writing symbolized within the document, while the statement's rhyming verbs and adjectives, grouped in threes, stylistically amplify the promise of tenurial power 'in all things' through aural ornament.[36] The supplement of ritual here increased the solemnity of the act of conveyance and affirmed the lasting security of the evidentiary document.

---

32 Pollock and Maitland, *History of English Law*, 2:90. See also Kelly, 'Anglo-Saxon Lay Society,' 43–6.
33 The rituals themselves have antecedents in Italian practice. See Kelly, *St Augustine's*, lxxxiiin39. A 'decimation' charter of King Æthelwulf dated to November of 844 (in which the king frees every tenth hide of bookland from certain taxes and burdens) states that Æthelwulf put the *cartulam* on the altar 'pro ampliore firmitate.' S 294a and 294b (formerly S 314 and 322). Kelly, *Malmesbury*, no. 16 at p. 181. For a discussion of the document's authenticity, see ibid., 80–7; and Keynes, 'West Saxon Charters,' 1115–16.
34 S 1164. Kelly, *Shaftesbury*, no. 1(a) at p. 3. Emphasis added. For similar ceremonies involving sods, see S 14 and 15 (Kelly, *St Augustine's*, nos. 43 and 44); S 33 (Campbell, *Rochester*, no. 8); S 239 (Kelly, *Abingdon*, no. 2); S 156 and 1258 (Brooks and Kelly, *Christ Church, Canterbury*, nos. 30 and 27); and S 1804–6 (Kelly, *Peterborough*, nos. 3, 4b, and 4c).
35 *EHD* I, 481.
36 For Frankish elements in this phrasing, see Levison, *England and the Continent*, 227–8.

A Peterborough memorandum describes a similar ritual which occurred sometime between 675 and 691. In this text Æthelred, king of the Mercians, confirms an earlier grant he had made to *Medeshamstede* (Peterborough) after a group of monks approached him 'quadam ob causam' (for a certain reason): 'ipse rex ob confirmatione et in testimonium suę donationis in proprio cubiculo et coram multis testibus glebam sumptam de prefata terra Leugttricdun imposuit super codicem euangeliorum'[37] (the king himself placed a clod obtained from the aforementioned land at *Leugttricdun* upon a gospel book as confirmation and evidence of his donation before many witnesses in his own chamber). A record of a synod held in 798 at *Clofesho* likewise describes how Æthelbald, 'famous king of the Mercians' (*rex inclitus Merciorum*), ordered sods and title deeds to be placed together on the altar at Christ Church, Canterbury, 'in order that his donation might be the more enduring.'[38] These public acts of conveyance and confirmation, carried out before witnesses, dramatize both the conceptual fusion of land and document and the conflation of royal and sacred endorsement. Karl Leyser observed of political ceremonial that, 'Only through ritual was clarity achieved, an idea made intelligible and communicated to participants and onlookers alike.'[39] These early Anglo-Saxon rituals effectively staged in public view the several forces conjoined in the land document to ensure the longevity of possession.

Charters might also be placed upon an altar some time after the original conveyance to confirm an earlier grant or provision.[40] A Sherborne charter dated to 864, for example, contains a postscript which states that King Æthelberht confirmed the privileges attendant upon an original grant by later placing a document on an altar before many witnesses.[41] The ceremony underscored the conflation of secular and sacred sanctions, but

---

37 S 1806. Kelly, *Peterborough*, no. 3 at p. 175.
38 S 1258. '… utque illius donacio perseverancior fieret' (*BCS*, vol. 1, no. 291 at p. 405). Translation, *EHD* I, 509. The charters were later stolen and delivered to Cynewulf, king of the West Saxons, who then 'took over for his own uses the aforesaid monastery with all things duly belonging to it' (ibid.). This fascinating narrative, too complex to cover here, foregrounds the instrumentality of documents in demonstrating possession as well as the potential for their misappropriation. The story also shows the vulnerability of property to shifts in political power – the land in question was located in an area contested by Mercia and Wessex during the eighth century.
39 Leyser, 'Ritual, Ceremony and Gesture: Ottonian Germany,' 211.
40 See Harmer, *Anglo-Saxon Writs*, 169–71 and 232.
41 S 333. O'Donovan, *Sherborne*, no. 6 at pp. 18–24. See also Keynes, 'West Saxon Charters,' 1123–8.

Æthelberht's confirmation – performed some months after the date of the original grant – seems to have been intended to salve some lingering concern over the original terms. A similar unease must have led the Peterborough monks to approach King Æthelred 'for a certain reason' and prompt him to arrange an ad hoc performance in his private rooms before witnesses. In both cases, public ceremony confirmed the grant through the spectacle of land and book joined together upon the sacred space of the altar. These early rituals, clearly designed to fortify the evidentiary status of the diploma, then, could also be performed after the original conveyance in order to quell some anxiety or ambiguity about the property. Grantees must have felt at times that the original document required supplementary activity – be it public ritual or even the insurance of additional writing – to ensure its authenticity and lasting value. The inherent prestige and solemnity of the original diploma, it seems, were not always enough.

Other sources indicate that these ceremonies could also be employed strategically in circumstances of disputed possession. A synod record dated to 824 documents the restoration of a disputed estate in Kent to Archbishop Wulfred. The land had been bequeathed to Wulfred by the siblings Ealdberht (*comes*) and Selethryth (*abbatissa*) so that he might possess it 'in sempiternam hereditatem' (in everlasting inheritance) after their deaths. Ealdberht confirmed the gift after Selethryth died, but when Ealdberht himself passed away sometime around 820, his kinsman Oswulf reneged on the original agreement:

Sed iuxta annorum curriculis contigit ut ille praefatus comes Aldberht repentina morte defunctus est . Tunc autem super hanc donationem et reconciliationem Osuulf comes propinquusque ipsius fraudulenter accipiens librum istius praenominati terre æt Oeswalum atque in praesentia Quoenðryðae abbatissae totiusque familiae illius monasterii quod dicitur Suðmynter in altare deposuit . Cumque hoc audisset episcopus continuo legatos misit ad Quoenðryðam abbatissam illamque familiam æt Suðmynstre obnixæque petens ut agillum illum quod ei ab Aldberhto in propriam hereditatem concessum est reddere illi debuissent . At illi .iiii. annorum spatium negauerunt et contradixerunt.[42]

---

42 S 1434. Brooks and Kelly, *Christ Church, Canterbury*, no. 56. The document survives in a contemporary single-sheet manuscript. Wormald, 'Handlist,' no. 13 at p. 265. See also Brooks, *Early History of the Church of Canterbury*, 184–5; and Kelly, *St Augustine's*, xxvii–xviii.

[But over the course of the years it also happened that the aforementioned nobleman Ealdberht died a sudden death. And then Oswulf, a nobleman and his kinsman, dishonestly took the deed for the aforementioned land at Easole in defiance of this grant and reconciliation and placed it on the altar in the presence of Abbess Cwoenthryth and of all the community at the monastery called Southminster. And when the bishop heard of this he immediately sent envoys to Abbess Cwoenthryth and the community at Southminster and firmly requested that the plot of land which Ealdberht had granted him in hereditary possession be returned to him. And they denied him for four years and spoke against him.]

Rather than surrender the estate to Wulfred, Oswulf conveyed the land to Minster-in-Thanet by placing the 'book' for the estate on the altar there in the presence of Abbess Cwoenthryth and the entire community.[43] In this particular situation, the ceremonial placement of the deeds on the altar seems to have been an attempt to lend legitimacy to the diversion of land that had been legitimately bequeathed to another party. The account clearly labels Oswulf's act as unjust (it was done *fraudulenter*) and the synod deliberates that both book (*librum*) and land (*agrum*) should go to Wulfred. In this case, the ceremonial display at the altar was clearly staged – albeit unsuccessfully – to remove the land from contested circumstances.

The few references to similar ceremonies in the tenth and early eleventh centuries seem to confirm the impression that such measures were employed to symbolize an end to lingering ambiguities or dispute. A contemporary single-sheet manuscript written sometime around 959, for example, describes Eadgifu placing 'books' for two estates upon the altar when she grants them to Christ Church, Canterbury: 'Þa nam Eadgifu, be þæs cynincges leafe ʒ gewitnesse ʒ ealra his bisceopa, þa bec, ʒ land betæhte in to Cristes cyrcean, mid hire agenum handum upon þone altare lede, þan hyrede on ecnesse to are ʒ hire sawle to reste; ʒ cwæþ þæt Crist sylf mid eallum heofonlicum mægne þane awyrgde on ecnesse þe þas gife æfre awende oþþe gewanude'[44] (Then Eadgifu, with the permission and witness of the king and all his bishops, took the deeds and gave the estates to Christ Church, and laid them upon the altar with her own hands for the eternal benefit of the community and for the repose of her soul; and she said that Christ Himself with all the heavenly host would forever curse any man who should ever divert or diminish this gift). Like the Latin diploma, this ritual conflated royal and

---

43 Minster-at-Thanet was known as Southminster at the time. Kelly, *St Augustine's*, xxviiin45.
44 S 1211. Harmer, *SEHD*, no. 23 at p. 38.

sacred endorsement with the added insurance of Christ's prohibition against any person who might challenge the grant. Prior to the passage given above, the document describes how the two estates in question had been embroiled in dispute for over fifty years.[45] This was clearly land with a troubled history. It seems likely that the ceremony at the altar was intended to mark a determinative end to a long and tenacious disputation. In cases like this one, solemn documents already invested with sacred and royal endorsement were publicly reconsecrated at problematic moments in order to remove them from dispute and doubt.[46] Judging by the extant evidence, such public ceremony by the tenth century had become reserved for extreme circumstances. During that same time period, the level of rhetorical craftsmanship had dramatically increased in diplomas as the performative element, originally intended to bolster the prestige and authority of the document, shifted away from public ritual and into conspicuous literary display within the diplomatic text itself. This chapter next examines several cases of such display in tenth- and early eleventh-century diplomas as it manifests in two distinct forms, stylized rhetoric and embedded narrative content, and also considers the ways in which such content introduces contradictory elements (particularly the awareness of potential loss) which can trouble the formal and conceptual coherence of the diplomatic text.

Literary Display in Anglo-Saxon Diplomas

Literary display in tenth-century diplomas is generally most evident in the proem.[47] The pronounced ostentation in many proems has often been dismissed as superfluous or even absurd by modern readers. Indeed, some scholarship has been slow to modify long-held assumptions about the 'excessive' language and style of some Anglo-Saxon diplomas. In 1865, for

---

45 See Wormald, 'Handlist,' nos. 32–5 at pp. 266–7.

46 A writ dated sometime between 1017 and 1020 (S 985) describes King Cnut performing a similar ceremony to confirm the liberties of Christ Church, Canterbury. Cnut states that he had given Archbishop Lyfing permission 'to draw up a new charter of freedom in my name,' but the archbishop had answered that 'he had charters of freedom in plenty if only they were good for anything.' Cnut later placed charters (*þa freolsas*) on the altar at Christ Church to visibly confirm Canterbury's rights. See Harmer, *Anglo-Saxon Writs*, no. 26 at pp. 181–2; and Brooks, *Early History of the Church of Canterbury*, 288–9.

47 Although proems had become a standard component of diplomas by the tenth century, not all diplomas include them. See Thompson, *Anglo-Saxon Royal Diplomas*, 28. One group of mid-tenth-century diplomas known as the 'Dunstan B' charters, for example, omits both the invocation and proem entirely (Keynes, 'The "Dunstan B" Charters,' 180).

example, Benjamin Thorpe described a proem as 'usually a pious effusion, sometimes, particularly in later documents, of inordinate length, and not seldom hardly intelligible.'[48] More recently, Susan D. Thompson has defined the proem as 'an introductory paragraph, often stressing the eternal joys of heaven and the transitoriness of earthly treasures, which may have no particular relevance to the document in which it is contained.'[49] Proems are thus distinguished by their excess and irrelevance. Such assessments are largely driven by the view that diplomas are formulaic texts of practice, intended only to fulfil a specific evidentiary function. The ornamental bombast of many proems can certainly offend against such an assumption. Frank Barlow once wrote, for example, that Anglo-Saxon charters were 'almost perverse' in style because their 'moralizing pomposities usually denied the very utility and purpose of earthly government.' In other words, the contents of the proem at best seem to have nothing to do with the document's bureaucratic function and at worst contradict that function outright. Barlow describes such 'hysterical expressions of disgust for the theatre of the world' as 'bizarre trappings for an efficient government.'[50] Barlow's comments, overwrought as they are, do indicate how the stylistic pretensions of some proems can seem 'bizarre' within the general context of an operative document.

Alice Rio has recently proposed that proems feature 'a highly conservative and often deliberately difficult style' intended to convey a sense of dignity and power through stylized and occasionally impenetrable language; such inscrutable moments, however, would not 'have had a significant impact on the understanding of the essence of the agreement recorded in the document.'[51] Rio's valuable point about multiple registers within a single text raises productive questions about the associative impact of elevated style and content within a 'practical' land document. What effects might such 'extraneous' content have within the contained environment of a diplomatic text? Proems can reflect and reify the pressing awareness that, regardless of the rhetoric of perpetuity, the possession of land was

---

48 Thorpe, *Diplomatarium Anglicum Ævi Saxonici*, xix.
49 Thompson, *Anglo-Saxon Royal Diplomas*, 27.
50 Barlow, *Edward the Confessor*, 159. Barlow adds, 'It is this contempt for the transitory world which discouraged rational thought, political effort, and planning for the generations to come. It is what explains the Middle Ages' (ibid., 159–60). The diploma in question (S 1006), issued by Edward the Confessor in 1044, recycles a proem which first appeared in S 416, an early effort of 'Æthelstan A' (see pp. 39–46 below).
51 Rio, *Legal Practice and the Written Word*, 17. See also Foot, *Æthelstan*, 133–4 and 214–15.

contingent upon and vulnerable to historical forces. Such tensions frequently emerge through elaborate meditations on the impermanence of earthly things and the converse value of the permanence which can be achieved only through writing or salvation. Rhetorical ornamentation adds to the prestige of the document, but the actual content of a highly wrought proem can concurrently charge the diplomatic text with negative or contradictory energy. The proem in this way introduces a theoretical dimension to the diplomatic text which actively shapes, and occasionally vexes, the document's terms of possession.

The general form and style of West Saxon diplomas had been fairly stable and consistent from the 840s into the 920s.[52] Between 928 and 935, however, a draftsman known to us only as 'Æthelstan A' introduced a standardized flamboyance that marked a stunning shift in West-Saxon diplomatic.[53] Richard Drögereit first identified 'Æthelstan A' in 1935, observing of his work, 'Unser Schreiber stilisiert ganz individuell. Er hat einen an Worten und Wendungen überreichen, mit Bildern geschmückten Stil. Stellenweise kann man ihn kaum übersetzen'[54] (The style of our scribe is completely individual. He has a style that is rich in words and idiom and adorned with imagery. At times he can hardly be translated).[55] The diplomas attributed to this draftsman are generally characterized by a rich pleonastic style with aggressively literary proems and anathemas, ostentatious language and imagery throughout, decorative rhetorical figures, elaborate dating clauses, and extensive witness lists. These are clearly documents with stylistic ambitions. 'Æthelstan A' also seems to have been a great admirer of Aldhelm as he generally imitates his bombastic style and quotes specific phrases from his works. In his 1898 lectures on Anglo-Saxon diplomas, W.H. Stevenson, apparently moved by a mix of admiration and irritation, described the style of these documents as a 'highly embroidered, flatulent Latinity' with a fondness for

---

52 Keynes, 'West Saxon Charters.'
53 For 'Æthelstan A,' see Drögereit, 'Gab es eine angelsächsische Königskanzlei?' 361–9; Bullough, 'Educational Tradition in England,' 303–8; Keynes, *Diplomas*, 42–4; Keynes, 'King Athelstan's Books,' 156–7; Lapidge, 'Schools, Learning and Literature in Tenth-Century England,' 20–1; Gretsch, *Intellectual Foundations*, 334–5; Kelly, *Abingdon*, 102–3; and Foot, *Æthelstan*, 70–3, 82–90, and 213–15. The phrase 'standardized flamboyance' is adopted from Kelly, *Abingdon*, 90.
54 Drögereit, 'Gab es eine angelsächsische Königskanzlei?' 361.
55 Translation by Rosemary Bootiman for *Kemble: The Anglo-Saxon Charters Website*. http://www.kemble.asnc.cam.ac.uk/sites/default/files/files/Drogereit.pdf.

grandiloquence and grecisms.[56] These qualities describe what Michael Lapidge has since categorized as the hermeneutic style, which he defines as 'a style whose most striking feature is the ostentatious parade of unusual, often very arcane and apparently learned vocabulary.'[57] As the style enjoyed its full vogue in England during the later tenth century, Æthelstan's ambitious draftsman would seem to have been an early practitioner. The identity of 'Æthelstan A' currently remains unknown although Lapidge has suggested that he was a foreign scholar at Æthelstan's court and perhaps a Breton.[58] Some twenty-one charters have been attributed to him, including two documents which survive as contemporary single-sheets.[59]

'Æthelstan A' preserved the traditional form of the diploma but stylistically amplified several of its regular components to a remarkable degree. One of King Æthelstan's early diplomas dated to 926 (and thus issued two years before the established career of 'Æthelstan A') provides a useful point of comparison. This document, S 396, opens with a brief invocation followed by a proem on a conventional theme: 'In nomine Domini nostri Iesu Christi. Cuncta que humanis optutibus caducarum molimina rerum liquide uidentur decidunt; que uero abdita inuisaque sunt eterni arbitris moderamine perpetualiter constare. Haut dubium est his que illa adipisci, largiflua Dei largiente gratia, atque mercari posse merentibus diuina scripturarum documenta pollicentur'[60] (In the name of our Lord Jesus Christ. All undertakings of transitory affairs, which are clearly seen by human eyes, decay; those truly which are hidden and invisible remain for ever by the government of the eternal Judge. It is not to be doubted but that the divine teachings of the Scriptures promise to those deserving it that they can acquire and buy these things by the gift of the abundant grace of

---

56 Stevenson, 'The Anglo-Saxon Chancery,' 34.
57 Lapidge, 'Hermeneutic Style,' 105.
58 Lapidge, 'Schools, Learning and Literature in Tenth-Century England,' 21. For the presence and cultural influence of Bretons in England after the 910s, see Dumville, 'Æthelstan, First King of England,' 156–8; Brett, 'A Breton Pilgrim in England in the Reign of King Æthelstan'; Lapidge, 'Israel the Grammarian'; and Foot, Æthelstan, 103–6 and 190–2. It has also been suggested that 'Æthelstan A' was Bishop Ælle (Ælfwine) of Lichfield. See Kelly, Abingdon, 102; and Foot, Æthelstan, 72 and 98.
59 The charters attributed to 'Æthelstan A' include (in approximate chronological order): S 399, 400, 403, 405, 412, 413, 1604, 416–19, 379, 421–3, 425, 407, 426, 1792, 434, and 458 (Keynes, 'Regenbald the Chancellor [sic],' 186n4). S 416 and 425 are the only diplomas from the group to survive as contemporary single-sheets.
60 Kelly, Abingdon, no. 21 at p. 89.

God).[61] Susan Kelly has identified a number of symptoms which suggest that S 396 may represent 'an early effort' of 'Æthelstan A.'[62] The transience theme was to be developed to great heights in the charters of 'Æthelstan A,' for example, while the attention to the Last Judgment in S 396's anathema anticipates another of the draftsman's compositional predilections: 'Si quis uero hanc largitionis munificentiam, arrepto procacitatis stimulo, infringere uel mutare aut minuere temptauerit, sciat se in illa magni examinis die cum poli cardines terreque fundamenta simul et infernorum ima pauitando contremescent latibula, qua uniuscuisque patebit opus et conscientiam siue bonum siue malum quod gesserit, si non prius satisfaccione emendauerit'[63] (If anyone, indeed, incited by impudence, shall try to infringe or change or diminish this generous munificence, let him know that, on the day of the great Judgment, when the hinges of the pole and the foundations of the earth as well as the deepest dens of hell shall quake and tremble, on which each shall reveal his work and conscience, what he did, good or ill ... if he have not previously made emends with compensation).[64] As we have seen, the anathema was a standard component in diplomas, but in this case it shows a significant degree of expansion and ornamentation.[65] Moreover, like kings Alfred and Edward before him, Æthelstan is designated as *Angulsaxonum rex* in S 396, but the draftsman adds the phrase 'non modica infulatus, sublimatus dignitate.'[66] Both the anathema and royal title, then, show an instinct for embellishment and amplification. This particular diploma shows early steps toward rhetorical display with a preference for particular themes and topics which would become especially prominent in the work of 'Æthelstan A.'

S 416, dated to 931, is the only single-sheet original to survive from a group of diplomas produced by 'Æthelstan A' between 931 and 933.[67] This small corpus of texts represents the draftsman's mature style: the nascent fondness for adornment and amplification evident in S 396, issued five years earlier in 926, has now emerged fully formed. The group of diplomas shares a common proem, cited here from S 416:

---

61 *EHD* I, 546.
62 Kelly, *Abingdon*, 90–1.
63 Ibid., 89.
64 *EHD* I, 547.
65 The final position of *latibula* in its clause (separated from its adjective and attendant genitive by the participle and finite verb) may represent an attempt at hyperbaton.
66 Kelly, *Abingdon*, 89. '... adorned and elevated with no small dignity' (*EHD* I, 546).
67 The group includes S 412–13, 416–19, 422–3, and 1604. There is some minor variation across the texts. See Kelly, *Abingdon*, 103.

Flebilia fortiter detestanda . totillantis sæculi piacula . diris obscenæ horrendæque mortalitatis . circumsepta latratibus . non nos patria indoeptæ pacis securos . sed quasi foetidæ corruptelæ in voraginem casuros . provocando ammonent . ut ea toto mentis conamine cum casibus suis . non solum despiciendo . sed etiam velud fastidiosam melancoliæ nausiam . abhominando fugiamus . tendentes ad illud evvangelicum; 'date et dabitur vobis'; Qua de re infima . quasi peripsema . quisquiliarum abiciens . superna ad instar pretiosorum monilium eligens . animum sempiternis in gaudiis figens . ad adipiscendam mellifluæ dulcedinis misericordiam . perfruendamque infinit[ae] letitiæ jucunditatem.[68]

[The woeful sins – which are to be strongly abhorred – of the tottering world, encompassed by the dire howling of foul and horrible death, by their challenge remind us – we who are not secure in the peace obtained in the homeland but as if about to plummet into an abyss of stinking corruption – to shun them with their calamities through a full effort of mind, not only by despising them but also by loathing them as if the nauseating vomit of biliousness, aiming for the gospel, 'Give and it will be given to you,' and therefore casting off the basest things as if the off-scouring of waste, choosing heavenly things in the likeness of costly necklaces and fixing the mind in never-ending joy on gaining the mercy of honeyed sweetness and on enjoying fully the delight of infinite happiness.][69]

Because S 416 has no invocation aside from a standard pictorial cross, it begins straightaway with a single sprawling sentence of overwhelming rhetorical and lexical force. The general sentiment is common enough – we must turn away from sin and look to salvation – but the style is utterly remarkable, especially in comparison to the West Saxon diplomatic of previous decades. The grandiose proem essentially consists of two parts which are separated by the citation of Luke 6:38. The first part, the longer of the two, features a concentration of synonyms for danger, filth, and corruption: the decaying world staggers on the edge of disaster. The first two phrases – linked by *piacula* and *circumspecta* – each show chiasmus with the two phrases together following a larger chiastic pattern: 'flebilia fortiter detestanda totillantis sæculi piacula' (a x a b B A), and 'diris obscenæ horrendæque mortalitatis circumsepta latratibus' (a b· b B x A). Other

---

68 *BCS*, vol. 2, no. 677 at p. 363.
69 Because 'Æthelstan A' borrows from Aldhelm in this proem, my translation at the appropriate moments reflects translations given in Lapidge and Herren, *Aldhelm: The Prose Works*.

notable effects within the first section include the measured repetition of three ablative gerunds (*provocando, despiciendo, abhominando*) and two vivid similes tagged by the phrases 'sed quasi' and 'sed etiam velud.'

The first section also includes a significant amount of sound-play. The first phrase begins with an alliterative word pair (*flebilia fortiter*) followed directly by another word pair with a heavy repetition on the *t*-sound (*detestanda totillantis*) which echoes the doubled appearance of that sound in *fortiter*. The *ut*-clause following *ammonent* likewise features clustered repetitions of *t*-, *c*-, *s*-, and *m*-sounds: 'ut ea toto mentis conamine cum casibus suis . non solum despiciendo . sed etiam velud fastidiosam melancoliæ nausiam . abhominando fugiamus.' The end of the phrase additionally features chiastic end rhyme on -*am* and -*e/ando*. After the citation of Luke 6:38 – a brief moment of pellucid sense and syntax within a long and difficult sentence – the proem appropriately shifts into a culminating sequence of synonyms for joy, comfort and eternity: by putting aside the *infima* we can gain infinite security through the *superna*. A tricolon follows the gospel passage with each clause ending in a present participle (*abiciens, eligens, figens*), culminating in a pair of parallel chiastic phrases. The proem thus begins and ends with doubled chiastic units, an effect which creates an envelope pattern for the full sentence. This sustained structural device thematically moves the reader out of worldly decay and into heavenly ecstasy with the scriptural passage providing a transitive fulcrum. 'Æthelstan A' was clearly an accomplished writer with a fondness for intricate patterning and rhetorical play.

'Æthelstan A' also weaves several borrowings from Aldhelm into this proem. Sean Miller has identified two citations from the prose *De uirginitate*:[70] 'uelud fastidiosam melancoliæ nausiam' echoes Aldhelm's 'velut fetidam melancoliae nausiam,'[71] and 'quasi peripsema quisquiliarum' approximates his 'velut quisquiliarum peripsema.'[72] The latter borrowing is especially appropriate as it appears during Aldhelm's praise of those faithful who have embraced chastity after knowing 'the legitimate fertility of marriage.' These exemplary souls eschew sin and aspire to eternal life

---

70 Miller, *New Minster, Winchester*, 57.

71 Ehwald, *Aldhelmi Opera*, 274.1–2. 'Like the stinking vomit of biliousness' (Lapidge and Herren, *Prose Works*, 94). Aldhelm likens the phrase to a prostitute's false claim that the virgin Athanasius had visited a brothel.

72 Ehwald, *Aldhelmi Opera*, 238.11. 'Like the scourings of filth' (Lapidge and Herren, *Prose Works*, 66). Aldhelm likens the 'scourings of filth' to those *mundi blandimenta* which are rejected by the faithful.

through Christ: 'et qui contempta mundi blandimenta velut quisquiliarum peripsema respuens ac carnalis luxus lenocinia refutans in sancto proposito successor extiterat, sumpto viriliter castae conversationis tirocinio horrendum gehennae tartarum tremescens et aeternae vitae desiderio flagrans gratuita Christi gratia fretus cum sudoris industria efficiatur antecessor'[73] (And he who had been merely a follower in pious resolve, rejecting the pleasures of the world with contempt like the scourings of filth and repressing the enticements of carnal delight, and having undertaken manfully the novitiate of a chaste way of life and, trembling at the horrifying abyss of hell and burning with desire for eternal life, relying on the freely given grace of Christ, becomes the leader through the diligence of his labour).[74] Sailing past the 'perilous shipwreck of this world,' these diligent faithful survive horrible storms, skirt by Scylla and Charybdis, and arrive safely in 'the harbour of the monastic life' with Christ as the pilot of their battered boat.[75] 'Æthelstan A' shows a similar fondness for elaborate similes which warn against the dangers of worldly sin and which celebrate the eternal security to be found in heaven. In addition to the two examples cited by Miller, the S 416 proem includes several other notable borrowings from Aldhelm:

S 416	Aldhelm
diris obscenæ horrendæque mortalitatis	*dirae mortalitatis horrendae mortis* (prDV) [76]
non nos patria indoeptæ pacis securos	*non est tuta indeptae pacis prosperitas* (prDV)[77]
pretiosorum monilium	*auratis virtutum monilibus* (prDV)[78]
mellifluæ dulcedinis	*mellifluam dogmatum dulcedinem* (prDV)[79]
toto mentis conamine	*toto conamine mentis* (CdV)[80]

None of these borrowings are exact – 'Æthelstan A' seems to have cultivated his own minor variations – but the exuberant vocabulary and imagery in the

---

73 Ehwald, *Aldhelmi Opera*, 238.10–14.
74 Lapidge and Herren, *Prose Works*, 66–7.
75 Ibid., 67.
76 Ehwald, *Aldhelmi Opera*, 247.4 and 10 (prDV = the prose *De uirginitate*).
77 Ibid., 240.23–4.
78 Ibid., 246.11.
79 Ibid., 260.6.
80 Ibid., 357, line 89 (CdV = *Carmen de uirginitate*).

S 416 proem clearly emulate the model of Aldhelm.[81] 'Æthelstan A' aspires to a full-throttle *Kunstprosa* which transforms the proem into a contained space for literary showmanship.

Stylistically, the S 416 proem practices a kind of rhetorical repulsion which renders the physical world in amplified figures of danger and disgust; conversely, the heavenly realm appears positively as an eternal space of security and bliss. The world becomes sickening and grotesque, and its aversion the only sensible course of action. Indeed, the proem dedicates most of its considerable energy to rendering the sublunary realm as a filthy slough of despond that pulls the unwary down into sin and death – the tone is wholly negative until the gospel citation introduces a decrescendo affirmation of the higher realm. But the heavy notes of doom still resound past the closing motif of heavenly reward. The insistent claim that the world is in decay contradicts the notion that anything on the earth could endure or maintain a lasting value, much less that it might be held in the eternal possession promised by royal diploma. Even the biblical citation ('date et dabitur') favours the one who gives rather than the one who receives: the grantor acquires the lasting benefit while the grantee gains something of a more limited and temporary value.

After the proem, Æthelstan, designated 'rex Anglorum per omnipatrantis dexteram totius Bryttaniæ regni solio sublimatus'[82] (King of the English, elevated by the right hand of All-Accomplishing God to the seat of dominion over all Britain), grants nine hides of land to his thegn (*minister*) Wulfgar. The king conveys the land to Wulfgar so that he might 'possess it freely and eternally as long as he lives' with the additional benefit that he may leave the estate *in perpetuum* to whomever he wishes after his death.[83] The diploma thus provides two key elements of bookland, perpetual possession and the freedom of alienation,[84] but the more restrained language of the disposition pales in comparison to the stylistic pyrotechnics of the proem. The proem makes a clear claim about the value of heavenly bliss, but its sustained fascination with worldly filth and disaster establishes a tonal precedent which lingers beyond the confines of the proem. And like the proem, the disposition – standard enough in its terms – features claims

---

81 See Winterbottom, 'Aldhelm's Prose Style.'
82 *BCS*, 2:363. For the 'imperial ambitions' in such nomenclature, see Wormald, *Making of English Law*, 444–9.
83 'liberaliter ac æternaliter quamdiu vivat habeat' (*BCS*, 2:363).
84 The grant also includes the freedom from secular burdens. Wulfgar will hold the land 'sine jugo exosæ servitutis' (ibid.) [without the yoke of odious servitude].

about the eternal which are yoked to intimations of mortality. Wulfgar will possess the estate 'liberaliter et æternaliter' but only as long as he lives ('quamdiu vivat'). The vision of eternal possession is fixed within the temporal limits of a human lifetime and the promise of perpetuity inextricably bound to the inevitability of death.

After the disposition comes a long vernacular boundary clause followed by a vivid anathema. The careful delineation of the bounds in English puts the land itself in writing, codifying it for human possession and inheritance. Immediately after that act of textual representation, however, the diploma's sanction imagines the contradiction of the document's proprietary terms. As is typical for the Anglo-Saxon diploma, the anathema reserves its punishment for the afterlife, but in this text that deferred scenario is rendered in striking terms: 'Si autem quod absit . aliquis diabolico inflatus spiritu . hanc meæ compositionis ac confirmationis breviculam . infringere vel elidere temptaverit . sciat se novissima ac magna examinationis die . stridula clangente archangeli salpice . bustis sponte dehiscentibus . somata jam rediviva relinquentibus . elementis omnibus pavefactis . cum Iuda proditore . qui a satoris pio sato . "filius perditionis" dicitur[85] . æterna confusione . edacibus ineffabilium tormentorum flammis periturum'[86] (If, however, God forbid, anyone swollen with diabolic spirit should be tempted to diminish or annul this brief document of my arrangement and confirmation, let him know that on the final and great day of judgment, when the archangel's shrill trumpet rings out, when graves burst open by themselves and give up the bodies now revived, when every element trembles, with the traitor Judas, who is called 'son of perdition' by the Sower's merciful Offspring, he is to perish in eternal confusion within the hungry flames of unspeakable torments). The stylized vision of the graves spewing out the reanimated dead at the Last Judgment clearly echoes the imagistic bombast of the proem. 'Æthelstan A' warms to such moments as he brings his rhetorical arsenal fully to bear on their violent amplification. In addition to its arresting content, the anathema features a significant degree of rhetorical ornamentation: a concentration of word pairs early in the set-piece, a number of which contain alliteration and end-rhyme (*compositionis ac confirmationis, infringere vel elidere, novissima ac magna*); clusters of alliteration, particularly on *s* and *r*; and an accumulative string of four consecutive ablative absolutes after *sciat se*. The anathema, like the proem, also features chiastic phrases near its beginning

---

85 John 17:12.
86 *BCS*, 2:364.

and end: 'hanc meæ compositionis ac confirmationis breviculam' (a b B B A) and 'edacibus ineffabilium tormentorum flammis' (a b B A). And like the proem, the anathema contains Aldhelmian borrowings in conjunction with scriptural citation. The description of the last Trump and of the dead rising from graves clearly echoes the *Carmen de uirginitate*:[87]

> Omnia de nigris resurgent corpora bustis
> Clausae per campos et tumbae sponte patescunt,
> Dum salpix crepat et clangit vox clara tubarum
> Adventante Deo, qui cunctis praemia pensat
> Seu pia perfectis seu certe saeva profanis.[88] (278–82)

> [All the bodies will rise from their dark graves, and the tombs throughout the field, having been closed, will open by themselves when the trumpet blasts and the clear call of the horn resounds with God's advent, Who metes out rewards to all – either divine rewards to the excellent or obviously cruel ones to the sinful.][89]

As he does in the proem, 'Æthelstan A' makes some alterations to his source, including a substitution of the grecism *somata* (*soma*) for the more pedestrian *corpora*. The parallels between the anathema and Aldhelm's poem are clear:

S 416	Aldhelm
stridula clangente[90]	*crepat et clangit*
salpice	*salpix*
bustis	*bustis*
bustis sponte dehiscentibus	*clausae ... tumbae sponte patescunt*
somata jam rediviva relinquentibus	*resurgent corpora*

Like Aldhelm, 'Æthelstan A' revels in expansion and amplification. The diplomas attributed to 'Æthelstan A' meet that stylistic imperative most intensely in the proem and the anathema, components which appear at the very beginning and near the end of the text. Moreover, the S 416 proem

---

87 Miller, *New Minster, Winchester*, 57.
88 Ehwald, *Aldhelmi Opera*, 364–5.
89 Lapidge and Rosier, *Aldhelm: The Poetic Works*, 109.
90 One might also compare this phrase with 'horrendus salpicum clangor' from the prose *De uirginitate* (Ehwald, *Aldhelmi Opera*, 252.14).

and anathema both begin with a large capital letter in the manuscript, the only parts of the text to do so; the material text thus provides visual cues to the stylistic prominence of the proem and anathema within the diploma. Consequently, the style and content of those two sections tonally frame the transaction memorialized in the diploma. The fascination with mortality and reversal accordingly becomes a prominent aspect of tenurial discourse in these texts. The diploma bears wild witness to the squalor and impermanence of earthly possessions even as it solemnly presents itself as authoritative and abiding evidence for the eternal possession of land within a transitory world.

More than ever before, 'Æthelstan A' established the royal diploma as an occasion for literary showmanship. Many of the royal diplomas produced later in the tenth century follow his precedent to some degree as proems remained a space for rhetorical display. The general form of the royal diploma would remain consistent, but its local contents were now open to variation and innovation. After 'Æthelstan A,' royal diplomas in the tenth century often – but not always – featured elaborate proems and anathemas.[91] Moreover, not all literary proems in this period expound upon earthly transience and inevitable loss: a number of them prominently take creation and divine order as their theme.[92] One of Edmund's diplomas dated to 941, for example, features an inordinately long proem on this theme with an extended interest in law and obedience.[93] After 'Æthelstan A,' however, earthly loss and impermanence endured as a favourite topos within proems.[94] A few examples should illustrate the motif's perennial appeal. In a diploma dated to 943, King Edmund gives ten hides to his *minister* Eadric *perpetualiter possideat*. The opening invocation celebrates the divine order: 'In nomine Dei summi et altitroni qui omnia de summo celi apice uisibilia et inuisibilia ordinabiliter gubernans atque moderans,

---

91 Some noteworthy examples include S 842, 865 (Miller, *New Minster, Winchester*, nos. 26 and 28), and S 858 (Kelly, *Abingdon*, no. 123).

92 For specific examples see Stafford, 'Political Ideas,' 70n14.

93 S 478. Kelly, *Shaftesbury*, no. 12 at pp. 47–53. Kelly notes that the document is atypical: 'The draftsman does not appear to have been familiar with the mainstream of contemporary diplomatic, or else did not feel constrained to produce a conventional text; he made no use of standard formulas or wording in the business clauses of the dispositive section, and he has allowed himself great license in the immensely long proem and in the lengthy sanction' (ibid., 51).

94 Later draftsmen would recycle the proem from S 416 in part or in whole in their own texts. Examples include S 692, 777, 781, 919, 928, and 1006. See Kelly, *Malmesbury*, 221–2; and Kelly, *Bath and Wells*, 119.

presentisque uite curriculo cotidie temporales possessiones et uniuerse diuitiarum facultates nostris humanis obtutibus cernimus deficientes et decrescentes. Sic mutando fragilitas mortalis uite marcescit et rotunda seculorum uolubilitas inanescit ac in carorum propinquorum amicorumque amissione conqueritur ac defletur'[95] (In the name of highest God enthroned in heaven, who from the highest summit of heaven governs and controls all things visible and invisible in good order, we in the course of present life discern with the human eye that temporal possessions and all the power of wealth fail and fade away. Thus life's mortal frailty withers through change and the world's wheel-like rotation turns to emptiness and is lamented and mourned in the loss of beloved family and friends). The initial statement affirms God's complete control over all things, imagining an ordered universe which moves according to divine will. That image of perfect order is followed, however, by the dire claim that material possessions never last and that human life always turns to loss. This statement furthermore appears as a particular expression of the divine order within the syntactical logic of the diploma's opening statement. All these things happen *ordinabiliter*, the text affirms – the natural course of events defies permanence and security. This maxim offers a bleak preface to the optimistic terms of land granted in perpetuity. Land becomes both an eternal possession and one of those *temporales possessiones* which, much like human life, will eventually fade to nothing.

A similar tension appears in one of King Eadwig's diplomas dated to 956. In this document the king gives a small tract of woods to Abingdon *in eternam hereditatem*. The proem begins with the familiar contrast between the ephemeral and the eternal: 'Nichil in hoc seculo prolixa felicitate fruitur, nichil diuturna dominatione potitur, nichil quod non ad fatalem uite terminum ueloci cursu tendatur. Ideoque ut ortodoxorum demonstrant paradigmata sic nobis mundanarum rerum patrimonie sunt perfruende, ut tamen eterne patrie emolumentis numquam fraudemur'[96] (Nothing in this world is enjoyed with enduring happiness; nothing is held with lasting power; there is nothing that is not pressed on to the fatal end of life with swift speed. And therefore as the examples of the orthodox show, the inheritance of worldly things must be enjoyed in such a way that we are never cheated of the benefits of the eternal homeland). The first sentence's patterned repetitions underscore its fatalistic content – each clause begins with

---

95 S 491. Kelly, *Abingdon*, no. 37 at p. 154.
96 S 607. Kelly, *Abingdon*, no. 57 at p. 242.

nichil and ends with a singular passive verb, producing a measured repetition and end rhyme. Material *patrimonia* may have a limited use value, but the inheritance of real worth is located elsewhere. The tenurial rhetoric of perpetuity approximates the value of that *eterne patrie* but it also affirms earthly possession as a temporary and lesser commodity. These two proems may lack the stylistic exuberance typical of 'Æthelstan A,' but they do maintain the idea of the inexorable perishability of all worldly things (including, one would presume, the ownership of land). This idea furthermore is not merely formulaic or conventional, but it rather becomes an ideological component of a discursive field. Through sustained repetition, the trope of transience becomes embedded in tenurial discourse as an established component of diplomatic rhetoric, one which typically receives literary amplification and also constructs a paradoxical value for property.

The solemnity of the royal diploma thus bolsters the terms of its grants and privileges while its ornamental features can cast those very terms in doubt. This same effect appears in a diploma of King Edward the Martyr dated to 977. In this document, Edward books several estates to his ealdorman Æthelweard *in perpetuam hereditatem* with the assurance that he may leave the land to whomever he wishes after his death. The proem extols the lasting value of writing in an otherwise unreliable world.

> Regnante inperpetuum domino nostro ihesu christo. Cunctis sophię studium ferme rimantibus stabili notum constat ratione . quod presentis esentię periculis incumbantibus et curis euanescentium rerum inopinate crebrescentibus [h]umana mortalium rerum cognitio quasi ros minuendo elabitur et obliuioni tantundem traditur . nisi aliqua certa ratione prenotetur . quia non sunt æterna quę hic conspiciuntur sed terrena . ut imbutus sermone tonantis apostolus inquit. Nunc uelut umbra cito sic corpore[ae] fugiunt res. Sed decus æternum hoc uisu stat certius omni.[97]

> [Our Lord Jesus Christ reigning for ever. It is known by firm reason to almost all who pursue the study of wisdom, that, as the dangers of the present existence are threatening and the cares of evanescent things unexpectedly increasing, human knowledge of mortal affairs, vanishing like dew, fades away, and is at length given to oblivion, unless it is noted down before by some secure means, because the things which are seen here are not eternal but temporal, as the Apostle, inspired with speech of the Thunderer, says. Now, like

---

97 S 832. Earle, *Hand-book to the Land-Charters*, 295.

a shadow, the corporal things quickly flee; but the eternal glory stands more certain than all that is visible.][98]

The longevity and reliability of writing is a stock theme in Anglo-Saxon diplomas,[99] and the conceit appears here in close association with the equally common theme of worldly decay. The central point is clear enough – writing offers the best defence against unforeseen events and the failure of human memory – but its stylized delivery amplifies the transience trope to the point that it threatens to overwhelm the enduring value of writing. The statement that 'the things which are seen here are not eternal but temporal' quietly undermines the promise of eternal possession of property – indeed the text's use of *terrena* to signify temporary things makes the link between transience and land (*terra*) explicit. And is not the document itself, with its written terms and record of witnesses, a visible token created for and from the material world? Is the royal diploma itself, and the form of land tenure it provides, then, one of the world's illusive shadows? Moreover, the proem's closing advocacy of the *decus æternum* over 'all that is visible' again defers lasting security into a space located elsewhere. The document problematizes its own terms before the actual business of the grant itself can even appear in the disposition.

The inevitability of earthly loss, then, had become a standard theoretical component in tenth-century royal diplomas. The tensions already implicit within a discourse that could promise eternal possession in a world which was intrinsically defined by change and loss often become more vexed in the royal diplomas produced after the 930s. Prominent motifs of earthly impermanence furthermore often fixed that debilitative idea as a 'truth' within an immutable divine order. The invocation generally signifies divine endorsement of the document, but the proem also commonly invokes divine authority (through biblical citation, for example) in support of its own statements. When the proem presents its claims about impermanence and the limited value of earthly possession as an orthodox truth, it enables competing ways of thinking about land: God sanctions both the diploma's conveyance of eternal possession (in earthly time) and its insistence that all things of this world are limited and finite. One of the key pillars of documentary support, an immutable and always-just divine order, can

---

98 *EHD* I, 566.
99 See Wormald, 'Bede and the Conversion of England,' 144 and 151; Keynes, 'Royal Government and the Written Word,' 226; and Foot, 'Reading Anglo-Saxon Charters,' 39–40.

thus prove problematic as supplemental writing in the diplomatic text both confirms and challenges the recorded provisions. Literary display in Anglo-Saxon diplomas amplified the grandeur and sacral air of the official document, but it also often enabled potentially disruptive moments within a composite text for articulating uncertainties about the stability of tenurial discourse and practice.

Troubling Evidence

Expansions or additions intended to confirm rather than question the security and longevity of the grant can likewise unsettle the reliability of the second cornerstone of diplomatic sanction, the king's confirmation and the enduring royal support of the written provisions. This effect is particularly evident in the diplomas of King Æthelred II produced in and after 993. A substantial number of these documents contain what Simon Keynes has described as 'an account of the circumstances leading up to the transaction that in some cases amounts to a description of the recent history of the estate, and that considerably augments the length of the text.'[100] These embedded narratives generally give details of recent estate history: some specifically discuss crimes which have led to past forfeiture of the estates in question,[101] while others show the king expressing regret for past 'mistakes' he made as a youth.[102] This development, not entirely unprecedented,[103] established a new potential component in Latin diplomas, and it represents another innovation in Anglo-Saxon diplomatic during the tenth century.[104]

---

100 Keynes, *Diplomas*, 95. See also Stenton, *Latin Charters*, 74–82; Keynes, *Diplomas*, 95–103; Stafford, 'Political Ideas'; and Kelly, *Abingdon*, 492–3.

101 S 883 (A.D. 995), 886 (A.D. 995), 877 (A.D. 996), 896 (A.D. 999), 926 (A.D. 1012), 927 (A.D. 1012), and 934 (A.D. 1015).

102 S 876 (A.D. 993), 885 (A.D. 995), 891 (A.D. 997), and 893 (A.D. 998). See also Keynes, 'Re-Reading King Æthelred the Unready,' 90–4, with special attention to S 876.

103 See Keynes, *Diplomas*, 95–7; and Stafford, 'Political Ideas,' 69–70.

104 Susan Kelly has described an 'outbreak of scribal originality' under Æthelred: 'During the course of Æthelred's reign, the draftsmen of royal charters became increasingly less inclined to use standard and repeated formulation, preferring instead to produce their own, unique compositions. This is particularly noticeable in the case of proems, which are sometimes long and exceedingly complex literary exercises, apparently composed for a single occasion; despite the effort which must have gone into devising these passages, they are rarely seen more than once in surviving documents' (*Abingdon*, 460). See also Keynes, *Diplomas*, 115–18.

This chapter next examines three of these 'discursive' diplomas and the ways in which their added content affects the whole text. What happens when history is introduced into a textual environment which typically refuses temporal limitation or alteration? How does narrativity impact the essentially declarative mode of the diploma? Discursive material was primarily intended to provide protection against future disputes in situations which had involved past forfeiture or problematic estate histories. At the same time, the narrative content in diplomas foregrounds the unpredictable factor of human activity – an influence which the royal diploma typically denies or conceals – in the exchange and possession of land. Supplemental material intended to clarify estate history and to fortify current possession accordingly can destabilize the conceptual apparatus of eternal possession by introducing the evidence of change within the diplomatic text. The absolute security of bookland is thus exposed as vulnerable to accident and reversal.

A number of Æthelred's diplomas include 'a narrative section describing the crimes of an individual, serving to explain why his estates had been forfeited and thus to demonstrate that the king had the right to dispose of the particular estate in question.'[105] Whereas diplomas typically had omitted conditions for legal forfeiture, this group of texts renders that penalty visible through embedded narratives of past cases. Bookland thus becomes something that the king or his representatives can legally reclaim in response to certain transgressions, its benefits conditional. In the process, holding property becomes a vulnerable enterprise and the land itself carries the traces of past human activity and claims. These contingent aspects can clash against the otherwise solemn aspect of the diploma and its language of timeless possession. S 886, dated to 995, offers a particularly rich example of emergent strain between the various structural elements and stylistic registers in a single text.[106] In this diploma, King Æthelred grants two-and-a-half hides at Dumbleton, Gloucestershire to his *minister* Wulfric.[107] The elaborate proem, which is unique to this document, rehearses the conventional theme of worldly decay and extols the gain of heavenly joy through

---

105 Keynes, *Diplomas*, 97.
106 Kelly, *Abingdon*, no. 126 at pp. 489–93. The original manuscript has been lost, but the text survives in two thirteenth-century copies and in a transcript of a lost single-sheet made in the sixteenth century by Robert Talbot (ibid., 492).
107 This individual is Wulfric Spot ('Wulfric 52,' PASE), a thegn and wealthy landowner who founded Burton Abbey. See Sawyer, *Burton*, xv–xlv; Keynes, *Diplomas*, 188–9 and 193; and Kelly, *Abingdon*, 493. Wulfric's will survives as S 1536 (Sawyer, *Burton*, no. 29 at pp. 53–6).

the distribution of earthly treasures. The text thus frames an entirely secular transaction within an elevated rhetoric of salvation:

> Regnante in eona eonum cæli terręque dispositore herebiquę triumphatore. Vacillantis status cosmi undecumque vergitur, ac rigidibus turbinibus quatitur, sed succurrente diuinitatis omnipotentia ita tamen heroum fulcimento roboratur, ne titillando eneruiter pessumdari improuide videatur, dum tantorum auctoritate primatum moderatur, quamdiu Christiani onomatis pollet uigor ac regnorum iura prouida dispensatione gubernantur. Unde quos istius eui fortuna manu tepidę euectionis alludit, summopere ad nanciscendam ea inuigilandum est gaudia quę minime sunt annua sed continua, quatinus distributione temporalium gazarum æternę dapsilitatis adipisci mereantur adminicula.[108]

> [The Disposer of heaven and earth and Vanquisher of hell reigning from age to age. The condition of the tottering universe declines on every side and is shaken with severe whirlwinds, but by the help of the divine omnipotence it is nevertheless strengthened with the support of great men, lest it should seem improvidently to be ruined by feeble vacillation; while it is regulated by the authority of such great primates as long as the strength of the Christian name prevails and the rights of kingdoms are governed by provident dispensation; whence those whom the fortune of this age sports with by its feeble motion, ought especially to be vigilant to acquire those joys which are not for one year but for ever, that by the distribution of temporal treasures they may deserve to gain the support of the eternal bounty.][109]

This singular proem, which Susan Kelly has described as 'a personal literary effort by the draftsman of this particular charter,'[110] shows some rhetorical elaboration beyond the general extravagance of its contents. The invocation notably shows polyptoton in 'eona eonum,' for example, while the proem's sustained repetition of passive verbal endings in final position across a series of six clauses creates homoeoteleuton and rhyme. Again, we have a proem distinguished by its decorative language. The proem first disavows the earthly as failing and finite but finally affirms the distribution of temporal goods (*temporalium gazarum*) – presumably land in this case – as a means of obtaining eternal bounties (*æternę dapsilitatis*). These admittedly are not paradoxical concepts, but they do present a conflicting

---

108 Kelly, *Abingdon*, 489–90. Emphasis added.
109 *EHD* I, 573.
110 Kelly, *Abingdon*, 492.

estimation of earthly property as land assumes variable value in the proem: it is useful only insomuch as it facilitates the eventual acquisition of eternal bounty. And as we have seen, this notion of exchange favours the grantor rather than the beneficiary: the king presumably acquires eternal goods by giving away land while the recipient gains a temporal commodity within a failing cosmos.

Through its amplification of standard themes, then, the proem generates concepts which can worry the provisions given later in the diplomatic text. We have seen how rhetorical display in the proem can enable such tensions, but the effect can also occur in other components of the composite text. The disposition of S 886 follows standard patterns of diplomatic,[111] but it delivers its terms with some degree of flair:

> Quapropter ego ÆÐELREDUS totius Albionis Dei prouidentia imperator cuidam dilectissimo mihi ministro, cui parentelæ nobilitas WLFRIC indidit nomen, pro fidissimo quo mihi affabiliter obsecundatus est obsequio, quandam ruris particulam, id est duas mansas et dimidiam in loco ubi solicolæ ÆT DUMALTVN appellant, in perpetuam concedo hereditatem, quatenus ille bene perfruatur ac prospere possideat quamdiu huius eui incolatum vitali flamine rotabilique meatu percurrere cernitur, et post istius labilis uitę excessum cuicumque sibi libuerit successori derelinquat.[112]

> [On this account, I, Ethelred, emperor by the providence of God of all Albion, concede as a perpetual inheritance to a certain thegn most dear to me, on whom nobility of kindred conferred the name Wulfric, on account of the most faithful obedience with which he has courteously served me, a certain parcel of land, namely two and a half hides in the place which the inhabitants call Dumbleton; in order that he may enjoy it well and possess it in prosperity, as long as he is seen to pass through the habitation of this life with vital spirit and rotary course; and after his departure from this fleeting life, that he may leave it to whatever successor he shall please.][113]

Æthelred's statement that he gives the property *in perpetuam hereditatem* defies the proem's declaration that the goods of this world will pass away in time. In other words, the diploma promises something that it has just claimed does not exist. The disposition delivers the standard elements of

---

111 Ibid.
112 Ibid., 490.
113 *EHD* I, 573–4.

bookland – perpetual tenure and freedom of alienation – but it quickly returns to the rhetoric of transience which was so apparent in the proem: after his departure from 'this fleeting life' (*labilis uitę*) Wulfric is free to bequeath the land to whomever he wishes. On one level, this statement might be regarded as inflated but standard diplomatic rhetoric. Conventional content, however, is not ipso facto semantically or theoretically vacant. The disposition attaches the language of mortality to the permanence of the grant, enabling an ambivalence which sustains the tensions already active within the proem.

After its anathema, the diploma introduces an embedded account of the land's recent history. The property had been forfeited by a previous owner, one Æthelsige, as a penalty for theft. The diploma delivers a grave preamble before relating the specifics of the offence. Such a heavy transgression, the king affirms, must be preserved in writing so that it may never be forgotten. 'Nam quod hominis memoria transsilit litterarum indago reseruat; unde hec legentibus est intimandum quia hoc prefatum rus per cuiusdam uiri infandę presumptionis culpam qua audacter furtiue se obligare non abhorruit, cui nomen Æðelsige parentes indidere, licet foedo nomen dehonestauerit flagitio, ad mei iuris deuenit arbitrium atque per me reuerendo ut iam ante præfatus sum conlatum est ministro. Cuius culpę notam Anglica relatione hic ratum duximus esse notandum'[114] (For, what the memory of man lets slip, the circumscription in letters preserves; hence it ought to be made known to readers that this aforesaid estate came into the control of my possession through a crime of unspeakable presumption of a certain man, to whom his parents gave the name of Æthelsige, although he disgraced the name by a base and shameful act; in that he did not shrink from audaciously committing theft; and, as I have said above, it was conferred by me on the honourable thegn. We have approved that the account of his crime should be noted here with a report in English).[115] The passage indulges in several embellishments: the statement that writing can preserve what is lost to memory; a play on the meaning of Æthelsige's name;[116] and the rhetorical amplification of the enormity of his crime. Such a prelude builds anticipation. How exactly did Æthelsige betray his name? What was his 'crime of unspeakable presumption'? The diploma gives the details in English:

---

114 Kelly, *Abingdon*, 490.
115 *EHD* I, 574.
116 Æthelsige means 'noble victory.' A similar onomastic play appears in S 885 (also dated to 995), there in reference to the name Godwine. See Keynes, *Diplomas*, 102.

Ðus wæs þæt land forworht æt Dumaltun ðe Ælþelsige forworhte Æþelrede cyninge to handa, þæt wæs ðænne þæt he forstæl Æthelwines swyn Æþelmæres suna ealdermannes. Ða ridon his men to ⁊ tugon ut þæt spic of Æðelsiges huse ⁊ he oð bærst to wuda ⁊ man hine aflymde ða ⁊ man gerehte Æðelrede cynge þæt land and his æhta. Ða forgef he þæt land Hawase his men on ece yrfe ⁊ Wulfric Wulfrune sunu hit siððan æt him gehwyrfde mid ðam ðe he gecwemre wæs be ðæs cynges leafe ⁊ his witena gewitnesse.[117]

[Thus was the land at Dumbleton forfeited which Æthelsige forfeited into King Ethelred's possession: it was because he stole the swine of Æthelwine, the son of Ealdorman Æthelmær; then his men rode thither and brought out the bacon from Æthelsige's house, and he escaped to the wood. And he was then outlawed and his land and his goods were assigned to King Ethelred. Then he granted the land in perpetual inheritance to his man Hawas; and Wulfric, son of Wulfrun, afterwards obtained it from him by exchange with what was more convenient to him, with the king's permission and the witness of his councillors.][118]

Æthelsige's great crime was stealing pigs. After the elevated tone of the prefatory matter, the more informal register of the vernacular jars against the solemn pitch of the document as a whole. The episode was included most likely as insurance against future claims by Æthelsige's kindred,[119] and it was probably based on an older vernacular memorandum which had been produced for Hawas back when he had received the property from Æthelred.[120] The account marks a shift in language, register, and style, but it also notably introduces traces of past activity – human and documentary – into the environment of the diplomatic text. The account shows that the land had been held *on ece yrfe* by several individuals over

---

117 Kelly, *Abingdon*, 490. Abbreviations expanded.
118 *EHD* I, 574.
119 See Keynes, 'Crime and Punishment,' 77; and Wormald, *Making of English Law*, 149. Wormald suggests that vernacular accounts may have been read aloud in court: 'Families losing their estates might well hang on to the deeds so as later to adduce prior title before an ignorant court. Unambiguous accounts of their loss could stop them' (ibid.). One other of Æthelred's diplomas, S 877 (A.D. 996), includes a vernacular account of past crimes.
120 Kelly, *Abingdon*, 493. See also Keynes, 'Crime and Punishment,' 79: 'Indeed, it is likely in general that such accounts of crimes in the charters were derived from written records made when the case was settled, and that the draftsmen of the charters either incorporated them more or less verbatim, or re-cast them into the body of the text.'

the years and that eternal possession was subject to exchange over time. The sequence of events furthermore makes it clear that S 886 was drafted to confirm Wulfric's current possession of the property. In other words, the formal surface of the diplomatic apparatus initially conceals the social circumstances that necessitated additional documentation. S 886 represents not a new grant of bookland, but a confirmation of a previous exchange that was probably produced in apprehension of dispute. The evidence of past forfeiture also reveals another limitation of possession: the legal mechanism that allowed kings to reclaim bookland in the event of certain crimes or failures to meet established obligations. S 886 demonstrates how diplomas could make grand promises of undisturbed continuity while also preserving evidence of past forfeiture and negotiation. In the witness list, King Æthelred confirms the diploma *indeclinabiliter* (without change), but this particular text contains abundant evidence that confirmations of land were anything but fixed in Anglo-Saxon England.

Whereas the supplemental narrative in S 886 recounts a case in which the king repossessed land for legitimate reasons, another group of Æthelred's diplomas contain apologetic narratives of past situations when the king had seized property under more questionable circumstances. The young king had appropriated land from several churches in the years after Bishop Æthelwold's death in 984, and in several charters issued between 993 and 998 the king expressed his regret over these actions.[121] These open apologies were surely meant to reassure beneficiaries who had already been wronged by the king, but they also reinscribe the troubling evidence that the possession of land was vulnerable to human scheming and the aggressions of the powerful.

One of Æthelred's diplomas issued in 998 provides an example of this double effect and its potential to unsettle the security of the diploma's general purpose and claims. In S 893, Æthelred restores an estate at Bromley (Kent) to St Andrew's cathedral at Rochester.[122] The Anglo-Saxon Chronicle reports that King Æthelred had 'destroyed' (*fordyde*) the see of Rochester in 986, a statement which seems to indicate that the king despoiled the see of some of its lands (presumably including the estate at Bromley).[123] Indeed,

---

121   Keynes, *Diplomas*, 95–7 and 176–86 (Keynes describes Æthelred's reign between 984 and c. 993 as 'the period of youthful indiscretions'). This group of diplomas consists of S 876, 885, 891, and 893 (Keynes, *Diplomas*, 180n101). See also S 838 and 937; and Stafford, 'Political Ideas,' 80–2.

122   Campbell, *Rochester*, no. 32 at pp. 42–4.

123   'Her se cyning fordyde þæt bisceoprice æt Hrofeceastre' (O'Brien O'Keeffe, *MS C*, 85).

Æthelred apparently had already been at odds with Ælfstan, bishop of Rochester, for some time prior.[124] After the despoliation, the young king booked the Bromley estate to his *minister* Æthelsige in 987, giving the appropriated land *in perpetuam possessionem* so that 'habeat et possideat quamdiu uiuat in æternam hereditatem' (he may have and hold [it] in eternal inheritance as long as he lives) with the attendant freedom of alienation. That diploma, S 864, which survives as a contemporary single-sheet, says nothing of the land's recent history or the circumstances under which the king had acquired it.[125] The beneficiary Æthelsige was most likely the thegn who appears prominently in the witness lists of diplomas issued between 984 and 994, and a different individual entirely from the pig thief from S 886.[126] Some ten years after that grant, however, Æthelred confiscated the estate from Æthelsige and penitently returned it to St Andrew's.[127]

The diploma of restoration, dated to Easter of 998, begins with a lengthy proem which presents the holy festival as a time for the faithful to turn their minds away from the changeable world and toward the eternal joys of heaven.

Omnipotens Christus saluator mundi . cuius coęternum cum patre sanctoque spiritu regnum nec incipit nec desinit in seculum . qui in extremo caducorum margine per uterum beatę uirginis incarnatus . pro redemptione generis humani in ara sanctę crucis semetipsum patienter in odorem suauitatis immolari permisit . euangelicis nos edocet institutis . ut quanto magis mundanę uolubilitatis dies sicut umbra pretereunt . et caduca labentis seculi momenta uelut fumus deficiunt . tanto instantius illuc tendat nostrę mentis intentio . ubi non annua sed continua est et ineffabili dulcedine referta pascalium deliciarum refectio . ubi tranquilla est et suauis sanctorum in secula seculorum exultatio . et sine fine perpetua cum deo uiuo et uero omnium bonorum possessio . Cuius gratuitę pietati cum omni est affectu gratias agendum . quod suorum corda fidelium sancti spiritus illustratione in amorem sui nominis inflammat . et ut sanctos eius pia mente uenerentur inspirat . ut

---

124 See Campbell, *Rochester*, xx–xxii; Keynes, *Diplomas*, 178–80; Wormald, 'Charters, Law and the Settlement of Disputes,' 298–311; and Flight, 'Four Vernacular Texts from the Pre-Conquest Archive of Rochester Cathedral.'

125 Campbell, *Rochester*, no. 30 at pp. 37–9. Oddly enough, Ælfstan, the bishop of Rochester, appears fourth in the witness list, apparently confirming the despoliation of St Andrew's.

126 Keynes, *Diplomas*, 184–5.

127 Measured at ten sulungs in S 864, the estate is here reckoned only at six sulungs. Æthelred seems to have returned a reduced estate.

quod nostra possibilitate consequi nequimus . eorum nobis suffragio posse
donari speremus . qui ei in illa diuinę contemplationis gloria adunati . aeternę
beatitudinis sunt diademate coronati.[128]

[Omnipotent Christ, Saviour of the world, whose kingdom, co-eternal with
the Father and Holy Spirit, neither begins nor ever ends, who, having been
made flesh at the outermost edge of perishable things through the womb of
the blessed virgin, patiently allowed himself to be sacrificed in sweet fra-
grance on the altar of the Holy Cross for the redemption of humanity, in-
structs us through evangelical decrees that the more the changeable world's
days pass by like shadow and the expiring world's doomed moments fade
away like smoke, so the focus of our mind should aspire more urgently to
that place where there is refreshment filled with the ineffable sweetness of
paschal delights, not once a year but continually, where there is always the
exultation of the saints, tranquil, pleasant, and perpetual without end with
the living God, as well as the possession of all goods. We must give thanks
with total love for his freely-given compassion because he inflames the hearts
of his faithful with the Holy Spirit's radiance to a love of his own name, and
he inspires so that they might venerate his saints with devout mind, so that
what we cannot obtain through our own ability we may hope will be given to
us through the aid of those who, united by him in that glory of divine con-
templation, are crowned with the diadem of eternal beatitude.]

The reference to 'paschal delights' explicitly aligns the diplomatic text with
the festival of Easter, situating the tenurial act within sacred history and effectively juxtaposing the king's local act of restoration with Christ's redemption of mankind. The preliminary matter of the diploma thus appropriates
the holy value of the liturgical season. Christ's kingdom in the proem moreover exists entirely outside history – it neither begins nor ends in time – while
the days of human time pass like smoke and shadow. Indeed the language
of permanence pervades the opening text of the document: *coeternum, continua, in secula seculorum, sine fine perpetua*, and *aeternę*. This ideal of the
eternal is furthermore linked specifically to ownership: one can enjoy the
possession of all goods (*omnium bonorum possessio*) once they have entered
that eternal space. In addition to its benefit of full possession, God's kingdom also offers a sense of community in which all are one, joined in divine
glory before God. This vision of a polity untroubled by change or division

---

128 Campbell, *Rochester*, 42.

imagines an idealized alternative to the worldly kingdom, much like visions of heavenly permanence traditionally counterbalance themes of earthly impermanence in proems. S 893's proem, set within the season of Christ's resurrection, provides a solemn preliminary which frames the recorded act of restoration within ideals of salvation, eternal possession, and community.

The king's restoration of Bromley is presented consequently as a regenerative act for both the king's spiritual welfare and for the good of the political community. By returning the land to Rochester, the diploma suggests, the king moves the secular realm a step closer to the perfect order of the heavenly realm. In a long narrative which appears just after the disposition, Æthelred explains that he had been misled in his youth by one Æthelsige, a man who later revealed himself to be a base villain. The contrite king regrets his actions and now wishes to make amends:

Cuius tamen rapinę predationem . non tam crudeliter quam ignoranter . et maxime Æþelsino quodam infelice . dei omnipotentis ac totius populi inimico instigante . meque eius iniquę suasioni incaute consentiente fieri iussi . Qui inter cętera quę sepe commisit furti et rapinę flagitia publicus hostis inuentus . in tantum malitię suę frena laxauit . ut non solum uulgo quoscumque posset inuaderet . sed ut meam quoque puerilem ignorantiam calliditatis suę laqueo circumueniens inretiret . et ut tantum flagitii committerem . improbus prefati sancti loci predo incitaret . insuper idoneum et fidelem michi prepositum mea ab eius inuasione defendentem occideret . Vnde et iusto exigente iudicio disposui . merito eum omni dignitate priuari . ut qui iniuste rapuit aliena . iuste amitteret propria . Nunc autem quia superna michi parcente clementia ad intelligibilem ętatem perueni . et quę pueriliter gessi in melius emendare decreui . iccirco domini compunctus gratia quicquid tunc instigante maligno contra sanctum dei apostolum me inique egisse recogito . totum nunc coram deo cum flebili cordis contritione pęniteo . et quęque opportuna ad eundem locum pertinentia libenter restauro . sperans pęnitentię meę lacrimas suscipi . et prioris ignorantię uincula solui ab eo qui non uult mortem peccatoris . sed ut magis conuertatur et uiuat . credens me et gratiam inuenire in conspectu apostoli . qui in populo suo mitissimus apparuit . et pro crucifigentibus se exorauit.[129]

[Even so, more out of ignorance than cruelty, and most especially urged on by a certain Æthelsige, a wretched enemy of Almighty God and of all the people, and having rashly followed his wrong advice, I ordered its despoliation

---

129 Ibid., 43.

by robbery. Once exposed as a public enemy engaged in the other crimes of thievery and robbery that he often committed, he loosened the reins on his vice to such a degree that he not only openly attacked whomever he was able to, but the wicked robber of the aforementioned holy place also incited me so that he might encompass and entangle my childish ignorance in the snare of his cunning, and so that I would commit so great a shameful act. And more-over he killed my able and faithful reeve who was defending my possessions against his attack. And so, as just judgment requires, I decreed that he rightly be deprived of every honour so that he who had unjustly taken the possessions of others should justly lose his own. But because, having been spared by divine mercy, I have now reached the age of understanding and determined to make right the acts that I committed in childhood, therefore, inspired by the Lord's grace, I reconsider whatever I then did unjustly when incited by the wicked one. I repent it all now before God with tearful remorse in my heart and I gladly restore every advantage relating to that same place, hoping that the tears of my repentance will be received, and the chains of my old ignor-ance be loosed, by him who 'does not desire a sinner's death but rather that he might change and live,' and trusting that I will find favour in the sight of the Apostle who appeared the most gentle to his people and who prayed for those who crucified him.]

The passage's language is heavy with the rhetoric of grace and repentance, while the paraphrase of Ezekiel 33:11 accentuates even further the restora-tion of land as a salvatory act.[130] Furthermore, by prominently evoking St Andrew at the end of the account, Æthelred aligns himself with the holy patron of Rochester cathedral and appeals to the precedent of the saint forgiving his persecutors. The king may have wronged Rochester in the past, the narrative suggests, but he was himself also injured through that act – Æthelred presents himself as a victim who had fallen prey to bad in-fluence during his vulnerable youth and who thus deserves forgiveness. Now that he has recovered his senses and punished the old malefactor by confiscating his property, the matured king has set himself on a path of repentance and redemption. This personal recuperation is achieved in part through the rightful return of Bromley to Rochester.

---

130 'Dic ad eos vivo ego dicit Dominus Deus nolo mortem impii sed ut revertatur impius a via sua et vivat convertimini a viis vestris pessimis et quare moriemini domus Israhel' (Fischer, *Biblia sacra*, 1314) [Say to them, 'As I live,' says the Lord God, 'I do not wish for the death of the wicked, but that the wicked one should turn from his way and live. Turn back from your evil ways – why will you perish, O house of Israel?'].

The king restores Bromley, 'cum divinę maiestatis auctoritate et mea precipiens . ut nullus successorum meorum qui post me regnaturi sunt in gente Anglorum . sed nec ulla alia cuiuslibet altioris aut inferioris dignitatis persona hanc tellurem occasione qualibet inuadere presumat . sed semper in posterum portio ipsa ad usum praefatę episcopalis sedis episcopi qui nunc eam regit'[131] (with the authority of the divine majesty and my own, ordering that none of my successors after me who will rule among the English people, nor any other persons of any rank whatsoever, high or low, should presume to take this land on any pretext whatsoever, but that forever hereafter that part shall be for the use of the aforementioned episcopal see of the bishop who now rules it). The avowal of permanence for the endowment, with its all-inclusive proscription against any challenge or change in the future, affirms the lasting stability of the provisions, but it also ironically memorializes Æthelred's past conduct and its consequences for Rochester. This specific provision promises abiding royal protection while the diploma as a whole demonstrates that the king had been vulnerable in the past to manipulation and consequently been willing to divert land unjustly. The narrative which accompanies the king's personal assurance that he has changed, then, diminishes the reliability of royal support through its evidence of past alteration. Pauline Stafford has argued that the discursive content in Æthelred's diplomas essentially performs recuperative ideological work: 'A king changing his mind, undoing his own previous actions, was a problematic situation. In the 990s it was managed and naturalized through re-presentation as a shift from youth to maturity, and as a renewal of the actions of Æthelred's predecessors.'[132] S 893's 're-presentation' of past deeds, however, problematically establishes that royal favour was subject to change over time – the ideal of enduring support within tenurial discourse is thus exposed as uncertain. The diplomatic innovation of discursive content which was intended to reassure a once-wronged beneficiary signifies in multiple ways, bolstering but also unsettling the act of reconciliation confirmed in the document. In a positive sense, the double-story of past dispossession clarifies recent changes in possession and safeguards against future challenges from Æthelsige's kindred. Indeed the document's thorough character assassination leaves little doubt that the forfeiture was justified and thus the text works to forestall any lingering claims to the land. Still, the narrative element reveals

---

131 Campbell, *Rochester*, 43.
132 Stafford, 'Political Ideas,' 82.

that the royal prerogative of granting bookland also included the power to rescind that privilege for reasons which were not always legitimate or just.

S 886 and 893 both contain supplemental content which adds history to the formal matter of the Anglo-Saxon diploma. By embedding local history within its text, S 886 reveals the potential for human activity to change the tenurial order. Forfeiture in this document is presented as a legitimate response to criminal activity, and although it shows that the possession of land was always provisional, it does not appear as an unjust deprivation. The narrative content in S 893, however, bears more troubling implications for the double-edged capacity of royal power to give and take away. Both cases show how diplomas were instrumental texts for securing the possession of bookland and for cancelling that same possession in response to unforeseen events and interventions. In other words, the monumental text – and its desire for the eternal – is subject to change as an object within the world-in-time, the very temporal space that the diploma aspires to transcend. The 'pressure to record' that was felt in cases of forfeiture,[133] particularly in the diplomas of Æthelred II, introduces the unsettling evidence of historical forces – and the reversal such forces could effect – within the diplomatic text, just as the general impetus for amplification and expansion in tenth-century diplomas often generated conflicting ideas about the security, duration, and value of bookland.

We can see a powerful confluence of these effects in an original single-sheet document dated to the first week of Easter in 1019. In this diploma (S 956) King Cnut restores five hides of land at Drayton (Hampshire) to the New Minster at Winchester. Like several of Æthelred's diplomas, this document provides an account of how the king, having been misled by 'a certain youth,' had wrongly despoiled the church of its land, but is now returning that property to its rightful heirs. S 956 embroiders this act of royal atonement with exceptionally artful prose. Sean Miller has observed that Cnut's charters generally 'are more individual literary compositions than formula-bound productions,' and S 956 shows its singular character throughout its text.[134] Stenton described the language of this diploma as 'wildly flamboyant' and this is nowhere more evident than in the

---

133 Ibid., 72.
134 Miller, *New Minster, Winchester*, 162. See also Kelly, *Shaftesbury*, 125. In her commentary on S 955, Kelly notes a general trend 'towards literary elaboration and the rejection of standardization' in the diplomas of both Æthelred and Cnut.

document's opening passage.[135] In place of the proem, the diploma offers a sustained invocation which celebrates God's creation of the cosmos.

> Px Christo Iesu saluatore nostro . uero et summo Deo in unitate trino . in trinitate uno . atque incomprehensibili natiuitate omousios a coeterno patre genito qui pulcherrimus rerum pulchrum profunda mente gerens empyrium . ante materialem olimpi telluris et oceani specificationem . luminosam angelorum ierarchiam . ac preclara solis et lunae astrorumque igneorum uasa limpida . uarigenumque cosmi quadrifidi ornatum ac specimen . atque squamigeram neptunicę procellositatis copiam inexcogitabilem . solo dumtaxat uerbi protulit imperio . indeficienter regnante . ac triumphante . perpetualiterque omnia moderante.[136]

> [Christ Jesus our Saviour, true and highest God, three in Unity, one in Trinity, born by an incomprehensible birth of one substance with his co-eternal Father – who, most beautiful of things, bearing with profound mind the beautiful empyrean before the material formation of heaven, earth and ocean, brought forth by the power of a mere word alone the shining hierarchy of the angels, and the bright clear vessels of the sun, the moon and the fiery stars, and the various decoration and adornment of the four quarters of the universe, and the inconceivable abundance of fish in Neptune's tempestuous element – reigning continually and triumphing and perpetually guiding all things.][137]

The highly wrought text is replete with ornamental sound-play, architectural patterning, and impressive vocabulary. The invocation contains a remarkable amount of parallel syntax and chiastic patterning. The phrases 'in unitate trino' and 'in trinitate uno,' for example, employ parallel syntax, polyptoton (*unitate/uno* and *trino/trinitate*), and homoeoteleuton (which also creates end rhyme) to rhetorically frame the mystery of the Trinity.[138] Since the invocation mentions only Christ the Son and God the Father, it seems appropriate that it uses two phrases of three words each to do so. The Trinity-theme also emerges in the closing clause, 'indeficienter regnante . ac triumphante . perpetualiterque omnia moderante,' through its three present participles and their rhyming inflections. The first five

---

135 Stenton, *Latin Charters*, 83.
136 S 956. Miller, *New Minster, Winchester*, no. 33 at p. 159.
137 *EHD* I, 599–600.
138 The invocation contains another example of polyptoton in its proximate use of *pulcherrimus* and *pulchrum*.

words of the final clause, 'indeficienter regnante ac triumphante perpetualiterque,' additionally show chiasmus (adverb – present participle –
conjunction – present participle – adverb). Finally, the long relative clause
embedded within the main ablative absolute – dealing with the wonder of
God's creation of the universe through 'a mere word alone' – features a
dazzling array of ornamental effects. The beginning of the clause is marked
by clustered repetitions of *p* and *m* sounds (***pulcherrimus**, **pulchrum**, **pro-
funda mente**, **empyrium materialem** **olimpi***) and it shows homoeoteleuton
throughout (*materialem … specificationem, olimpi … oceani, luminosam
… ierarchiam, preclara … limpida vasa, astrorumque igneorum, uarigenumque cosmi quadrifidi ornatum, squamigeram … copiam*). The invocation represents God's creation of 'the four quarters of the universe'
(*cosmi quadrifidi*) appropriately enough in a series of four phrases linked
by conjunctions: (1) 'luminosam angelorum ierarchiam'; (2) 'ac preclara
solis et lunae astrorumque igneorum uasa limpida'; (3) 'uarigenumque
cosmi quadrifidi ornatum ac specimen'; and (4) 'atque squamigeram nep-
tunicę procellositatis copiam inexcogitabilem.' The four-fold list also features chiasmus in its last three phrases, which each exhibit a word order of
(A B B [B B] A A), where A represents an accusative noun/adjective and B
a genitive noun/adjective. Each of the three phrases ends with an accusative pair,[139] further accentuating the structural repetition within the series
through another grouping of three elements. In addition, the embedded
'creation clause' reiterates the Trinity-theme architecturally through its
two groups of three genitive nouns: 'olimpi telluris et oceani' and 'solis et
lunae astrorumque.' The invocation, teeming with rhetorical ornamentation, thus incorporates a remarkable degree of 'number play' in its several
groupings of three (the Trinity) and four (the *cosmi quadrifidi*).[140] This
invocation – with its many lexical, structural, and aural adornments – presents a carefully crafted set-piece.

---

139 Miller proposes that the doublets in this diploma 'might suggest that the draftsman
     was influenced by Wulfstan's prose style; such repetition is certainly not at all com-
     mon in contemporary charters' (*New Minster, Winchester*, 162).
140 The attention to groupings of four appears again in the second blessing added after the
     witness list: 'Gloria et diuitiae et felicitas et beatitudo cunctis huic libertati fauentibus
     in tabernaculis donetur iustorum' (ibid., 161). 'Glory and riches and happiness and
     blessing in the tabernacles of the righteous be granted to all promoting this privilege'
     (*EHD* I, 601). Among Cnut's charters, S 949 and 960 also have a second blessing after
     the witness list; like S 956, both discuss the past history of the estate (Miller, *New
     Minster, Winchester*, 162).

S 956 replaces the proem, frequently an occasion for voicing sentiments of impermanence, with a long and highly ordered invocation affirming a highly ordered world. S 956's prefatory matter remains altogether free of any hint of transience or loss – the diploma jettisons such troubling ideas from its initial matter entirely.[141] The diploma seems studiously to avoid intimations of worldly mortality and change, perhaps because of the particular situation that prompted its creation. The absence of a proem also means that the dispositive clause follows the invocation directly, allowing an immediate resonance between the two components. This associative effect is achieved in part through the common attention in both sections to the power of words to effect transformative change. God creates 'by the power of a mere word alone,' and King Cnut achieves and affirms the restoration of the New Minster's land through the power of writing: 'hanc membranulam grammatum carecteribus canna sulcante precepi exarari'[142] ([I] have ordered this parchment to be inscribed by the furrowing reed with the forms of letters).[143] Cnut's command, with its conspicuous attention to the characters and implements of writing, calls for documentary writing to memorialize the restoration of the land's *utilitatibus* (benefits) to the monks 'just as it was a long time before.'[144] This royal order echoes the verbal act of creation celebrated in the invocation, corroborating the idea that words can make a well-ordered and regulated world.

The tenor of the diploma thus far is wholly optimistic, but the following discursive section disturbs the text's carefully cultivated sense of order. The king recounts the troubling history that has made the restoration

---

141 The transience theme does appear among Cnut's diplomas prior to the drafting of S 956. Another of Cnut's single-sheet diplomas (S 950) issued earlier in 1018 features a proem which contrasts 'the aging world' and heavenly eternity: 'Uniuersa quae in seculo presenti humanis uidentur oculis cito deficiunt . quae uero superis locantur montibus . amoenitate uigent continua . in summitonantis regimine aeternaliter fixa manentia . et idcirco nobis inueterati filiis seculi studendum est . ut operibus iustis . frui mereamur bonis caelestibus . semper uicturi cum angelis sanctis' (Brooks and Kelly, *Christ Church, Canterbury*, no. 144) [All things which are seen by human eyes in this present world quickly pass away, but the things which are set on the mountains above flourish in continual delight, remaining fixed eternally under the control of the Highest Thunderer; and therefore we children of a dying world must devote ourselves so that through good works we may earn enjoyment of celestial goods, to live forever with the holy angels].

142 Miller, *New Minster, Winchester*, 159.

143 *EHD* I, 600.

144 'admodum ante multa deseruiebat tempora' (Miller, *New Minster, Winchester*, 160). Translation, *EHD* I, 600.

necessary: misled by the lies of a certain *inhabitator adolescens* in Winchester, Cnut had earlier deprived the monks of the estate and transferred it to the devious young man.[145] As in Æthelred's diplomas, the king assumes a penitent tone as he confesses his past mistakes:

> Hanc quippe terram quidam prefatę ciuitatis inhabitator adolescens animosus et instabilis calliditate et mendacio sibi a me adquisiuit . dicens terram meam fuisse . meque facile eam sibimet tradere posse . quod et feci . At ubi ueritatem agnoui . hereditatem Dei dignis heredibus ocius restitui feci . et ad testimonium et confirmationem hoc in presenti cartula manifestari precepi . Et quia penes prescriptum adolescentem litteras huic libertati contrarias . et calliditatis indagine adquisitas haberi comperimus . et illas sub anathemate dampnamus . et quascumque alias si alicubi sunt pro nihilo ducimus . Hancque dumtaxat litteraturam libertate perhenni ditamus ac corroboramus.[146]

> [This land, indeed, a certain inhabitant of the aforesaid city, young, daring and inconstant, acquired for himself from me with cunning and lying, saying that the land was mine and that I could easily give it to him, which also I did. But when I realised the truth, I caused the inheritance of God rather to be restored to worthy heirs, and ordered this to be manifested for testimony and confirmation in the present charter. And since we have discovered that there are in the possession of the afore-mentioned youth letters contrary to this privilege, and acquired by fraudulent investigation, we both condemn those under pain of anathema, and hold as worthless any other such if there are any anywhere; and we endow only this writing with perpetual liberty and confirm it.][147]

The story is unequivocally clear in its ethical landscape – truth (*ueritatem*) is on the side of the monks while the 'animosus et instabilis' youth works through falsehood and machination – but it also looks ahead to sustained conflict between those opposed interests. The account renders this anticipated dispute essentially as a clash between competing documents. The current document ('in presenti cartula') confirms the restoration, but Cnut remains acutely aware of precedent *litteras* acquired by the unnamed youth. The diploma claims to supersede these 'fraudulent' writings in a

---

145　A lease, S 1420, discusses some of the Drayton estate's past history with the New Minster. See Miller, *New Minster, Winchester*, no. 32 at pp. 157–9. The diploma Cnut presumably issued to the 'youth' has not survived.

146　Ibid., 160.

147　*EHD* I, 600.

fantasy of generative writing which echoes the content of the invocation and its own account of creation by word alone. S 956 combats the possibility of rival documents by condemning those imagined texts preemptively as 'worthless' (*pro nihilo*) even as it affirms the exclusivity of its own authority ('we endow only this writing with perpetual liberty and confirm it').[148] The use of *dumtaxat* in both this particular endorsement and in the prefatory account of divine creation – the word appears only these two times in the entire text – fortifies the link between the two moments of generative writing: God's word alone made the four-quartered universe just as the written text of Cnut's diploma alone signifies the New Minster's perpetual right over the five hides at Drayton. In this way, the diploma makes the case for the transformative and abiding power of its own written text.

S 956 casts its act of restoration in a strategically ordered and artful text. At the same time, it reinscribes the disturbing evidence of the king's mercurial behaviour – the added element of conciliatory writing reminds the beneficiary that royal support can change direction. Cnut's denunciation of competing documentation furthermore problematizes the singular authority of the diploma. The 'youth' apparently had evidentiary documents of his own, one of which had probably been issued by Cnut after the king had appropriated the land from the New Minster. These elements undermine two foundational authorities in the restoration: the singular authority of the written document and the enduring support of the king. Sarah Foot has argued that Anglo-Saxon diplomas present self-authenticating versions of events that countermand alternative stories and/or documents that might offer competing claims for possession. Of S 956 she specifically writes, 'The whole text is designed to be incontestable, but it recognizes the evidential weight of other – contrary – documents and seeks to render them invalid in the process. The temporal summation of what has gone before is part of what makes the text powerful.'[149] Cnut's diploma certainly aspires to power through its style and contents, but its 'temporal summation' also weakens that sense of authority through its reminder that the king always retains some claim on the land with the attendant ability to take the land and give it to someone else, legitimately or not. In S 956,

---

148 Tenth-century diplomas frequently condemn competing documents. See Stafford, 'Political Ideas,' 70n11. See also Wormald, 'Charters, Law and the Settlement of Disputes'; and Foot, 'Reading Anglo-Saxon Charters,' 41.
149 Foot, 'Reading Anglo-Saxon Charters,' 62.

writing is both the problem and the solution. Cnut takes corrective action by ordering new writing which aspires to replace and defeat old documents, but in celebrating the (re)generative power of the word, the diploma also intimates that documents can effect change perhaps too easily. The proliferation of writing generates contradiction between different texts and even within individual ones. The presence of supplemental narrative in S 956 thus works against the 'timeless' claims of the diploma by inscribing the unpredictable factor of human activity and its potential to reverse or revise established documentary provisions.

The individual elements of the royal diploma collaborate to represent the grant of land in a memorial text whose authority theoretically lasts forever. The diploma fossilizes a single authentic moment, the original grant of property, for all time within a material text; in this sense the document is at once precisely situated in time and effectively timeless. The diploma manages this conflation of the temporal and atemporal through various forms of textual display: the collaboration of royal and divine endorsement, sacral rhetoric among its provisions, and the incorporation of stylized content. Beginning in the tenth century, literary showmanship provided a key means of supplementing the solemn authority of the diploma, performing a function that had once been fulfilled by public ceremonies of conveyance and confirmation. As I have argued, these various elements within the formal text can enable competing concepts about land and its possession in time. This multivocal element furthermore appears most forcefully within moments of literary display which could achieve more than the production of an impressive document. Rhetorical content can transcend the function of mere ornamentation to trouble the integrity of the whole text: amplified tropes of transience contradict the tenurial conceit of eternal possession, while narrative content intended to clarify recent changes in possession (and thus to protect the beneficiary against dispute) introduces traces of historical forces which problematize the diploma's absolute claims. In this way, the diplomatic text generates dissonance and tensions within its compositional parts: land is both worthless and precious, a possession perpetually secure but always at risk, a temporary commodity to be exchanged for eternal goods elsewhere.

One of the more troubling elements within this vexed discourse is the disconcerting potential of dispute and/or dispossession. As we have seen, supplemental writing intended to reassure or reinforce can also reinscribe the threat of competing claims and the possibility of loss. The historical evidence makes it clear that this apprehension was well-founded – the possession of land was certainly more fluid and vulnerable than the ambitious terms of the royal diploma would suggest. The next chapter accordingly examines how one class of legal document, developed in response to the enduring problem of dispute, engaged this particular problem not through solemn declarations of ownership in a timeless Latin muniment but rather through vernacular narrativity and strategic storytelling in a situational text.

2 Storied Land

God sceal wið yfele, geogoð sceal wið yldo,
lif sceal wið deaþe, leoht sceal wið þystrum,
fyrd wið fyrde, feond wið oðrum,
lað wið laþe ymb land sacan,
synne stælan.[1]

– Maxims II

The Anglo-Saxons developed a range of documentary forms for recording and controlling various aspects of land tenure, but these legal instruments could often fail to ensure their recorded terms. Property disputes were common, overturning the assurances of eternal possession contained in Latin diplomas, and many vernacular charters record the complex and frequently incomplete details of these disputes and their outcomes.[2] Such documents have provided invaluable evidence for understanding dispute settlement in Anglo-Saxon England, but thus far less attention has been given to their narrative and rhetorical function. These charters essentially function as strategic narratives designed to establish the claim of a particular party on a piece of

---

1 Dobbie, *Minor Poems*, 57. 'Good must contend with evil, youth with age; life must contend with death, light with darkness; army must contend with army, one foe with another; the aggrieved must contend with the aggrieved over land, must place the blame' (50–4a).
2 A majority of the Anglo-Saxon lawsuits assembled by Patrick Wormald involved property disputes. See Wormald, 'Handlist.' For dispute settlement in England and on the continent, see White, '"*Pactum … Legem Vincit et Amor Judicium*"'; Kennedy, 'Disputes about *Bocland*'; Davies and Fouracre, *Settlement of Disputes*; Brown, *Unjust Seizure*; Hyams, *Rancor and Reconciliation*, esp. 71–110; and Bowman, *Shifting Landmarks*.

land.[3] In contrast to Latin diplomas, which declare eternal possession and construct an idea of land as existing outside time, vernacular charter accounts selectively arrange events within time to deliver authoritative stories of dispute and its resolution. The charter narrative stands as a preemptive argument against competing claims to possession. As supplemental written activity, these texts provide a retrospective intervention which assigns sense and order to the human actions which had complicated or contradicted the declarative provisions of established documents. The substantial corpus of these charters attests to the general proliferation of writing that accumulated around land in Anglo-Saxon England, but their very existence also demonstrates the worrying potential for official documents to falter or fail under social pressure. Possession might theoretically be achieved and witnessed through an originary act of documentation such as that provided by the Latin diploma, but its subsequent preservation often required additional measures.

While the Latin diploma imagines land (and its possession) as timeless and insulated from change, dispute charters show that the conceptual fusion of earthly property to eternal time often needed to be supplemented by additional documentation and human improvisation. The static place represented in the diploma, held by one individual or institution for all time, becomes in vernacular narrative a dynamic space of social activity. In these texts, land is defined and determined by human action and conflict as events unfold over time. In this sense, the vernacular narrative of dispute makes *timely* claims, in contrast to the Latin diploma which makes *timeless* claims that essentially defy historical change or complication. The diploma conceptualizes land as existing outside time as it promises eternal possession in a memorial document. The charter narrative, in contrast, imagines land as being open to the manipulation and intervention of multiple agents as circumstances change over time.

After a preliminary discussion of the mode and method of Anglo-Saxon dispute charters, this chapter offers an extended analysis of one tenth-century document, S 1447, and its remarkable use of strategic narrative. S 1447 also employs a range of formal devices which are typically associated with artful prose – such as direct and indirect speech, narrative transitions, and rhetorical ornament – in order to shape and enhance its presentation of events; moreover, in a pronounced example of what Warren Brown has

---

3 See Brown, 'Charters as Weapons,' for a discussion of Carolingian dispute charters and the ways in which church scribes manipulated narrative in order 'to create useful histories' for their communities.

elsewhere called 'deliberate design' in narrative charters,[4] S 1447 cultivates a powerful resonance with contemporary politics in order to assume an additional degree of associative force. Finally, even though its narrative underscores the instrumentality of documents in the conveyance and possession of land, this text quite clearly shows the dynamic nature of property within social practice, revealing the ability of land to change hands easily and even to escape legal protections and provisions. Land in the process becomes a fluid commodity, a thing separate from ideals of the eternal or immutable, and thus conceptually at odds with the diplomatic rhetoric of perpetual possession.

Tales of Dispute

The earliest accounts of property dispute in Anglo-Saxon England appear in Latin documents dated to the eighth and ninth centuries.[5] Some of these charters contain substantial narratives of specific cases. S 1439, for example, dated to 844, gives a long account of a struggle between the church and secular parties on two occasions over the inheritance of one Oswulf, *dux atque princeps* in East Kent.[6] By the early tenth century, however, a new kind of vernacular document had emerged for recording the history and resolution of property disputes. These texts were generally composed to provide evidence or pleas in current or anticipated disputes. Stenton described the function of such a document as follows: 'Its object is to record the settlement of a dispute or to indicate the stage which has been reached in its progress, and it proceeds by way of a narrative of events which is often elaborate and covers a long period.'[7] Stenton rightly emphasizes the narrativity of these texts. As they tell their stories about dispute, such charters frequently employ narrative tropes and techniques which provide events with a partisan sense of order and meaning.

Hayden White has argued of historical narrative that 'events must be not only registered within the chronological framework of their original occurrence but narrated as well, that is to say, revealed as possessing a

---

4 Ibid., 244.
5 See the cases listed in Wormald, 'Handlist,' 265–6. The eighth-century disputes are all ecclesiastical cases.
6 Brooks and Kelly, *Christ Church, Canterbury*, no. 74. See also Wormald, 'Handlist,' nos. 18 and 19 at p. 266; and Crick, 'Church, Land and Local Nobility in Early Ninth-Century Kent.'
7 Stenton, *Latin Charters*, 43.

structure, an order of meaning, which they do *not* possess as mere sequence.'[8] In White's view, historical narrative is predicated on an assumed system of meaning which provides sense and justification to the movement of events, 'a structure that was immanent in the events *all along*.'[9] This determinative logic, constructed through narrative, makes a particular claim about the real, one which displaces, discredits, or silences other competing accounts: 'In order to qualify as "historical," an event must be susceptible to at least two narrations of its occurrence. Unless at least two versions of the same set of events can be imagined, there is no reason for the historian to take upon himself the authority of giving the true account of what really happened. The authority of the historical narrative is the authority of reality itself; the historical account endows this reality with form and thereby makes it desirable, imposing upon its processes the formal coherency that only stories possess.'[10] By telling 'what really happened' in particular disputes, narrative charters deliver authoritative representations of past events and their outcome. Paul Strohm has similarly argued that legal texts can be read 'less as records of events than as interpretations of events, inevitably reliant to one degree or another upon invention, upon fictional devices. A text's fictionality may derive from acts of commission (its imputation, for example, of motive) or omission (by what it evades or excludes).'[11] In other words, we can read charter accounts of dispute as controlled fictions which make strategic claims through story. The fictionality in these texts typically provides some explanation or justification for the movement of property from owner to owner, especially if that movement has involved forfeiture or dispossession. In these cases the narrative frequently offers discernible signs which confirm the order of things claimed within the document. By establishing that the disenfranchised party had lost the land for reasons definitive and just, the charter account attempts to dispel competing interpretations of past events.

In cases of forfeiture, charter accounts often explain the loss of property through some moral or ethical logic imposed by the narrative.[12] Within this

---

8 White, 'Value of Narrativity,' 9.

9 Ibid., 23.

10 Ibid.

11 Strohm, *Hochon's Arrow*, 4.

12 Paul Fouracre sees a similar reflex in Merovingian dispute settlement and *placita* documents: 'The confiscation of property must be seen to be indisputably correct, for this is where visible injustice could occur and those monitoring the count, the *rachymburgi*,

logic, those who lost land only did so for transparent and justifiable reasons. Property would be forfeited, for example, if its owner were found guilty of theft or treason against the king; such examples appear in the charters of Edward the Elder,[13] and are especially prominent in the charters of Æthelred II.[14] Beyond these serious crimes, however, charters also contain cases of forfeiture for other offences both sensational and mundane. S 1377, for example, records an exchange of property between Bishop Æthelwold and Wulfstan Uccea which occurred sometime between 963 and 975. Æthelwold later distributed the estates to Thorney and Peterborough. One of the exchanged estates had previously been forfeited by a former owner, a widow who had been charged with practicing witchcraft:

> Her sutelað on þyssum gewrite þet Aþelwold bisceop ⁊ Wulstan Uccea hwyrfdon landa on Eadgares cyninges ⁊ on his witena gewytnesse. Se bisceop sealde Wulstane þet land æt Hwessingatune ⁊ Wulstan sealde him þet land æt Iaceslea ⁊ æt Ægeleswurðe. Þa sealde se bisceop þet land æt Iacleslea into Þornige ⁊ þet æt Ægeleswyrðe into Buruh. ⁊ þæt land æt Ægeleswyrðe headde an wyduwe ⁊ hire sune ær forwyrt for þan þe hi drifon serne stacan on Ælsie Wulfstanes feder ⁊ þæt werð æreafe ⁊ man teh þæt morð forð of hire inclifan. Þa nam man þæt wif ⁊ adrencte hi æt Lundene brigce ⁊ hire sune ætberst ⁊ werð utlah ⁊ þæt land eode þam kynge to handa ⁊ se kyng hit forgeaf þa Ælfsie ⁊ Wulstan Uccea his sunu hit sealde eft Adeluuolde bisceope swa swa hit her bufan sægð.

> [Here it is declared in this document that Bishop Æthelwold and Wulfstan Uccea have exchanged lands with the witness of King Edgar and his witan. The bishop gave Wulfstan the land at Washington [*Sussex*] and Wulfstan gave him the land at Yaxley [*Hunts.*] and at Ailsworth [*Northants.*]. Then the bishop gave the land at Yaxley to Thorney and that at Ailsworth to Peterborough. The land at Ailsworth had been forfeited by a widow and her son because they drove an iron pin into Ælfsige, the father of Wulfstan, and it was found out and the deadly image was dragged out of her room. Then the woman was taken and drowned at London bridge and her son escaped and became an

---

were themselves property owners, thus likely to have a strong interest in the protection of property through due legal procedure' ('Settlement of Disputes,' 40). See also Brown, *Unjust Seizure*, 102–23; and Rabin, 'Old English *Forespeca*,' 234.

13 S 362, dated to 901, for example, refers to property previously forfeited by one Wulfhere and his wife for treason against King Alfred. *BCS*, vol. 2, no. 595 at p. 243.

14 For specific examples and discussion, see Keynes, 'Crime and Punishment,' 76–81.

outlaw, and the land passed into the king's hands, and the king then gave it to Ælfsige, and his son Wulfstan Uccea afterwards gave it to Bishop Æthelwold, as is related above.][15]

The account of the crime prominently occupies the centre of the memorandum, interpolated between the exchanges of estates. An extant diploma, S 533, dates King Eadred's grant of the Ailsworth estate to Ælfsige to 948, although it says nothing of the forfeiture that preceded the grant.[16] The crime and forfeiture, then, must have occurred some twenty years prior to the arrangement between Æthelwold and Wulfstan Uccea. The compressed account of that past case included within a matter-of-fact delineation of exchange and transmission effectively reinscribes contention in the land's history. The estate-in-writing thereby preserves an unsettling memory of a sensational crime and forfeiture. The account must have been included to establish that the property had passed to Ælfsige legitimately in 948: the nameless widow and son were rightly punished for their malicious plot and the king thereafter rewarded the property to Ælfsige, perhaps as recompense for his nearly fatal encounter with the dark arts. The account presents itself as a transparent statement of past events, a determinative record in which forfeiture was both justified and final.

To a sceptical reader, of course, the situation immediately seems suspect as Ælfsige clearly benefited from the accusation brought against the widow and her son.[17] The important point here, however, is not the bias in the account, but the process of documenting (and thereby justifying) the winding channels through which the Ailsworth estate finally came to Peterborough. Through both its moral logic and its attention to due procedure the memorandum erases the legitimacy of any potential claims brought by the kindred of the nameless widow and son. These 'criminals' (and their past claim to the property) disappear from the account in their respective moments of death and outlawry, to be replaced by the authoritative figure of the king and the legitimate transmission of land which his intervention represents. Interestingly enough, the worrisome trace of the old controversy at Ailsworth seems to have remained dormant. Trouble

---

15 S 1377. Kelly, *Peterborough*, no. 17 at pp. 275–6. Abbreviations expanded.
16 Ibid., no. 10 at pp. 221–5.
17 Andrew Rabin has pointed out that 'the widow's punishment here does not conform with the penalties found in either Old English legal or penitential texts. In neither tradition is the sticking of pins into an effigy considered sufficient justification for capital punishment' ('Anglo-Saxon Women Before the Law,' 43). See also Kelly, *Peterborough*, 276–7.

came instead when Wulfstan Uccea later attempted to renege on the original agreement about Yaxley, perhaps after King Edgar's death in 975.[18] The text of the Thorney foundation charter (S 792) preserved in the Peterborough archive indicates that Æthelwold was forced to repurchase the Yaxley estate after Wulfstan tried to alter the terms of the original exchange.[19] The anticipated dispute came not from the heirs of dead witches or lurking outlaws, but rather from banal greed and opportunism. New developments upset old arrangements – even those memorialized in writing – and additional measures were required to resecure and redocument possession over time.

While S 1377 focuses on a sensational crime which led to forfeiture, other charters dedicate their attention to documenting more fully the process and finality of a particular dispute's resolution. In these texts, the genesis of the dispute is less important than its end. S 1456 records the resolution of a dispute in the late tenth century over an estate at Snodland between Bishop Godwine (Rochester) and one Leofwine.[20] The undated document begins by immediately stating its purpose: 'Her cyð on ðysum gewrite . hu Godwine biscop on Hrofeceastre . ꝧ Leofwine Ælfeages sunu wurðon gesybsumode ymbe þæt land æt Snoddinglande . on Cantwarabyrig' (Here it is stated in this document how Godwine, Bishop of Rochester, and Leofwine, Ælfheah's son, were reconciled at Canterbury about the estate at Snodland).[21] This opening statement notably declares that the dispute is over – the story hence begins with the 'truth' of its ending. The narrative proper then begins with the archival discovery of written evidence. Soon after his appointment in 995, Bishop Godwine[22] found documents (*swutelunga*) showing St Andrew's claim to land at Snodland. Unfortunately, that property was currently in the possession of Leofwine.[23] Bishop Godwine moved to reclaim the land and the case soon became known to

---

18 There were widespread attacks on monastic landholdings after Edgar's death in 975. See Stenton, *Anglo-Saxon England*, 372–3; Fisher, 'The Anti-Monastic Reaction in the Reign of Edward the Marty'; Keynes, *Diplomas*, 176–86; Stafford, *Unification and Conquest*, 57–9; Williams, '*Princeps Merciorum gentis*,' 166–70; Keynes, 'Edgar, *rex admirabilis*,' 54–6; Jayakumar, 'Reform and Retribution'; and Lapidge, *Byrhtferth of Ramsey*, xx–xxi and 122n101.

19 See Kelly, *Peterborough*, 276–9 and 371.

20 Robertson, *Anglo-Saxon Charters*, no. 69 at pp. 140–3. See also Campbell, *Rochester*, no. 37 at pp. 54–5.

21 Robertson, *Anglo-Saxon Charters*, 140 and 141. Abbreviations expanded.

22 'Godwine 23,' PASE.

23 'Leofwine 37,' PASE.

King Æthelred II (r. 978–1016) and Ælfric, Archbishop of Canterbury (995–1005): 'ongan ða to specenne on ðæt land . ꝺ elles for Godes ege ne dorste . oððæt seo spræc wearð þam cynge cuð. Þa ða him seo talu cuð wæs . þa sende he gewrit ꝺ his insegl to þam arcebisceope Ælfrice . ꝺ bead him þæt he ꝺ hys þegenas on East Cent . ꝺ on West Cent . hy onriht gesemdon . be ontale . ꝺ be oftale' (Then he set about laying claim to the estate – and durst not do otherwise for the fear of God – until the suit became known to the king. When the claim was known to him, he sent a letter and his seal to Archbishop Ælfric, and gave orders that he and his thegns in East Kent and West Kent should settle the dispute between them justly, weighing both claim and counterclaim).[24] The account gives careful attention to procedural details. The words *ontale* (statement of the claimant) and *oftale* (counterstatement) could refer to either oral or written testimonies, but the detail of the king's *gewrit* and *insegl* clearly establishes the instrumental role of documents in moving the case forward to its legitimate resolution. After King Æthelred has ordered the archbishop to assemble the thegns in East and West Kent to settle the case, Bishop Godwine comes to Canterbury where 'eal seo duguð' meets to resolve the dispute.[25] The use of *duguð* is notable here. The word occurs mainly in poetry and it signifies generally a notion of excellence or power, or specifically a group of tried men or warriors.[26] *Duguð* in this context implies that the 'great men' who heard the case were experienced auditors, men not only of high social position but also of genuine prudence. The word thus begs credibility for the judicial decision that will be reached by the council.

After hearing the case, the assembled dignitaries propose that the bishop allow Leofwine to continue occupying the property during his lifetime, after which the estate would return to Rochester. Godwine agrees to the terms and Leofwine in turn consents to the compromise: 'ꝺ he behet þæs truwan þæt land æfter his dæge unbesacen eode eft into þære stowe þe hit ut alæned wæs . ꝺ ageaf þa swutelunga þe he to þam lande hæfde þe ær of þære stowe geutod wæs . ꝺ þa hagan ealle þe he bewestan þære cyrcan hæfde into þære halgan stowe' (and Leofwine gave his solemn assurance that after his death the estate should revert uncontested to the foundation from which it was leased, and gave up the deeds relating to the estate which he had and which had been alienated from the foundation, and all the

---

24 Robertson, *Anglo-Saxon Charters*, 140 and 141.
25 The account lists many thegns, a sheriff, two abbots, and the archbishop in attendance.
26 *DOE*, s.v. 'duguþ.'

messuages which he had west of the church to the holy foundation).[27] After this statement, the document records the names of the negotiators, gives a long list of the witnesses present, and then ends with a stylish anathema: 'Gif hwa þis ðence to awendenne . ⁊ þas foreword to abrecenne . awende him God fram his ansyne on þam miclan dome . swa þæt he si ascyred from heofenarices myrhðe . ⁊ sy eallum deoflum betæht into helle' (If anyone attempts to alter this or break this agreement, God shall avert his countenance from him at the great Judgment, so that he shall be cut off from the bliss of the kingdom of heaven and delivered over to all the devils in hell).[28] This closing sentence contains some embellishment in its rhythmical rhyme (*to awendenne* and *to abrecenne*), polyptoton (*awendenne* and *awende*), and vocabulary (*heofenarices*). Stylistic ornamentation thus collaborates with divine endorsement to bolster the document's solemnity in a closing flourish. The witness list and anathema furthermore emulate the prestigious form of the Latin diploma, approximating its powerful claims to permanence and its confluence of sacral and royal sanction. In this way, an authoritative form of writing finalizes and memorializes the brokered agreement.

Indeed, S 1456 predicates its claims aggressively upon the authority of writing. Documents notably act as 'plot devices' which advance the story: the case begins with an act of archival detection; the determinative council is assembled by the king's *gewrit* ⁊ *insegl*; and the resolution of the dispute is memorialized in a document which itself bears the trappings of a diploma. The process of the actual negotiation itself, however, is radically compressed in the account; additionally, the specific contents of the *ontalu* and *oftalu* are entirely absent. We read only that the bishop had shown his evidence before the council,[29] presumably meaning those documents that he had unearthed in the cathedral. This material evidence provides a tactile-visual sign of Rochester's claim and it is significant that the narrative promptly moves to settlement after that evidence has been displayed. The charter, which itself aspires to be a form of documentary proof, foregrounds the instrumentality of written evidence in resolving the dispute. Documents decide the case.[30]

---

27 Robertson, *Anglo-Saxon Charters*, 142 and 143. Abbreviations expanded.
28 Ibid.
29 '... se bisceop his swutelunge geeowod hæfde' (ibid., 140).
30 Patrick Wormald has argued that written evidence was just as instrumental in dispute settlement, if not more so, than the proof of an oath or verbal testimony ('Charters, Law and the Settlement of Disputes').

The narrative in S 1456 might seem somewhat workmanlike in its tone and style, but its account is entirely strategic. The charter says nothing, for example, about any basis for Leofwine's claim to the Snodland estate or how the land had been separated from Rochester. The substance of Leofwine's response to the terms of the settlement also adeptly eliminates any grounds for future challenges to Rochester's rights of possession. In this sense, the charter account provides an example of what Paul Hyams has called preventive law, 'the all-important effort to arrange matters in advance in order, above all, to avoid future dispute.'[31] Leofwine swears that the estate will go back to Rochester uncontested (*unbesacen*), while the given wording of 'into þære stowe þe hit ut alæned wæs' quietly classifies Leofwine's holding not as bookland but as land temporarily *alæned* (loaned) by its true possessor. In other words, the land never really belonged to Leofwine in the first place – his was always a limited right of possession. Furthermore, Leofwine surrenders all the documents representing his claim to the land along with 'all the messuages which he had west of the church of the holy foundation.'[32] In one powerful turn, Leofwine gives up the documents (*swutelunga*) and holdings (*þa hagan ealle*) that encroach upon Rochester's interests in a doubled act of submission which underscores the deep association between land and writing.

Trouble at Sunbury

Some dispute charters also enhance their persuasive storytelling by enfolding recent political events into their accounts of local history. This powerful juxtaposition can occur both within the workings of the text itself and through various extra-textual appeals to recent issues and events.[33] Since many Anglo-Saxon charters can be dated with some precision, they can be considered alongside other contemporary texts and events with some confidence. S 1447, which survives as a contemporary single-sheet manuscript dated to the late tenth century, delivers a strategic interpretation of past events which is tailored to a specific historical horizon.[34] Identified as

---

31 Hyams, 'The Charter as a Source for the Early Common Law,' 173.
32 'þa hagan ealle þe he bewestan þære cyrcan hæfde into þære halgan stowe' (Robertson, *Anglo-Saxon Charters*, 142 and 143). *Haga* can be defined as an enclosed site or area, such as a pasture or hedged field, or as a dwelling site. See BT, s.v. 'haga.'
33 For this process at work in the Fonthill Letter, see Smith, 'Of Kings and Cattle Thieves.'
34 See Robertson, *Anglo-Saxon Charters*, no. 44 at pp. 90–3. See also Tapp, *The Sunbury Charter*; and Kemble, 'Anglo-Saxon Document Relating to Lands at Send and

'Sunnanburge talu' on its dorse, this document tells the story of an estate at Sunbury (Middlesex) as it passes through the hands of several owners. The surveyed events begin in the early 950s and end when Archbishop Dunstan purchases the land in 968.[35] During that period, the Sunbury estate was subject to multiple forfeitures, failed bargains, and legitimate sales. S 1447 must have been written sometime between 968 and Dunstan's death in 988, probably in response to (or in anticipation of) some dispute. The carefully ordered narrative advances a particular interpretation of past events and their outcome, one which presents Dunstan's claim to the land as legitimate and final. S 1447 amplifies the persuasive force of its claims in several potent ways: strategic storytelling, an artful synthesis of legal and literary registers, and the juxtaposition of local and dynastic history.

The general contents of the document can be summarized as follows. The first owner mentioned in the account, one Æthelstan,[36] loses the Sunbury property after he fails to vouch warranty for the sale of a stolen slave.[37] Æthelstan's brother Edward[38] intervenes in an attempt to save the family property, but Æthelstan refuses his help and the land is declared forfeit. Æthelstan later attempts to reclaim the property after King Eadred's death (r. 946–55), but King Eadwig (r. 955–9) grants the property instead to one Beornric,[39] who expels Æthelstan from the estate. Æthelstan then appeals to Edgar, recently elected king by the Mercians, but Edgar refuses him and books the property to Ealdorman Æthelstan.[40] One

---

Sunbury.' For a facsimile, see Sanders, *Facsimiles of Anglo-Saxon Manuscripts*, vol. 2, Westminster Abbey 7.

35 For an overview of the property's history, see Korhammer, 'Bosworth Psalter,' 183–5.

36 'Æthelstan 42,' PASE. This is his only recorded appearance.

37 Vouching to warranty (*team*) involves cases in which stolen property is discovered in the possession of another party and then claimed by its rightful owner. The current holder of the stolen property attempts to show that he bought the property lawfully by calling on a witness to the transaction. This process would clear the owner of any charge of wrongdoing. See BT, s.v. 'team (III)'; and Keynes, 'Crime and Punishment,' 77.

38 'Edward 5,' PASE. This is his only recorded appearance.

39 PASE designates this individual as 'Beornric 2,' but a *minister* of the same name also appears low in the witness lists of several of Eadwig's charters: S 602 and 610 (dated to 956); S 641, 643, and 645 (dated to 957); and S 659 (dated to 958 for 959). This same individual, 'Beornric 3' (PASE), received estates in Wiltshire (S 612) and Hampshire (S 613) from Eadwig in 956. It may be that 'Beornric 2' and 'Beornric 3' represent the same person and that this Beornric was one of those 'new men' favoured by Eadwig early in his reign.

40 'Æthelstan 31,' PASE. His career as ealdorman apparently began in 940. He appears in the witness lists of charters issued under kings Edmund, Eadred, Eadwig, and Edgar.

Ecgfrith[41] then buys the land from Æthelstan and sometime later asks Archbishop Dunstan to act as the property's guardian for his widow and child. Dunstan attempts to fulfil his obligation after Ecgfrith's death, but King Edgar (r. 959–75) declares Ecgfrith's property forfeit and grants the estate to Ealdorman Ælfheah.[42] Ælfheah later sells the land to Dunstan in a transaction which concludes the account.

S 1447 is divided into four sections, each of which begins with a clear transitional phrase.[43] These divisions establish a general chronology for the related events and separate the narrative into discrete episodes. This sequence of transitions, each one different from the others, additionally creates a steady momentum in the account as it builds to its conclusion. The narrative is thus carefully organized in its presentation of events over time. The account begins with the phrase 'se fruma wæs' (the start of it was), establishing the first episode as the foundation for all that follows. The arresting opening sentence – 'It all started when someone stole a woman' – furthermore identifies the text not as a formal legal document,[44] but first and foremost as a story, one which begins with the theft of Thurwif,[45] a female slave. Her owner Ælfsige[46] later finds her in the company of one Wulfstan.[47]

Se fruma wæs þæt mon forstæl ænne wimman . æt Ieceslea Ælfsige Byrhsiges suna . Þurwif hatte se wimman . Þa befeng Ælfsige þone mann æt Wulfstane Wulfgares fæder . þa tymde Wulfstan hine to Æþelstane æt Sunnanbyrg . þa cende he tem . ⁊ let þone forberstan . ⁊ forbeh þone andagan . æfter þam bæd Ælfsige ægiftes his mannes . ⁊ he hine agef ⁊ forgeald him mid twam pundum .

---

41 'Ecgfrith 14,' PASE. This is his only recorded appearance.

42 'Ælfheah 33,' PASE.

43 Patrick Wormald divided the events into three distinct cases in his list of Anglo-Saxon lawsuits. See Wormald, 'Handlist,' nos. 38–40 at p. 267.

44 Narrative charters typically begin by identifying themselves as documents with specific contents. S 1454, a Christ Church, Canterbury document dated to 900 x 902, for example, begins, 'Her cyþ on þysum gewrite hu Wynflæd gelædde hyre gewitnesse æt Wulfamere beforan Æþelrede cyninge' (Robertson, *Anglo-Saxon Charters*, no. 66 at p. 136). S 1456, the Rochester document discussed above, similarly begins, 'Her cyð on ðysum gewrite hu Godwine biscop on Hrofeceastre ⁊ Leofwine Ælfeages sunu wurðon gesybsumode ymbe þæt land æt Snoddinglande on Cantwarabyrig' (ibid., no. 69 at p. 140).

45 'Thurwif 1,' PASE. She appears only in S 1447.

46 'Ælfsige 58,' PASE. He appears only in S 1447.

47 'Wulfstan 25,' PASE. He appears only in S 1447.

þa bæd Byrhferð ealdormann Æþelstan hys wer . for þam tembyrste . þa
cwæð Æðelstan þæt he næfde him to syllanne.[48]

[The start of it was that someone stole a woman at Yaxley from Ælfsige, son
of Beorhtsige. The woman was named Thurwif. Then Ælfsige laid claim to
her from Wulfstan, father of Wulfgar. Then Wulfstan called Æthelstan of
Sunbury to vouch for her sale. Then Æthelstan promised to vouch warranty
but he let it come to nothing and failed to appear on the set day. After that
Ælfsige asked for the woman's return and he returned her and compensated
him with two pounds. Then Ealdorman Beorhtfrith asked Æthelstan for his
fee because of the failure to vouch warranty. Then Æthelstan said he had
nothing to give him.]

Wulfstan asks Æthelstan to stand witness that he had bought the woman
in a legitimate sale; Æthelstan accepts Wulfstan's request but fails to appear at the appointed time. Æthelstan subsequently returns Thurwif to
Ælfsige and pays him a penalty of two pounds, a price equivalent to the
value of a slave,[49] but he cannot pay the additional fine for his failure to
vouch warranty. This default brings the Sunbury property into danger of
forfeiture. Through its legal terminology and procedural detail, the account establishes that Æthelstan lost the Sunbury property for good reason: he apparently stole a slave and then sold her under false pretence,
subsequently failed in his promise to vouch warranty, and finally defaulted
on the attendant legal penalty. Æthelstan, the narrative would have us be-
lieve, was a bad man whose bad decisions had finally caught up to him.

Æthelstan's brother Edward then appears with the *boc* for the estate.
This important detail of a produced diploma (essentially a title-deed to the
land) indicates the prominent role documents will play throughout the
account. S 1447's recurrent attention to the authority of documents in
establishing the transmission of property underscores its own instrumentality in declaring and protecting Dunstan's closing claim to the property.
The exact situation of Sunbury's possession at this point in the account is
uncertain, but Liebermann suggested that the land was once held jointly by
the two brothers as bookland.[50] Edward seems to have taken his brother's

---

48 Robertson, *Anglo-Saxon Charters*, 90. Abbreviations expanded.
49 Pelteret, *Slavery in Early Mediaeval England*, 166.
50 Liebermann, *Gesetze*, 2:327, s.v. 'Bocland (25b).' The *Liber Eliensis* (2.11) describes a
   case from Bishop Æthelwold's time of two brothers who held two hides in common.
   Æthelwold wants to purchase the property but the brothers for a long while cannot

vulnerability as an opportunity to secure the sole right of possession. The tension between the two brothers provides the text's first dramatic scene: 'þa cleopode Eadweard Æðelstanes broðor . ꝛ cwæð . ic . hæbbe Sunnanburges boc ðe uncre yldran me læfdon . læt me þæt land to handa ic agife þinne wer ðam cynge . þa cwæð Æðelstan þæt him leofre wære þæt hit to fyre oððe flode gewurde . þonne he hit æfre gebide . ða cwæð Eadweard hit is wyrse þæt uncer naðor hit næbbe . þa wæs þæt swa . ꝛ forbead Byrhferð þæt land Æðelstane . ꝛ he of ferde ꝛ gebeh under Wulfgare æt Norðhealum'[51] (Then Edward, Æthelstan's brother, spoke out and said, 'I have the Sunbury deed that our parents left us. Give me possession of the land and I will pay your fine to the king.' Then Æthelstan said he would rather it were lost to fire or flood than ever allow that. Then Edward said, 'It will be worse that neither of us should have it.' Then that was so. Beorhtfrith denied the land to Æthelstan and he went away and lived under Wulfgar at *Norðhealum*). This confrontation is remarkable both for its charged dialogue and for the intensity of Æthelstan's refusal to accept his brother's offer. While Edward's words appear as direct speech, Æthelstan's words are represented only as indirect speech. This tactic diminishes Æthelstan and his claim to Sunbury through the fictive mechanisms of story. The problem of what appears to be two brothers jointly owning bookland also introduces a moment of tenurial tension to the account, adding another unsettling element to the proceedings. At the end of the episode, Æthelstan leaves for elsewhere after Ealdorman Beorhtfrith[52] denies him the estate. The account notably says nothing of what happened with the property after Æthelstan's removal: the land in effect becomes an empty space awaiting a more worthy possessor. This first episode effectively stages an initial scene of two brothers at odds over family property. The story accordingly begins with the land in questionable circumstances, beset by legal transgression, fraternal discord, and forfeiture.

The brief second episode opens with the death of King Eadred and the succession of King Eadwig. Æthelstan returns to Sunbury, perhaps hoping that his reoccupation will go unnoticed: 'binnan ðam wendun gewyrda . ꝛ gewat Eadræd cyng . ꝛ feng Eadwig to rice . ꝛ wende Æðelstan hine eft into Sunnanbyrg . ungebetra þinga . þa geahsode þæt Eadwig cyng . ꝛ gesealde

---

agree on a sale price: 'quamdiu illi duo fratres eandem terram simul habuerunt, nullatenus huic rei finem imponere potuerunt' (Blake, *Liber Eliensis*, 87) [as long as the two brothers held the land together, they were in no way able to bring the matter to an end].
51 Robertson, *Anglo-Saxon Charters*, 90. Abbreviations expanded.
52 'Beorhtfrith 9,' PASE.

þæt land Byrnrice . ꞇ he feng to . ꞇ wearp Æðelstan ut'[53] (In the meantime things changed and King Eadred died and Eadwig succeeded to the kingdom and Æthelstan returned to Sunbury with things no better. Then King Eadwig heard of that and granted the land to Beornric and he took it and threw Æthelstan out). The action here comes in a paratactic rush, ending in Æthelstan's second ejection from the estate. The events seem brusque, particularly the unceremonious statement that Beornric 'threw Æthelstan out' after he had received the property from King Eadwig. The account furthermore says that Eadwig simply granted the land to Beornric with no indication that the king had booked the land to his thegn. This subtle detail again leaves the land in uncertain circumstances – the estate clearly changes hands, but its possession lacks the documentary confirmation of a *boc*. At this point the property itself seems less important to the story than the human activity – including but not limited to writing – that has determined its possession over time.

The third episode effectively moves the Sunbury land out of contention and into channels of legitimate transmission and possession. This section begins with Edgar's election as king of the Mercians (r. 957–9) – like the previous episode, this one explicitly juxtaposes local events and dynastic history. Once again, Æthelstan seizes upon a moment of political change for another attempt to regain the Sunbury estate. Æthelstan appeals to the young Edgar for judgment, but the Mercian witan demands that he first make good on his outstanding debt. Æthelstan again cannot pay: 'gemang þam getidde þæt Myrce gecuran Eadgar to cynge . ꞇ him anweald gesealdan ealra cynerihta . þa gesohte Æðelstan Eadgar cyng ꞇ bæd domes . þa ætdemdon him Myrcna witan land buton he his wer agulde þam cynge swa he oðrum ær sceolde . þa næfde he hwanon . ne he hit Eadwearde his breðer geðafian nolde . þa gesealde se cyng . ꞇ gebecte þæt land Æðelstane ealdormenn . to hæbbenne . ꞇ to syllanne for life . ꞇ for legere þam him leofost wære'[54] (At that time it happened that the Mercians chose Edgar as king and gave him sovereignty in all royal rights. And then Æthelstan sought out King Edgar and asked for judgment. Then the Mercian council refused him the land unless he would pay his fee to the king as he should have done before to the other one. Then he had nothing with which to pay, nor would he allow his brother to do it. Then the king granted and booked that land to Ealdorman Æthelstan, to hold and to give in life or at death to whomever

---

53 Robertson, *Anglo-Saxon Charters*, 90.
54 Ibid. Abbreviations expanded.

he wished). The statement that Æthelstan again refused his brother's intervention echoes the fraternal tension that was rendered so dramatically in the first episode. The brothers' common inheritance comes under risk through Æthelstan's reckless actions and his defiance of his brother's move to gain full possession. Æthelstan would rather see the property lost to his family entirely than surrender his own interest. After Æthelstan again fails to settle his debt, Edgar 'grants and books' the land to Ealdorman Æthelstan. This conveyance immediately raises the problem of two conflicting grants: each king has given the same estate to a different individual. As we have seen, the account indicates that Eadwig had simply 'gesealde þæt land' to Beornric, with no mention of a proper 'book' for the grant. The statement that Edgar 'booked' the estate to Ealdorman Æthelstan (*gesealde ꞇ gebecte þæt land*) settles the question of possession. Significantly, the language in both scenarios is identical aside from the additional detail of 'booking' that accompanies Edgar's grant of the property.

Ealdorman Æthelstan hence becomes the first owner of the estate with an unequivocal right to the property. The ealdorman's *boc* cancels out the contentious tenure shared by the two brothers and effectively trumps the competing claim that Beornric received (without a *boc*) from Eadwig. The account furthermore appropriates the solemn language of bookland in its statement that Edgar booked the property to Ealdorman Æthelstan 'to hæbbenne . ꞇ to syllanne for life . ꞇ for legere þam him leofost wære,' lightly adorning the claim with repetition and alliteration.[55] This moment in the text establishes that potential claims on the Sunbury estate which might be grounded in old interests are now invalid, eclipsed by the authority of the *boc* that Ealdorman Æthelstan has received from King Edgar. Æthelstan, Edward, and Beornric all disappear from the account at this precise point, never to be mentioned again – the land can now move out of prolonged dispute and its ambiguities of possession. This tenurial 'cleansing,' facilitated through documents, initiates a sequence of legitimate possessions which will eventually culminate in Dunstan's claim to the estate. Before that point, however, the land must pass through another controversy which ends in forfeiture.

The fourth episode features a legitimate change in possession, conducted with all the necessary documentation and confirmation, which is followed by an unsettling and inscrutable reversal. The section begins with Ecgfrith's purchase of the Sunbury estate from Ealdorman Æthelstan. The

---

55 The first phrase is also rhythmical.

account notably represents the sale as entirely legitimate: 'æfter þam getidde þæt Ecgferð gebohte boc ⁊ land æt Æðelstane ealdormenn . on cynges gewitnesse . ⁊ his witena swa his gemedo wæron . hæfde ⁊ breac oð his
ende'[56] (After that it happened that Ecgfrith bought the deed and land
from Ealdorman Æthelstan with the witness of the king and his councillors, as they were agreeable to it; he held and enjoyed it until his end). The
pairing *boc ⁊ land* maintains the attention to the instrumental function of
the diploma, and the witness of the king and his *witan* further underscores
the legitimacy of the sale. These details bear witness to the transfer of possession through the acquisition of both land and book. This particular
change in possession, the narrative makes clear, was entirely legitimate and
properly documented. At some point after he had bought the land, Ecgfrith
asked Dunstan to act as guardian for the property in the interest of his wife
and child: 'þa betæhte Ecgferð on halre tungan . land ⁊ boc on cynges gewitnesse Dunstane arcebisceope to mundgenne his lafe . ⁊ his bearne'[57]
(Then with the witness of the king, Ecgfrith clearly gave the land and deed
over to Dunstan as guardian to his widow and child). The procedural details here, like those given for Ecgfrith's purchase of the land, suggest that
the guardianship was properly established with the king's endorsement.[58]
The meaning of the expression *on halre tungan* (with a hale tongue) is not
entirely clear, but it seems to signify a full capacity or clarity of speech.[59]

---

56 Robertson, *Anglo-Saxon Charters*, 90 and 92. Abbreviations expanded.

57 Ibid., 92.

58 For the position of *mund*, or guardian, for a will, see Sheehan, *The Will in Medieval
England*, 40–4. Sheehan states, 'so far as can be seen, the *mund* did not receive any right
in the legacy of which he was to oversee the delivery. His function was often the protection of the owner and his property during the latter's life, and the protection of the
owner's arrangements for that property after his death' (ibid., 44). The role seems to
have had many similarities with that of *forespeca*. See Rabin, 'Old English *Forespeca*.'

59 The phrase appears elsewhere in S 1122, a writ of Edward the Confessor for
Westminster Abbey dated to the later 1040s (Harmer, *Anglo-Saxon Writs*, no. 78 at pp.
345–46); in S 357, a spurious charter written in the name of King Alfred, with versions
in both English and Latin (Kelly, *Shaftesbury*, no. 7 at pp. 28–30); and in S 1458, a vernacular single-sheet dated 964 x 988 with a later Latin translation (Campbell, *Rochester*,
nos. 34 and 34b at pp. 47–50). See the comments of Robertson (*Anglo-Saxon Charters*,
284 and 338) and Harmer (*Anglo-Saxon Writs*, 500). The Latin version of S 357 renders
'halre tungan' as 'uiuens et in prosperitate adhuc uigens' (while living and still thriving
in prosperity), while the Latin translation of S 1458, speaking of a secured inheritance,
provides 'omnino confirmauit totum quod pater suus in uita sua fecerat' (fully concluded every thing which his father had done while alive). See also *DOE*, s.v. 'belucan
(2.b.i)' for a suggestion of orality in the case of 'on halre tungon' in S 1458. Ælfric uses
the expression in his *Life of St Martin* in a way that would seem to indicate a clarity or

The expression dispels any potential ambiguity in the declaration of guardianship and thereby continues the account's commitment to proper procedure. Through chiastic repetition, the word pair *land ⁊ boc* also associates the guardianship with the legitimacy of Edgar's earlier grant of *boc ⁊ land* to Ealdorman Æthelstan. The two pairs together reinforce the conceptual link between land and writing and underscore the general endorsement of the diploma as the evidentiary instrument for longstanding possession.

Dunstan approaches the king about the guardianship after Ecgfrith's death, but unanticipated developments keep him from fulfilling his duties as *mund*. The archbishop learns that Edgar's *witan* has declared all Ecgfrith's property forfeit: 'þa he geendod wæs þa rad se bisceop to þam cynge myngude þære munde ⁊ his gewitnesse . þa cwæð se cyng him to andsware mine witan habbað ætrecð Ecgferðe ealle his are . þurh þæt swyrd þe him on hype hangode þa he adranc'[60] (When Ecgfrith met his end the bishop rode to the king and reminded him of the guardianship and his witness. Then the king said to him in answer, 'My council has declared all of Ecgfrith's property forfeit because of the sword that hung on his hip when he drowned'). These circumstances, which are both evocative and unclear, present a narrative scenario in which 'an occurrence sufficiently confused in itself is very obscurely narrated.'[61] What exactly was the significance of the sword that hung on Ecgfrith's hip? How or why did he drown? Kemble and Liebermann both held that Ecgfrith had committed suicide, but Robertson rejected this view, noting the 'entire absence of any reference elsewhere to forfeiture in the case of suicide.'[62] More recently, Nicholas Brooks has proposed that Ecgfrith drowned during an ordeal undertaken on account of 'some major crime,' a point supported by his

---

fullness of speech. The father of a twelve-year old girl who had been born mute appeals to Martin that he 'hire tungan unlysde' (unloosen her tongue). The bishop anoints her mouth with blessed oil and asks the girl to speak the name of her father: 'Þæt mæden sæde sona hire fæder naman . and hæfde hire spræce mid halre tungan' (Skeat, *Ælfric's Lives of Saints*, 2:288).

60 Robertson, *Anglo-Saxon Charters*, 92. Abbreviations expanded.
61 Auerbach, *Mimesis*, 81.
62 Robertson, *Anglo-Saxon Charters*, 338. See also Liebermann, *Gesetze*, 2:479, s.v. 'Grab (D).' For the practice of isolated burials in unconsecrated ground, including cases of suicide and (possibly) estate forfeiture, see Reynolds, *Anglo-Saxon Deviant Burial Customs*, 209–18.

being denied burial in consecrated ground.[63] Whatever Ecgfrith's actual offence may have been, the account prominently frames the forfeiture in a scene distinguished by dramatic detail and direct speech. This narrative method is reminiscent of that described by Auerbach in his analysis of Gregory of Tours. According to Auerbach, Gregory in his storytelling endeavoured 'to make the proceedings vividly visible.'[64] Gregory uses incidental detail and direct discourse at decisive moments to achieve a powerful presence of human action in the story: his style, in Auerbach's assessment, achieves 'a reawakening of the directly sensible.'[65] S 1447 stages the unanticipated moment of forfeiture in exactly such a way in order to deliver a narrative shock in which the protections and provisions gained by proper legal procedure and documentation dead-end in one spectacular moment.

After this vivid account of a second forfeiture, the charter states that King Edgar granted the property to Ealdorman Ælfheah. The entire loss of Ecgfrith's *are* prevents the archbishop from fulfilling his duty to Ecgfrith's widow and child: 'nam þa se cyng ða are þe he ahte .xx. hyda æt Sendan .x. æt Sunnanbyrg . ꞃ forgef Ælfhege ealdormenn . þa bead se bisceop his wer þam cynge . þa cwæð se cyng . þæt mihte beon geboden him wið clænum legere . ac ic hæbbe ealle þa spæce to Ælfhege læten'[66] (Then the king took the property that he owned, twenty hides at Send and ten at Sunbury, and granted it to Ealdorman Ælfheah. Then the bishop offered his fee to the king. Then the king said, 'That might afford him a consecrated grave, but I have decided the entire case for Ælfheah'). The account says nothing about a diploma in its statement that King Edgar granted the land to Ealdorman Ælfheah. This omission seems somewhat curious considering the earlier attention to such details in the narrative: the 'Sunnanburges boc' held by Edward, King Edgar 'booking' (*gebecte*) the estate to Ealdorman Æthelstan, Ecgfrith's purchase of *boc* ꞃ *land* from Ealdorman Æthelstan, and Ecgfrith's entrustment of *land* ꞃ *boc* to Dunstan. In this case, the account simply states that the king 'granted' (*forgef*) to Ealdorman Ælfheah, with the aforementioned estates at Sunbury and Send being the understood objects of the verb. Why the conspicuous absence of a *boc* at

---

63 Brooks, *Early History of the Church of Canterbury*, 249. Brooks observes, 'One might conjecture that the archbishop had less confidence than the king in the efficacy of proof by ordeal. Certainly when the king's relations with his nobles and the letter of the law were at stake, Edgar was not prepared to show especial favour to his archbishop.'
64 Auerbach, *Mimesis*, 85.
65 Ibid., 94.
66 Robertson, *Anglo-Saxon Charters*, 92. Abbreviations expanded.

this particular moment? Because the verb *forgyfan* can be defined as 'to grant land, privileges, goods, etc. by bequest or charter,'[67] we might understand the conveyance of the land by diploma to be implied in this case, and indeed a surviving single-sheet diploma dated to 962 does record this very grant.[68] Nonetheless, the silence about a document evidencing this particular grant of land – a procedural detail which has hitherto been consistently prominent in the account – momentarily unsettles the narrative.

Moreover, the fourth episode as a whole recalls the first episode and its own agitated examples of direct speech, forfeiture, and the matter of an outstanding *wer*. The fourth episode, unlike the first, however, lacks either a readily apparent antagonist (such as Æthelstan) or a transparent justification for forfeiture. By never divulging the details of Ecgfrith's transgression, the account denies the crime specificity in the narrative. Nor does the narrative censure Edgar for his decision to give the land to Ælfheah – the entire account is free of the partisan vilification that appears in some dispute narratives. Edgar's conciliatory statement that he will allow Ecgfrith a consecrated burial now that Dunstan has settled his *wer* manages to soften both the severity of the forfeiture and Edgar's defiance of the archbishop. The case may have gone against Dunstan's interests at this particular moment, but the narrative still presents the resolution as just. More importantly, this turn of events separates the Sunbury and Send estates from Ecgfrith's family, clearing the way for its purchase by Dunstan and its eventual distribution to Westminster Abbey.[69] What had initially begun as a frustration of Dunstan's interests ends in his gain. This negation of

---

67 *DOE*, s.v. 'forgyfan (A.3.c).'

68 S 702. Dunstan appears in second position in the witness list. See Korhammer, 'Bosworth Psalter,' 182–7. Nicholas Brooks has argued that the S 702 manuscript is a later copy 'unlikely to have been written before 968 when Dunstan acquired both the estate and the original charter, and seems to have been made for the benefit of the monks of Westminster who preserved the copy in their archives' (*Early History of the Church of Canterbury*, 252).

69 Sometime after 968, Dunstan gave Sunbury to Westminster Abbey. Domesday Book lists Sunbury among the Westminster holdings and two Westminster charters, S 894 (dated to 998) and 1293 (dated, impossibly, to 959), include the estate among Dunstan's gifts to Westminster. Both charters are later forgeries, but they seem to have some basis in earlier documents. S 894 states that Dunstan bought the estate from *dux* Ælfheah and then gave usufruct to a widow named Æthelflæd for her lifetime, after which time the land was to go back (*redeat*) to Westminster. See Korhammer, 'Bosworth Psalter,' 183–5. The information in S 894 suggests that Dunstan maintained possession of the estate but allowed Ecgfrith's widow the benefits of its use. If this was indeed the case it would indicate that Dunstan did fulfil his obligation as *mund* as promised (if not perhaps as anticipated).

competing claims from past owners maintains the plotted progression of the property out of dispute and into legitimate channels of transmission.

The last sentences of S 1447 record Dunstan's purchase of the two estates six years after Ælfheah received them from the king. The interests of Ecgfrith's survivors have fallen out of story, erased by forfeiture. The closing statement specifies the price Dunstan paid for the estates and emphasizes in a rhythmic and rhyming doublet that the purchase was entirely uncontested: 'Þæs on syxtan gere gebohte se arcebisceop æt Ælfhege ealdormenn . þæt land æt Sendan . mid .xc. pundum . ך æt Sunnanbyrg mid .cc. mancussan goldes . *unbecwedene* . ך *unforbodene* wið ælcne mann to þære dægtide . ך he him swa þa land geagnian derr . swa him se sealde ðe to syllenne ahte . ך hi þam se cyng sealde . swa hi him his witan gerehton'[70] (Six years later the archbishop bought the land at Send from Ealdorman Ælfheah for ninety pounds and that at Sunbury for two hundred mancuses of gold, uncontested and unopposed by anyone at that time. And so he dares to claim those lands as his own, as he who owned them to give, and to whom the king had given them just as they, his councillors, had advised him, gave to him). The dense final sentence labouriously maps the transmission of the estates from Edgar to Ælfheah and finally from Ælfheah to Dunstan. The syntax in S 1447 is generally paratactic and free of subordination, but the twisting final sentence breaks this precedent with its hypotactic succession of *swa* clauses and its thick clusters of pronouns. The core of this closing statement seems to have been modeled on part of a longer formulaic oath recorded in the legal text *Hit becwæð*: 'swa ic hit hæbbe, swa hit se sealde, ðe to syllanne ahte, unbryde ך unforboden.'[71] The final sentence of S 1447, however, contains a much more elaborate construction. The clause 'swa him se sealde ðe to syllenne ahte' matches the source nearly exactly, but the remainder of the statement elaborates the formula to the point of strained sense. This is in part due to the several rhetorical devices which decorate Dunstan's claim. In order to present

---

70 Robertson, *Anglo-Saxon Charters*, 92. Abbreviations expanded. Emphasis added.

71 Ibid., 339. 'So I have it, as he who had it to give gave it honestly and lawfully.' See also Liebermann, *Gesetze*, 1:400. Patrick Wormald described the full oath as 'a formula ... for emphasizing an owner's freedom to do as he wished with a property, and to hold it for his lifetime. It is the position inherent in the whole principle of bookland, though the sort of usufruct that is hinted at here only became prominent in the evidence from the ninth century' (*Making of English Law*, 385). *Hit becwæð* survives in two legal collections, each dated to the early twelfth century: Cambridge, Corpus Christi College 383 (Ker, *Catalogue*, no. 65) and Rochester Cathedral, *Textus Roffensis* (Ker, *Catalogue*, no. 373).

these embellishments more clearly, I have arranged the sentence in separate lines by the pointing in the manuscript:

⁊ he him swa þa land geagnian derr .
swa him se sealde ðe to syllenne ahte .
⁊ hi þam se cyng sealde .
swa hi him his witan gerehton.

These clauses present several examples of parallel syntax: the first two both end in an infinitive form followed by a finite verb; the last two feature parallel word order (conjunction / accusative or nominative pronoun [*hi* in both cases] / dative article or pronoun / nominative noun phrase / finite verb); and each of the four begins with a conjunction in the sequence of ⁊ … *swa*. These parallelisms indicate some attempt at achieving an ornamental prose style in the vernacular, perhaps in imitation of the literary display evident in Latin diplomas of the tenth century. In his *De schematibus et tropis*, Bede describes the use of such an elevated style in Latin prose: 'Solet aliquoties in Scripturis ordo verborum causa decoris aliter quam vulgaris via dicendi habet figuratus inveniri. Quod grammatici Grece »schema« vocant, nos habitum vel formam vel figuram recte nominamus, quia per hoc quodam modo vestitur et ornatur oratio' (The language of the Scriptures is sometimes found to be arranged, for beauty's sake, differently from the way common usage would dictate. Scholars call an artificial arrangement of words a *schema* in Greek; speakers of Latin properly call such an arrangement a »habit«, or an »adornment«, or a »figure«, because in this way language is so to speak clothed and adorned).[72] S 1447's final sentence uses several of the figures outlined by Bede in his treatise, including hyperbaton, polysyndeton (each phrase begins with a connecting conjunction), and perhaps polyptoton (*he* [1x], *him* [3x], *hi* [2x], *his* [2x]). The first two clauses are also chiastic in initial wording with 'he him swa' in the first line and 'swa him se' in the second. This concentration of rhetorical devices in a single sentence, used at the expense of the direct syntax typical of the account as a whole, indicates vernacular composition *causa decoris*. These flourishes provide a kind of rhetorical crescendo for Dunstan's final claim to the land. S 1447 thus strategically bolsters its

---

72 Bede, *De schematibus et tropis*, 168 and 169. For the knowledge and use of rhetorical figures in Anglo-Saxon England, see Knappe, 'Classical Rhetoric in Anglo-Saxon England'; Gneuss, 'The Study of Language in Anglo-Saxon England,' 98–101; and Steen, *Verse and Virtuosity*, 3–34.

closing argument with artful prose, employing literary display to deliver a persuasive declaration of enduring possession.

This element of verbal showmanship is most prominent in the final sentence, but S 1447 also contains other concentrations of lexical and rhetorical ornamentation throughout its text. The charter features a number of alliterative phrases, for example, several of which contain assonance, rhyme, or repetition:[73]

- *forberstan ⁊ forbeh*

- *læfdon læt me þæt land*

- *fyre oððe flode*

- *naðor hit næbbe*

- *wendun gewyrda ⁊ gewat*

- *for life ⁊ for legere þam him leofost*

- *on cynges gewitnesse ⁊ his witena*

- *myngude þære munde*

- *ætrecð Ecgferðe ealle his are*

- *on hype hangode*

- *ða are þe he ahte*

The document also contains three hapax legomena (*ætdeman*, *tembyrst*, and *cyneriht*), two of them compounds, while another compound word, *dægtide*, appears only nine times in the corpus with four of those appearances being in poetry. The verb *ætreccan* appears only three times, twice in charters and once in 'King Edgar's Establishment of the Monasteries,' a

---

73 Anglo-Saxon writs often feature similar embellishments. See Harmer, *Anglo-Saxon Writs*, 85–92.

prose text attributed to Bishop Æthelwold.[74] S 1447 additionally contains the only occurrence of which I am aware of the word *wyrd* in any charter.[75] In this way, the document delivers its story of dispute and resolution in an artful blend of legalistic and literary diction. Such embellishments provide a key means of fortifying the authority of the written word as the text represents events in a strategic narrative.

S 1447 also employs ornamentation in its two accounts of forfeiture in order to make sense of those losses as legitimate events in the land's history. The first episode contains two examples of polyptoton in three-word clusters: (1) *ægiftes*, *agef*, and *agife*; and (2) *tymde*, *tem*, and *tembyrste*. Additionally, the first episode contains five different verbs with the *for*-prefix, with each verb appearing a single time in the entire account: *forstæl* (*forstelan*), *forberstan*, *forbeh* (*forbugan*), *forgeald* (*forgyldan*), and *forbead* (*forbeodan*). Four of these verbs have distinct legal meanings related to theft or default, and only one other *for-* verb (*forgef*) occurs elsewhere in the charter.[76] This distribution suggests a deliberate concentration of such words early in the account. The fourth episode in turn shows several notable repetitions of its own: the chiastic repetition of *boc* ⁊ *land* and *land* ⁊ *boc*, two occurrences in close proximity of the phrase 'on cynges gewitnesse' followed soon after by 'to þam cynge ... ⁊ his gewitnesse,' another case of polyptoton in *mund* and *mundgenne*, and the repetition of *ar* twice in close proximity. Since these two episodes also contain the only examples of direct speech in the entire account, these particular scenes must have been felt especially to merit rhetorical and narrative embellishment. The account thus makes forfeiture sensible, something that is both vividly present and clearly justified in the narrative.

---

74 'Gif cinges gerefena hwylc gyltig biþ wiþ God oþþe wiþ men, hwa is manna to þam ungescead and ungewittig þæt he þæm cyninge his are <u>ætrecce</u> forþi þe his gerefa forwyrh[t] biþ?' (If any of the king's reeves is convicted of crime against God or men, what man is so foolish or senseless as to deprive the king of his property because his reeve is convicted?). Whitelock, Brett and Brooke, *Councils and Synods*, 1:154, emphasis added. The *DOE* defines *ætreccan* as 'to declare (something *acc.*) forfeited.' The verb also appears in S 1211 (dated to 959).

75 *Wyrd* appears predominately in poetry and Alfredian prose. My findings are based on a search on *wyrd* in the Dictionary of Old English Web Corpus, accessed June 2011.

76 For *forstelan*, see Schwyter, *Old English Legal Language*, 41–53 and 155. Schwyter locates six occurrences of the verb across only three lawsuit documents: S 1445 (2x), 1447 (1x), and 1457 (3x). By way of comparison, the verb appears 25 times across the law-codes.

Between Brothers

In addition to its narrative and stylistic craft, S 1447 magnifies its claims through the parallels it builds between local and dynastic history and the common element of familial conflict. The document most potently evokes the division of the Anglo-Saxon kingdom between Eadwig and Edgar in 957. Two parallel stories emerge in S 1447 of brothers at odds over family land: the Sunbury brothers, Æthelstan and Edward, appear in the present action, while the history of the kingdom divided between two young kings stands in the background and informs the ordering of local events. The correspondence between the two scenarios remains more evocative than exact, but the account of the history of the Sunbury estate clearly resonates with that of royal domain during the 950s. It is surely a coincidence that the Sunbury brothers both share names with recent West Saxon rulers, but the cluster of royal names in the account underscores, even if accidently, its associative connections with dynastic history.

Æthelstan plays the rogue in the Sunbury story as his irresponsible actions and ineffectual schemes ultimately lead to the loss of family property, while Edward attempts to secure the land for himself by seizing on his brother's weakness in a most mercenary way. Both brothers consequently appear to be of dubious character in the account. The standoff between them keeps the Sunbury estate in jeopardy: Æthelstan and Edward each want sole possession no matter the cost or consequence. The story of the Sunbury brothers thus provides a dramatic case of family land lost through fraternal strife. Active in the background, the dynastic story provides a positive counterpoint to that local story of loss as Edgar's good management shepherds family land (in this case, the entire realm) out of jeopardy. The Sunbury estate likewise can only move out of dispute and into legitimate and longstanding possession *after* it has been denied to Æthelstan by King Edgar. These narrative juxtapositions echo contemporary depictions of Edgar's succession to a reunited kingdom as a transition from a time of corruption and division to one of justice and concord. At the same time, the forfeiture of the Sunbury estate gives a disquieting reminder of the consequences that can arise from bitter disputes over property and inheritance within the family group.

In order to demonstrate how S 1447 resonates with contemporary politics, I first provide an overview of the political events and ideologies that inform the document's strategic storytelling. King Eadred died childless in 955, leaving the two young sons of his brother King Edmund (r. 939–46), Eadwig and Edgar, as the nearest candidates for the throne. Eadwig became king in 955 and ruled until his death in October of 959. Sometime between May and December of 957, however, the Mercians and Northumbrians declared allegiance to the younger Edgar, leading to a division of the kingdom. After 957, charters issued in Eadwig's name are witnessed only by bishops and ealdormen with authority south of the River Thames while those with offices 'north of the Thames, or in East Anglia, disappear from view.'[77] Charters issued in Edgar's name for 958 and 959 generally call him 'king of the Mercians' while Eadwig's charters name him 'king of the English.'[78] The division seems to have been free of civil violence and Edgar succeeded to a reunified kingdom after Eadwig's death in 959.[79]

The Anglo-Saxon Chronicle's bare account of those four years undoubtedly mutes their fraught politics.[80] The succession of a young king in 955 must have created a ready opportunity for competing groups to advance their particular interests, and substantial shifts in political fortune in the first years of Eadwig's reign do suggest some degree of turbulence at court. Certain bequests of land in King Eadred's will, for example, seem to have been inexplicably disregarded.[81] The year 956 saw Dunstan exiled and Eadgifu, mother of kings Edmund and Eadred, dispossessed of her estates. In 956 Eadwig also issued an extraordinary number of charters in which he advanced a number of 'new' men, and although he did maintain the interests of established families,[82] the complexion of the court changed significantly

---

77 Keynes, 'Edgar, *rex admirabilis*,' 8.

78 Ibid., 7–8 and 13–14. See also Keynes, 'Conspectus of the Charters of King Edgar.'

79 For an overview of the politics leading to the division of the kingdom in 957, see Stafford, *Unification and Conquest*, 40–50. See also Williams, '*Princeps Merciorum gentis*'; Yorke, 'Æthelwold and the Politics of the Tenth Century'; and Jayakumar, 'Eadwig and Edgar.' For an argument that joint kingship had already been established for Eadwig and Edgar in 955, see Biggs, 'Edgar's Path to the Throne.'

80 MS B, for example, with its dates off by one year, offers only a scant outline for the years 955–9: 'AN.dccclvi. Her forðferde Eadred cing,] Eadwig feng to rice. / AN.dccclvii. Her Eadgar æþeling feng to Myrcna rice. / AN.dccclviiii. Her forðferde Eadwig cing;] Eadgar his broðor feng to rice ægðer ge on Westseaxum ge on Myrcum ge on Norðhymbrum,] he wæs þa .xvi. wintre' (Taylor, *MS B*, 54) [956: Here King Eadred died, and Eadwig succeeded to the kingdom / 957: Here æþeling Edgar succeeded to the kingdom of the Mercians / 959: Here King Eadwig died, and his brother Edgar succeeded to the kingdom of the West-Saxons, and of the Mercians, and of the Northumbrians, and he was sixteen years old]. MS A contains even less information, with no mention at all of Edgar's election by the Mercians (Bately, *MS A*, 74–5).

81 See Keynes, 'The "Dunstan B" Charters,' 188–91; and Miller, *New Minster, Winchester*, 76–81.

82 Pauline Stafford has observed that, 'The men advanced or wooed were members of established families, though often the sons of established men. Eadwig did not

with his marriage to Ælfgifu in 955/6.[83] In 957 came the division of the king-dom between Eadwig and Edgar. Charter attestations show Archbishop Oda's absence from court beginning in 957, perhaps due to political tensions, and in 958 Oda separated Eadwig and Ælfgifu on grounds of consanguinity.[84] Eadwig's short reign clearly saw substantial agitation in the political arena.

S 1447 was probably written sometime between 968 and 975 and no later than Dunstan's death in May 988. Contemporary attitudes to the events of the late 950s are documented primarily in ecclesiastical writings generally predisposed to favour Edgar for his strong support of monastic reform. The two stories of brothers-at-odds in S 1447 seem to draw upon those same sentiments, especially their polemic contrast between Eadwig and Edgar. Monastic sources often vilify Eadwig as a poor king and celebrate Edgar as the sanctified redeemer of church and state. 'King Edgar's Establishment of Monasteries' (hereafter EEM), a vernacular prose text probably written by Bishop Æthelwold in the mid-960s, for example, scorns Eadwig as an immature ruler overly susceptible to the manipulations of greedy sycophants.[85] In contrast, Æthelwold lauds Edgar as an exemplary ruler who, favoured by God, far surpasses the excellence of his predecessors:

> Nęs lang to þy þæt his broþor þyses lænan lifes timan geendode, se þurh his cildhades nyteness þis rice tostencte ⁊ his annesse todælde, ⁊ eac swa halegra cyricena land incuþum reaferum todælde. Æfter his forðsiþe Eadgar, se fore-sæda cynincg, þurh Godes gyfe ealne Angelcynnes anweald begeat ⁊ þæs rices twislunge eft to annesse brohte, ⁊ swa gesundlice ealles weold þæt þa þe on æran timan lifes węron ⁊ his hyldran gemundon ⁊ heora dæda gefyrn to-cneowan, þearle swiþe wundredon ⁊ wafiende cwædon: 'Hit is la formicel Godes wunder þæt þysum cildgeongum cynincge þus gesundfullice eallu þing underþeodde synt on his cynelicum anwealde; his foregengan, þe geþun-gene wæron on ylde ⁊ on gleawscype swiþe bescawede ⁊ forewittige, [⁊] on

---

inaugurate a revolution at court but bound it closer to himself in a new generation ... The charters of this year point to unease, but not as yet crisis' (*Unification and Conquest*, 48). See also Keynes, 'Edgar, *rex admirabilis*,' 29–31.

83 See Jayakumar, 'Eadwig and Edgar,' 84–90; and Yorke, 'Æthelwold and the Politics of the Tenth Century,' 75–8. Ælfgifu appears to have been the sister of the ealdorman and chronicler Æthelweard and thus would have been descended from King Æthelred I (r. 865–71).

84 Brooks, *Early History of the Church of Canterbury*, 224–6.

85 For EEM, see Gretsch, *Intellectual Foundations*, 121–4, 230–3, and 240–1.

ænegum gewinne earfoþwylde, næfre þisne andweald on swa micelre sibbe smyltnesse gehealdan ne mihton, naþor ne mid gefeohte, ne med scette.'

[It was not long before his brother ended the time of this transitory life, who had through the ignorance of childhood dispersed this kingdom and divided its unity, and also distributed the lands of holy churches to rapacious strangers. After his death, Edgar, the aforesaid king, obtained by God's grace the whole dominion of England, and brought back to unity the division of the kingdom, and ruled everything so prosperously that those who had lived in former times and remembered his ancestors and knew their deeds of old, wondered very greatly and said in amazement: 'It is indeed a very great miracle of God that all things in his royal dominion are thus prosperously subjected to this youthful king; his predecessors, who were mature in age and very prudent and farseeing in wisdom (and) hard to overcome in any strife, never could maintain this dominion in so great peace and tranquility, neither by battle, nor by tribute.']⁸⁶

This account damns Eadwig for dividing the kingdom and most especially for doling out lands that he had taken from churches. The repetition of *todælde* in the passage emphasizes its preoccupation with division. Edgar, by contrast, heals the rifts created by his older brother and brings unity and prosperity to the realm: Edgar holds *anweald* over 'ealne Angelcynnes'; he mends partition (*twislunge*); and he restores the kingdom 'eft to annesse.' Æthelwold presents the transition from Eadwig to Edgar as a move from disarray to order and he idealizes Edgar's rule as the fulfilment of divine providence.

Another monastic source composed a few decades after Æthelwold's account features a similar contrast between Eadwig and Edgar. The earliest *uita* of St Dunstan, written sometime in the late 990s by the author known only as B.,⁸⁷ aggressively censures Eadwig as a foolish ruler and celebrates Edgar as a just king who fulfils God's plan. The author introduces Eadwig

---

86 Whitelock, Brett and Brooke, *Councils and Synods*, 1:146. Emphasis added.

87 In his preface, B. dedicates the work to Ælfric, archbishop of Canterbury (995–1005), and describes himself as 'omnium extimus sacerdotum B. vilisque Saxonum indigena' (Stubbs, *Memorials*, 3–52 at 3) [B., the most foreign of all priests and a lowly native of the Saxon people]. For discussion of B., see Stubbs, *Memorials*, x–xxx; Brooks, *Early History of the Church of Canterbury*, 245–6; and Lapidge, 'Hermeneutic Style,' 119–21. Lapidge elsewhere argues that B. was Byrhthelm, an English scholar who was trained at Glastonbury and later served as one of Dunstan's personal secretaries. Byrhthelm was a canon at Liège at the time when he wrote the *uita*. See Lapidge, 'B. and the *Vita S. Dunstani*.'

as 'a youth indeed in age and endowed with little wisdom in government'[88] before relating the tawdry tale of the young king shamefully slipping away from his consecration feast for a dalliance with a mother and daughter.[89] The kingdom is later divided due to Eadwig's poor leadership and the disaffected north (apparently inspired by divine guidance) chooses Edgar as their king:

> Factum est autem ut rex præfatus in prætereuntibus annis penitus a brumali populo relinqueretur contemptus, quoniam in commisso regimine insipienter egisset, sagaces vel sapientes odio vanitatis disperdens, et ignaros quosque sibi consimiles studio dilectionis adsciscens. Hunc ita omnium conspiratione relictum, elegere sibi, Deo dictante, Eadgarum ejusdem Eadwigi germanum in regem, qui virga imperiali injustos juste percuteret, benignos autem sub eadem æquitatis virgula pacifice custodiret. Sicque universo populo testante publica res regum ex diffinitione sagacium sejuncta est, ut famosum flumen Tamesæ regnum disterminaret amborum.[90]

> [It came about that the aforesaid king in the passage of years was wholly deserted by the northern people, being despised because he acted foolishly in the government committed to him, ruining with vain hatred the shrewd and wise, and admitting with loving zeal the ignorant and those like himself. When he had been thus deserted by the agreement of them all, they chose as king for themselves by God's guidance the brother of the same Eadwig, Edgar, who should strike down the wicked with the imperial rod, but peacefully guard the good under the same rod of equity. And thus in the witness of the whole people the state was divided between the kings as determined by wise men, so that the famous river Thames separated the realms of both.][91]

B. here emphasizes a number of key points. First, both Eadwig's political failings and God's will (*Deo dictante*) inspired the division of the kingdom. Second, the unanimous decision of the northern peoples supported

---

88   *EHD* I, 900. 'ætate quidem juvenis parvaque regnandi prudentia pollens' (Stubbs, *Memorials*, 32).

89   B. clearly sensationalizes the account. The 'wanton' daughter was Ælfgifu, Eadwig's future wife. Their marriage would be annulled later on grounds of consanguinity. See Yorke, 'Æthelwold and the Politics of the Tenth Century,' 76. MS D of the Anglo-Saxon Chronicle records the separation s.a. 958.

90   Stubbs, *Memorials*, 35–6.

91   *EHD* I, 901.

and guided the division – after they abandon Eadwig *omnium conspiratione*, the state is divided *universo populo testante*. Third, Edgar was a king who would bring justice to the realm and peace to deserving citizens (the *benignos*). Freed of ambiguity or complexity, politics here proceed according to a simple and unequivocal narrative logic.

Like Æthelwold, B. presents Eadwig as something of a caricature, a profligate ruler whose death clears the way for the better brother to assume the throne. 'Interea germanus ejusdem Eadgari, quia justa Dei sui judicia deviando dereliquit, novissimum flatum misera morte exspiravit; et regnum illius ipse, velut æquus hæres ab utroque populo electus, suscepit, divisaque regnorum jura in unum sibi sceptrum subdendo copulavit'[92] (Meanwhile the brother of this same Edgar, because he turned from and deserted the just judgments of his God, breathed his last by a miserable death, and Edgar received his kingdom, being elected by both peoples as true heir, and united the divided rule of the kingdoms, subjecting them to himself under one sceptre).[93] This passage stresses the return of unity to the point of over-determination: Edgar is elected by both peoples ('ab utroque populo'), he unites a kingdom divided ('divisaque regnorum iura'), and he rules with singular authority ('in unum sceptrum'). B. seems to have substantially amplified the partisan view of Eadwig that was already in place among the monastic reformers prior to the 970s. Indeed, B. was probably working from impressions he had gained during the years he spent with Dunstan in England. Michael Lapidge has shown that the 'eye-witness' material in the *uita* appears prominently for the years 939–60; this concentration of material is among the evidence which indicates that B. had been living outside England since 960.[94] It would seem that his presentation of events from the later 950s represents a contemporary view of that time, remembered many years later and informed by his close personal contact with Dunstan during those years. This 'dated' quality in B. seems all the more likely if we compare the presentation of Eadwig in Byrhtferth's *Vita S. Oswaldi*, written at Ramsey sometime between 997 and 1002 at approximately the same time that B. completed his *uita* of Dunstan.[95] The monastic rancour against Eadwig seems to have cooled in Byrhtferth; the young king appears only briefly as an 'insolens iuuentus'

---

92 Stubbs, *Memorials*, 36.
93 *EHD* I, 902.
94 Lapidge, 'B. and the *Vita S. Dunstani*,' 280–3.
95 Lapidge, *Byrhtferth*, lxvii–lxviii.

(immoderate youth) who eventually repents his wicked ways before Archbishop Oda. The division of the kingdom is not even mentioned.[96]

The situation in S 1447 is of course far more complex than the clear-cut oppositions and resolutions we find in the ecclesiastical sources. The account suggests more than it speaks directly, employing devices of repetition, parallelism, and implication. As we have seen, the first episode, featuring the brothers Æthelstan and Edward, dramatizes the consequences of fraternal discord for the enduring possession of family property. The scenario suggests that the brothers held the property jointly as bookland, even though Edward seems to have been the one in possession of the landboc. The mix of first-person and dual pronouns in Edward's first speech underscores this tenurial problem: 'ic hæbbe Sunnanburges boc ðe uncre yldran me læfdon.' The intensity of the impasse emerges in Æthelstan's apocalyptic statement that he would rather see the land destroyed by fire and flood than succumb to Edward's strong-arm tactics. Edward's prophetic response that it would be worse if neither of them had the land transforms the scene into a negative exemplum on how family discord can end in proprietary loss. This initial scenario effectively prepares the way for the convergence between the local and dynastic which emerges in the next episode.

As we have seen, the second episode begins with a paratactic string of short sentences which rapidly conflates the dynastic and local: King Eadred dies, Eadwig succeeds to the throne, and Æthelstan returns to Sunbury. These statements are immediately followed by the phrase 'ungebetra þinga,' apparently a genitive absolute (a construction which is exceptionally rare in Old English).[97] The absolute function can be understood generally as an accompanying circumstance, in which case 'ungebetra þinga' would seem to be attached to the statement that Æthelstan had gone back to Sunbury 'with things no better.'[98] Due to the paratactic syntax which precedes 'ungebetra þinga,' however, the absolute construction could be flexibly attached to both of the statements that precede it. In other words,

---

96 Ibid., 12–14.

97 Robertson identified the phrase as a genitive absolute, but Bruce Mitchell later denied the existence of a genitive absolute in Old English entirely. See Robertson, *Anglo-Saxon Charters*, 337; and Mitchell, *Old English Syntax*, 2:940. Despite the rarity of the construction, I can see no other way to translate the phrase other than as some form of an absolute.

98 Robertson translates the phrase loosely as, 'Then Æthelstan went back to Sunbury without making amends' (*Anglo-Saxon Charters*, 91). See also the discussion of absolute constructions in Mitchell, *Old English Syntax*, 2:914–40.

'things are no better' when Æthelstan reoccupies Sunbury *and* when Eadwig becomes king after Eadred's death. This link between local and dynastic history becomes more apparent through the repetition of *feng*: Eadwig 'feng to rice' and Beornric 'feng to' the Sunbury estate after he receives it from Eadwig. In both situations, land changes hands. Taken together, these several connections indicate strategic juxtaposition. The account accomplishes its slight on Eadwig not only through its critical genitive absolute, but also through the simple laconic language in which it represents the king's actions: 'ך gesealde þæt land Byrnrice . ך he feng to . ך wearp Æðelstan ut' (and [he] granted the land to Beornric and he took it and threw Æthelstan out). There is little solemnity here, especially in comparison to the more prestigious political diction given to Edgar when he receives *anweald ealra cynerihta* (sovereignty in all royal rights) from the Mercians in the following episode. This vocabulary of political power underscores the full legitimacy of Edgar's royal authority north of the Thames – Eadwig receives no such lexical distinction. S 1447 thus diminishes Eadwig even as it clearly invests Edgar with political prestige.

Finally, the two competing grants of the Sunbury estate in the second and third episodes – Eadwig gives the land to Beornric, Edgar to Ealdorman Æthelstan – create a narrative tension between Eadwig and Edgar which resonates with the story of Æthelstan and Edward. Which grant is more legitimate? As we have seen, the account resolves the difficulty through its careful use of language. Edgar books (*gebecte*) the land whereas Eadwig simply gives it (*gesealde*) – the presence of the document signifies abiding possession. The text furthermore renders Edgar's grant of bookland in a legalistic diction embellished by repetition and alliteration. Again, the account rhetorically distinguishes Edgar over Eadwig. When Edgar refuses Æthelstan's appeal and books the Sunbury estate to Ealdorman Æthelstan, Æthelstan and Eadwig each disappear from the narrative and the initial stage of dispute ends. Local and dynastic land both move toward legitimate and longstanding possession at the same narrative moment. In this way, S 1447 echoes the idea, so prominent in monastic texts, that Eadwig's death cleared the way for Edgar to shepherd a unified kingdom into a time of justice and peace. While S 1447's first brother story ends in loss, its second concludes with the recovery and regeneration of family land. In this way, the charter's presentation of events resonates with recent dynastic history and the celebratory ideology which had formed around Edgar's kingship.

The fourth episode, however, also presents an apparent problem for the account's alignment with Edgar's contemporary prestige. The king clearly defies Dunstan when he grants Ecgfrith's land to Ealdorman Ælfheah; the

forfeiture itself even implies a conflation of tenurial and political instability. The account handles those events in a politic way by avoiding open
criticism. As we have seen, the dramatic detail in the scene renders the
forfeiture both sensible and just. Edgar's actions make further sense if we
consider the myriad political pressures the young king would have faced
early in his reign. The reunification brought with it many political challenges. As Pauline Stafford has described, 'Edgar's accession to Wessex in
959 was later presented as a restoration of unity, a prelude to a prosperous
and tranquil reign. The reality was more fraught. Dispute and division
meant that nobles had openly taken sides, some opposing Edgar. Edgar
added a legacy of debts owed to supporters north of the Thames to his
new need to reconcile his brother's former allies in Wessex.'[99] Stafford sees
Edgar's grant of the property to Ælfheah as a political maneuver engi-
neered to secure support in Wessex. Ælfheah and his brother Ælfhere had
both been appointed as ealdormen by Eadwig: first Ælfhere in Mercia in
956 and later Ælfheah in East Wessex in 959.[100] After the division in 957,
Ælfheah stayed with Eadwig in Wessex while Ælfhere, already an ealdorman, supported Edgar in Mercia.[101] Edgar's gift of the Sunbury and Send
estates in 962 may have been a move to maintain the crown's relationship
with a powerful family, even if it meant defying Dunstan on this particular
occasion. S 1447 gives us a glimpse of the various demands and obligations
Edgar must have faced as he consolidated support early in his reign. The
account does not censure Edgar for his decision but rather adopts a view
which seems more pragmatic than moral. In this way, S 1447 tells a story
which justifies Dunstan's final claim to the estates and still maintains respect for the king.

As we have seen, celebrations of Edgar's kingship are most pronounced
in contemporary monastic sources. S 1447 and EEM seem to have been
produced at approximately the same time: the charter was most likely
written soon after 968 while Æthelwold wrote his text in the 960s, perhaps
in 964.[102] Moreover, according to the scenario outlined by Lapidge, the
author B. left England for Liège in 960 or very soon after, taking with him
opinions of Eadwig and Edgar which he had formed during the many
years he spent in Dunstan's entourage. All three texts draw upon the same

---

99 Stafford, *Unification and Conquest*, 51.
100 For the political career of this powerful family, see Williams, '*Princeps Merciorum gen-
    tis.*' For specific discussion of Ælfheah, see ibid., 147–54.
101 Ibid., 148.
102 Gretsch, *Intellectual Foundations*, 241.

polemical narrative in which Edgar, a king favoured by God, saves the kingdom from the dissolute Eadwig.

This ideological investment in Edgar as a redeemer of a land divided was not restricted to ecclesiastical productions. Edgar's charters, for example, also observe the reunification of the kingdom in their nomenclature for the king. Diplomas for the years 957 to 959 appropriately limit Edgar's political authority to the Mercian territory and peoples.[103] After his succession to a full kingdom in 959, however, Edgar's diplomas regularly emphasize his authority over all of Britain. This practice is clearly evident in the royal titles found in the five original single-sheet diplomas attributed to 'Edgar A,' a royal draftsman prominently active from 959/60 to 963.[104] Royal titles in these charters include, for example, 'totius Brittanniæ gubernator et rector'[105] and 'totius Brittanniae basileus.'[106] The clear transition from the more circumscribed titles of Mercian authority in the charters of 958 and 959 to the more expansive claims over all Britain in later charters indicates some attention within the royal writing office to territorial reunification under Edgar. S 1447 appropriates the prestige of an actively celebrated

---

103 Not all charters dated before Edgar's succession to a full kingdom follow this pattern. S 674, a Peterborough charter dated to 958, calls Edgar 'industrius Anglorum rex ceterarumque gentium in circuitu persistentium gubernator et rector' (Kelly, *Peterborough*, no. 13 at pp. 237–8) [diligent king of the English and leader and ruler of the other peoples present in that environs]. S 679, from the York archive and also dated to 958, contains a nearly identical formulation: 'ego EADGARUS industrius Anglorum rex ceterarumque gentium persistentium gubernator et rector' (*BCS*, vol. 3, no. 1044 at p. 249). Simon Keynes explains these anomalies as the work of scribes using an established exemplar 'without thought for its implications' since an identical formulation appears in charters of the early 940s under Edmund and again in 956 under Eadwig (*Diplomas*, 69n135 and 66n124).

104 See Keynes, 'Edgar, *rex admirabilis*,' 14–20. 'Edgar A' has been identified as the scribe responsible for the following single-sheet diplomas: S 687, 690, 703, 706, and 717. See also Drögereit, 'Gab es eine angelsächsische Königskanzlei?' 394–400; and Keynes, *Diplomas*, 69–76. The single-sheet S 702 is an imitative copy of an 'Edgar A' original, likely produced as additional documentation for Ælfheah's sale of the property to Dunstan. See Korhammer, 'Bosworth Psalter,' 182–5. There has long been conjecture (never fully substantiated) that 'Edgar A' was actually Æthelwold or one of his close associates. Æthelwold went to Winchester in 963, the same year in which 'Edgar A' apparently ended his term as royal draftsman. See Kelly, *Abingdon*, cxv–cxxv; and Kelly, *Peterborough*, 242–3.

105 'Ruler and leader of all Britain.' S 687 (Kelly, *Abingdon*, no. 86 at p. 352); S 690 (Kelly, *Abingdon*, no. 87 at p. 355); and S 703 (*BCS*, vol. 3, no. 1082 at p. 312).

106 'Ruler of all Britain.' S 702 (*BCS*, vol. 3, no. 1085 at p. 315); S 706 (*BCS*, vol. 3, no. 1083 at p. 313); and S 717 (*BCS*, vol. 3, no. 1101 at p. 334).

king, but it also evokes the memory of recent political disturbance in order to add weight to its particular claims about local possession.

While the partition and reunification of the kingdom were both apparently free of violence, the diplomas attributed to the draftsman 'Edgar A' still show some concern over the potential dangers of political division. Several proems in this diplomatic group quote Christ's statement in Luke 21:10 regarding the early signs of Doomsday, '"Surget gens contra gentem et regnum adversus regnum" et reliqua' ('People will rise up against people and kingdom against kingdom,' and so on). The end of the world will be heralded first by wars and insurrections, followed by earthquakes, pestilence, famine, and finally by the destruction of Jerusalem and the exile of its people. This biblical allusion to conflict between kingdoms must have assumed particular urgency in the years immediately before and after 959. The first citation of Luke 21:10 by 'Edgar A' likely occurs in S 681, dated to 959 and written when Edgar was still 'King of the Mercians':

> Uacillante practice vite statu eius finis nimium teste diuine auctoritatis eloquio accelerare dinoscitur. 'Surget enim,' ut ueredica promulgat sententia, 'gens contra gentem et regnum aduersus regnum' et reliqua. Nam uniuersa instantis vite patrimonia incertis successorum cleronomis deseruntur et omnis mundi gloria appropinquante leti termino ad nichilum reciproca fatescit. Iccirco recidiuis caducarum possessiunculis rerum eterna superne patrie emolumenta lucrando, altithrono patrocinante, adipisci magnopere satagamus.[107]

> [As the condition of active life falters, its end is perceived to hasten greatly through the eloquent witness of divine authority. For as the true statement proclaims, 'People will rise up against people, kingdom against kingdom' and so on. For all inheritances of the present life are forsaken by the inconstant heirs of future generations, and all the glory of the world fails as the end of joy draws near, receding to nothing. Therefore let us greatly busy ourselves to gain the eternal rewards of the heavenly homeland by acquiring the protection of the high throne through the perishable little possessions of impermanent things.]

Simon Keynes has located a number of features in S 681 which are typical of the 'Edgar A' diplomas produced between 960 and 963, including the quotation from Luke. S 681 contains the first citation of Luke 21:10 among

---

107   Kelly, *Peterborough*, no. 14 at p. 241.

the 'Edgar A' group, but this particular proem appears only in this single document.[108] The S 681 proem uniquely links impending apocalypse to the uncertain transmission of property. This potent blend of biblical allusion with the language of doomed inheritance speaks to the unsettled situation of a recently divided kingdom. S 681 thus gives timely voice to current fears about political instability and the uncertain inheritance of dynastic land. Like S 1447, this proem implicitly juxtaposes property and politics in order to assume a greater degree of urgency and authority.

Citations of Luke 21:10 are less topical after Edgar becomes king of all England in 959.[109] In S 706, dated to 962, for example, the verse appears within a traditional eschatological context free of any apparent legal dimension: '[XP] Altithrono in æternum regnante universis sophiæ studium intento mentis conamine sedulo rimantibus liquido patescit quod huius vitæ periculis nimio ingruentibus terrore recidivi terminus cosmi appropinquare dinoscitur ut veridica Christi promulgat sententia qua dicit . "Surget gens contra gentem et regnum adversus regnum" et reliqua'[110] (With Jesus Christ ruling forever enthroned on high, it is clearly evident to all assiduously seeking the pursuit of wisdom through eager effort of mind that the end of the failing universe can be discerned through the pressing dangers of this life to approach with great terror, as the true statement of Christ proclaims, saying, 'People will rise up against people and kingdom against kingdom,' and so on). This proem occurs identically or with slight variation in S 700 and 702 (dated to 962); S 710, 711, 714, and 716 (dated to 963); S 767 (dated to 968); and S 824 (undated). Such regularity, concentrated in the early 960s, indicates a diplomatic formula which had probably lost the original resonance of the juxtaposition of apocalypse and failed inheritance which is evident in S 681. Such sentiments seem to have become less urgent as the kingdom moved into a time of stability in the 960s and perhaps put aside some of the uneasiness born from division and reunification.

Nonetheless, the continuing citation of Luke 21:10 in Edgar's charters might still have preserved some trace of old political fears. Patristic explications of Luke 21 highlight both inner and outer conflict as harbingers of Doomsday, particularly in Christ's statement in Luke 21:9 that the disciples

---

108 Kelly notes that the proem 'has no precise parallels, but it incorporates a biblical citation used in a number of "Edgar A" diplomas (S 700, 702, 706, 710–11, 714, 716), and the second part has elements in common with the proems of S 708, 709' (ibid., 243).

109 For a general discussion of apocalyptic content in Edgar's charters, see Bremmer, 'Apocalyptic Expectations in Anglo-Saxon Charters,' 501–14.

110 *BCS*, vol. 3, no. 1083 at p. 313.

will hear of *proelia* and *seditiones*. Gregory the Great explicates that verse as follows: 'Pensanda sunt uerba Redemptoris nostri, per quae nos aliud interius, aliud exterius passuros esse denuntiat. Bella quippe ad hostes pertinent, seditiones ad ciues. Vt ergo nos indicet interius exteriusque turbari, aliud nos fatetur ab hostibus, <u>aliud a fratribus perpeti</u>'[111] (We must ponder the words of our Redeemer, through which he announces that we will suffer one thing from within and another from outside. War of course pertains to an enemy force, insurrection to fellow citizens. Therefore when he proclaims that we are to be disturbed from within and without, he reveals that we are to endure one thing from enemies and another from brothers). Gregory twice uses *hostis* to describe those who will attack from outside, but his description of the threat from within becomes more precise as it moves from *ciues* to *fratribus*. Internal conflict, in other words, will arise from within both the general body politic and the individual family.[112] Strife within the dynastic kindred uniquely fulfils both conditions simultaneously – interfamilial discord begets division within the kingdom. A dispute between royal brothers, then, would potently match Gregory's description of one of the precursors to the Last Days. Despite its formulaic use in the 960s, then, the enduring currency of such content in the 'Edgar A' proems may suggest some lingering preoccupation with the dangers of division and the delayed consequences of old dynastic conflicts.

Considered alongside these various contemporary texts and events, S 1447's account of two brothers fighting over and subsequently losing family property to outsiders could easily have gained associative force through its parallels with recent politics. Stenton insightfully remarked that narrative charters 'have unique interest as illustrations of the way in which the fortunes of individuals were affected by the salient events of history.'[113] S 1447 clearly demonstrates the ways in which strategic storytelling and artful prose could fashion and accentuate those very connections in order to achieve greater persuasive effect and to impose a conjoined sense of the local and national past.

---

111 Gregory the Great, *Homiliae in Evangelia*, 321 (no. 35). Emphasis added. Bede glosses Luke 21:9 much as Gregory does, explaining that, 'Proelia ad hostes pertinent seditiones ad cives' (*In Lucae Evangelium Expositio*, 365).

112 The disastrous consequence of division is a common biblical motif. See especially Matt. 12:25: 'omne regnum divisum contra se desolatur et omnis civitas vel domus divisa contra se non stabit' (Fischer, *Biblia sacra*, 1543) [Every kingdom divided against itself is made desolate and no city or house divided against itself will stand]. See also Luke 11:17.

113 Stenton, *Latin Charters*, 44.

Both the royal diploma and dispute charter provided a powerful means for knowing land and determining its possession in writing, but the narrative form of the charter, in contrast to the declarative mode of the diploma, selectively arranges historical contingencies and reversals into a partisan argument for legitimate and lasting possession. In other words, while the Latin diploma solemnly denies mutability, the vernacular narrative accepts and appropriates historical change in the service of its particular interests. The royal diploma makes claims through monolithic assertion, the dispute charter through incremental story. The latter cannot directly acknowledge the limitations of those claims provided by the Latin diploma – especially on those occasions when it draws upon the authority of those documents in its own telling of events – but the very existence of such documents shows that stable and longstanding possession of land could easily become a contested point in Anglo-Saxon England. As they work to justify the possession of property and forestall dispute, these charters underscore how vulnerable tenurial claims could be in actual social practice. The insistent declaration that property could be held with some degree of stability over time is driven in part by the uneasy knowledge that such stability could all too often prove an ephemeral fiction in lived experience.

The classes of legal documents examined in these first two chapters, the Latin royal diploma and vernacular dispute charter, each show pronounced elements of strategic ornamentation and invention during the tenth century. In practical terms, such stylistic embellishment serves to bolster the authority of the document in question and to underscore various extra-textual endorsements or appeals (royal and divine); at the same time, I argue, such content can also import troubling evidence (forfeiture) or dissonant concepts (transience) within the environment of the text. In the process, landholding assumes a multivalent significance which transcends pragmatic or economic considerations; it becomes an enterprise which can be associated with the eternal and salvation while it is at the same time shadowed by the apprehension of loss. Through the operations of writing, land becomes a thing both permanent and impermanent, secure yet always vulnerable. This accumulation of value charges tenurial discourse with a flexible signification which allows it to migrate to and inform textual modes beyond the legal or practical. The next three chapters examine this phenomenon as it manifests across several different vernacular genres, with the next chapter attending specifically to how the vocabulary and practices of land tenure could provide a versatile medium for instructive metaphor and exhortation.

3 Tenure in Translation

Ne sylle ge þæt land on ece yrfe for þam þe hit ys Godes and ge synd utacymene and mine tilian.[1]

– Leviticus 25:23

This chapter considers how the discourse of land tenure – its tropes, concepts, written instruments, practices, and word-stock – provided a versatile conceptual field which crossed language and genre. The title of this chapter, 'Tenure in Translation,' gestures not to the translation of texts from Latin into Old English, but rather to the textual mobility of tenurial discourse and its potential to inform different kinds of vernacular writing in productive ways. This chapter specifically considers how tenurial discourse could be appropriated in order to engage and move contemporary audiences rhetorically. I examine three texts – legal, philosophical, homiletic – for the ways in which they incorporate tenurial metaphor in order to persuade or instruct at key moments. Each of these texts uses conceits drawn from estate management and land tenure in various ways specifically to explain the ways of God and the logic of salvation. Metaphors grounded in tenurial discourse provide a conceptual key in these texts for accessing spiritual mysteries which might evade easy understanding or acceptance despite a readily available orthodox explanation. While any early medieval Christian would be familiar with the idea that a just God rewards the faithful, for example, it might be difficult for an individual to reconcile that concept with the disparities and uncertainties of lived experience. Situational and

---

1 Marsden, *Old English Heptateuch*, 135. 'Do not give that land into eternal inheritance because it is God's and you are outsiders and my laborers.'

lexical examples drawn from land tenure and estate management help explain and justify issues of spiritual obligation and salvation in these texts.[2]
Moreover, the tenurial motif also frequently provides a contained occasion
in each text for rhetorical embellishment and literary performance.

IV Edgar: Sudden Death and Overdue Rent

King Edgar's second law-code (designated as IV Edgar in Liebermann's
foundational edition) was issued in an unknown year after a meeting held at
a place known only as *Wihtbordesstan*. The code cites and confirms early
legislation, presumably the double set of laws promulgated by the king and
his *witan* earlier at Andover (II–III Edgar). IV Edgar is perhaps best known
for its attention to the Danelaw and its specific provisions for its own copying and distribution,[3] but the code is also remarkable for its style and form.
While both parts of II–III Edgar designate themselves as a *gerædnes* (ordinance), IV Edgar notably presents itself as a *gewrit* which publishes the king's
thoughts on a possible remedy for a 'sudden pestilence' that has afflicted the
entire realm: 'Her is geswutelod on þisum gewrite, hu Eadgar cyncg wæs
smeagende, hwæt to bote mihte æt þam færcwealme, þe his leodscype
swyðe drehte] wanode wide gynd his anweald'[4] (Here it is made known in
this document how King Edgar inquired what could be a remedy in the
sudden pestilence which greatly oppressed and reduced his people far and
wide throughout his dominion).[5] The code begins as a public address target-
ing a specific public issue, the *færcwealm*. The word *færcwealm* itself is rare,
appearing only twice in the extant corpus, and in IV Edgar it suggests
an epidemic that kills indiscriminately and with uncanny speed.[6] The
Anglo-Saxon Chronicle records a great mortality ('micel mancwealm') in

---

2 Emily Steiner has argued that legal documents could be 'instrumental in communicating
   or corroborating divine truth' in English poetry of the later medieval period (*Documentary Culture*, 17). This chapter shows that Anglo-Saxon writers exploited legal discourse
   in similarly productive ways.
3 See Lund, 'King Edgar and the Danelaw'; and Wormald, *Making of English Law*, 313–20.
4 Liebermann, *Gesetze*, 1:206.
5 *EHD* I, 434.
6 *Færcwealm* may have been newly coined in IV Edgar. It otherwise appears only once in
   a late homily of Wulfstan, Napier 50, written sometime in the early eleventh century. See
   Wulfstan, *Sammlung*, no. 50, pp. 266–74 at 271. In the homily *færcwealm* appears among
   a short list of evils which can fall upon the people suddenly and for which they must
   seek remedy (*bot*) from God. For Napier 50 in general, see Bethurum, *Homilies of
   Wulfstan*, 39–41; and Lionarons, 'Napier Homily L.'

962,[7] presumably a major pestilence of some kind, but Simon Keynes and Patrick Wormald have both suggested that IV Edgar was issued a decade later in the early 970s.[8] If the later date is correct, then the *færcwealm* would have been the second plague during Edgar's reign and thus may have posed an even more serious threat. Keynes has cogently described IV Edgar as 'a response of royal government in a moment of crisis,'[9] and the code does indeed assume a tone of special urgency, particularly in its lengthy prologue.

The opening sentence achieves its sense of pressing need in part through its lexical and formal innovations in legislative writing. Dorothy Whitelock commented that IV Edgar 'affords an example of a homiletic style before the period of the great homilists Ælfric and Wulfstan.'[10] Patrick Wormald likewise remarked that Edgar's second law-code 'was rhetorical as no previous Anglo-Saxon laws had been.' Its cultivated personal tone, he argued, enabled 'a more informal, and at the same time more flamboyant, legislative mode.'[11] These stylistic qualities are especially evident in the prologue. Before it declares any provision whatsoever, IV Edgar moves to persuade its audience of the need for the various measures it will proclaim. The *færcwealm* represents a fatal mystery which requires an immediate solution, and the preface both identifies the plague's cause and proposes a remedy. Much like a homily, the law-code engages an audience on a timely issue and advocates the proper observance of Christian duties. The preface's evocative language and form thus frame the issue as an occasion for instruction.

The plague presents an unsettling and seemingly incomprehensible emergency. How can this deadly contagion which has afflicted the entire realm with such speed be explained? More importantly, how might it be stopped? After careful deliberation the king and his advisors deem the *færcwealm* to be a manifestation of God's just anger. By neglecting the payment of church tithes, the English have provoked His divine wrath: '[1] Ðæt is þonne ærest, þæt him ðuhte ꝼ his witum, þæt ðus gerad ungelimp mid synnum ꝼ mid oferhyrnysse Godes beboda geearnod wære, ꝼ swyðost mid þam oftige þæs neadgafoles, þe Cristene men Gode gelæstan scoldon on heora teoðingsceattum'[12] (First, namely, that it seemed to him and his

---

7 Bately, *MS A*, 75.
8 Keynes, 'Edgar, *rex admirabilis*,' 11n41; Wormald, *Making of English Law*, 441–2.
9 Keynes, 'Edgar, *rex admirabilis*,' 12.
10 *EHD* I, 434.
11 Wormald, *Making of English Law*, 318–19.
12 Liebermann, *Gesetze*, 1:206.

councillors that a calamity of this kind was merited by sins and by contempt of God's commands, and especially by the withholding of the tribute
which Christian men ought to render to God in their tithes).[13] This statement attempts to make sense of apparently random events and to situate
them within a logic of divine justice. The English have earned their suffering
through the defiance of their deity. At the same time, the code proposes an
interpretation rather than simply declaring a truth – the crisis of the
færcwealm seems traumatic and widespread enough that a simple statement
might not be enough. The preface importantly attempts to persuade its
audience – all those dwelling under Edgar's dominion – of the value of both
its explanation and its proposed solution. The situation can best be understood, the *gewrit* suggests, by considering the inaccessible ways of the divine (*godcund*) through the example of worldly customs: 'He beðohte ꝺ
asmeade þæt godcunde be woruldgewunan'[14] (He has pondered and considered the ways of God by comparison with worldly usage).[15] By way of
illustration, the preface then offers an analogy drawn from the practices of
estate management and the obligations of tenants to their lord. This instructive scenario provides an exemplum which will both explain the crisis
and reveal its remedy.

This explanation of the *færcwealm* is delivered in two statements which
proceed from the general (*ærest*) to the specific (*swyðost*). The precise cause,
the failure to render tithes to God, introduces the word *neadgafol*, a rare
compound whose lexical elements together assume the necessity of payment – the obligation may seem a burden, but its fulfilment is imperative.
Gafol generally signifies tribute, but the word also frequently means a due
payment such as a rent or tax,[16] and these fiscal connotations effectively
prepare the way for the conceit which follows as the preface provides a
figurative argument to illustrate and support its claim about the cause of
the *færcwealm*. The text presents a scenario in which a *geneatman*[17] (I will
say more about this word shortly) resists paying the rent he owes to his
hlaford. This syllogistic analogy contains two propositions consisting of

---

13 *EHD* I, 434.
14 Liebermann, *Gesetze*, 1:206.
15 *EHD* I, 434.
16 *DOE*, s.v. 'gafol.'
17 The word *geneat* originally meant 'companion' or 'member of a household,' but by the
    eleventh century the word had come to represent a rank of men who held land from a
    lord in exchange for rent and other occasional duties. See Chadwick, *Studies on Anglo-
    Saxon Institutions*, 136–9; and Stenton, *Anglo-Saxon England*, 470–88.

conditional statements (if/then) with parallel syntax: '[1.1] <u>Gif</u> geneat-manna hwylc forgymeleasað his hlafordes gafol ꝺ hit him to ðæm rihtan-dagan ne gelæst, <u>wen is</u>, gyf se hlaford mildheort bið, þæt he ða gymeleaste to forgyfenesse læte ꝺ to his gafole buton witnunge fo; [1.2] <u>gyf</u> he ðonne gelomlice þurh his bydelas his gafoles myngað, ꝺ he ðonne aheardað ꝺ hit þencð to ætstrengenne, <u>wen is</u>, þæt ðæs hlafordes grama to ðam swyðe weaxe, þæt he him ne unne naðer ne æhta ne lifes'[18] (If any tenant dis-regards the rent to his lord, and does not pay it to him at the appointed day, it is to be expected, if the lord is merciful, that he may forgive the neglect and take his rent without exacting a penalty. If, however, he frequently through his bailiffs demands his rent, and the other then proves obstinate and intends to withhold it with defiance, it is to be expected that the lord's anger will so increase that he may grant him neither possessions nor life).[19] Because the verb *ætstrengan*, a hapax legomenon, implies physical force, it would seem that the tenant intends some form of resistance, but the lord's final response seems even more extreme. Are we to understand that a land-lord can murder a recalcitrant tenant with impunity? Much of the passage's vocabulary, moreover, is distinctly homiletic (*forgymeleasað*, *mildheort*, *forgyfenesse*, *aheardað*), infusing the quotidian matter of overdue rent with religious signification. This rhetorical amplification accentuates the start-ling scenario in which an angry landlord seemingly confiscates both life and property from his negligent tenant.

   This portrait of a murderous landlord has long been met with scepticism among modern commentators. Indeed there are no provisions in the law-codes or any evidence in the charters which might suggest that a landlord had such power over his tenants. A.J. Robertson sensibly remarked that the statement is 'perhaps not to be taken too literally.'[20] Vinogradoff too observed much earlier that, 'The obligations of the *geneat*, the follower, towards the lord are stated with some exaggeration and a scriptural tinge.'[21] H.P.R. Finberg likewise regarded the scene as a fanciful one: 'The sensa-tional picture of a recalcitrant *geneat* barricading himself in his farmhouse and holding out there to death does credit to the lawgiver's imagination, but can seldom indeed have been realized in practice.'[22] Surely this scenario should be read as a parable, a hyperbolic moment whose figurative veneer

---

18 Liebermann, *Gesetze*, 1:206. Emphasis added.
19 *EHD* I, 434.
20 Robertson, *Laws of the Kings of England*, 306.
21 Vinogradoff, *Growth of the Manor*, 238.
22 Finberg, 'Anglo-Saxon England to 1042,' 515.

delivers a cautionary message.[23] The embedded narrative shocks the audience to a recognition that there are consequences when we neglect to render what we owe to a superior power. The preface strategically uses a *woruldgewunan*, in this case the obligations attendant upon landholding, to illustrate the necessity of fulfilling duties to God.

After its parable of the punished tenant, the preface takes a turn which, much like the sestet of an Italian sonnet, completes the scenario developed in the previous section: '[1.3] Swa is wen, þæt ure Drihten do þurh ða gedyrstignysse, þe folces men wiðhæfton þære gelomlican myngunge, þe ure lareowas dydon ymbe þæt neadgafol ures Drihtnes: þæt syn ure teoðunga ꞇ cyricsceattas'[24] (So it is to be expected that our Lord will act on account of the audacity with which the laymen have resisted the frequent admonitions which our teachers have given about our Lord's tribute, namely our tithes and church-scot).[25] The transition *swa is wen* signals a change through its chiastic variation of the two previous *wen is* clauses, while the incremental repetition of *neadgafol* echoes the preface's opening claim. IV Edgar 1.3 thus pulls together various strands and terms from the preceding material in order to culminate and clarify the analogy in an instructive moment. The *hlaford* now becomes *drihten*, a common poetic word for God, and the idea of lordship ascends from the manorial to the divine. The beadles (*bydelas*) become teachers (*lareowas*) who patiently remind the faithful that God requires his own rent (*neadgafol*). This associative shift from beadle to teacher, from the punitive to the instructive, is formed in part through polyptoton: the beadles remind the negligent tenant (*gafoles _myngað_*) just as the *lareowas*, a word with clear connotations of preaching, deliver frequent _myngunge_ to laymen (*folces men*).[26] The section concludes with a final clarification of the *neadgafol* due to God ('þæt syn ure teoðunga ꞇ cyricsceattas') which recalls those tithes which the English have wrongly withheld from God. This technique of symmetrical repetition also manifests in a subtle case of tmesis, or the separation of a word into two parts: the *teoðingsceattum* in the initial claim

---

23 The parable of the landowner and the tenants from Matt. 21:33–44 provides an instructive biblical parallel. In this scenario the landlord eventually puts the bad tenants to death and leases the vineyard to others who will render him the produce at the proper time.

24 Liebermann, *Gesetze*, 1:206.

25 *EHD* I, 434.

26 *Bydel* commonly means a herald or messenger of God in addition to a secular or estate officer (*DOE*, s.v. 'bydel'). Interestingly enough, I Cnut 26 and II Cnut 84.4 mention beadles and teachers together (Liebermann, *Gesetze*, 1:304 and 368). According to I Cnut 26, for example, 'bisceopas syndan bydelas ꞇ Godes lage lareowas.'

appear in final position as _teoðunga_ ⁊ _cyricsceattas_. Rhetorical effects thus adorn the preface's teaching moment, delivering its lesson in a finely embellished package.

The turn at IV Edgar 1.3 is further distinguished by its transition from third- to first-person voice. Four genitive plural first-person pronouns prominently signal the shift.[27] This change amplifies the homiletic register already evident in the preface's vocabulary and appropriately enough introduces a direct appeal to the audience: '[1.4] Ðonne beode ic ⁊ se arcebisceop, þæt ge God ne gremian, ne naðer ne geearnian ne þone færlican deað þises andweardan lifes, ne huru þone toweardan ecere helle mid anigum oftige Godes gerihta; ac ægðer ge earm ge eadig, þe ænige teolunga hæbbe, gelæste Gode his teoðunga mid ealra blisse ⁊ mid eallum unnan, swa seo gerædnys tæce, þe mine witan æt Andeferan geræddon ⁊ nu eft æt Wihtbordesstane mid wedde gefæstnodon'[28] (Therefore I and the archbishop command that you do not anger God, nor merit either sudden death in this present life or indeed the future death in everlasting hell by any withholding of God's dues; but both poor man and rich, who has any produce, is to render his tithes to God with all gladness and with all willingness, as the ordinance directs which my councillors decreed at Andover, and have now again confirmed with pledging at _Wihtbordesstan_).[29] The first-person address aligns the singular voice of the king with the saving exhortation which concludes the preface's instructional function. The figurative element has fallen away entirely: _hlaford_ became _drihten_ in IV Edgar 1.3, and _drihten_ now becomes _God_ as the preface turns to explicit admonition. The first sentence in the passage above, peppered with five negatives (_ne_), appropriately employs anathematic language (also evident, as we have seen, in Latin diplomas) as it extends the fatal suffering of the mortal realm to the afterlife: transgressors will endure an endless death in an eternal hell.[30] The only way to avoid such a fate is to honour both the rights due to God and the law promulgated by the king. IV Edgar 1.4

---

27 These pronominal phrases include _ure Drihten_, _ure lareowas_, _ures Drihtnes_, and _ure teoðunga_.

28 Liebermann, _Gesetze_, 1:206 and 208.

29 _EHD_ I, 434.

30 The same logic is repeated in the section following: '[1.5a] Gyf he swa earm bið, þæt he aþer deð oððe þa Godes wanað, his sawla to forwyrde, oððe waccor mid modes graman hy behwyrð þonne þæt he him to agenum teleð, þonne him micele agenre is, þæt him æfre on ecnysse gelæst, gyf he hit mid unnan ⁊ fulre blisse don wolde' (Liebermann, _Gesetze_, 1:208). 'If he is so contemptible, that he either curtails God's [dues] to the perdition of his soul, or with reluctance at heart attends to them less diligently than to

provides a forceful crescendo to the scenario developed in the preface, one which seems designed both to convince the audience of its thesis and to move the audience to reparative action. The text decorates this appeal with a number of rhetorical effects: polyptoton (*gerædnys* and *geræddon*); repetition and sound-play (*andweardan* and *toweardan*, *teolunga* and *teoðunga*, *ge earm ge eadig*); and symmetrical phrases (*mid ealra blisse ꞇ mid eallum unnan*). Several repetitions also link the sentence to earlier material: *God ne gremian* echoes *ðæs hlafordes grama* (1.2); *þone færlican deað* echoes *færcwealm*; *teoðunga* echoes *teoðingsceattum* (1) and *teoðunga* (1.3); *gelæste* echoes *gelæstan* and *gelæst* (1.1); and *unnan* echoes *unne* (1.2). As we can see, incremental repetition in the preface clarifies thematic connections and advances the argument through analogy.

The element of personal address in the code also echoes the hierarchical scenario envisioned in the parable of the tenant and its attendant message of obligations due to a superior power. King Edgar delivers his injunctions in a tone which Patrick Wormald neatly described as both intimate and threatening.[31] The royal voice notably speaks to all the people of the realm, cutting across divisions of ethnicity, geography, and class. Edgar states, for example, that his laws are for the good of the entire people (*eallum leodscype*), and that the new provisions against theft and the sale of stolen goods will benefit English, Danes, and Britons alike, be they rich or poor.[32] Alongside this egalitarian vision, however, we also find measures which seem more severe and unyielding. The king threatens lax reeves with the loss of 'my friendship and all that they own' and orders them to carry out their duties without exception or favouritism. There shall be no forgiveness for those who break the law: '[1.5] Ðonne beode ic minum gerefan, be minum freondscype ꞇ be eallum þam ðe hi agon, þæt hi styran ælcum þara ðe þis ne gelæste ꞇ minra witena wed abrecan mid ænegum wacscype wille, swa swa him seo foresæde geradnes tæce; ꞇ on ðære steore ne sy nan forgyfnes'[33] (Moreover, I command my reeves, on pain of losing my friendship

---

what he accounts his own; then much more his own is what endures for him for ever into eternity if he would pay it with willingness and full gladness' (*EHD* I, 435).

31 Wormald, *Making of English Law*, 319.

32 '[2.2] Sy þeahhwæðere þes ræd gemæne eallum leodscype, ægðer ge Englum ge Denum ge Bryttum, on ælcum ende mines anwealdes, to ðy þæt earm ꞇ eadig mote agan þæt hi mid rihte gestrynað' (Liebermann, *Gesetze*, 1:210). 'Nevertheless, this measure is to be common to all the nation, whether Englishmen, Danes or Britons, in every province of my dominion, to the end that poor man and rich may possess what they rightly acquire' (*EHD* I, 435). Compare IV Edgar 1.6, 2, 3, 6, 12.1, 14.2, and 16 for similarly inclusive language.

33 Liebermann, *Gesetze*, 1:208.

and all that they own, that they punish each of those who does not perform this and who wishes to break the pledge of my councillors by any
remissness, just as the aforesaid ordinance directs them; and there is to be
no remission of that punishment).[34] Later, Edgar declares that any herdsmen who fail to notify the hundred of newly purchased (and potentially
stolen) livestock on the common pasture after five days time will be beaten
for their negligence. Again, there shall be no mercy in administering punishment, despite the fact that the herdsmen would neither have been owners of the livestock in question nor party to its purchase or theft: '[9] Gif
hit þonne ofer V niht ungecyd on gemænre læse wunað, þolige þæs orfes,
swa we ær cwædon, ⁊ ðara hyrda ælc ðolige ðære hyde; ⁊ ðæs ne sy nan
forgyfnes, gesecan þæt hi gesecan'[35] (If, however, it remains on the common pasture more than five days unannounced, he is to forfeit the cattle, as
we have said above, and each of the herdsmen is to be flogged; and there is
to be no remission of that, no matter what refuge they reach).[36] The code
imagines an unforgiving and inescapable justice in which Edgar assumes
the role of a munificent ruler who turns grim only when his subjects defy
his law.[37] In other words, Edgar resembles the *hlaford* of the code's preface:
merciful at first with the 'negligent tenant,' but finally vengeful upon subsequent offence and resistance. The parallel emerges again in the law-code's
closing statement: 'Ic beo eow swyðe hold hlaford þa hwyle þe me lif

---

34 *EHD* I, 434–5.
35 Liebermann, *Gesetze*, 1:212. Compare IV Edg 10 and 11.
36 *EHD* I, 436.
37 Edgar's laws were on occasion remembered for their severity. Lantfred of Winchester's
   Translatio et miracula S. Swithuni, written in the early 970s, describes a grotesque punishment prescribed for theft: 'Prenotato denique tempore, glorioso rege Eadgaro
   precipiente, ad deterrendos quosque malos horribili poena talis lex est constituta in
   Anglorum prouincia: ut si quispiam cleptes in tota uel predo inueniretur patria, caeca-
   tis luminibus, truncatis manibus, auulsis auribus, incisis naribus, et subtractis pedibus
   excruciaretur diutius; et sic demum decoriata pelle capitis cum crinibus, per omnia
   pene membra mortuus relinqueretur in agris, deuorandus a feris et auibus atque noc-
   turnicanibus' (At the aforesaid time and at the command of the glorious King Edgar, a
   law of great severity was promulgated throughout England to serve as a deterrent
   against all sorts of crime by means of a dreadful punishment: that, if any thief or robber were found anywhere in the country, he would be tortured at length by having his
   eyes put out, his hands cut off, his ears torn off, his nostrils carved open and his feet
   removed; and finally, with the skin and hair of his head flayed off, he would be abandoned in the open fields, dead in respect of nearly all his limbs, to be devoured by wild
   beasts and birds and hounds of the night). Lapidge, *Cult of St Swithun*, 310–13. See
   also Whitelock, 'Wulfstan *Cantor* and Anglo-Saxon Law'; and Wormald, *Making of
   English Law*, 125–8.

gelæst, ך eow eallum swyðe bliðe eom, for ði þe ge swa georne ymbe frið syndon'[38] (I will be a very gracious lord to you as long as my life lasts, and I am very well pleased with you all, because you are so zealous about the maintenance of the peace).[39] Edgar presents himself not as *cyng*, as he is titled in the law-code's opening sentence, but as a *hlaford* dedicated to his subjects and grateful for their commitment to peace. The stern tone retreats as the code ends in an ideal vision of lordship and community. The use of *hlaford* in the final statement furthermore echoes the scenario laid out in the preface, creating an envelope structure predicated on the concept of lordship and the obligations of tenancy. Like God, the king can be seen as a figural landlord who makes certain demands upon those who live on his land. In each case, the continuing support of the superior power – landlord, king, God – is contingent on a subordinate's fulfilment of set duties.

The question remains why IV Edgar assigns the role of defiant tenant to the *geneatman*. What exactly was a *geneatman*? And to what end does this particular individual represent the subordinate who fails to meet his obligations? In order to answer these questions, we must first consider the social context for the preface's analogy in more detail. The preface builds its worldly metaphor on the model of estate management and the ways in which a lord received certain benefits from his holdings in land and men. When the king alienated property to a beneficiary, he also transferred those goods and service which had traditionally been due from the land and its inhabitants. These considerable benefits included renders of food and goods (*feorm*) as well as a range of services and labour due from those living on the land; many of these obligations were customary and had long been in place under old systems of tribute and extensive lordship.[40] Organization varied by time and place, but an estate typically consisted of two different categories of land, *inland* (inland) and *utland* (outland), with each carrying distinct obligations to the lord.[41]

---

38 IV Edgar 16. Liebermann, *Gesetze*, 1:214.
39 *EHD* I, 437.
40 Faith, *English Peasantry*, 1–14.
41 Extensive estates with widely scattered lands are especially evident in Domesday Book for the northern counties and northeast midlands. These estates were 'usually made up of the following elements: an estate centre to which services and dues were rendered (Latin *manerium*); intensively exploited demesne which was either contiguous or located close to the estate centre (OE *inland*); topographically detached parcels of demesne known as berewicks (OE *agenland* or *berewic*, Latin *berewica*); and further, less heavily dependent tributary land known as sokeland (OE *socn* or *socnland*, Latin *soca*)' (Baxter, *Earls of Mercia*, 258). See also Stenton, *Types of Manorial Structure*. This

The lord had proprietary rights over inland while the 'characteristic feature of outland was that the lord possessed over the landholders, whose scattered tenements formed it, merely seigniorial rights, and enjoyed only those customs which had once been rendered to the king.'[42] Inland was mainly worked by a resident and dependent peasantry, a heterogeneous labour force which consisted of both free and enslaved tenants who were largely dedicated to the production of essential supplies and services for the manor or 'home farm' (*heafodbotl*).[43] These tenants typically were obligated to work a set numbers of days each week for their lord (week-work), and while many of them were technically free, they were still dependent on the lord and frequently tied to his land.[44] Those who lived on an estate's outland, by contrast, owed customary obligations but were otherwise free.[45]

Among this free peasantry, the *geneat* would have been an individual of some means and status. Even so, he would still have been attached to a lord,[46] and his status and privileges were determined in part by his obligations to that social superior.[47] He would also have lived on land which carried certain obligations to a lord but over which the lord had no direct

---

model of the extended estate was not a geographically limited phenomenon, however: 'this structure is widely accepted as typical of – indeed it constitutes the common denominator of – the multiple or complex estate' (Faith, *English Peasantry*, 43). See also Reynolds, *Later Anglo-Saxon England*, 81–4; and Lavelle, 'Geographies of Power.'

42 Barlow, *Feudal Kingdom of England*, 11. See also *EHD* II, 71–3.
43 Faith, *English Peasantry*, 56–88.
44 Harvey, 'Life of the Manor,' 54.
45 Faith, *English Peasantry*, 89–152. Outland was later known as warland or sokeland. Note, for example, the distinction between 'inland' and 'warland' in the twelfth-century estates surveys from Burton Abbey (*EHD* II, no. 176 at pp. 884–92). See also Stenton, *Types of Manorial Structure*, 10–11; Vinogradoff, *Growth of the Manor*, 224–7; Faith, *English Peasantry*, 89–91; and Baxter, *Earls of Mercia*, 210–11.
46 An 'eald geneat' stands among those loyal to Byrhtnoth in *The Battle of Maldon* (at line 310a). This character, Byrhtwold, delivers the poem's celebrated speech on loyalty and heroism at lines 312–19 ('The mind must be firmer …'). A 'cynges geneat' is also named among the prominent casualities of a naval skirmish between the English and the Danes in the Anglo-Saxon Chronicle, s.a. 896 (Bately, *MS A*, 60).
47 Maitland outlined three bonds of lordship, the personal, the tenurial, and the jurisdictional (*Domesday Book and Beyond*, 66–107 at 67), and Stephen Baxter has recently discussed how frequently these various bonds overlapped in pre-Conquest England (*Earls of Mercia*, 204–69 at 208–15). See also Stenton, *Anglo-Saxon England*, 490–2; Sawyer, '1066–1086: A Tenurial Revolution?'; and Reynolds, *Fiefs and Vassals*, 338–42.

proprietary rights.[48] The precise conditions of landholding for *geneatmen* in late Anglo-Saxon England are difficult to ascertain, and there would undoubtedly have been considerable variation in the size and circumstance of their holdings. Some may have held their land on lease,[49] while others likely would have inherited family land through customary law (*folcriht*) with the property remaining subject to longstanding customary obligations. Rosamond Faith has argued that many among the free peasantry would have 'considered that they owned their own land and ... expected to pass it on in some way to their descendants.'[50] Domesday Book suggests that many small landholders before the Conquest did have the power to alienate their land, but whether or not the *geneat* would have typically been among them remains uncertain.[51]

We know much more about the duties and services owed by the *geneat* to his lord. The *Rectitudines singularum personarum*, a vernacular treatise on estate management composed sometime between the mid-tenth and early eleventh century, lists these duties in some detail.[52] The thegn appears first in the survey where he is distinguished by his *bocriht* (a hapax legomenon), that is, the privileges of bookland; this right differentiates the thegn's tenure from that of the groups which follow him in the text.[53] The *geneat* appears in second place with the following obligations: 'Geneatriht is mistlic be ðam ðe on lande stænt: on sumon he sceal landgafol syllan ꝼ gærsswyn

---

48 II Edgar 1.1, for example, distinguishes between the lord's demesne and the holdings of free tenants when it states that church tithes are to be paid from both *ðegnes inland* and *geneatland*. See Liebermann, *Gesetze*, 1:196.

49 Lease tenants typically owed some combination of rent and services for their land. In a letter reputedly written to King Edgar (S 1368), Bishop Oswald states that his lease tenants owed substantial duties, many of which resemble those typically expected of the *geneat*. Oswald's tenants all must pay church dues. They must fulfil the 'law of riding' (*equitandi lex*) and they must be ready to ride for the bishop and to build hedges for his hunting. The letter survives as a late eleventh-century copy in Hemming's Cartulary at Worcester (London, BL, Cotton Tiberius A. xiii [Gneuss 366]). For Hemming's Cartulary, see Tinti, *Sustaining Belief*, 137–47.

50 Faith, *English Peasantry*, 127. Maitland also believed that some of the *uillani* recorded in Domesday may have held their own land with customary demands of goods and services remaining in place (*Domesday Book and Beyond*, 60 and 76–8).

51 Baxter, *Earls of Mercia*, 215–36. See also Reynolds, *Fiefs and Vassals*, 338.

52 See Seebohm, *The English Village Community*, 129–47; Vinogradoff, *Growth of the Manor*, 231–5; Harvey, 'Rectitudines Singularum Personarum and Gerefa'; and Wormald, *Making of English Law*, 387–9.

53 The thegn held *bocriht*, but his land could still carry obligations beyond the three common burdens, including the maintenance of the deer-fence (*deorhege*) at the king's residence, various guard duties, church dues, 'and many other different things.'

on geare ꝺ ridan ꝺ auerian ꝺ lade lædan, wyrcan ꝺ hlaford feormian, ripan ꝺ mawan, deorhege heawan ꝺ sæte haldan, bytlian ꝺ burh hegegian, nigefaran to tune feccan, cyricsceat syllan ꝺ ælmesfeoh, heafodwearde healdan ꝺ horsdwearde, ærendian fyr swa nyr, swa hwyder swa him mon to tæcð'[54] (*Geneat* duty varies according to what is in place for the land: on some [estates] he must give land-rent and a pig for pasture each year, and ride and carry and lead the way, work and entertain his lord, reap and mow, hew the deer hedge and keep up blinds, build and fence the borough, bring new-comers to the manor, pay church dues and almsfee, keep guard over his lord and watch the horses, carry messages far and near wherever he is directed). Several of these services notably involve work which would have required the *geneat* to own a horse and equipment.[55] A Worcester charter dated to 896, for example, describes a *geneat* riding along the boundaries of a wood-land tract as a priest reads out the bounds from an old charter as part of an effort to settle a dispute.[56]

Some of the *geneat*'s obligations also suggest a degree of personal con-tact with the lord and thus would have been of a more prestigious nature than the agricultural labour typically required of other peasants. The *kot-setla* and *gebur*, the two groups which follow the *geneat* in *Rectitudines*, for example, owe regular week-work on the lord's estate as well as addi-tional seasonal plowing. The *geneat* class furthermore seems to have been economically prosperous – Stenton memorably described *geneatas* as

---

54 Liebermann, *Gesetze*, 1:445.

55 An estate survey for Tidenham (Gloucestershire), composed sometime between 956 and 1065, describes similar obligations for the *geneat*: 'Se geneat sceal wyrcan, swa on lande, swa of lande, swa hweðer swa him man byt, ꝺ ridan ꝺ auerian ꝺ lade lædan, drafe drifan, ꝺ fela oðra ðinga don' (S 1555; Kelly, *Bath and Wells*, no. 24 at p. 147). The verb *averian* appears only three times in the corpus: once in S 1555 and twice in *Rectitudines singularum personarum*. The *DOE* defines the word as follows: 'in context outlining service or obligation due to a lord, probably "to provide a carrying-service by draught-horse."' The word may have been confused with OE *aferian* (*DOE*, s.v. 'averian'). Domesday Book at one point speaks of seven sokemen (i.e., free holders with certain obligations and dues under the jurisdiction [OE *socn*] of a lord) of King Edward in Hertfordshire who supplied *averae* to the local sheriff (Maitland, *Domesday Book and Beyond*, 138). A twelfth-century survey of estates in the 'Black Book' of Peterborough similarly lists a sokeman 'who performs service with a horse' as well as a group of fifty sokemen who 'must work by custom each year for 6 days at the deer hedge' (*EHD* II, no. 177 at p. 893). The variations in terminology within Domesday probably obscure similarities between *geneatas*, radknights, and sokemen.

56 S 1441. *BCS*, vol. 2, no. 574 at pp. 216–17. See also Harmer, *SEHD*, no. 14 at pp. 24–5; and Wormald, 'Handlist,' no. 21 at p. 266.

'a peasant aristocracy.'[57] A.J. Robertson equated them with the *gafolgelda* (rent-payer) mentioned in Ine's laws, and while the terminology in the provisions is not entirely precise, these earlier rent-payers apparently enjoyed a high standing among the peasantry.[58] Later evidence suggests that the *geneat* was an antecessor to Domesday's *radcniht* (whose name clearly suggests riding duties of some kind), some of whom held a substantial amount of land with subtenants of their own in 1066.[59] In Tewkesbury (Gloucestershire), for example, three radknights held estates of six, three, and two hides 'in the time King Edward.'[60] While a *geneat* may have owed agricultural services such as reaping and mowing, he probably would not have needed to perform that work with his own hands.[61] The *geneat* may not have enjoyed the status or *bocriht* of a thegn, then, but he did occupy a privileged position among the free peasantry.

What made this class of peasant freeholders particularly appropriate for exemplary metaphor in the preface to IV Edgar? The *geneat* may have been a free and relatively prosperous man with his status poised somewhere between *ceorl* and thegn, but his land still carried customary obligations to a higher authority.[62] The *geneat* held a more distinguished position than the *ceorl*, but he still owed a more extensive set of duties than would be typically associated with a thegn – he thus occupied a middle position in the

---

57 Stenton, *Anglo-Saxon England*, 473.

58 Robertson, *Laws of the Kings of England*, 302. The provisions in question are Ine 6.3 and 23.3. Whitelock commented that the Welsh *gafolgelda* in Ine 23.3 seems to have been 'the highest class of Welsh peasant' (*EHD* I, 401n6). H. Munro Chadwick distinguished the *gafolgelda* and *gebur* mentioned in Ine 6.3 as follows: the *gafolgelda* 'was a ceorl who possessed a certain amount of land, though less than five hides. The gebur on the other hand seems to have been a man who received from his lord both land and livestock, which at his death both returned to the lord' (*Anglo-Saxon Institutions*, 87n1).

59 Harvey, 'Domesday England,' 80–5. See also Campbell, 'Some Agents and Agencies of the Late Anglo-Saxon State,' 211–14.

60 Faith, *English Peasantry*, 107–8. At the same time, Domesday records that radknights in Deerhurst and Tewkesbury did do some plowing and harrowing. This information may have been recorded, however, because it was exceptional – the radknights at Deerhurst are designated as 'free men' who *tamen* (nevertheless) plowed and harrowed. See Lennard, *Rural England*, 370.

61 The twelfth-century legal compilation *Quadripartitus* translates *geneat* as *uillanus*. Likewise, while *geneatas* and *geburas* both appear in the Tidenham survey, Domesday only records *uillani* and *bordarii* on the estate in 1066. The classification of the peasantry in Domesday can be elusive and terminology varies by circuit. See Lennard, *Rural England*, 339–92; Stafford, *Unification and Conquest*, 207–10; and Williams, 'How Land was Held Before and After the Norman Conquest.'

62 Is there a paronomastic pun in the similar sounds of *geneatman* and *neadgafol*?

social and tenurial hierarchy, between the peasantry and the nobility. And his land was not held by book. He instead likely held family land by customary right with the expectation (rather than the written guarantee) that he would pass that property on to his heirs. His holding furthermore had long carried a set of obligations and would continue to do so for his successors; those obligations may have been relatively light and intermittent, but they nonetheless had to be met. In effect, the *geneat* provides a lesson at the local level that all landholding was contingent upon obedience to a superior power. The *geneat*, presumably an esteemed member of the free peasantry who held a prestigious position close to his lord, illustrates well the principle that all tenants, even the most prosperous and respected, were beholden to maintain the duties and dues they owed in return for their holding. The small parable of the disobedient tenant forfeiting life and land to an offended lord, then, speaks both to the value of property and to the limitations and obligations attendant upon its possession.

Within the parabolic logic of the law-code's preface, the entire realm faces fatal consequences when it neglects its obligations to church and God. The king acts as a mediator in IV Edgar, reminding the people of what they owe and of the consequence of failing to meet that debt. Indeed, even the sovereign is not exempt from the hierarchal network of obligation and the limits of life and tenure. His final promise to his people is notably conditional: he will be their devoted lord (*hold hlaford*) 'as long as his life lasts.' This phrase suggests that proprietary rights are always temporary, even for the highest earthly power; at the same time, the preface demonstrates that landholding always carries obligations to a superior power which must be maintained. The text thus imprints land with networks of power, both human and divine, within which the observance of subordinate duties proves to be a matter of life and death.

A Transformative Leap: From *Cotlif* to *Bocland*

While IV Edgar uses its disquieting parable of the negligent tenant to admonish its audience, the preface to the Old English adaptation of Augustine's *Soliloquia* features a more positive example of the diligent tenant rewarded by his lord. The preface to the Old English *Soliloquies* (hereafter *OESol*), which has no known source and is presumed to be an original composition, contains perhaps the best known use of tenurial language for exemplary purposes in the vernacular: the tenant whose *læn* is transmuted to *bocland* by his gracious lord. *OESol* survives only in the Southwick Codex, a mid-twelfth-century manuscript now bound with the Beowulf manuscript in London, BL, Cotton Vitellius A. xv.[63] A colophon attributes the text to King Alfred and scholars have generally accepted his role in its original production.[64] The preface presents two distinct but related metaphors. The first metaphor of cutting and gathering timber ends in the speaker's wish that he might find an eternal home through the writings of the holy fathers; the second metaphor features a tenant who hopes to gain the eternal inheritance of bookland, followed by an apparent notice of Augustine's *Soliloquia* as a source text. The two metaphors are distinguished by their use of voice – the building metaphor is written entirely in first person while the tenurial metaphor mainly employs a general third-person voice – but they nonetheless share prominent lexical and structural elements. Each features the same opposition, delivered in the same wording, between the transitory (*læne stoclif*) and the eternal (*ece ham*), for example, and each ends with the citation of textual authorities. Of the two sections, the woodcutting metaphor has proven the most attractive for modern scholars who, not surprisingly, have appreciated the value it places on intellectual work. As a consequence, critical appraisals of the preface typically give less attention to the tenurial metaphor.[65] This second conceit is integral to the preface's exemplary function, however, as it extends motifs and concepts from the first metaphor in important ways.

The first section presents the famous set-piece in which the speaker gathers wood for building in an extended metaphor for reading and reflection.[66] The speaker encourages others to follow his example and bring back enough timber to build their own 'ænlic hus' (singular houses) where they may live peacefully throughout the year. The speaker,

---

63 See Ker, *Catalogue*, no. 215 at pp. 279–81. The manuscript copy of *OESol* presents several textual difficulties: 'Because so much time lies between the date of Alfred's translation and the date of the manuscript, it is not surprising that the text as preserved contains numerous errors and lacunas and at least one substantial dislocation, as well as being incomplete at beginning and end' (Keynes and Lapidge, *Alfred the Great*, 299). For a useful overview of the work's textual history, see Potter, 'King Alfred's Last Preface,' 25–6; and Gatch, 'King Alfred's Version of Augustine's *Soliloquia*.'

64 For a challenge to this attribution see Godden, 'Alfredian Project and its Aftermath,' 114–22. The preface to *OESol*, unlike the prefaces to several other works attributed to Alfred, does not name the king. The first sentence of the preface to *OESol*, however, also seems to be incomplete, indicating that some text has been lost.

65 Examples include Potter, 'King Alfred's Last Preface'; Greenfield and Calder, *New Critical History*, 52; Fulk and Cain, *History of Old English Literature*, 59–60; and Irvine, 'Old English Prose: King Alfred and His Books,' 261–2.

66 See Heuchan, 'God's Co-Workers and Powerful Tools,' on possible sources for the preface's building metaphor.

regrettably, has not yet had the opportunity to enjoy such an end to his own labours: 'swa swa ic nu ne gyt ne dyde'[67] (as I now have not yet done). Still, he hopes that 'se þe me lærde' (he who taught me) may allow that, 'ic softor eardian (mæge) ægðer ge on þisum lænan stoclife be þis wæge ða while þe ic on þisse weorulde beo, ge eac on þam ecan hame ðe he us gehaten hefð þurh sanctus Augustinus and sanctus Gregorius and sanctus Ieronimus, and þurh manege oððre halie fædras'[68] (I may dwell more quietly both in this temporary habitation along the way as long as I am in this world, and also in the eternal home which he has promised us through St Augustine and St Gregory and St Jerome and through many other holy fathers). The contrast in this passage between a temporary dwelling and an eternal home will be repeated in nearly identical terms in the second section. The speaker's labour will help him find the way 'to þam ecan hame, and to þam ecan are, and to þare ecan reste'[69] (to the eternal home, and to the eternal glory, and to the eternal rest). The measured cadence and repetition in this phrase envision a particular progression in a threefold sequence. The phrase begins with the hope of home, moves to an idea of honour coupled with the possession of land, and then ends in lasting rest. The noun *ar* commonly means 'glory' or 'honour,' but it can also mean 'landed property' or 'estate,' particularly in legal writing.[70] The word's potential range of meaning allows 'ecan are' to signify at once both eternal glory and eternal land, with an associative connection between the two senses. Salvation thus assumes a tenurial dimension which will become more pronounced in the second metaphor.

The central conceit in the second section of the preface imagines a tenant who, after living for a time on a land loaned by his lord, receives from him a munificent grant of bookland. This tenurial upgrade provides an 'eternal inheritance' which prefigures 'eternal homes' elsewhere – the association between landholding and salvation is clear.

ac ælcne man lyst, siððan he ænig cotlyf on his hlafordes læne myd his fultume getimbred hæfð, þæt he hine mote hwilum þar-on gerestan, and huntigan, and fuglian, and fiscian, and his on gehwilce wisan to þere lænan tilian, ægþær ge on se ge on lande, oð þone fyrst þe he bocland and æce yrfe þurh

---

67 Carnicelli, *Soliloquies*, 47.1–12.
68 Ibid., 47.13–16.
69 Ibid., 48.2.
70 *DOE*, s.v. 'ar (C.1 and C.2).'

his hlafordes miltse geearnige. swa gedo se weliga gifola, se ðe egðer wilt ge
þissa lænena stoclife ge þara ecena hama. Se ðe ægþer gescop and ægðeres
wilt, forgife me þæt me to ægðrum onhagige: ge her nytwyrde to beonne, ge
huru þider to cumane.[71]

[But it is pleasing to any man, after he has built any dwelling on land loaned
by his lord with his lord's help, that he may rest there for a time, and hunt and
fowl and fish, and provide for himself from the loaned land in many ways,
both on sea and on land, until the time when through his lord's mercy he
might earn bookland and an eternal inheritance. May he who is wealthy and
generous make it so, he who rules both these temporary habitations and the
eternal homes. May he who created both and rules both grant that I be fit for
each: both to be useful here and especially to arrive there.]

Bocland represents the *ece yrfe* of heaven, the eternal land promised by a
religion of the book and made more accessible through the writings of
the holy fathers.[72] The tenurial distinction between *bocland* and *lænland*
thus provides a figural analogue for the distinction between an eternal
heaven and the transitory world, but the conceit extends beyond the familiar opposition between the eternal and transitory. The preface says
nothing about the size of the tenant's holding, nor does it contain any
legal vocabulary which would indicate social or economic status – indeed
the metaphor's turn to third-person voice presents a generalized scenario
for exemplary purposes.[73] At the same time, the passage implies the condition of a temporary and dependent holding transformed into free and
eternal possession. Several words and phrases in the preface suggest a
dependent and potentially servile tenant occupying a small piece of his
lord's property in return for obligatory labour. Such a scenario would

---

71 Carnicelli, *Soliloquies*, 48.5–12.

72 *Boc* can mean both charter and the gospels in Old English, a lexical connection which
    facilitates the association between land tenure and salvation. See Fell, 'Perceptions of
    Transience,' 173–4. As a nominal compound, *bocland* is richly figurative in a way which
    resembles the semantic play between word elements found in poetic compounds. *Bocland*
    enables a powerful range of associations between writing, land, proprietary rights, salva-
    tion, and the eternal; these associations are amplified even further by the conflation of
    royal and sacral endorsement which booked land carries in tenurial discourse. For poetic
    compounds in Latin and Old English generally, see Lapidge, 'Old English Compounds:
    A Latin Perspective.'

73 A similar technique frequently appears in elegiac poems and wisdom literature.

envision a much more dramatic transformation than has been hitherto appreciated for the dutiful tenant imagined in the *OESol* preface.

The metaphor begins with the statement that the tenant has built a *cotlif* on his lord's loan with his lord's help. What exactly is a *cotlif*? Carnicelli simply defines it as a cottage while the *DOE* offers the more substantial 'habitation, small holding; after ca. 1000 and in all uses quoted, a dependent small holding.'[74] Neither definition is entirely adequate for understanding the word's place in the preface. The matter is further complicated by the fact that the word's meaning seems to have changed over time.[75] *Cotlif* occurs fourteen times in the extant corpus, appearing almost exclusively in eleventh-century texts. In its annal for 1001, Anglo-Saxon Chronicle MS A records that marauding Danes 'forbærndon ðone ham æt Wealtham ๅ oðra cotlifa fela'[76] (burned down the manor at Waltham and many other dwellings). In this case, *cotlif* is synonymous with *ham* and seems to mean some kind of building or even a small settlement.[77] Context in this case does not allow for a more precise definition. In later texts, however, *cotlif* clearly means some kind of estate. The word appears in the long annal for 963 in

---

74 Carnicelli, *Soliloquies*, 111; *DOE*, s.v. 'cottlif.' BT defined the word as 'a village.' BTs later added that the word could be 'used of a single habitation' (*cott* typically means 'cottage' in Old English). The *Oxford English Dictionary* equivocates on its own definition of *cotlif*: 'A cot-house, a cottage; or (as some think) a village.' The word also appears in the Middle English text *The Proverbs of Alfred*: 'Wo is him þat vuel wif. / bryngeþ to his cotlyf.' See Arngart, *Proverbs of Alfred*, lines 274–5 at 2:101. Arngart defines *cotlif* quite broadly as 'dwelling, manor, village' (ibid, 2:243), but the sense in the relevant passage seems to be that of a single dwelling. The *Oxford English Dictionary* lists several later derivations of OE *cott* and *cotsetla*, including *cotset*, *cotsetland*, *cotland*, *cotman*, and *coterell*.

75 See Andrews, *The Old English Manor*, 94–5n1. Andrews endorses Seebohm's earlier interpretation of the *OESol* preface as a 'vivid little glimpse' into the creation of a new estate from deforested folkland (Seebohm, *English Village Community*, 170–1). For a more comprehensive discussion of the meaning of *cotlif*, see Förster, *Reliquienkultus*, 66–7n3.

76 Bately, *MS A*, 80. The annal was written by Bately's 'Hand 5' (who 'was responsible for annals 973–1001') in the very early eleventh century (ibid., xxxvii–xxxviii).

77 Swanton observed that the word in this case 'applied to something that could be burned down' (*Anglo-Saxon Chronicle*, 133n10). Perhaps the word specifies a structure made of wood? Whitelock translated *cotlifa* more broadly as 'villages' (*EHD* I, 238). BTs cites the relevant passage from the *OESol* as the sole authority for its definition, 'used of a single habitation' (s.v. 'cotlif [I]'). The supplement also adds that 'in the charters of Edward the Confessor the word seems used in the sense of *manor*' (ibid., s.v. 'cotlif, [II]'), a suggestion which Harmer perhaps dismissed too quickly (*Anglo-Saxon Writs*, 496). While 'manor' was not an operative Anglo-Saxon term, the system of estate management it represents was already well in place before 1066.

the Peterborough Chronicle (Oxford, Bodleian Library, Laud Misc. 636) during its description of the refoundation and endowment of Ely. After a community of monks has been established there, Bishop Æthelwold 'bohte þa feola cotlif æt se king ꝸ macode hit swyðe rice'[78] (bought many estates from the king and made it very rich). Here *cotlif* must mean an estate capable of generating considerable income and services rather than a small village or a single domicile. *Cotlif* has a similar meaning in its ten appearances among the vernacular writs issued for Westminster.[79] Some of the estates recorded in these documents were of modest size,[80] but others were quite large. S 1146, for example, confirms estates at Pershore (two hundred hides) and Deerhurst (fifty-nine hides).[81] *Cotlif* clearly means more than a 'dependent small holding' in the Westminster writs.[82] Finally, *cotlif* appears in a vernacular record of King Æthelstan's donations of relics to Exeter. This text survives in a late eleventh-century addition (fos 8r–14r) to an early tenth-century Breton gospel book, which was one of the manuscripts that Bishop Leofric gifted to Exeter sometime before his death in 1072.[83] In addition to a full third of his relic collection, the text states, King Æthelstan generously endowed a new minster dedicated to St Mary and St Peter with twenty-six *cottlifa*.[84] As in the other eleventh-century texts, the word in this case seems to mean estate.[85]

---

78 Irvine, *MS E*, 57. Wulfstan of Winchester's *Vita S. Æthelwoldi*, composed c. 996, tells how Æthelwold, after buying Ely from King Edgar for a large sum of money, renovated the place and 'eumque terrarum possessionibus affluentissime locupletatum' (enriched it lavishly with possessions in land). *Life of St Æthelwold*, 38 and 39, 41. Irvine notes several correspondences between the Peterborough annal and the *Vita S. Æthelwoldi*, but cautions that the *uita* may not have been a direct source for the vernacular text (*MS E*, xciv–xcvi). At any rate, the *cotlifan* in the Peterborough annal clearly mean estates.

79 The relevant documents include S 1120 (Harmer, *Anglo-Saxon Writs*, no. 76), S 1128 (ibid., no. 84), S 1129 (ibid., no. 85), S 1135 (ibid., no. 91), S 1142 (ibid., no. 98), S 1146 (ibid., no. 102), and S 1148 (ibid., no. 104).

80 The property of Ayot (Hertfordshire) in S 1135, for example, was valued at two and a half hides (ibid., 511).

81 Ibid., 521.

82 At the same time, it should be noted that the Westminster writs all survive in questionable copies of the later eleventh or thirteenth centuries.

83 Oxford, Bodleian Library, Auct. D.2.16 (Gneuss 530). See also Ker, *Catalogue*, no. 291; Förster, *Reliquienkultus*; Conner, *Anglo-Saxon Exeter*, 171–205; and Foot, *Æthelstan*, 200–3.

84 Conner, *Anglo-Saxon Exeter*, 176.

85 The manuscript hand dates to the second half of the eleventh century, but the text may be a later recension of an older copy, one composed much nearer in date to Æthelstan's

The single appearance of *cotlif* in the preface to *OESol*, then, seems to predate all other attestations by more than a century. The unequivocal attestation closest in time is found in the Anglo-Saxon Chronicle (MS A), where the word could mean a single dwelling or small settlement. In all other cases *cotlif* means 'estate' in a general sense with no specific indication of the tenurial conditions or size of the holding. The surviving evidence suggests that the word's meaning changed over time from 'a small holding with an attached dwelling' to the more general 'estate.' This hypothesis accords well with the conclusion reached by Max Förster in his 1943 edition of the Æthelstan donation list. In a substantial note, Förster suggested that the original meaning of *cotlif* was 'a cottar's wooden house' or 'a cottar's individual holding' and that over time the word came to mean 'a village of cottars dependent on a lord.'[86] In both situations the holding would have been dependent on a lord or attached to a manorial centre. Förster's attention to the cottar (i.e., cottager) provides valuable insight into the rank of the tenant in the *OESol* preface and the size of his holding. The word element *cot-* suggests a much more modest condition than we would expect for a thegn or even a *geneat*.

This possibility seems all the more likely if we consider *cotlif* in conjunction with the related noun *cotsetla*. While *cotlif* describes a holding in land, probably with an attached dwelling, *cotsetla* designates a particular class of tenant. The word appears only five times in the corpus, with two attestations in the *Rectitudines singularum personarum*. That estate survey describes the duties of the *cotsetla* (cottager/cottar) as follows:

Kotesetlan riht be ðam ðe on lande stent: on sumon he sceal ælce Mondæge ofer geares fyrst his [h]laforde wyrcan oðð III dagas ælcre wucan on hærfest. Ne ðearf he landgafol syllan. Him gebyriað V æceres to habbanne; mare, gyf hit on lande ðeaw sy; ⁊ to lytel hit bið, beo hit a læsse; forðan his weorc sceal beon oftræde. Sylle his heorðpænig on halgan Ðunresdæg, ealswa ælcan frigean men gebyreð, ⁊ werige his hlafordes inland, gif him

---

original donation. Förster dated the composition of the list to 1010 (*Reliquienkultus*, 23–40), but Conner later questioned some of Förster's claims about the text's earliest possible date of composition (*Anglo-Saxon Exeter*, 172–4).

86 Förster, *Reliquienkultus*, 66–7n3 and 135, s.v. 'cot-lif.' The definitions as given in German are 'Blockhaus eines Kötters,' 'Einzelanwesen eines Kötters,' and 'Kossätendorf, das von einem Herrschaftsgut abhängig ist.'

man beode, æt sæwearde ꞇ æt cyninges deorhege ꞇ æt swilcan ðingan, swilc his mæð sy, ꞇ sylle his cyricsceat to Martinus mæssan.[87]

[The cottager's duty is according to what is set on the land: on some (estates) he must work for his lord every Monday throughout the year or three days each week during harvest. He does not need to pay rent. It is fitting that he have five acres, more if it be the custom on the estate; and it is too little if it ever be less, for his labour must always be available. He is to pay his hearth-penny on Holy Thursday as every free man should, and he is to serve on his lord's inland if anyone orders him, at coast-watch and at the king's deer-hedge and at such things befitting his rank, and he is to pay his church-dues at Martinmas.]

The *cotsetla* has a very small holding in land with the attendant obligation of regular labour.[88] He owes no rent but he must perform week-work for his lord with extra days owed during the busy harvest season. In addition he must work on his lord's *inland* whenever he is ordered to do so.[89] An estate survey from the 'Black Book' of Peterborough (early twelfth century) gives a similar account of the cottager and his duties: 'And [there are] 8 cottars each of whom has 5 acres and they work (for the lord) 1 day each week, and twice a year they make malt. And each one of them gives 1 penny for a he-goat (if he has one) and 1 halfpenny for a nanny-goat.'[90] A Burton survey (also early twelfth century) records that, 'Alwi the cottar has 1 dwelling and a croft on the "inland," and 1 acre of meadow, and he works for 1 day in the week.'[91] These post-Conquest sources most likely record longstanding arrangements and thus provide valuable evidence for arrangements in late Anglo-Saxon England. The surveys yield several important points: the cottar has a dwelling with a small piece of land attached; his holding is on the lord's demesne; and he owes week-work. Some cottagers may also have been freed slaves, part of 'a class of servile

---

87 Liebermann, *Gesetze*, 1:445–6. The *DOE* adapts its definition entirely from this passage: 'cottager with at least 5 acres of land who pays no rent but works a certain number of days for his lord; he pays a "hearth-penny" tax and is thus a free man' (s.v. 'cottsetla').
88 See Stenton, *Anglo-Saxon England*, 473–5.
89 'In the phrase *werian land* the word refers to the performance of services that might be demanded from the holders of land' (BT, s.v. 'werian [IIIc]'). Warland in post-Conquest texts thus signifies land which carries certain obligations of tax and services. See Faith, *English Peasantry*, 89–93.
90 *EHD* II, no. 177 at p. 892.
91 Ibid., no. 176 at p. 891. The Burton surveys record similar information for several other cottars.

tenants who were legally free but still dependent' and who were attached to the inland of an estate.[92] 'In such cases,' H.P.R. Finberg observed, the lord 'might allow the freedman enough timber to build himself a cabin, and with it a few acres of land.'[93] Finberg also described the cottager as 'unfree or half-free' in his classification of social classes in late Anglo-Saxon England, placing him between the slave and the *gebur*.[94] A smallholder with limited means and freedom, then, the *cotsetla* held a most humble position among the peasantry.

Can we see anything of this condition in the preface to the *OESol*? While *cotlif* and *cotsetla* share a common first element, there initially seems to be nothing in the preface which would indicate servile status. Nonetheless, several aspects in the passage do suggest a condition of dependent tenure much like that held by the cottager. The first of these aspects involves the statement that the imagined tenant builds a *cotlif* on land held on loan from his lord: 'ac ælcne man lyst, siððan he ænig cotlyf on his hlafordes læne myd his fultume getimbred hæfð, þæt he hine mote hwilum þar-on gerestan, and huntigan, and fuglian, and fiscian, and his on gehwilce wisan to þere lænan tilian, ægþær ge on se ge on lande'[95] (But it is pleasing to any man, after he has built any dwelling on land loaned by his lord with his lord's help, that he may rest there for a time, and hunt and fowl and fish, and provide for himself from the loaned land in many ways, both on sea and on land). Landlords frequently provided materials and goods, the *fultum* mentioned in the above passage, for their dependent peasants.[96] The land is furthermore clearly designated as the lord's possession; the tenant is an occupant with no proprietary claim to the holding. Second, the statement that the tenant might rest 'at times' implies the pressure of other demands on his time. The cottager owed his lord regular week-work in addition to whatever labour was required for his own support – time for rest would have been precious

---

92 Faith, *English Peasantry*, 64. Cottars 'probably included freed and "housed" ex-slaves,' Faith observes, and they 'generally had no land other than their *cotagium* or cottage plot' (ibid., 72).

93 Finberg, 'Anglo-Saxon England to 1042,' 510–11. Finberg assumed that the tenant in the preface of the *OESol* was a thegn and that his lord was the king (ibid., 458–61).

94 Ibid., 508. The *gebur* appears immediately after the *cotsetla* in *Rectitudines*. The *gebur* paid rent, but he held more land than the *cotsetla*, typically a yardland (one quarter of a hide) or more.

95 Carnicelli, *Soliloquies*, 48.5–8.

96 Faith, *English Peasantry*, 56–88.

indeed.[97] Additionally, the phrase 'and his on gehwilce wisan to þere lænan tilian' suggests that the tenant also works the land for his own subsistence.[98] The verb *tilian* (with *his* as its genitive object) indicates that the tenant works the *læne* to provide for himself.[99] The 'hunting and fowling and fishing' furthermore may have been more a matter of necessity than of leisure if the smallholder needed food for his table. The above passage suggests a modest existence of work and service in which the tenant ekes out a small living from a plot of land not his own.

An additional indication that the imagined tenant might be interpreted as a dependent smallholder comes from the word *stoclif*. The preface uses the word twice, once at the end of the building metaphor and once again near the end of tenant metaphor.[100] The word appears only four times in the extant corpus: twice in *OESol* and twice as a gloss for *oppidum* and *ciuitas*.[101] Carnicelli defines the word as 'dwelling place' while Bosworth and Toller offer 'a town, habitation.' These definitions seem unduly cautious. The first element, *stoc-*, suggests a much more precise definition for this uncommon compound. In place-names, OE *stoc* typically indicates an enclosed area or habitation, a dependent settlement, or even an outlying farmstead.[102] Recent research also suggests that stockland 'seems to have been a distinct category of land' frequently attached to a village or to the core area of an estate; stockland was generally 'inhabited land, not simply farmland,' and likely contained the smallholdings of dependent tenants clustered around a central area.[103] Meaning more than just a simple

---

97 The promise of eventual rest notably appears twice in the preface's first section. The speaker laments that he has not yet had the chance to live 'softly' in his newly built home (Carnicelli, *Soliloquies*, 47.11), and later longs for 'the eternal rest' promised through the holy fathers (ibid., 48.2–3). The desire for rest, then, is active throughout the preface.

98 A final noun may be missing from the phrase 'to þere lænan.' See Carnicelli, *Soliloquies*, 48.

99 See BT, s.v. 'tilian (III.2).' The related noun *tilia* means 'cultivator of land.' It also appears as a gloss for *colonus*, meaning peasant or farmer (ibid., s.v. 'tilia'; *DMLBS*, s.v. 'colonus').

100 Carnicelli, *Soliloquies*, 47.13–14 and 48.10. In both cases *læne stoclif* stands in contrast to *ece ham*.

101 My findings are based on a search of the Dictionary of Old English Web Corpus.

102 Smith, *English Place-Name Elements*, 2:153–6. Smith notes that *stoc* rarely appears 'in literary documents' but he fails to note the presence of *stoclif* in *OESol* (ibid., 153–4). Ekwall later observed, 'The fact that Stoke is such a common name indicates that the places so named were once dependent on some village or manor' (*Concise Oxford Dictionary of English Place-Names*, s.v. 'stoc,' 443).

103 Faith, *English Peasantry*, 19–21.

habitation, *stoclif* suggests a servile existence on the inland of an estate. With their common second element, *stoclif* and *cotlif* together suggest the life of a dependent tenant who holds a modest dwelling and small plot of land from a lord in return for regular labour.

At the same time, *stoclif* acts as a multivalent compound which links the first and second metaphors of the preface. As a simplex OE *stoc(c)* can mean a log or the trunk of a tree, and as a place-name element it can indicate cleared woodland or buildings constructed of wood.[104] The place-name Stockleigh, for example, means 'the wood from which timber was got.'[105] One thinks immediately of the speaker harvesting timber in the preface's first metaphor. The *stoc(c)-* element in *stoclif*, then, contextually suggests both the clearance of woodland and the smallholding of the cottager. Another possible point of connection emerges from the evidence that cottagers likely provided part of the labour-force for clearing forested areas in order to claim more arable land.[106] Sally Harvey has described the Domesday bordars as 'a class of people, perhaps formerly servile, who dwell in cottages on the edge of the existing village and its fields, who have taken in a few acres of land from the waste, common, or woodland, to form a smallholding.'[107] Bordar and cottar are near-equivalent terms in Domesday Book and Harvey's description clearly resembles the situation of the cottager as it is presented in the written sources. Domesday Book is of course a much later text than the *OESol*, but the clearing of forest for agricultural use (a process known as assarting) was not a Norman innovation. The plowman (or his ox) is 'har holtes feond' (an old enemy of the woods) in Exeter Riddle 21,[108] for example, while the Cotton Tiberius calendar shows scenes of workers clearing land in March and cutting wood in July.[109] Alfred's law-code also contains provisions for special situations which might arise during the cutting of timber, including accidental deaths from falling trees: '[13] Gif mon oðerne æt gemænan weorce offelle ungewealdes, agife mon þam mægum þæt treow, ꝛ hi hit hæbben ær XXX niht of þam lande, oðða him fo se to se ðe ðone wudu age'[110] (If someone accidentally

---

104 Smith, *English Place-Name Elements*, 2:156–7.

105 Ekwall, *Studies on English Place- and Personal Names*, 95–7.

106 Harvey, 'Life of the Manor,' 58–9. See also Lennard, *Rural England*, 14–16; and Hooke, *Landscape of Anglo-Saxon England*, 162–8.

107 Harvey, 'Evidence for Settlement Study: Domesday Book,' 197. Harvey adds that cottars and bordars appear 'to be basically the same class of person' (ibid.).

108 Krapp and Dobbie, *Exeter Book*, 191 (line 3a).

109 Hooke, *Landscape of Anglo-Saxon England*, 163–4.

110 Liebermann, *Gesetze*, 1:56.

kills another man at common labour, let him give the tree to the kinsmen, and they should have it from that land within thirty days, or he who owns the woods is to have it). The men described here are working on someone else's property and the prescribed compensation for the victim is modest enough to suggest that such workers would have been of low status. Finberg imagined the scene as follows: 'Here we may picture a landlord employing servile dependants to clear part of his woodland, perhaps with the intention of settling them as *coliberti* on the soil thus cleared.'[111] This scenario, which appears in a text contemporary to the *OESol*, accords with the later evidence of bordars and cottagers clearing forest for their lord or for hire.[112] The repetition of *stoclif* in both the first and second metaphors in the *OESol* preface thus enables a continuity between the work envisioned in the first metaphor and the dependent holding suggested in the second.

The lexical evidence, then, suggests a dependent smallholder more than an already prosperous and relatively unburdened thegn. The preface additionally implies a low condition through the disparity of status and means it establishes between the tenant and his lord. The double repetition of both *hlaford* and *læn* in the text underscores the point that the tenant is subordinate to his lord with no proprietary claim whatsoever to the land on which he lives. The phrase 'swa gedo se weliga gifola' (may he who is wealthy and generous make it so) in turn emphasizes the lord's considerable riches. Indeed the distinctive *gifola*, a hapax legomenon, invites the audience to consider the remarkable munificence made possible by wealth.[113] The preface's tenant clearly occupies a subordinate position socially and economically. Antonina Harbus has underscored this hierarchical dynamic within the text in her analysis of the Alfredian prefaces. According to Harbus, Alfred generally claims authority in his prefaces through metaphors of power. In the *OESol* preface, she argues, this 'metaphor of power is focalised from the subordinate's point of view' in order 'to show how the power dynamic should be apprehended from the less powerful side of the relationship.'[114] Whether or not we accept the 'subordinate perspective' as a

---

111 Finberg, 'Anglo-Saxon England to 1042,' 456.
112 See also Verhulst, *Carolingian Economy*, 37; and Hooke, *Trees in Anglo-Saxon England*, 138–64.
113 This is the only appearance of *gifola* in the corpus. The related adjective *gyfol* appears only four times, with three of those appearances being in the Old English Pastoral Care and Boethius. See *DOE*, s.v. 'gyfola.'
114 Harbus, 'Metaphors of Authority in Alfred's Prefaces,' 724. See also Waterhouse, 'Tone in Alfred's Version of Augustine's *Soliloquies*,' 50.

rhetorical pose assumed by Alfred for strategic purposes, Harbus clearly identifies the remarkable imbalance of power imagined in the text. The tenant's hope for advancement is entirely dependent on his lord's favour.

What might be gained rhetorically from such a scenario of a dependent tenant with a smallholding? The preface evokes the life of the cottager, but it notably does not present that condition as low or servile – the 'half-free' peasant instead becomes an exemplary figure who models the virtues of work and service. In social and economic terms, the scenario imagines a transformative reward of wondrous proportion. The occupation of a small piece of land which carries the constant burden of obligatory labour and a constrained freedom – all these limiting conditions fall away at once with the lord's grant of bookland. This striking turn testifies to the lord's mercy and the considerable benefits of his munificence – an apt parable indeed for the gift of salvation. At the same time, the preface indicates that such a gift is earned and not merely received: 'oð þone fyrst þe he bocland and æce yrfe þurh his hlafordes miltse geearnige' (until the time when through his lord's mercy he might earn bookland and an eternal inheritance). Labour becomes not a burden, but a productive activity which, if sustained over time, can yield both an essential livelihood and the benefits of prosperity. Interestingly enough, a similar view of work as productive activity later appears in Book III of the *OESol*: 'nis þæs æac na to wenanne þæt ealle men hæbben gelicne wisdom on heofenum Ac ælc hefð be þam andefnum þe he ær æfter æarnað; swa ær he hær swiðor swincð and swiðor giornð wisdomes and rihtwisnesse, swa he hys þær mare hæft, and æac maren are and maren wuldor'[115] (It is also not to be supposed that all men will have the same kind of wisdom in heaven. But each will have it according to how much he had earned it before: as he works harder and strives harder for wisdom and rightness here, so he will have more of it there, and he will also have more honour and more glory). Wisdom is a hard-won commodity which yields exponential gains in heaven – purposeful work ends in a deferred but substantial reward. The speaker of the preface likewise hopes that he may merit both earthly and heavenly reward: 'Se ðe ægðer gescop and ægðeres wilt, forgife me þæt me to ægðrum onhagie: ge her nytwyrde to beonne, ge huru þider to cumane'[116] (May he who created both and rules both grant that I be fit for each: both to be useful here and especially to arrive there). The preface's ideal of the useful life is exemplified in the figure of a diligent tenant who lives on a small plot provided by his lord in return

---

115 Carnicelli, *Soliloquies*, 94.9–13.
116 Ibid., 48.10–12.

for obligatory labour. Within the preface, however, those obligations are not oppressive but redemptive as the cottager's constrained circumstances are transformed through the mercy of a powerful lord.

The preface's tenurial framework, then, accomplishes more than a familiar opposition between the transitory and the eternal. It incorporates ideals of obligation, service, and reward which are drawn from the social structures of estate management and lordship. For those peasants who worked the inland of an estate, however, being useful was not a philosophical ideal – it was a requirement of daily life. The preface boldly reconceptualizes the heavy demands of obligation and service as transformative experience. The preface's tenant gains eternal inheritance because he earns it; his lord is merciful, but his gift importantly comes after a time of rendered service. Much like the speaker in the building metaphor labours to gather timber for his house of learning, the gift of bookland yields the highest return after sustained work and diligence. Eternal possession and salvation come to the faithful tenant as a reward for his dedication and perseverance over time. The fantastic level of mobility imagined in the scenario dramatizes the conventional motif of salvation within a fresh conceit, and the presence of the lowly cottager within that conceit makes its exemplary force all the more powerful.

Christ and the First Charter

While IV Edgar and the *OESol* preface look to the practices of tenancy and estate management for instructive metaphor, we can find in the vernacular homily Vercelli X a more extensive integration of conceits grounded in the social practices of inheritance and land tenure. Vercelli X underscores even more forcefully the idea that landholding brings with it a set of obligations to a superior authority who has the power both to issue and to remove certain privileges of possession. This tenurial material, however, forms only one stratum of a variegated text. The anonymous homily adapts several Latin sources into a sustained exposition on the conventional theme of the fleeting nature of worldly prosperity. The homily must have enjoyed some popularity as it survives in part or whole in nine different copies with three different manuscripts preserving a complete text.[117] The text contains several distinct movements, and Donald

---

117 For manuscript details, see Scragg, *Vercelli Homilies*, 191–5 (hereafter *VH*); and
     Wilcox, 'Variant Texts of an Old English Homily.'

Scragg, the text's most recent editor, has usefully divided the homily into seven sections:

1. A preamble on the power of the Gospel, with an emphasis on speech (lines 1–8)
2. Christ's Incarnation and the promise of salvation (lines 9–54)
3. A dramatic scene of the Last Judgment (lines 55–110)
4. A call to good works (lines 111–21)
5. A plea for charity and Christ's parable of the rich man from Luke 12:16–21 (lines 122–99)
6. The transience of worldly goods (lines 200–45)
7. A plea to turn from the world and look to salvation (lines 246–75)[118]

Scragg identifies three main Latin sources for the homily: Paulinus of Aquileia's *Liber exhortationis ad Henricum comitem*; pseudo-Augustine's *Sermo* 310; and Isidore's *Synonyma* II.[119] At the same time, some parts of the homily, such as the second section on the Incarnation, seem to be original compositions with no known source in either Latin or the vernacular. Despite its range of content and different sources, Scragg argues that the homily is a unified text rather than rote patchwork.[120] Paul E. Szarmach likewise praises the anonymous homilist as a master craftsman with 'a flare for poetic and dramatic effects, all artfully joined.'[121] Samantha Zacher has recently made an extended case for a single accomplished author: 'The respective changes made by the homilist to each of his individual sources,' she argues, 'together suggest considerable confidence both in his command of the source material and in his own vernacular prose style; the author of Vercelli X emerges as a talented writer of Old English prose working under the twin influences of the imported Latin and inherited vernacular rhetorical traditions.'[122] The different sections of the homily furthermore adhere thematically, Zacher argues, through the careful

---

118 Scragg, *VH*, 191–2.
119 Ibid. See also Zacher, *Preaching the Converted*, 109–12. For the reception and circulation of Isidore's *Synonyma* in Anglo-Saxon England, see Di Sciacca, *Finding the Right Words*.
120 Scragg, *VH*, 192.
121 Szarmach, 'The Vercelli Prose and Anglo-Saxon Literary History,' 36. See also Szarmach, 'The Vercelli Homilies: Style & Structure.' In this earlier formal analysis, Szarmach praises the homily as 'a seamless *tour de force* in its structure' (ibid., 244).
122 Zacher, *Preaching the Converted*, 112–13.

repetition of key concepts throughout the homily.[123] In short, Vercelli X presents us with a carefully structured and highly rhetorical text.

One recurrent concept in the homily which has not yet been fully recognized is its concern with land and inheritance. Within its general discourse on the futility of worldly wealth, the text incorporates concepts and vocabulary drawn from land tenure into an extended meditation on redemption, good works, and salvation. That these lexical and thematic elements appear most frequently within the homily's original content indicates a deliberate aspect to their development within the text. Issues of land tenure and inheritance form a *leitmotiv* in the homily, providing one of the structural links across its various sections. The role of the document in securing the possession and transmission of property occupies a particularly prominent place within this thematic strand. Tenurial metaphors furthermore provide both positive and negative exempla – the royal diploma in particular provides a flexible symbol, capable of representing both the promise of salvation and the hopeless vanity of worldly wealth. The homily consequently enacts a familiar tension within tenurial discourse: the assurance of eternal possession through documentation, shadowed by an abiding suspicion that such provisions are a legal fiction.

The first intimation of tenurial content occurs in the homily's second section. This section begins by recalling the many prophecies of Christ's coming to earth from heaven, 'þæt se wolde of ðam <u>rice</u> cuman ⁊ of ðam <u>cyne</u>stole ⁊ of ðam þrym<u>rice</u> hyder on þas eorðan, ⁊ him þas <u>cynerico</u> on his anes æht ealle geagnian' (X.12–14)[124] [that from that kingdom and from that royal seat and from that kingdom of glory he would come here onto this earth to claim this royal kingdom for himself completely into his possession]. A threefold sequence of clauses, each beginning with *of ðam*, marks Christ's movement from the heavenly kingdom 'onto this earth' while the alternating repetitions of *rice* and *cyne-* emphasize Christ's royal power both in heaven and on earth. The structure of the passage accordingly emphasizes its content as Christ's royal power is transferred from the heavenly to the earthly realm. Christ will maintain a strong dramatic presence throughout the homily and it is notable that he begins his textual incarnation as a political ruler. The subsequent description of Christ during his days among men, however, largely emphasizes his mercy (*mildheortnesse*) and his role as redeemer as the language of kingship and royal

---

123 Ibid., 112.
124 All quotations from Vercelli X are cited by line number in Scragg, *VH*, 196–213. Emphasis added.

authority temporarily retreats from the homily (X.16–34). The material which comes immediately thereafter, however, fuses royal power and divine mercy in a single striking conceit of legal documentation.

The homily dramatizes Christ's redemption of mankind through a remarkable metaphor of salvation accomplished through a written act. Before the coming of Christ, the homilist says, we were as orphans dispossessed of an inheritance in heaven. Through the Saviour's mercy, however, our right to the heavenly kingdom has been reinscribed and renewed: 'Ær þan we wæron steopcild gewordene, ða we wæron bewerede þæs hiofoncundan rices, ᚱ we wæron adilgode of þam þryðfullan frumgewrite ða we wæron to hiofonum awritene. Wæron we nu syðþan amearcode þurh þone soðan scyppend ᚱ þurh þone lyfigendan [God] ᚱ þurh þone acennedan sunu, urne dryhten, to þan gefean neorxnawanges' (X.35–40) [Before then we had become orphans when we were excluded from the heavenly kingdom and we were erased from the glorious original charter when we were recorded for heaven. We now have been marked down again through the true Creator and through the living God and through the born Son, our Lord, into the joys of paradise]. As no vernacular or Latin source has been identified for these lines, we may assume them to be original content tailored to this particular text. The central image of the *frumgewrit* imagines a foundational document, the prelapsarian written deed which granted humankind an eternal right to *neorxnawang*. Even though this privilege was lost through the transgression of original sin, Christ has restored the rights of humanity through his own sacrifice.[125] The word *frumgewrit* appears only in this homily and it may have been coined specifically for this passage. Christ importantly gives salvation through a charter, and redemption is figured as an act of textual revision: salvation is both delivered and denied through a master document and it is the hand of Christ that updates the mythic text.

The metaphor is clearly based on the practice of granting land by royal diploma, which is itself predicated in part on the deep associations between landholding and salvation. The *frumgewrit* represents the very first diploma, issued by the King of kings. We have seen how the royal voice (and the authority it represents) grants land within the Latin diploma and also how the royal prerogative could later rescind that privilege. Forfeiture of land was a prescribed legal penalty for certain crimes, but kings could

---

125 This documentary metaphor anticipates some aspects of the popular English lyrics known as the 'Charters of Christ' which circulated in the fourteenth and fifteenth centuries. See Steiner, *Documentary Culture*, 47–90.

also take lands under circumstances which might have seemed less than legitimate (especially to the dispossessed). The *frumgewrit* exemplifies this process of a powerful privilege delivered through a document and then revoked as a penalty for transgression. Through sin, the metaphor suggests, our name was struck from the charter that recorded our place in heaven. Christ's role in recovering that lost right places him in the dual role of Redeemer and Ruler. The only earthly authority that could restore forfeited lands in actual social practice was that of the king.[126] In 960, for example, King Edgar restored lands to one Wulfric which the thegn had earlier forfeited for some unknown offence.[127] By emending the already altered text of the *frumgewrit*, Christ performs a similar act of restoration through his own singular authority, an act which recalls the homily's earlier language of kingship and political power. As one who holds both an earthly *cynerice* and a heavenly *cynestole*, Christ the King has the power to alter old punishments and issue new rewards through the written instrument of the *frumgewrit*.

The passage also delivers its striking metaphor in finely embellished prose. Zacher has shown how generally 'the homilist uses a variety of rhetorical strategies to highlight important passages,' and that practice is clearly evident here.[128] The first sentence features a fourfold sequence of paratactic clauses, each beginning with 'we wæron.' This measured repetition occurs over a sequence which is chiastic in structure: the first and fourth clauses are of approximately the same length in syllable count, as are the longer second and third clauses.[129] The sustained consonance on *w* additionally creates a sustained aural effect, while the repetitions of *hiofon-* and *-writ-* underscore the conceptual link between salvation and the written document. Moreover, the repetition of the *a-* prefix in *adilgode* and *awritene* enables a contrast between the two verbs and their respective senses of erasure and inscription. This contrastive element is further amplified by the opposite position of each verb in its respective clause: *adilgode* appears immediately after 'we wæron' while *awritene* appears in final position in its own clause.

---

126 We have already seen cases in which Æthelred II and Cnut returned lands which they had previously appropriated from the church (see pp. 56–68 above).

127 S 687. Kelly, *Abingdon*, no. 86 at pp. 351–5. The diploma survives as an original single-sheet. Edgar also restored lands in 959 to his grandmother Eadgifu which had been confiscated earlier by Eadwig (S 1211).

128 Zacher, *Preaching the Converted*, 122.

129 The first clause has eleven syllables and the fourth has twelve; the second clause has fifteen syllables and the third has seventeen.

The next sentence begins with 'wæron we,' a phrase which notably reverses the word order of the 'we wæron' repeated across the previous sentence. This syntactical reversal artfully signals a positive reversal in the exposition – through Christ's actions, the names of the fallen are returned to the charter of salvation. The *a-* prefix appears again in *amearcode*, linking the original act of writing (*awritene*) with the later reinscription made possible through redemption. Christ's instrumental role in this restoration is then emphasized in a threefold sequence of *þurh þone* clauses which repeat some of the descriptions given to Christ earlier in the homily.[130] This sequence furthermore forms a *tricolon crescens*, a three-unit pattern in which each part progressively increases in size. The tricolon skilfully interweaves consonance on *-d-* as it leads, appropriately enough, into the metaphor's culminating reward, 'the joy of paradise' promised in the *frumgewrit*. Structure and content again work in well-aligned tandem.

The homily's next movement, a dramatic Doomsday scene, shows the punitive aspect of Christ's authority and its conflation of royal and divine power. While the episode makes no reference to tenurial documents and contains no explicitly legal vocabulary, it does stage a judgment scene in which the damned are deprived of a place in paradise, the very privilege which Christ had regranted through his written intervention in the *frumgewrit*. Christ here appears not as a merciful redeemer, but as a grim judge and offended lord who punishes those who have betrayed him.[131] This set-piece greatly expands on its Latin source,[132] casting the devil as an eloquent plaintiff pleading his case in a long speech.[133] 'Se wiðerwearda feond' (X.64–5) [the acrimonious enemy] boldly claims his right to those souls whose bad deeds have outweighed their good works. Such individuals, the fiend says, have broken the law set by the judge: 'Dem be ðam þe þine bebodu forhogodon, ꝸ þine æ abræcon, ꝸ symle hie besmiton mid synnum ꝸ gebysmeredon' (X. 67–9) [Judge according as they have ignored your commandments, and as they have broken your law, and as they have continually defiled and mocked it through sin]. The law-breakers have stopped their ears to the Gospel but gladly heeded the beguiling music of the

---

130 'ꝸ þa ealra fæmnena wuldor <u>cende</u> þone soðan <u>scyppend</u> ... ða se ælmihtega <u>dryhten</u> in þas woruld becwom' (X.18–21). Emphasis added.

131 The *OESol* presents the sinner's betrayal of God in similar social terms. See Gatch, 'King Alfred's Version of Augustine's *Soliloquia*,' 28.

132 Chapter 62 of Paulinus of Aquileia's *Liber exhortationis ad Henricum comitem*.

133 For a discussion of this and similar episodes in other Vercelli homilies, see Haines, 'Courtroom Drama and the Homiletic Monologues of *The Vercelli Book*.'

fiend's harp: 'Ac ðonne ic mine hearpan genam ⁊ mine strengas styrian ongan, hie ðæt lustlice gehyrdon, ⁊ fram þe cyrdon ⁊ to me urnon' (X.83–5) [And when I took my harp and began to stroke my strings, they heard that with pleasure and turned from you and ran to me]. The devil argues that the sinners have betrayed their lord as traitors who 'þin cynerice eal forgeaton' (X.88) [all forgot your kingdom] and 'mishyrnesse gewrecan' (X.100) [made disobedience]. *Þin cynerice* artfully echoes the early description of Christ as the holder of a *cynerice* (X.14), amplifying further the motif of the ruler betrayed.

After its conclusion, the homilist notably describes the devil's speech as having been made to the *hælend* (X.102). When Christ addresses the damned, however, he speaks not as a mild Saviour, but as a righteous Judge who damns the traitorous sinners with 'worda grimmost' (X.104) [the sternest of words].[134] The loss of paradise as a punishment for disobedience recalls the penalties for treason against the king as they appear in the law-codes – those who trespass against the sovereign suffer dispossession, exile, or death. In this legalistic vision of the Last Judgment, the damned forfeit their place in paradise, a right which was once lost but then resecured by Christ. The offended Ruler/Judge revokes the privilege he had once restored in the *frumgewrit*. This scene thus underscores the fact that the security promised by documents was always contingent to some extent upon the beneficiary maintaining obligations to the issuing authority.

This legal element emerges more precisely in tenurial terms in the homily's fifth section. This part of the text, with its admonition to exercise charity, draws from pseudo-Augustine sermon 310,[135] but as Scragg points out, the homilist has taken the parable of the rich man from Luke 12:16–21 (which appears only at the end of the Latin source) and transformed it into a structural frame for the entire section.[136] Christ's voice dominates this section of the homily as he delivers through epiplexis a long and stinging rebuke to the wealthy fool. Paul E. Szarmach has memorably described the

---

134 Christ's short speech is delivered in verse. See Zacher, *Preaching the Converted*, 113–16.

135 PL 39:2340–2. The homilist seems to have used a version of the sermon as it is preserved in the early twelfth-century portion of Salisbury, Cathedral Library 9. Salisbury 9 contains a copy of an earlier tenth-century version of the text (Scragg, *VH*, 192n1). See also Becker, 'The Latin Manuscript Sources of the Old English Translations of the Sermon *Remedia Peccatorum*'; Becker, 'The Manuscript Source of Ælfric's Catholic Homily II 7'; Cross, 'A *Sermo de Misericordia* in Old English Prose'; and Webber, *Scribes and Scholars at Salisbury Cathedral*, 160–2. Scragg quotes from the Salisbury 9 version in his edition.

136 Scragg, *VH*, 192.

scene's rhetoric as a 'direct verbal attack' in which 'the Lord asks question after question of the mute and inglorious sinner, while declarative statements and commands further render the sinner helpless before the severe Judge.'[137] In this lengthy monologue Christ repeats his earlier role as *dema* from the courtroom drama of the Doomsday scene, but in this case his stern address is more intimate as it is addressed to a single character in a specific context. Christ's speech also importantly incorporates legal terminology of land and inheritance in order to suggest in forceful terms that the human possession and control of land is only a man-made fantasy.[138]

Christ first chastises the rich man for his perverse aversion to charity – through his covetousness the fool neglects (*areceleasodest*) those gifts he has himself received from God (X.142–3). This language recalls the earlier Doomsday scene in which the devil portrays the sinner as one who disregards God's law and commandments. The greedy man has betrayed his Lord by failing to distribute his goods among the needy and by hoarding them instead for himself and his family. For this presumption, Christ withdraws his favour from the rich fool: 'Ic þe nu afyrre fram mine sylene þe ic þe ær forgeaf' (X.143–4) [I now remove you from my gift that I granted you before]; and later, 'æghwæt þæs ðe ðu hafast, ic þe sealde. Eall hit is min, Ᵹ þin ic afyrre fram þe' (X.151–2) [everything that you have, I gave to you. It is all mine and I remove what is yours from you]. The rich man has failed to meet the reciprocal obligations he has assumed through his lord's support. The repetition of *afyrre* (remove) – each time with Christ as the subject – underscores the point that whatever possessions the wealthy man presumes to be his own can be taken away at any time by God. Christ reminds the fool that he really owns nothing. What he has now he holds on loan through his Lord's favour.

The homily applies this principle directly to the possession of land when Christ threatens to leave the miser to suffer the same hardships he has ignored in others:

---

137 Szarmach, 'The Vercelli Prose and Anglo-Saxon Literary History,' 37.

138 The parable of the rich man in Luke begins after a man asks Christ to settle an inheritance dispute (Luke 12:13): 'Ait autem quidam ei de turba magister dic fratri meo ut dividat mecum hereditatem at ille dixit ei homo quis me constituit iudicem aut divisorem supra uos' (Fischer, *Biblia sacra*, 1632–3) [And someone in the crowd said to him, 'Teacher, tell my brother that he should divide the inheritance with me.' But he said to him, 'Man, who made me a judge or executor over you?']. Would the parable have been contextually associated with contested or uncertain inheritance? Christ's question about playing the part of *iudicem* also resonates with the vernacular homily in interesting ways.

To hwan heold ðu hit þe sylfum ⁊ þinum bearnum, þæt meahte manegum mannum genihtsumian? Unyðe þe wæs þæt ðu hit eal ne meahtest gefæstnigan, ne mid insigelum eal beclysan. Wenst ðu ðæt hit þin sie þæt sio eorðe forðbringeð, hio þe groweð ⁊ bloweð ⁊ [sæd lædeð ⁊] onlif[an] bringeð? Eall ic nu afyrre minne fultum from ðe. Hafa æt þinum gewinne þæt ðu mæge ⁊ on þinum geswince. Ic ofteo mine renas þæt hie þine eorðan ne onhrinað, ⁊ ic afyrre from þe mine mildheortnesse, ⁊ þonne bið sona gecyðed ⁊ ætiewed þinra yrmða dæl. Gif ðu wene þæt hit þin bocland sie ⁊ on agene æht geseald, hit þonne wæron mine wæter þa ðe on heofonum wæron, þanon ic mine gife dæle eorðwærum. Gif ðu mihta hæbbe, dæl regnas ofer þine eorðan. Gif ðu strang sy, syle wæstm þinre eorðan. Ic ahyrde mine sunnan ⁊ hie gebyrhte; þon[n]e forbærneð hio ealle þine æceras. Þonne bist ðu dælleas mines renes, ⁊ þe þin eorðe bið idel ⁊ unnyt goda gehwylces. (X.162–76)

[Why do you hold for yourself and your sons what would be enough for many people? It was no easy thing for you that you could not secure it all, nor seal it all up. Do you think that what the earth brings forth could be yours, the earth which grows and blooms and bears seed and brings food? I now remove my help from you completely. Have what you can from your toil and from your labour. I withhold my rains so that they will not touch your earth, and I remove my mercy from you, and then your share of misery will be shown and revealed soon enough. If you think that it is your book-land and given into your own possession, then it was my waters that were in the heavens from where I share my gift with earth-dwellers. If you have the power, distribute rains over your earth. If you are strong, give fruit to your earth. I will harden my sun and it will grow bright; then it will burn all your fields. Then you will be without a share of my rain, and your earth will be empty and useless for any good.]

The homily follows the general contour of the Latin source but significantly intensifies issues of land tenure and inheritance through addition and accentuation. The opening question follows the source text closely enough,[139] but the next sentence, 'Unyðe þe wæs þæt ðu hit eal ne meahtest gefæstnigan, ne mid insigelum eal beclysan,' has no precedent in the Latin sermon. Two words in this original content suggest documentary practice: the verb 'gefæstnigan' and the noun 'insigelum.' The most common definition of *gefæstnian* is 'to fix something firmly in place,' but the verb can

---

139 'Quid te filiis tuis fingis seruare quod potest omnibus sufficere?' (Scragg, *VH*, 205)
    [Why do you scheme to preserve for yourself and your sons what can suffice for all?].

also mean 'to confirm a document,' especially by signature.[140] This possible sense becomes all the more likely when we consider the presence of *insegl* (seal) in the same sentence. Seals affixed to documents were used as marks of authentication as early as the ninth century by royal and non-royal persons, lay and ecclesiastical, for a variety of purposes, including the settlement of disputes and the confirmation of tenurial and jurisdictional rights.[141] The vocabulary of documentary practice in the Vercelli X passage suggests a futile flurry of legal activity to protect proprietary interests and provisions for inheritance. The passage more pointedly associates such activity with greed and presumption, turning the documentary motif toward negative exemplarity.

The appearance of *bocland* in the passage culminates the text's emergent interest in land tenure and its written instruments. The homilist renders *terra tua* as *bocland*,[142] an accurate enough translation, but one which also introduces an unmistakable legal register to the text. Moreover, this choice of translation appears to have been strategic since the homily provides *þin eorðe* for the other three appearances of *terra tua* in the Latin sermon. What does the text gain by using the word *bocland* at this particular point? By expanding the compact 'si terra tua est' into 'Gif ðu wene þæt hit þin bocland sie ꝺ on agene æht geseald,' the homilist specifically includes bookland among the rich man's presumptions. The ideas of eternal possession and freedom of alienation inherent in bookland, the text implies, are legal fictions authored by covetous men. The rich man's land carries value and yields benefits only because it receives support (rain, crops, etc.) from God – the man has no control whatsoever over his property. The appearance of *bocland* in this passage most immediately evokes the royal diploma as a written testament and guarantee of possession, but it also recalls the *frumgewrit* as a written instrument of salvation from

140 *DOE*, s.v. 'gefæstnian (B.2.a).'
141 For a survey of the evidence, see Keynes, 'Royal Government and the Written Word,' 244–8. See also Harmer, *Anglo-Saxon Writs*, 10–24; and Heslop, 'English Seals from the Mid Ninth Century to 1100.' The *OESol* presents the example of a lord's *ærend-gewrit* and *insegl* in a way which suggests that its audience would have been familiar with the practice: 'geþenc nu gyf ðines hlafordes ærendgewrit and hys insegel to ðe cymð, hwæðer þu mæge cweðan þæt ðu hine be ðam ongytan ne mægæ, ne hys willan þær-on gecnawan ne mæge' (Carnicelli, *Soliloquies*, 62.22–5) [Consider now if your lord's message and his seal came to you, whether you could say that you could not recognize him by those things and could not perceive his will therein].
142 'Si terra tua est, mea est pluuia quae super terram tuam discendit' (Scragg, *VH*, 206) [If it is your land, it is my rain which falls over your land].

earlier in the homily. The mode of tenure promised by royal diploma thus becomes a pale imitation of those eternal rights granted through the mythic document of the *frumgewrit*. Christ's rebuke to the wealthy fool mocks the idea and instruments of bookland as empty human scribblings.

The *bocland* passage, like the earlier *frumgewrit* passage, also features several stylistic and structural elements which complement its thematic content. Samantha Zacher has noted several embellishments in this passage, including 'the use of rhyme (*groweð ⁊ bloweð*), paronomasia (*renas* and *onhrinað*), and repetition (*forbringeð* and *bringeð*).'[143] To this list we can add polyptoton evident in several word-forms which share a common root: *dæl* (X.170), a noun; *dæle* (X.172), a finite verb; *dæl* (X.172), an imperative; and *dælleas* (X.175), an adjective. The two appearances of the verb *afyrre* in the passage also echo the two uses of the same verb earlier in the section (X.143, 152). In each case, Christ is the grammatical subject, removing his favour from the rich fool. This interwoven repetition provides a structural cohesion within the larger section, but it also underscores the polemic point that worldly goods (including land) are always held on loan from a higher power.[144] Finally, the repetition of *þin eorðe* across the passage exponentially derides the idea that land can be held in eternal possession within earthly time. As we have seen, *þin eorðe* translates the recurrent *terra tua* in the Latin sermon, but the sermon adds one additional *þin eorðe* beyond what is found in the source.[145] The choice of *eorðe* for *terra*, especially if we consider it alongside the single use of the more precise *bocland*, has significant implications. OE *eorðe* rarely carries proprietary associations – it typically means 'ground' or 'earth' in the most general sense.[146] Old English generally prefers some form of *-land-* to indicate tenurial information,[147] and *land* as a simplex often means 'landed property'

---

143 Zacher, *Preaching the Converted*, 122.

144 Zacher points out that a form of *afyrre* also appears in Christ's grim words to the condemned in the earlier Doomsday scene (X.106). This repetition, she argues, connects the two sections: 'the homilist's use of envelope-patterning to frame speeches taken from distinct sources promotes unity in the structure of the homily at large' (ibid.).

145 Compare 'Gif ðu mihta hæbbe, dæl regnas ofer þine eorðan. Gif ðu strang sy, syle wæstm þinre eorðan' (X.172–3) to 'Plue super terram tuam si potes; si producat germen suum si uales' (Scragg, *VH*, 206). Emphasis added.

146 None of the definitions offered in the *DOE* give 'estate' or indicate that *eorðe* can mean privately owned land.

147 Charters typically introduce the boundary clause with *terra* or *land*.

or 'estate.'[148] By consistently translating *terra* as *eorðe* (aside from the single use of *bocland*) the homily troubles the conceptual viability of bookland. What the wealthy man thinks is his bookland, the text suggests, is in actuality God's earth. The homily thus systematically implodes the idea of proprietary rights over land, especially the vaulting idea of eternal possession which adheres to bookland. The idea of 'your earth' becomes an empty jangle through its chiming repetition, the vacant fantasy of a rich fool unaware that he is on the cusp of losing everything.

The 'parable of the rich man' section of the homily ends powerfully in a vision of doomed inheritance. Christ tells the fool that he will die that same night and then asks him who will receive his riches now that his heirs, like their father, have offended God (X.190–6). The designation of the heirs as *yrfeweardas* (X.194–5) [guardians of the inheritance] is darkly ironic: the rich man's children will die that same night and the family's *yrfe* will pass uncontested to strangers: 'Sona þa on þone welegan mann on þære ilcan nihte deaþ on becwom, ⁊ on his bearn ealle. Fengon þa to gestreonum fremde syþþan' (X. 197–9) [Then, that same night, death suddenly came upon the wealthy man along with his children. Strangers then took their riches afterwards]. This moment of disappointment and deprivation appears to be another of the homilist's original contributions – the Latin source says nothing about the man's children nor does it contain the detail that the family property was dispersed among outsiders.[149] These added elements, which occupy an emphatic position at the end of the section, provide a blunt conclusion to Christ's long harangue to the miser. This nightmarish moment thus conflates the loss of inheritance with the loss of life as it evokes fears over the stability of written provisions in controlling the possession and transmission of land.

This same anxiety emerges once again in the final lines of the homily's *ubi sunt* catalogue.[150] The catalogue appropriately enough ends on the transience

---

148 Modern English has retained this distinction. One rarely encounters expressions such as 'he worked the family earth,' or 'There will be an earth auction next weekend.'

149 'O uanitas huius diuitis! Nescit si uiuat, et de fructibus tediat nocte moriturus, fabricare disponit ubi non es[t] mansurus' (Scragg, *VH*, 208) [Oh, the foolishness of this rich man! He does not know if he lives and he is weary with his profits, soon to die in the night. He plans to build where he cannot remain]. PL 39:2342 reads, 'O uanitas huius diuitis! Nescit si uiuat, et de fructibus cogitat; nocte moriturus, fabricare disponit' (Oh, the foolishness of this rich man! He does not know if he lives, and he thinks of his profits; about to die in the night, he plans to build).

150 This section of the homily is based largely on Isidore's *Synonyma* II.89–91. See Cross, '*Ubi Sunt* Passages in Old English'; Szarmach, 'A Return to Cotton Tiberius A. III'; Di Sciacca, *Finding the Right Words*, 105–48; and Zacher, *Preaching the Converted*, 106–39.

of worldly wealth: 'Hwær coman middangeardes gestreon? Hwær com worulde wela? Hwær cwom foldan fægernes? Hwær coman þa þe geornlicost æhta tiledon ך oðrum eft yrfe læfdon? Swa læne is sio oferlufu eorðan gestreona, emne hit bið gelice rena scurum, þonne he of heofenum swiðost dreoseð ך eft hraðe eal toglideð – bið fæger weder ך beorht sunne' (X.238–43) [Where have the treasures of the earth gone? Where has the prosperity of the world gone? Where has the land's beauty gone? Where are those who so diligently tended to their property and later left an inheritance to others? So temporary is the immoderate love of earthly riches, just like a shower of rain; when it falls from heaven so heavily and then quickly vanishes altogether, there will be fine weather and a bright sun]. The last two sentences of the passage are independent of the homilist's Isidorian source.[151] The image of someone working to accumulate possessions for his or her heirs has no counterpart in the *Synonyma*, and the rain simile replaces that of a passing shadow while still preserving its underlying premise.[152] These changes to the source recall several words and themes from the *bocland* passage and the subsequent notice of doomed inheritance: *yrfe* echoes *yrfeweardas* (X.194–5); *eorðan* echoes the several appearances of *þin eorðe*; and the rain simile echoes the reference to rain in Christ's rebuke (X.172–3). Original content or embellishment appears at the end of both sections and the motif of inheritance consequently assumes prominent place in both movements. The

---

151 In Isidore the passage reads, 'Brevis est hujus mundi felicitas, modica est hujus saeculi gloria, caduca est et fragilis temporalis potentia. Dic ubi sunt reges? ubi principes? ubi imperatores? ubi locupletes rerum? ubi potentes saeculi? ubi divites mundi? quasi umbra transierunt, velut somnium evanuerunt. Quaeruntur, et non sunt' (*Synonyma* II.91; PL 83.865) [The good fortune of the world is brief, the renown of the age is short, temporal power is fleeting and frail. Tell where are the kings? Where are the princes? Where are the emperors? Where are those prosperous in goods? Where are the world's powerful men? Where are the world's riches? They have passed away like a shadow, as if faded into dream. They are sought out and they are not there]. Claudia Di Sciacca has described the addition as 'an intentional and artful *uariatio* on the part of the Anglo-Saxon homilist' (*Finding the Right Words*, 123).

152 Szarmach gives an insightful discussion of this passage: 'That fair weather and bright sun follow the passing shower at once describe the passing nature of earthly treasures and suggest a better alternative to them. The dual function of the image in summarizing the exposition of mutability and yet looking ahead to the conclusion shows this homilist's characteristic way of linking his major structural units. The homilist continually presents a major theme from which he develops the next with a degree of surprise or unexpectedness' ('The Vercelli Homilies: Style & Structure,' 247). The homilist employs this tactic of surprise, I would add, in both positive and negative ways (i.e., the sudden death of the rich man and his entire family, followed by the despoliation of their possessions by strangers).

homily thus links bookland effectively to failed inheritance, casting it as one of the many earthly vanities which fade to nothing.

In these several ways, the homilist uses tenurial language and concerns to amplify exemplary content at key moments. The success of this tactic testifies to the resonance that matters of land tenure and inheritance must have held for contemporary audiences. Vercelli X uses its tenurial motifs to generate awe and to move its audience through rhetorical and emotional appeals. Christ appears as both a merciful power who brings redemption through a master document and as a grim lord who berates negligent subjects before turning away from them at their moment of destruction. The homily thus associates land with both salvation and death. The text furthermore situates a document at the centre of both conceits. Salvation comes through the renewed right which is granted in the *frumgewrit*, while the wealthy man's misplaced faith in bookland affords him and his heirs nothing in their time of dying. In this sense, the homily navigates something of a paradox: it dismisses the royal diploma as a futile instrument which traffics in false promises of eternal possession, yet its main metaphor of salvation is predicated entirely on that same documentary practice. Vercelli X thus repeats the conceptual tensions evident in other tenurial texts when the assurance of a longstanding and secure possession carries the worrying elements of its own contradiction.

The three texts examined in this chapter demonstrate the potential for tenurial concepts and practice to inform multiple written genres. Land tenure provides a versatile conceptual field which is available for adaptation across different modes of writing for varied purposes. This chapter has specifically considered several texts in which land tenure provides the matter for rhetorical or figural elements in exemplary writing. IV Edgar builds an analogy of tenancy and rent in order to explain a widespread plague and to admonish its audience to adopt a course of corrective action. The parable of the recalcitrant tenant who is punished by his angry lord offers a warning, but it also provides a theoretical foundation for the imperative of obligation and obedience. The preface to the *OESol*, by contrast, features a positive conceit of salvation in which a dependent tenant receives reward rather than punishment from his lord. This text seems untroubled by intimations of loss as it portrays the obligations of holding land as dramatically productive. Vercelli X, however, features a more ranging use of tenurial motifs with significant variations in tone and rhetorical techniques. The homily specifically uses the royal diploma to represent both the promise of heavenly salvation and the inevitability of worldly loss. These figural moments additionally identify the potential for revision and reversion in even the most authoritative of documents. That the homily effectively uses this point to represent both hope (eternal salvation) and futility (earthly wealth) testifies to the flexibility of the conceit. The transformation and translation of tenurial motifs allow these three texts to frame orthodox concepts in startling new ways through compelling rhetorical content.

Through the apparatus of writing, land becomes an intellectual and philosophical concept which emerges from but also transcends those social mechanisms which determine its use and transmission as a possession. In the process, property generates a highly productive thematic and lexical field across different textual modes and genres. The final two chapters of *Land and Book* consider how tenurial discourse and land issues inform other textual productions which are typically deemed non-legal. The possession of the land, the ability both to acquire and to control it over time, provides an occasion in these texts for engaging or proclaiming an array of claims, beliefs, potentialities, and anxieties. Prominent among these forces is the challenge of history, the evidence of rupture and crisis which contradicts the ideals of continuity and eternity which often circulate in tenurial discourse. The possession of land distinguishes the holder, but that valuation often contends with a sense of precarious tenure, a felt vulnerability to dispossession or dispute which typically must be sublimated within a formal or ideological order. The next chapter specifically considers how the early tenth-century annals of the Anglo-Saxon Chronicle appropriate aspects of tenurial discourse in order to inscribe an expanding realm ruled by an uninterrupted line of celebrated dynastic figures. In the process, the Chronicle's selective account conflates territorial expansion and dynastic succession in an affirmation of political power over collective lands and peoples. These annals thus constitute an aggregate *landboc* which selectively records the territorial claims of West Saxon rulers in an accumulative chronological narrative.

4 The Anglo-Saxon Chronicle as Dynastic Landbook

Bide me and ic þe sylle þeoda to agnum yrfe, and þinne anwald ic gebræde ofer ðeoda gemæro.[1]

– Psalm 2:8

In his prefatory letter to the Old English translation of Gregory's *Regula pastoralis*, King Alfred turns a nostalgic look back to better times when 'ða kyningas ðe ðone onwald hæfdon ðæs folces [on ðam dagum] Gode & his ærendwrecum hersumedon; & hie ægðer ge hiora sibbe ge hiora siodo ge hiora onweald innanbordes gehioldon, & eac ut hiora eðel gerymdon'[2] (those kings who had dominion over the people in those days obeyed God and his representatives; and they upheld peace, good conduct, and dominion within, and also expanded their homeland outwards). Alfred's admiring appraisal of past rulers communicates his views on the right use of *anweald* (power, sovereignty): a good king both maintains domestic order within the kingdom itself (*rice*) and expands the lands of the realm (*eðel*). *Eðel* generally signifies 'homeland,' but it can more specifically connote hereditary land or ancestral domain.[3] Alfred's pairing of *rice* and *eðel* understands *anweald* as something that can be passed down and maintained over familial generations, thereby providing a longstanding political authority over dynastic lands.

---

1 O'Neill, *King Alfred's Old English Prose Translation of the First Fifty Psalms*, 101. 'Appeal to me and I shall grant nations into your own inheritance, and I shall extend your authority over the borders of nations.'
2 Sweet, *King Alfred's West-Saxon Version of Gregory's Pastoral Care*, 3.
3 *DOE*, s.v. 'eðel.'

An interest in the concept of *anweald* appears widely in other vernacular texts associated with the Alfredian era, including the Anglo-Saxon Chronicle.[4] The word *anweald* appears frequently in the Chronicle, where it generally signifies political power and dominion over a group of territories and peoples.[5] The Chronicle's obituary notice for Alfred, for example, states that at the time of his death he was king over all the English except for those regions under Danish control: 'se wæs cyning ofer eall Ongelcyn butan ðæm dæle þe under Dena onwalde wæs.'[6] This clause notably attends to those lands that remained beyond the king's dominion. Alfred had halted the Scandinavian advances for a time and secured his kingdom, but lands under English control had still been much reduced; the Chronicle notice of Alfred's death acknowledges that territorial condition quietly but emphatically. Despite his many accomplishments, Alfred left to his son Edward what one historian has described as 'the united but much attenuated kingdom of Wessex and Mercia.'[7] It would fall to Alfred's descendants to realize the political ideal of both achieving domestic security and extending dynastic lands.

How might this sovereignty over expansive lands be attested in testamentary writing, especially as dominion changed over time? Secular and ecclesiastical powers in Anglo-Saxon England knew several means in the late ninth and early tenth centuries for declaring and preserving the ownership of land in writing. Latin diplomas represented royal grants of individual estates, leases granted the temporary use of property under limited terms, records of privileges specified the obligations and freedoms attendant on ownership, and narrive charters recorded the outcomes of property disputes. All these documentary forms work to record and control the

4 Kretzschmar, 'Adaptation and *Anweald*,' 142–5.
5 The main definitions provided by the *DOE* indicate the word's primary association with secular governance. *Anweald* also appears as a gloss for *ius, decretrum, lex, potestas*, and *spectrum* (A.1.a, A.1.a.ii, A.1.a.iv); in each case it signifies 'royal or imperial power, as if in the sense "power, dominion, sway"' (*DOE*, s.v. 'anweald'). These glosses indicate the legal connotations of the word as well as its association with governmental power. The word in the main seems reserved for royal power, and is only applied to authority over a large amount of territory (it is not used to indicate possession of individual estates). The word rarely appears in charters and when it does it usually denotes royal authority as in S 1447: 'gemang þam getidde þæt Myrce gecuran Eadgar to cynge ꞇ him anweald gesealdan ealra cynerihta' (Robertson, *Anglo-Saxon Charters*, 90) [At that time it happened that the Mercians chose Edgar as king and gave him sovereignty in all royal rights].
6 Bately, *MS A*, 61 (s.a. 900).
7 Hart, *Early Charters of Northern England and the North Midlands*, 16.

transmission of property, yet they also all deal in individual estates or small groups of local properties. *Anweald*, in contrast, involves the possession of land on a scale far beyond the representative capacity of an individual charter. Existing modes of tenurial writing were not suited for recording the possession of dynastic lands in dynamic or aggregate terms.

This chapter reads the tenth-century annals of the Anglo-Saxon Chronicle as a textual mode for asserting dynastic dominion over a growing amount of territory. The Chronicle has been frequently read as a political text promoting a dynastic agenda for the House of Wessex.[8] Thomas Bredehoft, for example, has argued that the early tenth-century annals functioned as an independent 'extension of the Alfredian chronicle into a dynastic chronicle following the fortunes of Alfred's offspring.'[9] Those generational 'fortunes' in the Chronicle, I contend, are inextricably tied to land and the assertion of an expansive *anweald*. While tenurial discourse in Anglo-Saxon England deals largely in individual units of property, the Chronicle works to write a collective territory held under the hereditary authority of the West Saxon dynasty. Its vernacular combination of genealogy, annalistic prose, and classical verse represents a synthesis of textual modes unavailable to established conventions of tenurial writing. Furthermore, the Chronicle was intended as a public text, an official record to be distributed regionally and added to over time.[10] Such a record can claim national property in ways which include but also extend beyond the parameters of standard tenurial modes. At the same time, discrete groups of tenth-century Chronicle annals specifically share certain techniques with contemporary royal diplomas: the delineation of property boundaries and the use of literary ornamentation to bolster claims of possession. These parallels clarify the ways in which the

---

8   Davis, 'Alfred the Great: Propaganda and Truth'; Wallace-Hadrill, 'The Franks and the English in the Ninth Century'; Thormann, '*Chronicle* Poems'; Bredehoft, *Textual Histories*; Keynes, 'The Power of the Written Word,' 175–82; Scragg, 'A Reading of *Brunanburh*'; Sheppard, *Families of the King*; Trilling, *Aesthetics of Nostalgia*, 175–213; and Brooks, 'Why is the *Anglo-Saxon Chronicle* about Kings?'

9   Bredehoft, *Textual Histories*, 65. See also Stafford, 'The Annals of Æthelflæd,' 108–11. Stafford argues, 'From the outset the question was of Alfred's inheritance. A chronicle which attached Edward's story to that of his father claimed the inheritance which Alfred's own writing of the past had defined' (ibid., 111).

10   Nicholas Brooks has argued most recently for a tradition of centralized production and dissemination of the Anglo-Saxon Chronicle from the royal household. See Brooks, 'Why is the *Anglo-Saxon Chronicle* about Kings?' In Brooks's view, the Chronicle exhibits a pronounced royal agenda. Part of this agenda, I contend, involves the affirmation of *anweald* and territorial power which can be transmitted over time within the dynastic line.

Anglo-Saxon Chronicle, particularly in its annals for the first half of the tenth century, incrementally records and affirms dynastic *anweald* over an expanding realm and its various peoples.

This chapter specifically examines the annals for 900–46 as they appear in Chronicle manuscripts A (Cambridge, Corpus Christi College 173 [Gneuss 52]) and B (London, BL, Cotton Tiberius A. vi + London, BL, Cotton Tiberius A. iii, fol. 178 [Gneuss 364]) in order to demonstrate two points: first, that these annals employ a textual practice most evident in royal diplomas – the writing of territorial bounds as a means of articulating the legitimate possession of land; and second, that similar to contemporary developments in diplomatic style, the Chronicle poems for 937 and 942 enhance territorial claims through conspicuous literary performance. 900–46AB function as an accumulative narrative of expanding dynastic territory, marking out the borders of *anweald* within sets of annals dedicated to individual rulers. This discursive process begins with the circumscription of territorial authority at the time of Alfred's death and continues through the accounts of his descendants bringing new lands within the ambit of West Saxon control. The Chronicle records the moving borders of dynastic territory specifically through its inventory of place-names and through its accounts of military activity on the edges of the English realm. This notation of events and places creates what Jacqueline A. Stodnick has called 'discursive mapping,' a dynamic textual process which produces 'a geographically-imagined category.'[11] As it marks the geographic borders of dominion as they change over time, the Chronicle creates and maintains the idea of a bounded realm held under the hereditary *anweald* of successive royal figures. In this fashion, the Chronicle fulfils at a national level a function similar to that served by the royal diploma at the level of the local estate.

Comparisons between the Anglo-Saxon Chronicle and contemporary diplomas raise preliminary questions of whether and to what extent Chronicle scribes would have been familiar with diplomas or involved in their production. While most scribes working in early and mid-tenth century England would certainly have been familiar with diplomas, arguments for Chronicle scribes also producing or copying such documents must to some degree remain tentative.[12] The scribal production of the Chronicle in its various forms is a complex issue, and this chapter is not the occasion to

---

11 Stodnick, 'What (and Where) is the *Anglo-Saxon Chronicle* About?' 90.
12 It is clear, however, that later Chronicle scribes worked with diplomatic materials. MS E incorporates material drawn from forged charters (Irvine, *MS E*, xc–xcvi), while several diplomatic forgeries have been attributed to the F-scribe (Baker, *MS F*, xxiii).

engage such questions fully.[13] The copying of annals 910–46 into manuscripts A and B has been dated with some precision,[14] thereby providing a
terminal date for the material's composition, but exact dating and proven-
ance for either the exemplars or the original composition of that material
remain conjectural. Nonetheless, the inclusion of vernacular bounds in
diplomas had been well established by the beginning of the tenth century,
and diplomas would certainly have been familiar to scribes working at
both monastic centres and the royal court. The textual model for the circumscription of property in English, with its functional indication of
ownership, would have been readily available to those writers responsible
for the original Chronicle material as well as to those scribes later responsible for copying that material into manuscripts A and B.

Could a scribe's experience with royal diplomas have informed his or
her work in other texts? One example would seem to indicate that this
indeed was the case. A gospel book produced on the continent in the late
ninth or early tenth century (London, BL, Cotton Tiberius A. ii) was later
given by King Æthelstan to Christ Church, Canterbury.[15] The gift is commemorated by an inscription written in Anglo-Saxon Square minuscule:

> Volumen hoc euuangelii . ÆÐELSTAN . Anglorum basyleos . et curagulus
> totius Bryttanniæ . devota mente . Dorobernensis cathedre primatui . tribuit
> ecclesiæ Christo dicatæ . quod etiam archiepiscopus . hujus ac ministri
> ecclesiæ . presentes successoresque . curiosis affectibus perenitter agnoscant .
> scilicet et custodire studeant . prout Deo rationem sunt reddituri . Ne quis in
> æternum furva fr[au]da deceptus . hinc illud arripere conetur . Sed manens hic
> maneat . honoris exemplumque cernentibus . perpetue sibi demonstret . Vos
> etenim obsecrando postulo . memores ut vestris mei mellifluis oraminibus .
> consonaque voce fieri prout confido . non desistatis.[16]

---

13 For scribal activity in MS A, see Bately, *MS A*, xxi–xlvi; Dumville, 'English Square
    Minuscule Script: The Background and Earliest Phases'; Dumville, 'The Anglo-Saxon
    Chronicle and the Origins of English Square Minuscule Script'; and Dumville, 'English
    Square Minuscule Script: The Mid-Century Phases.'
14 In MS A these annals were written by scribe 2 (annals 891 to 920) in the 920s and scribe 3
    (annals 924 to 955) in one stint during the mid-tenth century. See Dumville, 'The Anglo-
    Saxon Chronicle and the Origins of English Square Minuscule Script,' 56–70. All of MS
    B was written in a single hand sometime between 977 and 1000. Simon Taylor favours a
    date closer to 977 than 1000 since the hand displays none of the insular forms typical of
    eleventh-century script (*MS B*, xxiii–xxiv).
15 Gneuss 362. See Keynes, 'King Athelstan's Books,' 147–53.
16 *BCS*, vol. 2, no. 711 at pp. 417–18.

[Æthelstan, king of the English and guardian of all Britain, with a devout mind gave this book to the primatial see of Canterbury, a church dedicated to Christ. May the archbishop and his servants of the church, present and future, forever regard that book with diligent goodwill, and may they especially strive to keep it safe, as they are to render account to God, lest anyone hereafter, ensnared by dark deceit, should attempt to steal the book from here. But may it continue to remain here, and may it always provide an example of honour to those looking upon it. And I ask and pray that you will not cease to remember me in your sweet prayers, as I am sure will be made in harmonious voice.]

Chaplais identified the scribe of this inscription as the same Winchester scribe responsible for writing five charters between 944 and 949 during the reigns of kings Edmund and Eadred.[17] Simon Keynes subsequently observed that the scribe's inscription in Cotton Tiberius A. ii 'employs language which shows that he was already familiar with the conventions of charters, notably in his use of the royal style.'[18] The influence of diplomatic conventions also appears in the inscription's language of perpetuity and its petitions for prayers, both common rhetorical features in Latin diplomas. The incorporation of such language into the inscription could be attributed in part to its function as a statement of a royal gift – a scenario similar to a royal grant of property – but the dedication in Cotton Tiberius A. ii nonetheless provides one clear example of diplomatic style influencing composition in another context. We can see a similar influence within the Anglo-Saxon Chronicle, albeit one which works in a much more complex fashion.

Writing the Bounds

While the influence of diplomatic language in the Cotton Tiberius A. ii inscription occurs within a Latin environment, tenth-century diplomas also offered an established method for demarcating the limits of territorial possession in English: the vernacular boundary clause. Property bounds in diplomas of the seventh and eight centuries are generally brief and in Latin, primarily 'formed by supplying vernacular place-names within a framework

---

17 Chaplais, 'Origin and Authenticity,' 41.
18 Keynes, 'King Athelstan's Books,' 150. See also Gretsch, *Intellectual Foundations*, 337–8; and Foot, *Æthelstan*, 212–13.

of compass directions and landmarks in Latin.'[19] The following bounds, for example, appear in a single-sheet diploma dated to 759: 'confiniæ tamen ejusdem terræ . ab australi plaga Uuisleag . ab occidente Rindburna, a septemtrionale Meosgelegeo; ab oriente vero Onnanduun cum campis silvis pratis pascuis cum omnibus ad se pertinentibus'[20] (The boundaries of the land are Wistley on the southern side, *Rindburna* to the west, *Meosgelegeo* to the north, Andover Hill to the east, with the fields, woods, meadows, pastures, and everything belonging to it). Early bounds like these situate the property in general terms as they sketch the geographical limits of possession. Boundary clauses written in English first appear in the ninth century and then become a standard component of tenth-century diplomas, where they can become quite detailed and lengthy.[21] Most vernacular boundary clauses 'begin at a cardinal point on the estate boundary' and proceed clockwise on a walking tour through a series of landscape features back to the original starting point.[22] The boundary markers 'are either fixed points, such as a tree, a stump, a stone or some similar, isolated object, or else they are a linear feature, a stream, a road, a hedge or the boundary of an adjoining estate.'[23] The only single-sheet diploma to survive from the reign of Edward the Elder contains such a boundary clause in English:

Ðis synt þa land gemæro . Ærest of þam garan innan þa blacan hegcean . of þære hegcean nyþer innan þone fulan broc of ðam fulan broce wið westan randes æsc þanon on þæne ealdan dic wiþ westan þa herde wic . of þære dic þæt innan Wealdan hrigc on eadrices gemære . ꝺlang eadrices gemære þæt innan Cynebellinga gemære ꝺlang gemære þæt on Icenhylte . ꝺlang Icenhylte oþ þone hæðenan byrgels . þanon on cynges stræt . up ꝺlang stræte on welandes

---

19 Lowe, 'Development of the Anglo-Saxon Boundary Clause,' 68. See also Rabuck, 'The Imagined Boundary,' 149–65.

20 S 56. *BCS*, vol. 1, no. 187 at p. 266.

21 There is a gap in the production of royal diplomas during Edward's reign between 910 and 924, but the vernacular boundary clause was well established prior to this hiatus. Three single-sheet diplomas with vernacular boundary clauses survive from the ninth century (S 298, 327, and 331), with S 298 (dated to 847) containing remarkably detailed bounds. See Lowe, 'Development of the Anglo-Saxon Boundary Clause,' 68–9. Other single-sheets of the ninth century (such as S 293 and 328) also have more detailed perambulations in Latin which resemble the style of vernacular bounds. See also Thompson, *Anglo-Saxon Royal Diplomas*, 30 and 40.

22 Hooke, *Landscape of Anglo-Saxon England*, 95.

23 Reed, 'Anglo-Saxon Charter Boundaries,' 281.

stocc . of þam stocce nyþer ꝺlang rah heges þæt on Hegleage of ðære leage nyþer ðæt eft on ðæne garan.[24]

[These are the estate boundaries. First from the corner to the black hedge, from the hedge down to the dirty brook, from the dirty brook to the ash tree west of the bank, from there to the old ditch west of the herdsman's dwelling, then from the ditch into the wooded ridge up to Eadric's boundary, along Eadric's boundary then to the boundary of the Kimblings, along the boundary then to Icknield, along Icknield up to the heathen mounds, from there to King's Street, up along the street to Weland's Stump, from the stump down along the roe hedge then to the haying meadow, from the meadow down back to the corner.][25]

As we can see, tenth-century vernacular boundary clauses typically delineate estate bounds through a paratactic list of landscape features linked by transitional conjunctions and adverbs such as *þa*, *ðonne*, and *ðonan* in order to indicate perambulatory movement over time. While Latin bounds had been organized by cardinal direction, vernacular clauses create property boundaries incrementally, moving from point to point through an accumulative catalogue of markers.

Nicholas Howe has argued that diplomas essentially invent landscape in order to enable the human possession and transmission of property. According to Howe, boundary clauses 'never describe the parcel itself in any detail but only track its edges or boundaries,' thereby envisioning 'landscape as bounded, as contained by human-defined purposes.'[26] The ambulatory tracing of boundaries accordingly inscribes the spatial limits of possession, putting the land in writing and setting down borders through implied human action. This textual model for the circumscription of property in English, with its functional indication of ownership, would have been readily available to both the writers responsible for the original Chronicle material as well as to those scribes responsible for copying the material into manuscripts A and B in the tenth century. Indeed, Chronicle annals 912–46AB repetitively enact such a process in their accounts of Edward, Æthelflæd, Æthelstan, and Edmund,

---

24 S 367. The diploma is dated to 903, but debate over the script suggests that the document may be an imitative copy made in the later tenth century. See Brooks and Kelly, *Christ Church, Canterbury*, no. 101.

25 My translation has consulted Reed, 'Buckinghamshire Anglo-Saxon Charter Boundaries,' 178–81.

26 Howe, *Writing the Map of Anglo-Saxon England*, 39.

charting the expansion of dynastic territory in incremental units dedicated to individual rulers. The Chronicle sets out territorial borders by recording movement through a series of topographic markers and place-names; in the process, the annals demarcate the expanding periphery of dynastic lands. This textual operation represents what Margaret Clunies Ross in another context has called a 'cultural paradigm of spatial representation' for producing and legitimizing the division of land.[27] Like the vernacular boundary clause, the Chronicle creates an idea of territory in writing while its annalistic structure enables a restatement of that bounded realm under successive royal figures. Annals 900–46AB share with contemporary diplomas a common vision for writing land which fuses the textual representation of boundaries with the representation of power.

The Edwardian Annals

The annals for the reign of King Edward the Elder (r. 899–924) survive in different forms in the two tenth-century Chronicle manuscripts. MS A contains the more full set of annals, particularly for the years 915 to 920.[28] David Pelteret has identified these annals as part of a distinct set running from 912 to 920, with a single author proposed for the material.[29] Indeed, these annals give a remarkably detailed account of Edward's movement and construction of fortresses in the north and west during those years. MS B, in contrast, has less content, with its last annal appearing for 915 (equivalent to 914A) just prior to its inclusion of the Mercian Register. The Edwardian annals in MS B consequently feature the king's military success in important engagements, such as the battle of Tettenhall in 910, with very little mention of fortress construction. Despite their differences in content and style, the Edwardian annals in A and B both show the king successfully meeting those criteria for good rulership outlined by Alfred in his prefatory letter to the Old English *Regula pastoralis*: Edward first contains an internal threat to his power, thereby establishing peace within the realm, and then expands the bounds of the *eðel* outward throughout his reign. This accumulative narrative shows Edward

27 Clunies Ross, 'Land-Taking and Text-Making in Medieval Iceland,' 160.
28 The number of scribes responsible for these annals has been a matter of debate. Dumville concluded that the annals were 'written by a single scribe, on two occasions, and probably from two separate exemplars' ('The Anglo-Saxon Chronicle and the Origins of English Square Minuscule Script,' 68), while Bately sees 'three distinct hands and three minor ones' (*MS A*, xxv–xxxiv at xxx).
29 Pelteret, 'An Anonymous Historian of Edward the Elder's Reign.'

extending his *anweald* across new lands which will then be passed on to his heirs. In this way, the Chronicle records dynastic possession and the transmission of a heritable *eðel* over time.

The Edwardian annals in MS B begin with the revolt of *ætheling* Æthelwold against his newly-crowned cousin. In Stenton's memorable words, Edward 'was kept in unease by an enemy sprung from his own house' during the first years of his reign.[30] As the son of King Æthelred (r. 865–71), Alfred's older brother, and an *ætheling*, Æthelwold had valid expectation of the throne.[31] 901B notably includes two pieces of information about Æthelwold which are absent in MS A. First, unlike MS A, MS B refers to Æthelwold specifically as *ætheling*, thereby indicating his legitimate candidacy for kingship.[32] Second, MS B states that Æthelwold was accepted as king by the Northumbrians: '⁊ gesohte þone here on Norðhymbrum, ⁊ hie hine underfengon heom to cinge ⁊ him to bugan'[33] (And he sought out the enemy forces among the Northumbrians, and they accepted him as king, and submitted to him). MS A indicates only that Æthelwold 'gesohte þone here on Norðhymbrum'[34] (sought out enemy forces in Northumbria). MS B thus indicates both the legitimacy of Æthelwold's claim and the extent of his support. In fact, Æthelwold was accepted not only in Northumbria, but also in Essex,[35] and soon afterwards he also convinced the *here* in East Anglia to harry into Mercia.[36] As James Campbell has pointed out, 'for a few years Æthelwold had extensive success' before his death on the battlefield ended his bid for the throne (s.a. 905).[37]

---

30 Stenton, *Anglo-Saxon England*, 321.
31 Æthelwold appears just above Edward in the witness list in S 356, an undated lease-charter of King Alfred. Both Æthelwold and Edward are designated as *filius regis* (Kelly, *Malmesbury*, no. 20 at p. 195).
32 For a discussion of the *ætheling* status and its significance for determining royal succession, see Dumville, 'The Ætheling: A Study in Anglo-Saxon Constitutional History.' For Æthelwold's challenge to Edward, see Smyth, *Scandinavian York and Dublin*, 1:49–52.
33 Taylor, *MS B*, 46 (s.a. 901).
34 Bately, *MS A*, 62 (s.a. 900).
35 'Her com Aþelwold hider ofer sæ mid eallum þæm flotan þe he begitan mihte ⁊ him gebogen wæs on Eastsexum' (Taylor, *MS B*, 46, s.a. 904) [In this year Athelwold came here from over the sea with all the ships he could find and there was submission to him among the East Saxons].
36 'Her gelædde Æþelwold þone here on Eastenglum to unfriþe þæt hie hergodan ofer eall Myrcna land' (ibid., s.a. 905) [Here Athelwold led the enemy army in East Anglia to war so that they harried across all of Mercia].
37 Campbell, 'What is Not Known About the Reign of Edward the Elder,' 21–2 at 21. See also Stafford, 'Annals of Æthelflæd,' 110.

Æthelwold's story is one of struggle over kingship, but at its base it also involves a family dispute over property.[38] The Chronicle's focus on the West Saxon dynasty involves territorial claims on a scale far beyond local disputes over individual estates, but like narratives of local dispute, the Chronicle endorses the resolution of dispute through written testimony. As we have seen, MS A seems reluctant to acknowledge the basis and extent of Æthelwold's claim to the crown and lands of the West Saxon kingdom. Despite its additional details, however, MS B clearly presents Æthelwold's challenge as an insurrection fueled by the interests and support of groups outside of Wessex, and by extension, outside his family: the *here* in Northumbria (s.a. 901); the *flotan* gathered from 'over the sea' and men among the East Saxons (s.a. 904); and the *here* in East Anglia (s.a. 905). By contrast, Edward appears with the native *fyrd* in the annals for 901 and 905, clearly connecting him with West Saxon interests.[39] These points of nomenclature colour the dispute in Edward's favour and assume that his cousin acted outside his family's interests in more ways than one. The Chronicle account of Æthelwold's rebellion, then, supports Edward's legitimate claim to West Saxon lands and establishes him as a successful defender of family property.

After this resolution of internal dispute, MS B records the expansion of West Saxon authority in the north. After Æthelwold's threat is ended, Edward begins regular military action against the *norðhere* in his campaign to gain territory occupied by Scandinavian forces. Annals 910 and 911B state that Edward sent a combined force of West Saxons and Mercians against the *norðhere* that had been ravaging Mercia,[40] with the English forces overtaking and defeating the Danes at Tettenhall in Staffordshire. This defeat of the Northumbrian Danes greatly reduced Scandinavian strength in the north and, according to Stenton, 'opened the way to the great expansion of the West Saxon kingdom which occurred in the following years.'[41] 911B notably states that Edward gathered his *fyrd* from both Wessex and Mercia, indicating the cooperation of the two merging kingdoms; indeed, Edward's authority in Mercia will become a key concern in the Edwardian annals and later in the Mercian Register as well. After

38 See also Smith, 'Of Kings and Cattle Thieves.'
39 The Chronicle generally associates *here* with enemy forces and *fyrd* with English troops. Æthelwold is accordingly figured as an invader much like the Danes who had attacked England over the last decades. See Stodnick, 'Sentence to Story,' 107–8.
40 Taylor, *MS B*, 47.
41 Stenton, *Anglo-Saxon England*, 323.

Ealdorman Æthelred, Æthelflæd's husband, dies in Mercia in 911 (s.a. 912), Edward assumes authority in London and Oxford and finalizes (at least in the view of the Chronicle) the union of Mercia and Wessex.[42] The accumulation of individual annals demonstrates the ability of a dynastic protagonist, in this case Edward the Elder, to repel territorial challengers at the same time that it records the steady extension and consolidation of West Saxon *anweald* over new regions and peoples.

Beginning in 913, Edward begins a project in collaboration with his sister Æthelflæd of constructing fortified *burh*s (strongholds) at strategic points in order to contain possible Scandinavian aggression. This fortification project stabilized West Saxon lands and provided staging points for military expeditions into enemy-controlled areas. The Chronicle continues its depiction of Edward as a ruler capable of controlling territory not only by noting the specific locations of his *burh*s, which act as geographical markers of regional power, but also by recording the submission of peoples formerly under Scandinavian authority (s.a. 913) and the defeat and expulsion of *here* forces (s.a. 914 and 915).[43] The long annal for 915 gives a detailed account of the invasion of a *mycel sciphere* sailing from Brittany and its eventual repulsion by the West Saxons.[44] The annal highlights the instrumentality of the *burh*s in mounting forces effectively against nearby aggression: the invaders are soundly beaten at Archenfield by men mustered from Hereford and Gloucester, the two nearest *burh*s.[45] The diminished *here* is then driven into an enclosure (*pearroc*) where they are surrounded and forced to give hostages as a token that they will leave the king's dominion

---

42 'Her gefor Æþered ealdormann on Myrcum, ⁊ Eadweard cing feng to Lundenbyrig ⁊ to Oxnaforda ⁊ to eallum þam landum þe þærto hyrdon' (Taylor, *MS B*, 48) [Here Æthelred, ealdorman of the Mercians, died, and King Edward came to power over London and Oxford and to all the lands that were subject thereto].

43 The Chronicle does not indicate that Edward was present at all these battles. The 914 annal, for example, records that local men repelled the *here*: 'þa wurdan þa landleode his geware ⁊ him wið gefuhtan ⁊ gebrohtan hie on fullan fleame ⁊ ahreddan eall þæt hie genumen hæfdon ⁊ eac heora horsa ⁊ heora wæpna mycelne dæl' (ibid.) [then the local people were aware of this and they fought against them and put them to full flight and took back all that they had taken as well as their horses and a good part of their weapons].

44 See Hill, *Atlas of Anglo-Saxon England*, no. 88 at p. 57.

45 'ða gemetton þa menn hie of Hereforda ⁊ of Gleawceastre ⁊ of þam nehstan burgum ⁊ him wið gefuhtan ⁊ hie geflymdan ⁊ ofslogan þone eorl Hraold ⁊ þæs oþres eorles broðor Ohteres ⁊ mycel þæs herges' (Taylor, *MS B*, 48) [then the men from Hereford and Gloucester and from the nearest strongholds met them and fought against them and put them to flight and killed the leader Hroald and the brother of the other leader Ohtere and a large part of the enemy army].

('þæt hie of ðæs cinges <u>onwealde</u> faran woldan').[46] The *here* steals away in the night, but it is engaged again by West Saxon forces and the surviving invaders are forced to swim back to their ships.[47] In the end the beaten remnants of the *sciphere* huddle on an island where many of them starve until the last survivors are finally forced to flee to Dyfed and Ireland.[48] This account artfully tracks the *sciphere*'s increasingly constrained movement and the steady reduction of its numbers until it is finally forced off the mainland altogether. This systematic diminishment of the invading enemy effectively demonstrates West Saxon control of territory and the efficacy of English movement. 915B significantly concludes with Edward constructing *burh*s at Buckingham in a display of regional power which prompts the submission of Thurkytel and other *eorlas* in the area.[49] This narrative formula will importantly reappear in part or whole throughout the Mercian Register as well as in the poems for 937 and 942: an outside threat comes to ground only to be repelled by the English, followed by the submission of enemy forces (or peoples once under enemy control) to West Saxon authority.

Annals 900–46AB strategically record the expansion of dynastic lands in groups of annals dedicated to individual figures in the House of Wessex, thereby underwriting the inheritance and transmission of *anweald* within that family line. The Edwardian annals in MS B perform this function primarily by demonstrating the successful containment of several challenges to that *anweald* – the annals notably begin and end with the neutralization

---

46 Ibid. Emphasis added.

47 'þa sloh hie man æt ægþrum cyrre þæt heora feawa onweg coman butan ða ane þe þærut ætswymman mihton to þam scipum' (ibid., 49) [then they were struck on each occasion so that few of them came away except the one time when they were to able to swim away to their ships].

48 'ꝺ þa sæton hie ute on þam iglande æt Steapan Reolice oþ þone fyrst þe hie wurdon swiþe metelease, ꝺ manige menn hungre acwolen forðon hi ne mihton nanne mete geræcan; foran þa þonan to Deomedum ꝺ þanon to Yrlande' (ibid.) [and then they sat out on the island at Steapan Reolice until the time when they were sorely without food, and many men perished from hunger since they were unable to get any food; then they traveled from there to Dyfed and from there to Ireland].

49 'ꝺ þa æfter þam on þam ilcan geare foran to Martines mæssan þa for Eadweard cing to Buccingaham mid his fyrde ꝺ sæt þær .iiii. wucan ꝺ geworhte þa byrig buta on ægðre healfe ea ær he þonon fore; ꝺ Þurkytel eorl hine gesohte him to hlaforde ꝺ þa eorlas ealle ꝺ þa yldestan menn þe to Bedeforda hyrdan' (ibid.) [and then afterwards in the same year before Martinmas, King Edward traveled to Buckingham with his army and stayed there four weeks and he constructed both strongholds on each side of the river before he left there; and eorl Thurkytel sought him as lord and all the eorls and senior men who belonged to Bedeford].

of substantial threats to dynastic territory. In each case, Edward, or a force acting under his authority, successfully meets the threat and secures land. The failed revolt of Æthelwold and the defeat of the *mycel sciphere* in 915 effectively bookend the Edwardian material in MS B, creating a structural envelope for the entire group of annals. 901 and 915B further echo one another in their respective accounts of territorial challengers stealing away in the night: Æthelwold slips away from Wimbourne under the cover of darkness just as the besieged *here* escapes by night from their containment in a *pearroc*. These symmetrical details discredit Edward's enemies and affirm his ability to defend his lands against both internal and external threats. As a contained unit in MS B, these annals cast Edward both as Alfred's legitimate successor and as a royal protagonist capable of protecting and expanding dynastic property.

The Edwardian annals in MS A largely have the same material as MS B up to 914A (equivalent to 915B), but MS A also contains an additional group of detailed annals for 915–20. The Edwardian annals for 912–20A primarily record Edward's military campaigns in Danish regions to the north and east, his sustained construction of *burh*s, and the submission of the peoples resident in those areas.[50] The annals display close attention to matters of geography, direction, and time, and they indicate the crucial role which the construction and fortification of *burh*s played in the tenth-century expansion of West Saxon authority.[51] David Hill has characterized the methodical construction and maintenance of *burh*s as a central component of territorial expansion after the death of Alfred: 'The pattern of the campaigns was hardly dashing – it was a process of slowly strengthening the West Saxon and Mercian areas with *burh*s, then fortifying the frontier areas with more *burh*s, and finally pushing the *burh*s forward far enough to force the Danes to react.'[52] Within 912–20A, only the 913 annal does not record the construction or fortification of at least one *burh* under Edward's direction; the annals mention a sum total of twenty strongholds being constructed, fortified, or manned during the period. In addition, many of the annals are precise in situating individual locations. The 912 entry, for example, records that 'het Eadweard cy[ni]ng atimbran þa norðran burg æt

---

50 For a discussion of these campaigns and the submissions to Edward, see Abrams, 'Edward the Elder's Danelaw,' 138–40.

51 See Pelteret, 'An Anonymous Historian of Edward the Elder's Reign.'

52 Hill, *Atlas of Anglo-Saxon England*, 55. For a series of maps charting the construction of *burh*s under Edward and Æþelflæd, see ibid., 56–9. For *burh*s as civil defence, see Reynolds, *Later Anglo-Saxon England*, 86–92.

Heorotforda betweox Memeran ⁊ Beneficcan ⁊ Lygean' and that his forces 'worhte þa burg þa hwile æt Heorotforda on suþhealfe Lygean'[53] (King Edward ordered the northern stronghold at Hertford to be built between the Maran and the Beane and the Lea ... meanwhile [some of his forces] made the stronghold at Hertford on the southern side of the Lea). Other entries, such as that for 920, also exhibit a marked attention to both direction and location: 'Her on þysum gere foran to middum sumera for Eadweard cyning mid fierde to Snotingaham ⁊ het gewyrcan þa burg on suþhealfe þære eas ongean þa oþre ⁊ þa brycge ofer Treontan betwix þam twam burgum, ⁊ for þa þonan on Peaclond to Badecanwiellon ⁊ het gewyrcan ane burg þær on neaweste ⁊ gemannian'[54] (In this year King Edward traveled with his army before midsummer to Nottingham and ordered the stronghold to be built on the southern side of the river, opposite the other, and the bridge over Trent between the two strongholds, and from there he went to Bakewell in the Peak District and ordered one stronghold to be built and manned in that place). The attention to location and direction in 912–20A effectively records Edward's movements as he works to secure land and expand the territory held under his *anweald*.

This record of *burh*s located on the bounds of royal authority and the subsequent extension of those frontiers resembles the form and function of boundary clauses, which are typically 'concerned only with the boundaries or peripheries of estates.'[55] Each *burh* acts as a kind of boundary marker connected by the movement of Edward and his forces: many of the annals contain some variation on the formula, 'for Eadweard cyning [mid firde] to x,' followed by the construction or fortification of a *burh* at the noted location (s.a. 912, 914–20). Such a record of movement across the landscape creates not only an itinerary of military action, but also, like charter bounds, a network of place-names and landscape features which together represent the limits of territorial power.[56] This annalistic record of Edward's movement from place to place inscribes a periphery of his *anweald* which moves outward as the annals progress over time. Several of the annals also record Edward's movement both to and from different

53 Bately, *MS A*, 64.
54 Ibid., 69.
55 Reed, 'Anglo-Saxon Charter Boundaries,' 297.
56 See also Lavelle, 'Geographies of Power.' Lavelle discusses the significance of royal estates and itineraries as demonstrations of royal power (or the lack thereof) in the Chronicle, but his attention to the control of royal territory through a record of places and movement complements my own arguments here.

locations through the formula 'ær he þonan fore' (s.a. 914, 915, 916), amplifying further the connection of places through human movement so evident in the perambulations of vernacular boundary clauses.

The progressive connection of locations through human movement becomes more pronounced through the annals' frequent use of þonan, an adverb which also occurs regularly in vernacular boundary clauses. Þonan appears some seventeen times in its spelling variations in MS A, with eight of those occurrences falling within the annals for 912–20.[57] Approximately half of the occurrences of þonan as a directional adverb in MS A, then, fall within the annals for 912–20. Furthermore, þonan is followed by a place-name or directional indicator four times within the Edwardian annals (s.a. 914, 917, 918, 920), while the word appears three times in the formula 'ær he þonan fore' (s.a. 914, 915, 916). The concentration of this directional adverb within these annals reflects their commitment to delineating geographical location and movement. The distinctive use of þonan to connect human movement across named locations functions much as it does in the perambulations of charter bounds, but in the Chronicle it does so on the scale of the royal domain. The notation of burhs as territorial markers linked by Edward's movement inscribes the moving bounds of anweald and dominion over land and people.

This effect is especially clear in the annal for 918 in which Edward travels to Stamford and constructs a burh; then rides to the burh at Tamworth after Æthelflæd's death in order to secure his authority in Mercia; and finally travels to Nottingham to repair and man the burh there. In each instance, Edward's movement to a location on the bounds of his authority is followed by the political submission of the peoples in the region. Through this repetitive pattern, the Edwardian annals claim both land and resident peoples. For example, 912A states that after the construction of a burh at Witham, those people in the area formerly under Danish authority submitted to Edward.[58] This pattern of a burh being constructed or fortified, followed by the submission of nearby peoples, also appears s.a. 914, 915, 917

---

57 My tally ignores alternations of þ and ð. The spellings þonan/þonon/þanon appear in the Edwardian annals. Ðanon appears s.a. 606 and 993 (twice); þanon appears s.a. 917 and 1001 (twice); þonon appears s.a. 547, 891, 914, and 916; þonan appears s.a. 584, 904, 914, 915, 917, 918, and 920. In annal 547, the word functions as a temporal rather than a directional adverb.

58 'þa for Eadweard cyning mid sumum his fultume on Eastseaxe to Mældune ㄱ wicode þær þa hwile þe man þa burg worhte ㄱ getimbrede æt Witham, ㄱ him beag god dæl þæs folces to þe ær under deniscra manna anwalde wæron' (Bately, MS A, 64) [then King Edward went with some of his forces into Essex to Maldon and camped there while the

(on four separate occasions), 918, and 920.[59] The Edwardian annals thus systematically map the expansion of dynastic territory in a chronological narrative, predicated in large part on the strategic construction and maintenance of *burh*s which act as boundary markers for political authority.

Like boundary clauses, the Edwardian annals record the limits of territorial authority through the textual notation of movement across landscape. The annalistic format, however, allows the writing of bounded territory to function as an ongoing process. Whereas diplomas mark out estate borders and declare the right of possession within a single monumental text, the Chronicle annals record the expanding borders of dynastic authority in a composite text, accumulating lands for the West Saxon house through a yearly record. In this sense, the Chronicle dynamically records the possession and control of land within and across time, whereas the grant of property represented within a royal diploma exists outside of time; the diploma represents the original grant within a static material text, just as it fixes the political authority of the grantor and witnesses within the temporal moment represented by that text. Both textual forms, however, share a common project: the creation of bounded land through writing and the placement of that land within the legitimate possession of an individual or community, all of which is recorded within a memorial text. Annals 910–46A work as a boundary clause writ large, fashioning a powerful declaration of *anweald* held and passed on over generations.[60] Read as a whole, the Edwardian annals construct a story of an able dynastic hero who inherits the realm, protects it from internal dispute, repulses outside aggression, and then expands West Saxon *anweald* over a number of years.

---

stronghold was built and constructed at Witham, and a good part of the people who before had been under the power of the Danes submitted to him].

59 For the Chronicle account of the northern submission in 920, see Davidson, 'The (Non) submission of the Northern Kings in 920.' Davidson argues that the 920 entry works as part of a deliberate argument for the legitimacy of Edward's political authority, especially within Mercia.

60 The Chronicle's focus on fortress construction and military engagement notably passes over Edward and Æthelstan's strategic purchase of land within Scandinavian territories in preparation for future conquest. S 396 and 397, both diplomas of Æthelstan dated to 926, refer to thegns purchasing land from the Danes on the orders of Edward and Æthelred. See Stenton, *Anglo-Saxon England*, 322–3; and Dumville, 'Æthelstan, First King of England,' 151–2. These documents suggest a compelling connection between the financial acquisition of individual estates and the acquisition of aggregate territory through conquest.

The Mercian Register

A similar attention to writing territorial boundaries appears in the Mercian Register, a small group of annals (896–924) dedicated to the activities of Æþelflæd, Lady of the Mercians, as she collaborated with her brother Edward in acquiring and securing new territory.[61] These annals appear as a discrete unit in two Chronicle manuscripts, the late tenth-century MS B and the mid-eleventh-century MS C (London, BL, Cotton Tiberius B. i [Gneuss 370.2]); the content of the annals was also blended into the annals proper in the later eleventh-century MS D (London, BL, Cotton Tiberius B. iv [Gneuss 372]).[62] Manuscripts B and C present the Mercian Register as a separate unit, breaking established chronology by inserting the text after the annal for 915.[63] The Mercian Register begins in both MS B and MS C with a horizontal string of empty annals for the years 896 to 901, and concludes after its entry for 924 with another horizontal string of nine empty annals for 925 to 933.[64] This manuscript layout marks the Mercian Register as a distinct text and establishes Æthelflæd as a separate royal figure engaged in a long project of expanding and consolidating territory. MS A gives a full treatment of Edward's activities, but it records only Æthelflæd's death in 918 followed by the transfer of her authority to Edward.[65] Conversely,

---

61 See Stafford, 'Annals of Æthelflæd'; Wainwright, 'Lady of the Mercians'; Stenton, *Anglo-Saxon England*, 324–30; and Stafford, 'Political Women in Mercia.'

62 See Cubbin, *MS D*, xxx–xxxii and 36–41.

63 For the layout of the Mercian Register in B and C, see Szarmach, 'Æðelflæd of Mercia: *Mise en page*.' See also Taylor, *MS B*, xxxii and 49–51; O'Brien O'Keeffe, *MS C*, 74–6; and Stafford, 'Annals of Æthelflæd,' 106–7. The insertion of the Mercian Register in B and C has been seen as disruptive and clumsy. Commenting on the place of the Mercian Register in his proposed exemplar for B and C, Plummer noted, 'The question had been solved very crudely by the scribe of the MS. from which B and C are copied, who simply inserts the Register unaltered in the middle of his Chronicle' (*Two of the Saxon Chronicles Parallel*, 2: lxxii). F.T. Wainwright echoed Plummer's opinion: 'In MSS. B and C these fragmentary annals are crudely inserted into the structure of the main chronicle after the annal now dated 915; there is no attempt to avoid the consequent repetition and confusion' ('Chronology of the "Mercian Register,"' 385). A similar view appears in Hart, 'The B Text of the *Anglo-Saxon Chronicle*,' 255.

64 MS B mistakenly gives 816 to 819 for 896 to 899 by omitting a crucial roman numeral C in those annal numbers (i.e., *dcccxvi* instead of *dcccxcvi*). MS D obscures this distinct layout by collating the contents of the Register into the Edwardian material, but it still preserves a vestige of the design in its run of empty annals from 927 to 933.

65 'þa gefor Æþelflæd his swystar æt Tameworþige .xii. nihtum ær middum sumera, ⁊ þa gerad he þa burg æt Tameworþige, ⁊ him cierde to eall se þeodscype on Myrcna lande þe Æþelflæde ær underþeoded wæs, ⁊ þa cyningas on Norþwealum, Howel ⁊ Cledauc ⁊

the Mercian Register focuses nearly exclusively on Æthelflæd as 'Lady of the Mercians,' mentioning Edward only in its annals for 921 and 924.[66] Æthelflæd is clearly the dynastic protagonist of these annals. The Mercian Register consequently functions as a narrative both separate from and parallel to the preceding Edwardian annals, systematically detailing the fortification of *burh*s, the acquisition of territory, and the secured allegiance of peoples occupying those territories, all of which is accomplished under Æthelflæd's leadership.

Despite its focus on Æthelflæd, the Mercian Register does obliquely register the dynastic conflict from the early years of Edward's reign. The 904 and 905 annals record two fantastic events: a lunar eclipse and a comet.[67] This particular notation of spectacular natural events is unique within the Edwardian annals and the Mercian Register, both of which favour information on fortification and military action. When 904 and 905MR are read against the same years in the Edwardian annals, however, these accounts of environmental anomalies assume a new significance.[68] The darkening of the moon in 904 coincides with Æthelwold's marshalling of an army among the East Saxons while the comet of 905 coincides with the large battle that brought about Æthelwold's death. The comet bears special witness to the momentous danger of this internal conflict, for as Bede states in his *De natura rerum*, a comet can foretell a number of potentially traumatic events, including a change in royal power (*regni mutationem*).[69] Natural portents in the Mercian Register effectively echo political crisis in the Edwardian

---

Ieoþwel, ⁊ eall Norþweallcyn hine sohton him to hlaforde' (Bately, *MS A*, 68–9) [Then his sister Æthelflæd died at Tamworth twelve nights before midsummer, and then he rode to the fortress at Tamworth, and to him submitted all the people in the land of the Mercians which were before subject to Æthelflæd, and the kings among the northern Welsh – Howel and Cledauc and Ieothwel – and all the northern Welsh peoples sought him as lord]. The sparse mention of Æthelflæd outside the Mercian Register led Wainwright to protest that Æthelflæd's 'reputation has suffered from bad publicity, or rather from a conspiracy of silence among her West Saxon contemporaries' ('Lady of the Mercians,' 53).

66 The Mercian Register annal for 921 appears in MS C, but not in MS B.

67 '[904] Her mona aðeostrode. / [905] Her oþywde cometa' (Taylor, *MS B*, 49) [904: Here the moon grew dark. / 905: Here a comet appeared].

68 For a discussion of natural portents in the Chronicle, see Thormann, '*Chronicle* Poems,' 75–7.

69 'Cometae sunt stellae flammis crinitae, repente nascentes, regni mutationem aut pestilentiam aut bella, uel uentos aestusue, portendentes' (Bede, *De natura rerum*, 216) [Comets are stars with a hair-like flame which appear suddenly, foretelling a change in royal power, pestilence or wars, winds or heat].

annals through a juxtaposition which underscores the gravity of inter-familial conflicts over dynastic inheritance.

The Mercian Register gives primary attention, however, to the fortification project shared by Æthelflæd and Edward. The Mercian Register records the construction or maintenance of *burh*s in 907 (Chester), 910 (*Bremesburh*), 912 (*Scergeat*, Bridgnorth), 913 (Tamworth, Stafford), 914 (Eddisbury, Warwick), and 915 (Chirbury, *Weardburh*, Runcorn). These locations provided defensive points along the Welsh border to the west and against Scandinavian forces in the midlands and the north.[70] The Mercian Register's catalogue of *burh*s accordingly provides a set of textual markers for the territorial limits of political authority, functioning much like the Edwardian annals in MS A. The Mercian Register does not contain the level of directional detail evident in those annals, but it does display some geographical and temporal precision, as in its annal for 912: 'Her com Æþelflæd Myrcna hlæfdige on þone halgan æfen Inuentione Sancte Crucis to Scergeate ┐ þær ða burh getimbrede, ┐ þæs ilcan geares þa æt Bricge'[71] (In this year, Æthelflæd, Lady of the Mercians, came to Scergeat on the holy eve of the Invention of the Holy Cross, and constructed a stronghold there, and in the same year the one at Bridgnorth). Like the Edwardian annals, the Mercian Register also presents the occupation of a *burh* as a catalyst for the submission of neighbouring peoples. Æthelflæd seized the Danish stronghold at Derby in 917 and later took the stronghold at Leicester in 918, and the Chronicle states that the capture of the strongholds was followed by the submission of forces situated there.[72] Like the Edwardian annals in MS A, the Mercian Register carefully records territory secured through the construction and maintenance of *burh*s accompanied by the subsequent submission of resident peoples.

The manuscript layout of the Mercian Register in MS B further accentuates its sustained attention to inscribing the boundaries of dynastic territory.

---

70 See Hill, *Atlas of Anglo-Saxon England*, nos. 85–9 at pp. 56–7. See Wainwright, 'Lady of the Mercians,' 58–9 for discussion and map of these strategic locations, 'part of the long line of fortresses which by 916 stretched from the Mersey to Essex and menaced the Danes in their midland strongholds' (ibid., 59). See also S 223, a vernacular charter from the 890s which mentions the fortification of the *burh* at Worcester ordered by Æthelred and Æthelflæd (Harmer, *SEHD*, no. 13 at pp. 22–3).

71 Taylor, *MS B*, 49.

72 '[917] Her Æþelflæd Myrcna hlæfdige Gode fultmigendum foran to Hlafmæssan begeat þa burh mid eallum þam ðe þærto hyrde, þe is hatan Deoraby' (ibid., 50) [In this year, before Lammas, Æthelflæd, Lady of the Mercians, through the aid of God seized the stronghold called Derby, along with all those subject to it].

After its annual number for 908, MS B contains no other annal numbers until 925, while the entries for 914 and 915 contain no initial formulaic markers (such as *her* or *on þysum geare*) to indicate the beginning of a self-contained annal.[73] The three annals for 913–15 consequently run together to create a running itinerary of place-names linked by Æthelflæd's movement: 'Her Gode forgifendum for Æþelflæd Myrcna hlæfdige mid eallum Myrcum to Tamaweorðige ꞇ þa burh ðær getimbrede on foreweardne sumor, ꞇ þæs foran to Hlafmæssan þa æt Stæfforda; ða þæs oþre geare þa æt Eadesbyrig on foreweardne sumor, ꞇ þæs ilcan geares eft on ufeweardne hærfest þa æt Wæringwicon; ða þæs oþre geare on ufan midne winter þa æt Cyricbyrig, ꞇ þa æt Weardbyrig, ꞇ þy ilcan geare foran to middan wintra þa æt Rumcofan'[74] (In this year, through the grace of God, Æthelflæd, Lady of the Mercians, went with all the Mercians to Tamworth and built the stronghold there in early summer, and afterwards before Lammas the one at Stafford; then in the next year the one at Eddisbury in early summer, and later that same year, in late harvest, the one at Warwick; then in the next year, after midwinter, the one at Chirbury, and then at *Weardbyrig*, and in the same year before midwinter the one at Runcorn). I have presented the text without reproducing manuscript division and capitalization in order to highlight its structural resemblance to the paratactic catalogue of a vernacular boundary clause. The progression of the narrative pattern 'Æthelflæd went here and then here' effectively sketches out the geographic movement of power. The Mercian Register in this way delineates dynastic territory, functioning as a boundary clause developed and maintained over time. The bounded territory produced through this textual operation in the Edwardian annals and Mercian Register is furthermore explicitly tied to dynastic figures who effectively 'make' the land as they move across it.

The Mercian Register, then, offers a record of Æthelflæd expanding authority over territories that previously had been beyond her father's control. Moreover, this campaign was conducted in collaboration with Edward – Æthelflæd does not seem to have been an independent agent pursuing Mercian independence.[75] The title *Myrcna hlæfdige* does indicate

---

73 The annals are visually distinguished in the manuscript by initial capitals and indentation, but are syntactically linked by the conjunction *ða*. Of the Mercian Register's sixteen populated annals in MS B, all but four (s.a. 910, 911, 914, and 915) begin with *her*; none of the four annals lacking *her* have an annal-number in the manuscript.

74 Taylor, *MS B*, 50.

75 See Keynes, 'Edward, King of the Anglo-Saxons,' for a compelling assessment of an emerging 'kingdom of the Anglo-Saxons' under Edward in the early tenth century.

Æthelflæd's authority in Mercia while her obituary notice (s.a. 918) speci-fies that 'heo Myrcna anwald mid riht hlaforddome healdende wæs'[76] (she was holding power in Mercia with legitimate authority), but this does not mean that Æthelflæd ruled a separate Mercian kingdom.[77] She instead as-sumed the position of a satellite ruler previously occupied by her husband, Æthelred. In the view of the Chronicle at least, Mercia already had be-come part of those lands under Alfred's authority even though it still re-tained a distinct territorial identity. The Mercian Register does not record Edward's claim over London and Oxford after Æthelred's death in 911, an omission which might indicate disapproval, but the event does not seem to have interrupted Æthelflæd's fortification project in any way. Read together, the Edwardian annals and the Mercian Register show Edward and Æthelflæd's coordinated project of extending their family's territorial authority.

Still, some readers have seen the Mercian Register as a subversive element within a composite text that otherwise favours the interests of Wessex. Annal 919B in particular has inspired this view: 'Her eac wearð Æþeredes dohtar Myrcna hlafordes ælces onwealdes on Myrcum benumen ⁊ on Westsexe alæded ðrim wucan ær middum wintra; seo wæs haten Ælfwyn'[78] (Here also the daughter of Æthelred, lord of the Mercians, was deprived of any authority among the Mercians and taken into Wessex three weeks before midwinter; her name was Ælfwynn). The entry compels for a num-ber of reasons: *eac* assumes a syntactical precedent which seems to be ab-sent; the annal names Ælfwynn as Æthelred's daughter with no mention of Æthelflæd; it records a specific date for Ælfwynn's deposition but says nothing of her fate once taken into Wessex; and it specifies no agent re-sponsible for depriving her of authority.[79] Wainwright read this entry as a terse acknowledgment of a violent West Saxon suppression of Mercian independence with Edward playing the role of belligerent aggressor: 'The words of the annalist who wrote of the deposition of Ælfwyn in the

---

76 Taylor, *MS B*, 50.
77 The political relationship between Wessex and Mercia in the early tenth century was complex, but it is clear that Æthelflæd (like Æthelred before her) held power in Mercia under the authority of Wessex and that she acted in collaboration with her brother. See Keynes, 'King Alfred and the Mercians,' 19–39; Keynes, 'Mercia and Wessex in the Ninth Century'; and Stafford, 'Annals of Æthelflæd,' 111–16.
78 Taylor, *MS B*, 50.
79 For Ælfwynn in the historical record, see Bailey, 'Ælfwynn, Second Lady of the Mercians.' Bailey proposes that Ælfwynn entered the religious life at Wilton and died there sometime after 948.

Mercian Register are heavy with resentment, and even the West Saxon annalist implies that at least a display of force was required to secure the submission of the Mercians to Edward on Æthelflæd's death.'[80] The 919 annal, however, does not directly censure Edward in any way – in fact it does not name him at all. The trembling indignation that Wainwright saw in the 919 annal assumes a particular narrative in which Ælfwynn plays victim to Edward's villain.

This provocative annal, however, might also be interpreted in a way more consistent with the general ideological and territorial agenda advanced in the Chronicle annals for the first decades of the tenth century. If we consider the Mercian Register in conjunction with the Edwardian annals, the 919 annal might be read as a preemptive move to contain potential dissent within the West Saxon dynasty. Ælfwynn does not seem to have represented an active threat like that posed by Æthelwold, but her neutralization was likely intended to circumvent possible dispute over future succession or later challenges to West Saxon authority in Mercia. By recording Ælfwynn's loss of all *anweald* in Mercia, the Chronicle ostensibly eliminates any rival claim to Mercian territory. The textual consolidation of West Saxon *anweald* under Edward the Elder in the Anglo-Saxon Chronicle mirrors the historical consolidation of Mercia and Wessex in the early tenth century. Rather than challenging the West Saxon claim to Mercia, the Mercian Register confirms it. The Mercian Register's attention to territorial expansion and *anweald* remains consistent with the narrative strategies evident in the Edwardian annals.

The incomplete sentence which concludes the Mercian Register records the deaths of Edward and his son Ælfweard, followed by the Mercian confirmation of Æthelstan as king.[81] This notice notably elides Ælfweard's

---

80 Wainwright, 'Lady of the Mercians,' 68. Stenton likewise represents the event as Edward's final move in securing Mercian submission and quelling any remaining impulse toward Mercian separatism: '[The Mercian] wish for a ruler intermediate between themselves and [Edward] was met for the moment by the allowance of nominal authority to Ælfwynn, Æthelflæd's daughter. But in the winter of 919, by a violent act of power, Edward caused her to be carried off into Wessex, and thenceforward there remained no formal distinction between Mercia and the other English regions under his rule' (*Anglo-Saxon England*, 330). See also the more temperate assessment in Bailey, 'Ælfwynn, Second Lady of the Mercians,' 115–17.

81 'Her Eadweard cing gefor on Myrcum æt Fearndune, ꝺ Ælfweard his sunu swiþe hraþe þæs gefor on Oxnaforda, ꝺ heora lic licgað on Wintanceastre' (Taylor, *MS B*, 50) [Here King Edward died among the Mercians at Farndon, and very soon afterward his son Ælfweard died at Oxford, and their bodies lie at Winchester].

brief tenure as king,[82] thereby maintaining the Chronicle's selective tale of dynastic and territorial progress. MS A passes over Ælfweard entirely in its own annal for 924, omitting as well Edward's death in Mercia and the Mercian election of Æthelstan. 924A instead provides a cleanly compressed account of death followed immediately by succession: 'Her Eadweard cing forþferde, ⁊ Æþelstan his sunu feng to rice'[83] (Here King Edward died and his son Æthelstan succeeded to the kingdom). The Chronicle's priority on continuity and uninterrupted succession within the West Saxon line is readily apparent here. Despite their occasional differences in content and focus, the Chronicle annals 900–24AB share a commitment to recording the containment of dispute within the royal family and to charting the steady expansion of *anweald* under Alfred's children. In this way, these annals construct an affirmative record of dynastic property and inheritance.

The Turn to Verse

After the Edwardian and Mercian annals, the style of the Chronicle changes dramatically as annals 924–46AB turn to a sporadic mix of barren annal-numbers, brief prose entries, and, for the first time, poetry. This shift in content has been seen at times as a diminishment in both quality and quantity through which the Chronicle becomes something of a desiccated husk: David Dumville described this part of the Chronicle, for example, as 'an emaciated record, a shadow of its former self';[84] Dorothy Whitelock judged the post-Edwardian annals in MS A to be typical of a 'general decay in historical writing';[85] and Pauline Stafford observed that the Chronicle 'dries up in the tenth century.'[86] The material for the reign of Æthelstan (r. 924–39) is surprisingly brief, as is that for the reign of Edmund (r. 939–46), while the inclusion of poetic content in this section of the Chronicle, remarkable enough in its own right, is even more pronounced in the context of the sparse prose surrounding the poems. While the prose annals abandon the considerable level of detail evident in the preceding tenth-century annals, they do maintain the territorial interests

---

82 See Dumville, 'Æthelstan, First King of England,' 146; Stafford, 'Annals of Æthelflæd,' 103; and Foot, *Æthelstan*, 37–40.
83 Bately, *MS A*, 69.
84 Dumville, 'Æthelstan, First King of England,' 142.
85 *EHD* I, 110.
86 Stafford, *Unification and Conquest*, 6.

evident in that early material, albeit in a different register. Aside from local notices of ecclesiastical office, these annals record only changes in kingship or military action in border areas. 933A, for example, states that King Æthelstan harried Scotland by land and sea, while the annals for 944 and 945 show King Edmund asserting his power in Northumbria and Cumbria. Despite their brevity, these prose annals repeat the attention to dynastic succession and territorial control evident in the Edwardian annals and the Mercian Register even though they do not contain the same systematic attention to geographical movement.

The Chronicle poems in turn forge a link between land and ruler through their celebration of instrumental English victories under dynastic heroes. As Renée Trilling has recently argued, the first Chronicle poems are 'case-specific instruments of West Saxon ideology, inscribed into the official collective memory of Anglo-Saxon England.'[87] The two poems entered at 937 (*The Battle of Brunanburh*) and 942 (*The Capture of the Five Boroughs*) are historically-situated texts designed to publicize and preserve a specific idea about kingship and the relationship between ruler and realm. Both poems celebrate the protection or acquisition of territory by West Saxon kings just as they reiterate a line of legitimate succession, and by implication, the transmission of dynastic land within that line. The surrounding prose annals work with the poems to inscribe the protection and extension of *anweald* through the activity of individual royal figures over time.

The appearance of poetry in what has hitherto been a collection of prose annals introduces poetic diction and meter to the Chronicle, an innovation which contextually underscores the significance of those events commemorated in verse. Recent critical responses to the Chronicle poems have frequently regarded them as expressions of an emerging English nationalism driven by West Saxon interests.[88] In this view, the poems function as political texts which continue the Chronicle's ideological program of championing the West Saxon dynasty. As Trilling has observed, the first Chronicle poems connect 'the ruling Wessex dynasty to a long tradition of heroism and victory.'[89]

---

87 Trilling, *Aesthetics of Nostalgia*, 213.
88 Janet Thormann, for example, has claimed that 'the poems produce the idea of a national history that legitimizes West-Saxon power as national authority' ('*Chronicle* Poems,' 66). Thomas Bredehoft has argued that *Brunanburh* 'continues the dynastic focus of the Edwardian annals and the Mercian Register, but in the broader context of a nationalizing narrative' while *Capture* continues 'the focus on dynastic succession and English nationalism' within the Chronicle (*Textual Histories*, 102 and 103). See also Scragg, 'A Reading of *Brunanburh*.'
89 Trilling, *Aesthetics of Nostalgia*, 173.

But why might such a development have occurred in the Anglo-Saxon Chronicle at this particular time using this particular material? Panegyric verse committed to royal heroism could easily have found suitable matter in the reigns of both Alfred and Edward – the Chronicle records important victories for both kings which would seem just as worthy of special treatment. What made the particular accomplishments of Æthelstan and Edmund worthy of celebration in traditional vernacular verse? And why might this particular verse have been deemed fitting for inclusion in the Anglo-Saxon Chronicle?

One explanation might be found in the precedent and influence of contemporary Latin writings. A substantial number of Latin texts, including some occasional poems and a group of stylistically ambitious charters, survive from Æthelstan's reign while traces of other works now lost suggest a much larger corpus of Latin writing from the period.[90] William of Malmesbury, for example, mentions a long Latin poem composed in Æthelstan's time, while a Glastonbury library catalogue lists the item 'bella Etheltani regis' – neither work survives.[91] The two extant occasional poems, however, significantly celebrate both Æthelstan's military strength and his widespread territorial authority. *Carta dirige gressus*, probably the earlier of the two texts, seems to have been written in commemoration of Æthelstan's successful northern campaign in 927. Æthelstan at that time received the submission of Constantine II (r. 900–43) and other northern kings, signifying his dominion in the north.[92] The poem celebrates Æthelstan's rule over a complete kingdom ('perfecta Saxonia') now that he has proven his strength across all of Britain ('per totum Bryttanium').[93] A second poem, *Rex pius Æðelstan*, survives in a gospel book (London, BL, Cotton Tiberius A. ii) which was produced on the continent sometime during the late ninth or early tenth century but later donated to Christ Church, Canterbury by King Æthelstan.[94] The

90 See Robinson, *Times of Saint Dunstan*, 25–80; Lapidge, 'Schools, Learning and Literature in Tenth-Century England,' 16–24; and Gretsch, *Intellectual Foundations*, 332–83.
91 See Lapidge, 'Some Latin Poems'; Zacher, 'Multilingualism at the Court of King Æthelstan'; and Foot, *Æthelstan*, 251–8.
92 See Stenton, *Anglo-Saxon England*, 339–40; Lapidge, 'Some Latin Poems,' 78–80; and Foot, *Æthelstan*, 18–20 and 160–4.
93 Lapidge, 'Some Latin Poems,' 86.
94 See Keynes, 'King Athelstan's Books,' 147–53; and Gretsch, *Intellectual Foundations*, 337–9. The manuscript may have come to England sometime after the marriage of Otto I (r. 936–73) to Edith, daughter of Edward the Elder and Æthelstan's half-sister, in late 929 or early 930. For the prose preface which accompanies the poem, see pp. 154–5 above.

poem primarily celebrates the donation itself, but it also praises Æthelstan's military might in lines which may allude to the famed battle at Brunanburh: God has elevated Æthelstan 'ut ualeat reges rex ipse feroces / uincere bellipotens, colla superba terens' (so that this king himself, strong in war, might conquer defiant kings, treading upon their arrogant necks).[95] With their praise of the king's military triumphs and expansive dominion, these two poems suggest a court culture interested in royal panegyric with a specific attention to territorial and military power.[96] Such a Latin tradition might well have inspired the production of similar verse in English for inclusion within the vernacular environment of the Chronicle.[97]

Æthelstan's reign also witnessed a number of prominent developments in the production of Latin diplomas. Eric John observed that Æthelstan was the first king 'to grant bookland over the length and breadth of England,'[98] a fact which testifies to the extent of the king's territorial power. Moreover, when the regular production of royal diplomas resumed during Æthelstan's reign after the hiatus from 910 to 924, the documents displayed several innovative new features: 'Extant originals are large in format – partly because of increased text-size but chiefly as a result of the substantial numbers of witnesses ... and they are written in a script new to the charter-tradition, the Anglo-Saxon Square minuscule which was just reaching an advanced stage of development as a canonical script ... These royal charters are, then, striking documents which differ dramatically in appearance from their ninth-century counterparts.'[99] Royal diplomas at the time also began to assume a general uniformity in constitutive elements and manuscript layout while the vernacular boundary clause became a standard component of the document.[100] These several developments demonstrate an interest in the ways in which the rights of possession might be memorialized in a solemn written object.

---

95 Lapidge, 'Some Latin Poems,' 83 and 85n158. This line might also be a reference to the submissions recorded in the Anglo-Saxon Chronicle, s.a. 926, but not if the manuscript had traveled to England after the marriage between Otto and Edith in 929/30. See also Foot, *Æthelstan*, 94–5.

96 For Æthelstan as a 'patron of poets,' see Foot, *Æthelstan*, 110–17.

97 For an argument that the tenth-century Chronicle verse was influenced by contemporary Norse skaldic poetry, see Townend, 'Pre-Cnut Praise-Poetry in Viking Age England.' See also Frank, 'Did Anglo-Saxon Audiences Have a Skaldic Tooth?'; and Niles, 'Skaldic Technique in *Brunanburh*.'

98 John, *Orbis Britanniae*, 46.

99 Dumville, 'Æthelstan, First King of England,' 153.

100 See Thompson, *Anglo-Saxon Royal Diplomas*, 27–49.

In addition to these structural innovations, Æthelstan's diplomas were distinguished by the infusion of an elaborate literary diction within a formulaic prose environment. As we have seen, between 928 and 935 the draftsman known as 'Æthelstan A' transformed the style of royal diplomas through his ambitious use of hermeneutic Latin.[101] The proem in particular became a space within the diplomatic text for rhetorical and lexical display. S 425, a single-sheet diploma dated to 934, begins with a remarkable proem which is typical of the draftsman's elaborate style:

> Fortuna fallentis sæculi procax non lacteo inmarciscibilium liliorum candore amabilis . sed fellita hejulandæ corruptionis amaritudine odibilis foetentis filios valle in lacrimarum carnis . rictibus debacchando venenosis mordaciter dilacerat . quæ quamvis arridendo sit infelicibus adtractabilis Acherontici ad ima Cociti ni satus *alti subveniat boantis* . impudenter est decurribilis . et ideo quia ipsa ruinosa deficiendo tanaliter dilabitur . summopere festinandum est ad amoena indicibilis lætitiæ arva . ubi angelica ymnidicæ jubilationis organa . mellifluaque vernantium rosarum odoramina . a bonis beatisque naribus inestimabiliter dulcia capiuntur . sineque calce . auribus clivipparum suavia audiuntur.[102]

[The wanton fortune of the deceiving world, not lovely with the milky-white radiance of unfading lilies but odious with the galling bitterness of woeful corruption, raging with venomous jaws tears with its teeth the sons of fetid flesh in the vale of tears; although with its smiles it may be alluring to the unfortunate, it brazenly leads down to the lowest depths of Acherontic Cocytus unless the offspring of the High-Thunderer should intervene. And so because that ruinous [fortune] mortally fades away in its failing, one must especially hasten to pleasant fields of ineffable joy where the angelic music of hymnal jubilation and the mellifluous scent of blooming roses are sensed as sweet beyond measure by good and blessed noses and heard by ears as the delights of musical instruments without end.]

'Æthelstan A' has taken the allotted space for the proem, traditionally a brief opening meditation on some conventional theme, and exploded it in an effusive blast of ornate Latin. Donald Bullough and Michael Lapidge have both suggested a range of sources for the rarified vocabulary of the 'Æthelstan A' charters, including Aldhelm, Orosius, and the *Hisperica*

---

101 For a more detailed discussion of 'Æthelstan A,' see pp. 37–46 above.
102 S 425. *BCS*, vol. 2, no. 702 at pp. 402–3. Emphasis added.

Famina. Lapidge has pointed out, for example, that the adverb *tanaliter* is found elsewhere only in the 'Saint-Omer Hymn,' a Breton-Latin poem,[103] while Bullough has suggested a link between 'Æthelstan A' and the *Famina* based upon their common use of *Cocitus* in association with adjectival *Acheronticus*.[104] Moreover, the exceptionally enigmatic word *clivipparum* appears only in this particular proem.[105] This use of obscure vocabulary and arresting imagery introduces an elevated diction within a standardized prose environment. The proem in S 425 also displays some rhetorical embellishment through tmesis in the phrase 'alti subveniat boantis,' where the noun *altiboantis* (the High-Thunderer) is split by the verb *subveniat*. Chiasmus also appears arranged in clusters of three at the beginning and end of the proem. This figural and lexical ornamentation produces an intense moment of literary display within a composite text dedicated to demonstrating the enduring right of possession.

The royal titles in Æthelstan's charters also employ elevated diction to proclaim an expansive dominion for the king.[106] Beginning in 891, King Alfred's diplomas replaced the traditional 'Occidentalium Saxonum rex' (king of the West Saxons) with the new 'Anglorum Saxonum rex' (king of the Anglo-Saxons).[107] This new title envisioned a more extensive political authority for the West Saxon dynasty and it would become standard nomenclature in the diplomas of King Edward the Elder.[108] Æthelstan's early diplomas also maintain the title of 'Angul Saxonum rex,'[109] but beginning in 930 his diplomas introduce grander designations of kingship. A single-sheet charter dated to 931, for example, names Æthelstan 'rex Anglorum per omnipatrantis dexteram totius Bryttaniæ regni solio sublimatus' (King

---

103 Lapidge, 'Israel the Grammarian,' 95.
104 Bullough, 'Educational Tradition in England,' 305.
105 The word is defined as '(?) a sort of musical instrument' in *DMLBS*, s.v. 'clivippa.' The proem appears in a group of Æthelstan's diplomas issued between 28 May 934 and 21 December 935. See, Keynes, *Diplomas*, 44. Of the group, only S 425 survives in a contemporary form. S 407 (*BCS*, vol. 2, no. 703 at p. 405) mistakenly supplies *divipparum* for *clivipparum*, perhaps indicating the word's unfamiliarity to a later scribe. S 1166, a twelfth-century forgery ostensibly issued by Cenfrith, *comes* of the Mercians, to Aldhelm in 680, borrows the proem but notably omits the phrase 'clivipparum suavia' (Kelly, *Malmesbury*, no. 2 at p. 132).
106 See Foot, *Æthelstan*, 25–8, 197, and 212–26.
107 Keynes, 'West Saxon Charters,' 1147–8.
108 S 369, dated to 903, clearly distinguishes between Edward as 'Angul Saxonum rex' and his grandfather, King Æthelwulf, as 'occidentalium Saxonum rex' (king of the West Saxons). Kelly, *Abingdon*, no. 19 at p. 81.
109 S 394 (A.D. 925), 396 (A.D. 926), and 397 (A.D. 926).

of the English, raised up to the throne of the kingdom of all Britain by the right hand of the All-Accomplishing) while the witness list dubs him as 'florentis Bryt[t]aniæ monarchia præditus rex'[110] (king gifted with the absolute rule of flourishing Britain). This amplified nomenclature marks a stylistic turn in West Saxon diplomatic as royal titles imagine a dominion over all of Britain (totius Britanniae) which is expressed in ostentatious language. Another set of diplomas beginning in 935 maintains this vision of an all-encompassing sovereignty endorsed by God, naming Æthelstan 'nodante Dei gratia basileus Anglorum et equæ totius Bryttanniæ orbis curagulus'[111] (bound by the grace of God, king of the English and equally ruler of all the lands of Britain). These rhetorical flourishes, common throughout the 'Æthelstan A' charters, dignify the king by affirming his political dominion in grandiose terms; David Dumville described these royal styles as 'noticeably self-conscious, parading extravagant but by no means wholly insubstantial claims to quasi-imperial standing.'[112] Elevated style thus serves an ideological purpose.

The 'Æthelstan A' charters maintain the general form of the diploma, then, but substantially elevate the register of the document through their inclusion of specialized vocabulary and expansion of regular components such as the proem and the royal title. The stylized language of these charters glorifies the authority of the king to dispense land in writing, and it likewise enhances, at least in theory, the document's authority in demonstrating the legitimate and lasting possession of property. Later diplomas would retain some of the embellishments and amplifications pioneered by 'Æthelstan A,' although they would rarely assume the rhetorical exuberance evident in those charters produced under King Æthelstan. Still, many diplomas issued under kings Edmund and Eadred maintained the precedent of elaborate proems and ambitious royal nomenclature. Such embellishments became regular diplomatic practice in the tenth century, and by 950 – the terminus ante quem for the first two Chronicle poems – royal diplomas had become established as both functional and artistic texts. Latin diplomas, then, provide a prominent example of a conventional prose genre in Anglo-Saxon England which experienced significant stylistic innovation in the first half of the tenth century. These texts continued to represent the conveyance and possession

---

110 S 416. BCS, vol. 2, no. 677 at pp. 363 and 364.
111 S 430. BCS, vol. 2, no. 707 at p. 412. This title also appears with some variation in S 429, 431, 438, 440, 446, and 448.
112 Dumville, 'Æthelstan, First King of England,' 153.

of property, but they did so in elevated language which substantially amplified the grandeur of the document.

In sum, the conveyance and possession of property received aesthetic ornamentation in Æthelstan's charters, and diplomas from the 930s through the 950s continued to render claims upon land in self-consciously artistic language. These developments in diplomatic production provide a compelling analogue for the Chronicle's turn to verse: *Brunanburh* was composed sometime between 937 and 950 when it was copied into MS A; *Capture of the Five Boroughs* in turn must have been composed sometime between 942 and 950. In addition to their common practice of writing territorial boundaries, then, the vernacular Chronicle and Latin diplomas display a similar move toward formal and stylistic elaboration at approximately the same time. Diplomatic innovations altered the style and register of the document without disturbing its original form and purpose; the introduction of poetry to the Chronicle similarly alters the style of that text while still maintaining its established annalistic form. The 'Æthelstan A' charters and vernacular poetry furthermore both employ a specialized diction, and both bring complexities of imagery, vocabulary, and syntax which are in marked contrast to their more prosaic precedents. I do not mean to suggest a model of direct influence in which annalists consciously imitated the style of contemporary Latin diplomas, but rather a set of circulating discursive practices and priorities which was not limited to one particular group of texts or mode of writing. It is this diffuse tenurial discourse, I argue, that informs the Chronicle's innovative combination of prose and verse and its interest in dynastic territory and continuity in those annals dedicated to Æthelstan and Edmund.

Annals 924–46A were entered by a single hand working in one stint sometime around 950 and can subsequently be read as a contained unit.[113] The 924 annal records the death of Edward and succession of Æthelstan, omitting any reference to Ælfweard's brief moment on the throne (present in MS B); as we have seen, this omission facilitates a narrative of uninterrupted dynastic succession populated by effective and accepted leaders.[114]

---

113 Dumville, 'The Anglo-Saxon Chronicle and the Origins of English Square Minuscule Script,' 62–6. See also Dumville, 'English Square Minuscule Script: The Mid-Century Phases,' 144–51.

114 William of Malmesbury mentions that Æthelstan's succession met with some initial resistance. Æthelstan was crowned at Kingston in 924, William says, 'quamuis quidam Elfredus cum factiosis suis, quia seditio semper inuenit complices, obuiare temptasset' (despite the opposition of a certain Alfred and his supporters [for sedition is never in

933A records Æthelstan's military success in Scotland, establishing the king's efficacy in policing territorial borders. These brief annals – the only two in MS A to mention Æthelstan prior to the poem for 937 – effectively shorthand two of the key priorities evident in annals 900–46AB: royal succession and territorial control.

The poem entered s.a. 937, the longest of all the Chronicle poems, introduces the distinct diction and meter of vernacular verse to what has hitherto been a prose environment. *The Battle of Brunanburh* contains a range of highly conventional poetic vocabulary and expressions along with stock motifs such as the beasts-of-battle.[115] In this way, the piece conspicuously places itself within a recognizable poetic tradition. Sarah Foot has argued that the poem 'was by design highly contrived; its author sought deliberately to write in a manner different from everyday speech, more rhetorical and pointed than the workaday prose of the conventional annal.'[116] This careful employment of literary language to distinguish new content parallels the dramatic introduction of hermeneutic Latin in Æthelstan's royal diplomas. In both situations, artistic language dignifies strategic claims to territorial authority within an official text.

Brunanburh continues the attention to both the defence of territory and dynastic succession which is so evident in the earlier tenth century annals. In the early lines of the poem, Æthelstan and Edmund appear both as Edward's worthy heirs and as able guardians of the kingdom:

afaran Eadweardes,   swa him geæþele wæs
from cneomægum,   þæt hi æt campe oft
wiþ laþra gehwæne   land ealgodon,
hord and hamas.[117] (7–10a)

[Edward's heirs, as it was natural for them from their noble descent, that they in battle often protected land, treasure, and homes against any enemy.]

---

want of support]). William of Malmesbury, *Gesta regum Anglorum*, 1:206 and 207 (ii.131). S 436, a spurious Malmesbury charter dated to 937, also mentions a foiled plot to blind Æthelstan at Winchester (see Kelly, *Malmesbury*, no. 28 at pp. 225–7).
115 Campbell, *Brunanburh*, 38–42.
116 Foot, 'Where English Becomes British,' 129. Scragg, by contrast, argues that the 'many stock syntactic patterns' in the poem 'suggest a certain limitation on the poet's range and lexical variety' ('A Reading of *Brunanburh*,' 115).
117 Bately, *MS A*, 70–1.

While Æthelstan and Edmund are the rightful keepers of *land*, *hord*, and *hamas*, the allied Scots and Danes have come seeking *land*, arriving from 'ofer æra gebland / on lides bosme land gesohtun' [over the mingling waves in a ship's bosom, they came for land] (26b–27).[118] The stakes of the battle are territorial. The poem commemorates the English victory in part through its account of enemy forces driven from the island: the poem revels in detailing how the invading forces were cut down and disgraced in the battle, lingering over the particular losses and humiliations of the two enemy leaders, Anlaf and Constantine. The enemy survivors, shamed and beaten, can only flee to their ships and return to lands elsewhere:

> Gewitan him þa Norþmen   nægledcnearrum,
> dreorig daraða laf,   on Dingesmere
> ofer deop wæter   Difelin secan,
> Ᵹ eft Hiraland,   æwiscmode.[119] (53–6)

[Then the Northmen, the downcast survivors of spears, took themselves to nailed vessels, out onto Ding's Mere to seek Dublin over the deep water, back to Ireland, shamed in spirit.]

Brunanburh here features a pattern of events similar to that found in annal 914A/915B: a large enemy force arrives by sea only to be beaten back and then driven off the land entirely by the West Saxons and their allies. 914A/915B's stylized account of enemy humiliation as the diminished *sciphere* is driven from the mainland and forced to retreat back to Ireland thus anticipates the narrative trajectory of the 937 poem. Both texts affirm English control over territory, but *Brunanburh* more explicitly links that control to the ability and authority of royal leaders. Prominently featured in the poem, Æthelstan and Edmund lead the West Saxons to victory whereas the 914A/915B annal does not directly celebrate Edward as heroic war-leader.

In contrast to the beaten retreat of the invaders, Æthelstan and Edmund enjoy a triumphant homecoming: 'Swilce þa gebroþer begen ætsamne, / cyning Ᵹ æþeling, cyþþe sohton, / Wesseaxena land, wiges hremige' [Just as the brothers both together, king and ætheling, sought their home, the land of the West Saxons, triumphant in the fight] (57–9).[120] The opposition between

---

118 Ibid., 71.
119 Ibid., 72.
120 Ibid.

the glorious West Saxon leaders and their downcast enemies – linked by *swilce* at lines 37 and 57 – is clear. The humiliated invaders are forced off the very land they came to take, while the victorious brothers return to a realm unequivocally their own. The poem's closing lines bolster this claim to the land by linking the current English victory to the legendary past of the Germanic migrations:

> Ne wearð wæl mare
> on þis eiglande   æfer gieta
> folces gefylled   beforan þissum
> sweordes ecgum,   þæs þe us secgað bec,
> ealde uðwitan,   siþþan eastan hider
> Engle ⁊ Seaxe   up becoman,
> ofer brad brimu   Brytene sohtan,
> wlance wigsmiþas,   Weealles ofercoman,
> eorlas arhwate   eard begeatan.[121] (65b–73)

[Nor was there a greater slaughter of a people felled by the edges of swords ever yet on this island before this, as books tell us, old scholars, since the Angles and Saxons came here from the east, sought out Britain over the broad sea, bold makers of war overcame the Britons, glorious warriors took the land.]

These lines portray the arrival of the Anglo-Saxons as a foundational moment in which the Germanic peoples claim their new homeland.[122] Even though they came as invaders from across the sea much like the ignoble *Norðmen* repelled at Brunanburh had done, the poem distinguishes the Angles and Saxons with positive epithets such as 'wlance wigsmiþas' and 'eorlas arhwate.' The adjective *arhwæt* appears only in *Brunanburh* and can be translated as 'glory-bold' or 'active in glory, active and glorious.'[123] The noun *ar* can signify honour, worth, or glory, but in a legal sense it can

---

121 Ibid.
122 Nicholas Howe influentially argued that the *adventus Saxonum* served as a myth of cultural origin for the Anglo-Saxons and that its invocation in *Brunanburh* 'signifies that they remain worthy to hold the island that had been won by their ancestors' (*Migration and Mythmaking*, 31).
123 *DOE*, s.v. 'arhwæt.' See also Campbell, *Brunanburh*, 121n73. Campbell suggests that 'the likeliest meaning of *arhwæt* is "abounding in glory," "glorious."'

also mean 'landed property' or the possession of that property.[124] This unique poetic compound couples the idea of personal distinction with the holding of property. The poem suggests in a single word that the *eorlas* of old were worthy of the homeland they gained, just as the contemporary scions of the West Saxon dynasty are worthy holders of that same *eard* (73b). This ancestral *eard* historically prefigures the *land* placed under the protection of Æthelstan and Edmund in the poem's first lines. *Brunanburh* memorializes an important military victory for the English, but it also establishes a historical basis for the lasting authority of West Saxon kings over their collective lands.

Æthelstan's victory at Brunanburh demonstrated his ability to meet an organized allied threat to the kingdom's northern borders.[125] The Chronicle poem represents that event as a resounding victory for the West Saxon and Mercian forces, locating the impetus for that victory in both the present worthiness of Æthelstan and Edmund and the legendary precedent of the *adventus Saxonum*. The historical reality of the battle itself, however, must have been both more complex and more costly. The *Annals of Ulster*, for example, record a staggering number of casualties on both sides: 'Bellum ingens lacrimabile atque horribile inter Saxones atque Norddmannos crudeliter gestum est, in quo plurima milia Nordmannorum que non numerata sunt, ceciderunt, sed rex cum paucis euassit, id est Amlaiph. Ex altera autem parte multitudo Saxonum cecidit. Adalstan autem, rex Saxonum, magna uictoria ditatus est'[126] (A huge war, lamentable and horrible, was cruelly waged between the Saxons and Norsemen. Many thousands of Norsemen beyond number died although King Anlaf escaped with a few men. While a great number of the Saxons also fell on the other side, Æthelstan, king of the Saxons, was enriched by the great victory). Like the Chronicle poem, the annal contrasts Æthelstan's victory against Anlaf's retreat with only a few survivors, but the statement of heavy losses among the English challenges

---

124 *DOE*, s.v. 'ar (C.1 and C.3).'
125 For the significance of the battle and its enduring reputation, see Foot, *Æthelstan*, 169–83; and the various essays in Livingston, *The Battle of Brunanburh: A Casebook*.
126 Mac Airt and Mac Niocaill, *Annals of Ulster*, 384 and 386. Abbreviations expanded. The *Annals of Ulster* were compiled in the late fifteenth century from older materials, with annals written in both Irish and Latin. Alfred P. Smyth speculated that the 'earliest account of the battle may well be that in the *Annals of Ulster*, which is unusually long and includes details which by comparison even with other Irish entries is very extensive' (*Scandinavian York and Dublin*, 2:36). In Smyth's opinion the entry preserved in the *Annals of Ulster* represents a contemporary account written perhaps even before the Chronicle poem.

the monolithic triumphalism of the poem. Within the composite text of the Chronicle, *Brunanburh* provides an ideological fantasy of heroic glory and territorial power. As Trilling has recently argued, 'The poem simultaneously creates and reifies the image of the classical warrior king, and that image quickly becomes more important than the mere reality of the battle itself.'[127] That image of a warrior king is founded in no small part on dynastic continuity and the expansive reach of royal dominion, an ideal which conflates genealogy and territorial right.

Æthelstan's hard-won victory in 937 ensured the security of his far-flung polity during his lifetime. Æthelstan ruled over more territories and peoples than any of his predecessors and he successfully secured the kingdom's borders to the north and west. Not surprisingly, Æthelstan was well remembered by Anglo-Norman chroniclers for these substantial achievements. William of Malmesbury, for example, states that after his consecration Æthelstan, 'ne spem ciuium falleret et inferius opinione se ageret, omnem omnino Angliam solo nominis terrore subiugauit, preter solos Northanimbros' (intent on not disappointing the hopes of his countrymen and falling below their expectations, brought the whole of England entirely under his rule by the mere terror of his name, with the sole exception of the Northumbrians).[128] Æthelstan rectified this situation soon enough after the death of his Northumbrian ally Sihtric by invading the north and receiving the submission of several kings there in 927.[129] After enforcing his authority in the north, William says, Æthelstan then fixed his western border in the south at the Tamar and Wye rivers.[130] Æthelstan inherited an already enlarged kingdom, but he also realized the territorial ambitions of the West Saxon house to an unprecedented extent.[131] The Chronicle account of that dynastic inheritance and territorial expansion uniquely enables a record of progressive growth and an uninterrupted realization of ancestral right to land.

After Æthelstan's death in 939 Edmund faced renewed aggression in the north from Anlaf Guthfrithson, the same Norse leader who had been defeated at Brunanburh in 937. Anlaf gained control of the region known as

---

127 Trilling, *Aesthetics of Nostalgia*, 199.
128 William of Malmesbury, *Gesta regum Anglorum*, 1:212 and 213 (ii.134).
129 Sihtric was married to Æthelstan's sister. See Anglo-Saxon Chronicle MS D, s.a. 925 and 926 (Cubbin, *MS D*, 41); and Lapidge, 'Some Latin Poems,' 79–80. These events are not recorded in MSS AB.
130 William of Malmesbury, *Gesta regum Anglorum*, 1:216 (ii.134).
131 See Foot, *Æthelstan*, esp. 212–26.

the Five Boroughs, whose inhabitants had been part of the English state for two decades but were now under Norse rule. Stenton described the event as 'an ignominious surrender ... the first serious reverse suffered by the English monarchy since Edward the Elder began his great advance against the southern Danes.'[132] Chronicle manuscripts A and B say nothing of these events, noting only that Edmund succeeded Æthelstan in 939. By way of contrast, MS D includes Edmund's territorial loss in its record that the Northumbrians gave their allegiance to Anlaf in 941.[133] This omission in MSS AB maintains the narrative of uninterrupted succession and expansion initially begun in the Edwardian annals. Annals 900–46AB thus present a highly selective account of a bounded domain held securely over time under the *anweald* of the West Saxon dynasty. As we have seen, the elisions and emphases evident in these annals both conceal and reveal various disputes and reversals in the Chronicle's ideological narrative as it strategically writes the dynastic realm through a series of internal and external conflicts which are successfully contained by effectively heroic kings.

Edmund's succession after Æthelstan's death appears in annal 940A, but the first full entry for his reign offers a verse commemoration of his liberation of the Five Boroughs in 942. Like *Brunanburh*, this poem employs a distinct literary form and lexis to celebrate a king's ability to secure territory. The poem lauds Edmund with a number of epithets, beginning and ending with the half-line, 'Eadmund cyning' (1a and 13b). Within its several appositive titles for the king, the poem contains a catalogue of place-names for the Five Boroughs, followed by a description of the Anglo-Danes now freed from heathen bondage:

Her Eadmund cyning,   Engla þeoden,
maga mundbora,   Myrce geeode,
dyre dædfruma,   swa Dor scadeþ,
Hwitanwylles geat   ꠃ Humbra ea,
brada brimstream.   Burga fife,
Ligoraceaster   ꠃ Lindcylene
ꠃ Snotingaham,   swylce Stanford,
eac Deoraby.   Dæne wæran ær
under Norðmannum   nyde gebegde
on hæþenra   hæfteclommum

132 Stenton, *Anglo-Saxon England*, 357. See also Smyth, *Scandinavian York and Dublin*, 2:89–106.
133 Cubbin, *MS D*, 43.

lange þraga,   oþ hie alysde eft
for his weorþscipe   wiggendra hleo,
afera Eadweardes,   Eadmund cyning.[134]

[Here King Edmund, prince of the English, defender of men, bold doer of deeds, conquered Mercia, bounded by the Dore, Whitwell Gap, and the Humber river, a broad waterway, and five boroughs: Leicester, Lincoln, and Nottingham, as well as Stamford and Derby. The Danes previously had been under the Northmen, pressed by need into heathen bonds for a long time until King Edmund, Edward's heir, protector of warriors, through his worthiness freed them again.]

The greater part of the poem – 18 of its 26 half-lines – consists of either appositive phrases for Edmund or specific place-names and locations. The Dore, Whitwell Gap, and the Humber River 'marked the western and northern limits' of Edmund's push into Mercia,[135] and their notation here reinscribes the territorial limits of West Saxon authority. The envelope pattern on 'Eadmund cyning' links land to ruler, structurally placing the region of the Five Boroughs both within Edmund's authority and within specific geographical markers. The poem declares the extension of political authority over a specific region and its people, noting specific place-names (the Five Boroughs) and linear features (the river Humber) in order to establish a bounded territory. *Capture* thus exhibits two important textual strategies: (re)writing the bounds of the realm through the activity of a dynastic hero, and celebrating a king's territorial control through classical verse. This dual appearance of written bounds and stylistic display – two discursive methods which also appear in contemporary diplomas – demonstrates how different aspects of tenurial discourse can converge in a single poetic text.

The declaration of Edmund as Edward's heir in the poem's final line situates him within the genealogy of West Saxon kings, but it also directly links Edmund and his accomplishments to the work – specifically the protection and expansion of the realm – begun by his father. In Stenton's assessment, *Capture* was 'the first political poem in the English language, and its author understood political realities.'[136] Indeed, the political sense evident in the poem and throughout annals 900–46AB is clearly founded

---

134 Bately, *MS A*, 73.
135 Dobbie, *Minor Poems*, xlii. See also Hill, *Atlas of Anglo-Saxon England*, no. 102 at p. 60.
136 Stenton, *Anglo-Saxon England*, 359.

on the concept of *anweald* and its fusion of dynastic continuity with territorial dominion.[137]

The final three annals for Edmund's reign, all in prose, record his conquests in Northumbria (s.a. 944) and Cumbria (s.a. 945), his death in 946, and the succession of his brother Eadred in that same year. The 946 annal states that Eadred enforced his *geweald* in Northumbia and also received oaths from the Scots 'that they would do all that he wanted'; the annal's paratactic sequence of events assumes an immediate transition in kingship with no disruption of territorial power whatsoever.[138] These prose annals accordingly work in conjunction with the poem to maintain the Chronicle's steady attention to territorial power and royal succession.

946AB says nothing of Edmund's murder as it was recorded in later sources: Edmund was reportedly stabbed at the feast of St Augustine by a thief who had returned to England after exile.[139] The early Chronicle manuscripts omit this tragedy of a young king's life cut short. Indeed, such an event would most certainly have undercut the Chronicle's ongoing narrative of dynastic glory and progress.[140] The final three annals for Edmund's reign, then, even though they lack the methodical documentation evident in the Edwardian and Mercian annals, clearly maintain the attention to land and dynastic continuity established in the earlier tenth-century annals. The selective content in these short annals collaborates with the poems to write the bounds of the domain as they change over time, inscribing those geographic limits through the actions of effective royal leaders. Despite the pronounced change in style in 924–46A, the Chronicle continues to write the bounds of the domain through its accumulative record of the actions of triumphant dynastic protagonists.

---

137   See also Scragg, 'A Reading of *Brunanburh*,' 117.

138   'Her Eadmund cyning forðferde on Sanctes Agustinus mæssedæge, ⁊ he hæfde rice seofoþe healf gear. ⁊ þa feng Eadred æþeling his broþor to rice ⁊ gerad eal Norþhymbra land him to gewealde, ⁊ Scottas him aþas sealdan, þæt hie woldan eal þæt he wolde' (Bately, *MS A*, 74) [Her King Edmund died on St Augustine's Day, and he had the kingdom six and a half years. And then his brother, *æþeling* Eadred, succeeded to the kingdom and brought all Northumbria under his power, and the Scots gave him oaths that they would do all that he wanted]. The annal's double affirmation of Eadred as both *æþeling* and Edmund's brother might be an attempt to underscore Eadred's legitimacy as the next king, especially since Edmund was survived by two young sons, Eadwig and Edgar.

139   See Anglo-Saxon Chronicle MS D (s.a. 946) and MS E (s.a. 948); William of Malmesbury, *Gesta regum Anglorum*, 230–3 (ii.144); and John of Worcester, *Chronicle*, 398.

140   On the narrativity of annals, see Foot, 'Finding the Meaning of Form: Narrative in Annals and Chronicles.'

Historians have long recognized that the West Saxon rulers were careful stewards of their land resources as they worked to control the transmission of property and kingship within the family line.[141] We can see these same priorities at work in the tenth-century Anglo-Saxon Chronicle's own commitment to dynastic continuity and proprietary interests. The Chronicle's attention to *anweald* furthermore takes on significant tenurial and documentary aspects. Annals 900–46AB share with tenth-century diplomas a specific mode for writing land in the vernacular and for constituting an idea of bounded land which can then be passed into longstanding human possession. This story of inherited territory also functions in a way analogous to the tenth-century charter accounts of local property dispute and their resolution of family conflict: these annals show the West Saxon line resolving or containing disputes from within their own house at crucial moments. Furthermore, the introduction of verse in these annals parallels the development of literary ornamentation in contemporary diplomas. In these several ways, this unit of the Anglo-Saxon Chronicle, completed by the mid-tenth century, participates in broader cultural practices of writing land, both in its stylistic and discursive methods and in its attempt to contain or obscure dispute, disruption, and loss. The Chronicle, however, imagines land much differently than the tenurial modes evident in royal diplomas and narrative charters. The idea of *anweald* becomes a dynamic concept in the Chronicle for asserting the hereditary possession of accumulated lands and peoples over time. The Anglo-Saxon Chronicle may share certain techniques and concerns with established tenurial texts, but it writes land on the more ambitious scale of the royal domain.

---

141 See Dumville, 'Æthelstan, First King of England,' 151–3; Nelson, 'Reconstructing a Royal Family'; Wormald, '*On þa wæpnedhealfe*'; and Stafford, 'Succession and Inheritance.'

5 Poetic Possession

Custodite leges meas atque iudicia et facite ea ne et vos evomat terra quam intraturi estis et habitaturi.[1]

– Leviticus 20:22

ᛟ (eþel) byþ oferleof   æghwylcum men,
gif he mot ðær rihtes   and gerysena on
brucan on bolde   bleadum oftast.[2]

– *The Rune Poem*

While the previous two chapters have considered how tenurial discourse informs various instructive and ideological writings in English, this final chapter looks to manifestations of that same discursive field in vernacular poetry. This chapter specifically examines the significance of tenurial language and tropes in the poems *Guthlac A* and *Deor*. While these texts do not include direct references to legal documentation, each one cultivates lexical and topical elements which are grounded in the language and mechanisms of Anglo-Saxon tenurial practice. Dates of original composition for these two poems remain uncertain, but because each text appears solely in the Exeter Book, written most probably during the 960s or 970s, we may assume some circulation for the poems in the tenth century and consequently consider how these

---

1 Fischer, *Biblia sacra*, 163–4. 'Keep my laws and my judgments and observe them lest the land which you are to enter and inhabit should vomit you out.'
2 Dobbie, *Minor Poems*, 30. 'A homeland is over-dear to any man if he may enjoy in his house what is right and proper in lasting prosperity' (71–3).

texts might have resonated within that specific historical horizon.[3] This contextualization preserves my general interest in texts composed or copied in the tenth century without taking on questions of dating or authorial intent, and it allows me to situate literary texts within a particular field of cultural activity and interest, that is, the legal and rhetorical conventions of property.

Guthlac A and Deor employ legal and tenurial vocabulary toward different illustrative ends. Guthlac A uses property dispute as a narrative device to demonstrate sanctity, imagining the acquisition of contested land as a transformative and salvatory experience. Deor in contrast presents the loss of land as a kind of social erasure. This negative element culminates in the poem's resonant use of landriht, a word which appears in several legal texts as well as in several Old English poems, including Beowulf, Genesis A, and Exodus. I argue that Deor exploits the full range of the word's connotative legal and poetic senses in order to imagine dispossession as a trauma which effaces identity. Both Guthlac A and Deor engage key issues which have been considered in previous chapters – the link between land and status, the metaphorical potential of property, the problem of dispute, and the threat of forfeiture – but they do so in legendary spaces insulated in part from contemporary social pressures. I read these texts as poetic fantasies which draw upon and contribute to the symbolic weight of property within the Anglo-Saxon cultural imaginary. Moreover, each poem presents its tenurial conceit in extreme terms: because land signifies power, its possession (or lack thereof) accordingly shapes identity through the most intense forms of social elevation or exclusion. In this sense, each poem articulates the deep-seated and determinative value of property in Anglo-Saxon England.

Guthlac A: Salvation and the Productive Dispute

In Guthlac A, property dispute and land tenure become conceptual fields for modeling the endurance of faith and the reward of salvation through the figure of St Guthlac. The poem presents property dispute as spiritually productive, but it does so in part by imagining a scenario in which contested ground is entirely cleansed of competing claims. Even as the text advances this fantasy of perfect settlement and uncontested possession, however, it also presents forfeiture as the necessary precedent of

---

3 For the Exeter Book, see Sisam, 'The Exeter Book'; Conner, Anglo-Saxon Exeter; Gameson, 'Origin of the Exeter Book'; and Butler, 'Glastonbury and the Early History of the Exeter Book.'

possession. The places that Guthlac gains both on earth and in heaven were previously held by those fallen angels who rebelled against God – the saint's own entitlement is achieved through their deprivation, a narrative turn which imports disquieting implications about the vulnerability of holding land. The poem's conflation of land tenure and salvation in this way maintains the social qualification that possession is always contingent on one maintaining a set of obligations to the power who granted the property. Within its positive account of a saint rewarded with land and eternal salvation, then, *Guthlac A* maintains many of the negative or limiting elements common to tenurial discourse.

The legend of St Guthlac (c. 674–714) is perhaps best known for its protagonist's dramatic showdown with a troop of demons in the Crowland fens on the borderland of Mercia and East Anglia. Guthlac had spent his young life as a Mercian warrior, but at the age of twenty-four he abandoned the military vocation and entered the religious life at Repton. Two years later Guthlac searched the Crowland fens for a suitable hermitage and there he found an ancient barrow where he made his home. The saint afterwards defended himself against the temptations and assaults of resident spirits in order to maintain his solitary habitation. Guthlac remained at his wilderness retreat until his death, performing miracles and receiving visitors who sought his spiritual guidance and abilities. The legend of St Guthlac appears in several Anglo-Saxon texts, including the eighth-century Latin *uita* by Felix,[4] a vernacular prose translation of that text,[5] a homiletic text in the Vercelli Book,[6] and the two Old English poems in the Exeter Book (known respectively as *Guthlac A* and *Guthlac B*).[7] Guthlac's cult produced an impressively substantial corpus of commemorative material.

Among this corpus of texts, *Guthlac A* is remarkable for its sustained attention to the saint's confrontation with the demons.[8] The element of territorial contest in the poem has attracted significant scholarly

---

4 Colgrave, *Life of Saint Guthlac*, hereafter *VSG*. See also Colgrave, 'Earliest Saints' Lives,' 51–5.

5 Gonser, *Prosa-Leben*. The text survives in an eleventh-century manuscript: London, BL, Cotton Vespasian D. xxi, fols. 18–40v (Gneuss 657).

6 *VH*, 381–94 (Vercelli Homily 23). See also Zacher, *Preaching the Converted*, 225–68.

7 Roberts, *Guthlac Poems*. Guthlac also appears in the Old English Martyrology and the Anglo-Saxon Chronicle, s.a. 714. See Roberts, 'An Inventory of Early Guthlac Materials.'

8 This episode resembles the story of Cuthbert battling demons for the possession of Farne Island. See Colgrave, *Two Lives of Saint Cuthbert*, 96–7 and 214–17. Bede gives a much more detailed account of the conflict and cleansing (at ch. 17) than the earlier anonymous *uita*. For Felix's sources, see Love, 'Vita S. Guthlaci (L.E.2.1).'

interest, particularly to the ways in which the poem enfolds the political and spiritual in its account of conflict on *mearclond*,[9] but thus far less attention has been given to the poem's integration of tenurial language and mechanisms.[10] Through its strategic deployment of legal vocabulary – particularly words concerned with estate management and dispute settlement – *Guthlac A* emplots property dispute, typically a source of anxiety, as a transformative and salvatory activity. The poem furthermore compresses that motif into a single transformative contest which ends in a way which is free of lingering complications or the potential for renewed conflict.

Guthlac A begins with a meditation on the soul's journey to heaven and the individual perseverance needed to achieve salvation. For inspiration in this endeavour, the poet evokes the example of the saints,

ða þe him to heofonum   hyge staþeliað,
witon þæt se eðel   ece bideð
ealra þære mengu   þe geond middangeard
dryhtne þeowiað   ond þæs deoran ham
wilniað bi gewyrhtum.   Swa þas woruldgestreon
on þa mæran god   bimutad weorþað,
ðonne þæt gegyrnað   þa þe him godes egsa
hleonaþ ofer heafdum.[11] (66–73a)

[those who fix their mind on heaven, and those who know that the homeland endures as eternal for the host of all those who serve the Lord throughout the world and through their works aspire to that dear home. So these worldly treasures will be exchanged for those glorious goods, when those over whose heads leans the fear of God yearn for them.]

---

9   Jones, 'Envisioning the *Cenobium*'; O'Brien O'Keeffe, 'Guthlac's Crossings'; Cohen, *Medieval Identity Machines*, 116–53; Siewers, 'Landscapes of Conversion'; Michelet, *Creation, Migration, and Conquest*, 47–9 and 163–97; and Johnson, 'Spiritual Combat and the Land of Canaan in *Guthlac A*.'

10 David Johnson has recently observed that the poem's topos of spiritual warfare 'is specifically defined as territorial in nature' ('Spiritual Combat and the Land of Canaan in *Guthlac A*,' 308). For a more extensive discussion of tenurial themes in the poem, see Clark, 'Land Tenure in *Guthlac A*.' Clark sees 'Anglo-Saxon concepts of permanent and precarious tenure' as fundamental to the poem.

11 All citations from *Guthlac A* are from Krapp and Dobbie, *The Exeter Book*, 49–72.

The statement that 'worldly treasures will be exchanged for glorious goods' echoes a common theme in diplomatic proems from the seventh through the eleventh centuries.[12] Such statements are scriptural in basis and by no means unique to diplomatic discourse, but their appearance early in *Guthlac A* in proximity to ideas of service, reward, and land introduces a tenurial register to the text's presentation of salvation. The poem frames salvation as a territorial share in an everlasting hereditary land (*eðel ece*) which the faithful must earn through resolve and struggle. The image of *godes egsa* looming over the faithful furthermore suggests the divine sovereign's dual power to entitle or deprive, much like the possession and forfeiture of bookland was a prerogative of earthly kings. Moreover, the references to the fallen angels which appear later in the poem provide a negative example of this same logic as God punishes the rebel angels by casting them out of their seats in heaven. These vacant seats consequently become available to mankind through the gift of salvation, which is itself envisioned as a grant of land within eternal space. Guthlac's dispute at the *beorg* thus provides an exemplum which illustrates the gift of salvation as a territorial reward facilitated through the past forfeiture of others. In this paradigm the stress of worldly struggle is sublimated within an ideal of property dispute as a process both perilous and purifying.

The textual relationship between Felix's *uita* and *Guthlac A* remains uncertain,[13] but a preliminary comparison of the two texts can clarify the particular ways in which *Guthlac A* employs its tenurial topos in an exemplary mode.[14] Whereas Felix situates the confrontation between Guthlac and the demons within a definite historical and geographical environment,[15] the poem largely removes such specificity in favour of a more symbolic stage. *Guthlac A* predominantly focuses on the conflict between the lone saint and the throng of demons at a *beorg* – a conflict which is clearly framed as a struggle over land – but the topographical nature of this site is

---

12 See pp. 26–7 above.
13 Roberts, *Guthlac Poems*, 19–23. Roberts is sceptical of a direct link between Felix's *uita* and *Guthlac A* while still acknowledging that 'a great part of the poem (ll. 93–748) loosely resembles Felix's account of the saint's struggles against demons' (ibid., 19). See also Gerould, 'Old English Poems on St. Guthlac'; Kurtz, 'From St. Antony to St. Guthlac'; and Roberts, '*Guthlac A*: Sources and Source Hunting.'
14 Michelet observes generally that, 'Guðlac's fight against the demons is territorial at heart and the motif of land possession is of paramount importance in the poem' (*Creation, Migration, and Conquest*, 164). She does not expand, however, on the basis or significance of that importance.
15 See O'Brien O'Keeffe, 'Guthlac's Crossings.'

sketched in the broadest of strokes. First described as a *beorgseþel* (102a), and later simply as a *beorg* (140a), the place is revealed to Guthlac by God:

> Wæs seo londes stow
> bimiþen fore monnum,   oþþæt meotud onwrah
> beorg on bearwe,   þa se bytla cwom
> se þær haligne   ham arærde,
> nales þy he giemde   þurh gitsunga
> lænes lifwelan,   ac þæt lond gode
> fægre gefreoþode,   siþþan feond oferwon
> Cristes cempa. (146b–53a)

[The place of the land was concealed from men until the Creator revealed a mound in the wood when the builder arrived, the one who raised up a holy home there; he did not at all yearn with greed for the transitory wealth of the world, but he fairly protected that land for God after he had overcome the enemy as Christ's champion.]

The passage presents Guthlac not only as a *miles Christi*, but also as an agent capable of transforming and stewarding the land. He is a builder (*bytla*) who constructs a holy dwelling in the waste as well as one who protects (*gefriðian*) the land for God. The verb *friðian* also notably appears in *Gerefa*, a vernacular prose treatise on a reeve's duties in administering his lord's estate.[16] The sensible reeve, the treatise advises, should above all consider the foundational maxim, 'Hede se ðe scire healde, þæt he friðige ⁊ forðige ælce be ðam ðe hit selest sy'[17] (He who holds the office should take care that he protect and foster everything according to what is best for it). Guthlac fulfils a similar role in the poem, watching over the land as his Lord's faithful servant in expectation of a final reward, much like the speaker in the preface to the *OESol* hopes for the transformative grant of bookland after his own faithful service.[18]

---

16 For *Gerefa*, see Bethurum, 'Episcopal Magnificence in the Eleventh Century'; and Harvey, 'Rectitudines Singularum Personarum and Gerefa.'

17 Liebermann, *Gesetze*, 1:453.

18 Stephanie Clark underscores the point that Guthlac receives land in return for his service: 'As God's warrior, Guthlac is given a right to the land in return for his service of displacing the usurpers and thereafter keeping watch over the land faithfully for God rather than claiming it as his own independent domain. At this point the land is not confirmed to him as a permanent dwelling. The outcome of his service will determine the permanence of the grant' ('Land Tenure in *Guthlac A*'). In this sense, the poem

Despite its suggestive vocabulary of land and its use, the above passage attends more closely to the quality of Guthlac's conduct and character than to the nature of the place itself. The *beorg* becomes a figurative space in the poem, a staging ground for Guthlac's sanctity. This abstract description of place differs a great deal from the more detailed account in Felix. The *uita* says that Guthlac, inspired by his reading about 'priscorum monachorum solitariam vitam' (the solitary life of monks of former days), seeks out a *heremum* (desert) of his own.[19] He finds a suitable *solitudinem* in the fens between Mercia and East Anglia, a region which Felix describes in some detail.[20] He learns of an island within the marshland from Tatwine, a local man with some knowledge of the area. Guthlac travels there on a fisherman's skiff, and recognizing the place as a gift from God, decides to make it his permanent home.[21] After a thorough exploration, he returns to Repton and spends ninety days there before returning to his retreat. Guthlac then makes his wilderness home upon a plundered *tumulus* on the island: 'Erat itaque in praedicta insula tumulus agrestibus glaebis coacervatus, quem olim avari solitudinis frequentatores lucri ergo illic adquirendi defodientes scindebant, in cuius latere velut cisterna inesse videbatur; in qua vir beatae memoriae Guthlac desuper inposito tugurio habitare coepit' (Now there was in the said island a mound built of clods of earth which greedy comers to the waste had dug open, in the hope of finding treasure there; in the side of this there seemed to be a sort of cistern, and in this Guthlac the man of blessed memory began to dwell, after building a hut over it).[22] In Felix,

---

draws upon the same notions of service and obligation which are evident in other Anglo-Saxon tenurial texts (see pp. 117–35 above).

19 *VSG*, 86 and 87.

20 'Est in meditullaneis Brittanniae partibus inmensae magnitudinis aterrima palus, quae, a Grontae fluminis ripis incipiens, haud procul a castello quem dicunt nomine Gronte, nunc stagnis, nunc flactris, interdum nigris fusi vaporis laticibus, necnon et crebris insularum nemorumque intervenientibus flexuosis rivigarum anfractibus, ab austro in aquilonem mare tenus longissimo tractu protenditur' (There is in the midland district of Britain a most dismal fen of immense size, which begins at the banks of the river Granta not far from the camp which is called Cambridge, and stretches from the south as far north as the sea. It is a very long tract, now consisting of marshes, now of bogs, sometimes of black waters overhung by fog, sometimes studded with wooded islands and traversed by the windings of tortuous streams). Ibid.

21 'Igitur, adamato illius loci abdito situ velut a Deo sibi donato, omnes dies vitae suae illic degere directa mente devoverat' (He loved the remoteness of the spot seeing that God had given it him, and vowed with righteous purpose to spend all the days of his life there). Ibid., 88 and 89.

22 Ibid., 92–5.

Guthlac settles within a barrow, a landscape feature which indicates that the place had once been inhabited, or at the very least used, in the past. The detail that the *tumulus* had been opened by grave-robbers also signifies an additional, later presence on the island. Despite its presentation as a *heremum*, then, the site was both known to those living nearby and marked by traces of earlier human activity.[23]

Guthlac A employs very little of this material from Felix. The poem gives limited topographical detail and omits entirely any description of Guthlac's travel to his retreat. God directs Guthlac to the site, not Tatwine, and. Felix's account of the opened *tumulus* is only indirectly suggested (perhaps) in the statement that Guthlac did not choose the location based on a greed for worldly treasures (150–1a). Nonetheless, the use of the word *beorg* does suggest, at least initially, that the saint's new home was on a burial mound.[24] *Beorg* means 'hill' in its most general sense, but in charters the word frequently indicates a burial mound or barrow.[25] The Old English translation of Felix renders *tumulus* as *hlæw*,[26] a more precise word for barrow, but *beorg* is clearly attested in other poetic texts as a burial mound.[27] While it may lack the political and geographical specificity found in Felix, the landscape in *Guthlac A* still carries some trace of an earlier presence which implies a latent but potentially competitive claim to the land.

That rival element manifests in the poem through the many attacks from the demons which infest the place. These *ealdfeondas* struggle against the saint's intrusion into their habitat and attempt to dislodge

---

23 For a topographical and historical discussion of the area, see O'Brien O'Keeffe, 'Guthlac's Crossings,' 5–8.

24 The exact nature and significance of the *beorg* in *Guthlac A* has generated a good deal of critical discussion. See Liebermann, 'Ueber ostenglische Geschichtsquellen,' 245–7; Shook, 'The Burial Mound in *Guthlac A*'; Reichardt, '*Guthlac A* and the Landscape of Spiritual Perfection'; Wentersdorf, '*Guthlac A*: The Battle for the *Beorg*'; Siewers, 'Landscapes of Conversion'; and Reynolds, *Anglo-Saxon Deviant Burial Customs*, 247–50.

25 *DOE*, s.v. 'beorg.' The second meaning offered is 'barrow, tumulus, burial mound (both Saxon and pre-Saxon burial mounds; freq. in charters).' See also Grinsell, 'Barrows in the Anglo-Saxon Land Charters'; Semple, 'A Fear of the Past'; Williams, 'Monuments and the Past in Early Anglo-Saxon England'; and Gelling and Cole, *Landscape of Place-Names*, 145–52. Roberts maintains that *beorg* is simply a hill in *Guthlac A* even though she accepts the meaning of 'grave' for the same word in line 1193b of *Guthlac B* (*Guthlac Poems*, 20–2, 132, and 186).

26 Gonser, *Prosa-Leben*, 117.

27 See, for example, *Beowulf*, line 3163: 'Hi on beorg dydon beg ond siglu' (*Klaeber's Beowulf*, 108) [They put rings and jewels in the barrow].

him from the contested spot.²⁸ The fiends had 'þær ær fela / setla ge-
sæton' [established many residences there before] (143b–4a) and they
clearly view Guthlac as a trespasser on land which they consider to be
their own. In one provocative act early in the poem, Guthlac ascends
the *beorg* and raises a cross there to sanctify the *wong* (175–80). This
dual act of claim and consecration drives the demons into a frenzy of
relentless feud:

> þonne mengu cwom
> feonda færscytum   fæhðe ræran.
> Ne meahton hy æfeste   anforlætan,
> ac to Guðlaces   gæste gelæddun
> frasunga fela. (185b–9a)

[Then a host of enemies came to raise feud with sudden shots. In their malice they
were unable to let it go and they brought many temptations to Guthlac's spirit.]

This site of conflict and temptation, however, is also figured as a generative
space. The poet pauses to tell us that the place where Guthlac faced so
many dangers was the same one where '[f]rome wurdun monge / godes
þrowera' [many of God's martyrs became brave] (181b–2a). Guthlac's feud
helps him to gain personal salvation, but it also prepares a space for later
devotion to the Christian faith. Salvation and sanctity emerge from territorial dispute, demonstrating once again the ready consonance between
land and salvation in Anglo-Saxon texts.

Despite the presence of the demons at the *beorg*, the poem presents the
area as empty and inaccessible, a space in need of a more worthy tenant:

> Stod seo dygle stow   dryhtne in gemyndum
> idel ond æmen,   eþelriehte feor,
> bad bisæce   betran hyrdes. (215–17)

[The hidden place remained empty and uninhabited in the Lord's mind, far
from hereditary right. It awaited the claim of a better steward.]

---

28 *Ealdfeond*, which only appears in poetry, literally means 'old enemy' although the word
    is frequently translated in the plural as 'demons' or 'devils' (*DOE*, s.v. 'ealdfeond').

The words *eþelriht* and *bisæce* deserve special comment. *Eþelriht* occurs only three times in the extant corpus, in each case denoting a right to ancestral or hereditary land.[29] The phrase 'eþelriehte feor' suggests that the disputed *stow* is not only distant from any existing *eðel*,[30] some actual place, but also far removed from the condition of being an ancestral territory attached to any kindred or community – the land is void of any established traditional rights or expectation of possession. The *ealdfeondas* do not hold the land by hereditary right, then, but are temporary tenants with no legitimate or lasting claim. The immediately preceding lines make this point clear:

> þær hy bidinge,
> earme ondsacan,   æror mostun
> æfter tintergum   tidum brucan,
> ðonne hy of waþum   werge cwoman
> restan ryneþragum,   rowe gefegon;
> wæs him seo gelyfed   þurh lytel fæc.[31] (209b–14)

[where they, wretched adversaries, before could enjoy respite for a time after torments, when they came weary from wanderings to rest during stolen moments, savouring the silence. This was allowed to them for a short while.]

The demons' occupation of the place represents only a temporary relief from their ceaseless wandering. They cannot 'on eorþan eardes brucan' [enjoy earthly land], the poem states, and they are 'hleolease hama þoliað'

---

29 See *DOE*, s.v. 'eþel (1.a).' *Eþelriht* appears only in *Guthlac A* (216b), *Exodus* (211b), and *Beowulf* (2198a). In *Beowulf* the word refers to the Geatish realm under the joint rule of Hygelac and Beowulf; in *Exodus* it refers to the Promised Land. For the emotive force and range of *eðel* in Old English, see Howe, 'Looking for Home in Anglo-Saxon England,' 147.

30 Roberts recommends the interpretation of geographical distance here (*Guthlac Poems*, 137). Jones interprets the phrase as pertaining more specifically to Guthlac's socio-legal position: 'In effect, he has removed himself from the sphere of his clan's protection and placed himself under God's *wær*' ('Envisioning the *Cenobium*,' 281). I propose that the phrase more specifically indicates the tenurial condition of the land itself.

31 The noun *biding* is a hapax legomenon, appearing only at line 209b of *Guthlac A*. The *DOE* defines the word as 'an abode' but also indicates that it is related to the verb *bidan*, which primarily means 'to wait, stay, remain, dwell' (*DOE*, s.v. 'biding' and 'bidan'). In the context of the passage above the word implies a temporary dwelling with an expectation (or hope) of enduring possession. For the demons, of course, this expectation will be denied.

[without shelter and lack homes] (220–2). The *ealdfeondas* are drifters, finding only fleeting refuge on land that has yet to be claimed into heritable possession by any party. The contested *beorg* at this point remains an unformed tenurial space charged with potential energy: 'vacant' yet overrun by demonic squatters, 'empty' but awaiting its proper tenant.

This element of expectancy is most evident in the statement that the place 'bad bisæce betran hyrdes' [awaited the claim of a better steward] (217). The word *bisæce* presents a noteworthy example of legal diction in the poem. Roberts glosses the word as a feminine noun (*bisacu*) meaning 'dispute,' while Bosworth and Toller define the related *bisæce* as 'a visit' or 'persecution, dispute, litigation.'[32] The Wulfstanian treatise known as *Episcopus*, for example, states, 'gif ðær hwæt bisæces sy, seme se biscop'[33] (if there be some dispute, let the bishop settle it). The *DOE* defines the word as 'subject to legal process; disputed, contested' and lists four occurrences which include three Wulfstanian legal texts and *Guthlac A*.[34] In each case the word clearly has a legal resonance tied to matters of dispute. The related form *unbesacen* appears widely in charter descriptions of individual estates, where it consistently means 'undisputed.' An early eleventh-century survey of lands in Yorkshire, for example, indicates that a certain piece of plough land at *Ectune* is 'unbesacen agenland'[35] (undisputed land held in proprietary right). *Unbesacen* can also indicate a settled dispute, as when Leofwine promises Bishop Godwine in S 1456 that a contested estate will revert *unbesacen* to Rochester after his death.[36] The word also occurs with the same meaning in

---

32   BT, s.v. 'bisæce.' BTs, s.v. 'bisæce' gives 'a visitation' as a possible definition, citing *Guthlac A* as its sole example.

33   Whitelock, Brett and Brooke, *Councils and Synods*, 1:417–22 at 421 (ch. 12). *Episcopus* appears in Oxford, Bodleian Library, Junius 121 (Gneuss 644) where it is inserted within *Institutes of Polity*. A Latin version also appears in the *Quadripartitus*. See Wormald, '*Quadripartitus*'; and Wormald, *Making of English Law*, 242 and 391–2. *Quadripartitus* translates the vernacular passage cited above as, 'Et si aliquid controuersiarum intersit, discernat episcopus' (Liebermann, *Gesetze*, 1:479, emphasis added).

34   *DOE*, s.v. 'bigsæc.' In *Guthlac A* the word is 'of uncertain meaning and etymology: dispute (if *bigsacu*); visit, visitation (if *bigsēc*); or possession, taking possession (if emended to *bigsæt*)' (a.ii).'

35   S 1461a. Robertson, *Anglo-Saxon Charters*, no. 84 at p. 166. The text appears in a gospel-book, York, Minster Library, Add. 1 (Gneuss 774), written in a late tenth- or early eleventh-century script on 'the verso of the last page of St John's gospel' (Robertson, *Anglo-Saxon Charters*, 413). *Agenland* appears only in this text with three separate occurrences.

36   See chapter 2 for a discussion of this text. The word indicates that the property is to return without challenge upon termination of a lease. Similar examples include S 1280, 1454, and 1464.

Cnut's law-codes in reference to issues of land and inheritance.[37] In *Guthlac A*, 'bad bisæce betran hyrdes' introduces the legal language of dispute to the poem's account of contested ground. The land 'awaits' a productive dispute which will both demonstrate Guthlac's sanctity and provide an instructive metaphor in which salvation appears as a territorial reward won through faith and perseverance.

The poem consequently presents the clash at the *beorg* as a hybrid of property dispute and spiritual warfare. The demons try to drive away Guthlac by testing the limits of his faith and their attacks come primarily through speech and accusation:

> wæron teonsmiðas   tornes fulle,
> cwædon þæt him Guðlac   eac gode sylfum
> earfeþa mæst   ana gefremede,
> siþþan he for wlence   on westenne
> beorgas bræce. (205–9a)

[Filled with gall the slander-smiths said that besides God himself Guthlac alone had brought them the greatest trouble when he stormed the hills in the wilderness on account of pride.][38]

The description of the demons as *teonsmiðas* (a hapax legomenon) presents them as skilled artisans of accusation and slander.[39] The dispute is very much a battle of words and rhetorical attack.[40] Moreover, the demons project their own nature onto Guthlac and then ironically censure those same qualities – the poem later reveals, for example, that the fiends are without permanent place precisely because of their own pride. By using the verb *brecan* ('bræce,' 209a) the demons also portray Guthlac's arrival in the wilderness as a violent invasion. The verb generally denotes an act of

---

37 II Cnut 72 and 79 (Liebermann, *Gesetze*, 1:358 and 366).
38 The plural *beorgas* indicates hills rather than a barrow. The landscape of the poem begins to change.
39 The demons are later described as *edwitsprecan* (speakers of scorn) who use *tornum teoncwidum* (bitter slander) against the saint (447–8).
40 Laurence K. Shook regarded the poem as more a debate than narrative ('Burial Mound,' 2). This assessment calls attention to the many formal speeches in the poem in which Guthlac answers the charges and temptations of the demons.

aggression or destruction,[41] but it can also signify broken or ploughed ground.[42] The demons present the saint as a forceful interloper who has come to plunder and exploit their land.

Actual violence in the poem, however, is largely sublimated within aggressive speech. 'Godes ondsacan' [God's adversaries] (233b) can only attack Guthlac's spirit through cruel words, *hearmstafas* (229a) and *sarstafum* (234a), for they are not permitted to kill Guthlac or drive him away through physical force (226–8a). The saint in turn defends himself with discourse. Guthlac responds to the demons' threats with the claim that, bolstered by faith, he will drive the demons from the land. 'Mæg ic þis setl on eow / butan earfeðum ana geðringan' [I can wrest this seat from you, alone and without difficulty] (244b–5), he says, and build there his own 'hus and hleonað' [house and shelter] (251a).

> Gewitað nu, awyrgde,   werigmode,
> from þissum earde   þe ge her on stondað,
> fleoð on feorweg.   Ic me frið wille
> æt gode gegyrnan;   ne sceal min gæst mid eow
> gedwolan dreogan,   ac mec dryhtnes hond
> mundað mid mægne.   Her sceal min wesan
> eorðlic eþel,   nales eower leng. (255–61)

[Go now from this land on which you here stand, you accursed and downcast things, and flee on a far-off track. I will seek peace with God. My spirit shall not suffer error through you, for the Lord's hand protects me with its might. Here shall my earthly homeland be, yours no longer.]

Guthlac ends this speech by claiming a hereditary right to the land (*eorðlic eþel*) through the agency and protection of God,[43] a claim which is predicated on the displacement of the fiends. Possession can only come through the dispossession of others. The poem also

---

41   *DOE*, s.v. 'brecan' offers 'destroy; to break into; to take (something *acc.*) by storm; to break (something *acc.*) down' (2, 3a, 3b, 4b).

42   *DOE*, s.v. 'brecan' (7). The vernacular prose translation of Felix notably uses 'bræcon' to render Felix's 'scindebant' (tear, dig open) in its description of the plundered *hlæw* (Gonser, *Prosa-Leben*, 117).

43   Line 261a (*eorðlic eþel*) contains the second occurrence of *eðel* in the poem, effectively echoing the word's first appearance at line 67 (*eðel ece*) within a passage which conflates tenure and salvation.

significantly introduces Guthlac's speech with the half-line, 'Guðlac him ongean þingode' (239a), a statement which frames his words as part of a legalistic exchange within the negotiation of a dispute.[44] The use of *þingian* implies that the debate between saint and demons is working toward some kind of settlement, but the process is instead marked by intractable verbal aggression and rhetorical force. Neither party will concede or compromise.

The demons, riled and wailing in indignation, surround the *beorg* as their advocates, 'feonda foresprecan' (265a), formally respond to Guthlac's claim:

> Ðu þæt gehatest   þæt ðu ham on us
> gegan wille,   ðe eart godes yrming.
> Bi hwon scealt þu lifgan,   þæh þu lond age?
> Ne þec mon hider   mose fedeð;
> beoð þe hungor ond þurst   hearde gewinnan,
> gif þu gewitest   swa wilde deor
> ana from eþele.   Nis þæt onginn wiht!
> Geswic þisses setles! (271–8a)

[You promise that you will take a home from us, you who are God's wretch. How shall you live even if you do own the land? No one will bring you food here. Hunger and thirst will be hard opponents for you if you go off alone from your homeland like the wild animals. That is no kind of plan! Give up this seat!]

The demons' representatives mock Guthlac's rhetoric of ownership, casting his still hypothetical possession ('þæh þu lond age,' 273b) as a hard and lonely inheritance; indeed, their use of *eðel* (277a) seems a derisive rebuttal of Guthlac's aggressive claim in 261a. Moreover, the appearance of the word *foresprecan* (265a) importantly introduces another legal term from dispute settlement. In Anglo-Saxon law, the *forespreca* acted as a legal representative who performed 'duties as mediator, intercessor, and advocate' for another party.[45] A *forespreca* would typically represent his client's interests before a higher authority, such as the king or an assembly of powerful persons, and attempt to win a favourable judgment for them. This term, in conjunction with *þingian*, implies that the debate is working toward some kind of settlement, but the exchange of speeches, claims, and

---

44 See BT, s.v. 'þingian (II).'
45 Rabin, 'Old English *Forespeca*,' 236. See also *DOE*, s.v. 'forespreca.'

counter-claims remains a dispute without an arbiter, a verbal quarrel with no resolution in sight.

The back-and-forth contest eventually culminates in the baleful demons carrying Guthlac to the entrance of hell (*heldore*) where they torment him with more *torncwidum* (cutting speech) in the hope of bringing the saint to despair.[46] They taunt Guthlac by telling him that his many sins have already excluded him from a place in heaven – he will never receive 'heah-getimbru / seld on swegle' [high halls, a seat in the sky] (584b–5a). The fiends thus threaten the saint with dispossession and the possibility of being without place, the very condition which they themselves must endure. Guthlac's defiant answer dramatically reveals his tormentors to be the fallen angels who lost their own place in heaven after their revolt against God.[47] The restless spirits are homeless because they long ago had defied the divine sovereign. This revelation represents a decisive moment in the dispute by establishing an originary precedent for dispossession – the first forfeiture in heaven prefigures and justifies the subsequent loss of place on earth. Guthlac's rebuke grimly frames divine punishment as enforced forfeiture, a penalty paid for treason against God as Ruler:

Sindon ge wærlogan,   swa ge in wræcsiðe
longe lifdon,   lege bisencte,
swearte beswicene,   swegle benumene,
dreame bidrorene,   deaðe bifolene,
firenum bifongne,   feores orwenan,
þæt ge blindnesse   bote fundon.
Ge þa fægran gesceaft   in fyrndagum,
gæstlicne goddream,   gearo forsegon,
þa ge wiðhogdun   halgum dryhtne.
Ne mostun ge a wunian   in wyndagum,
ac mid scome scyldum   scofene wurdon

---

46 Lines 557–78 at 574b. For the prominence of this confrontation in the poem, see Hill, 'The Middle Way.' Hill examines two key (and spatially apt) temptations in the poem – 'the first when the demons lift Guthlac up in the air to see the sins of others, and the second when they draw him down to the gates of hell' – as tests of pride and terror (ibid., 183). Hill notes parallels of this same pattern in Gregory's *Moralia in Job* and in Felix.

47 This identification is repeated in lines 658–72. The fallen have lost their place in God's kingdom 'for þam oferhygdum þe eow in mod astag / þurh idel gylp ealles to swiðe' [because of the arrogance which excessively rose up in your spirit through idle boasting] (661–2); consequently they have 'þurh deopne dom dream afyrred, / engla gemana' [through solemn judgment been expelled from joy (and) the company of angels] (669–70a).

fore oferhygdum   in ece fyr,
ðær ge sceolon dreogan   deað ond þystro,
wop to widan ealdre;   næfre ge þæs wyrpe gebidað.⁴⁸ (623–36)

[You are traitors, so you have long lived in exile, plunged in flame, darkly deceived – deprived of the heavens, bereft of joy, consigned to death, ensnared in sins, hopeless of life – that you might find a remedy for blindness. In days long past you eagerly renounced a beautiful creation, spiritual joy in God, when you rejected the holy Lord. You could not live forever in pleasant days, but with shame in your crimes you were shoved into the eternal fire because of pride, where you must perpetually endure death, darkness, and lamentation; you will never have respite from it.]

These lines show a significant amount of embellishment. Beginning in 624 there are four consecutive lines of double alliteration with interlinear alliteration on *f* in lines 626–7 and lines 628–9. This sequence of lines furthermore features end rhyme on -*ene* across four consecutive half lines (625–6) as well as the chiming repetition of the prefixes *bi*- and *be*- across six consecutive half lines (624b–27a). In addition to this condensed cluster of ornamentation there is double alliteration at lines 630, 633, and 636; beginning at line 627 this effect furthermore occurs at regular intervals, falling on every third line. The elevated style in this passage amplifies its contents: the fallen angels have exchanged eternal joy for endless torments through their defiance of God. The empty seats they left behind in heaven now await those faithful who can win their way to eternal salvation.⁴⁹ Guthlac trusts that his faith and perseverance will earn him such a place:

               Eom ic soðlice
leohte geleafan   ond mid lufan dryhtnes
fægre gefylled   in minum feorhlocan,
breostum inbryrded   to þam betran ham,
leomum inlyhted   to þam leofestan
ecan earde,   þær is eþellond
fæger ond gefealic   in fæder wuldre,

---

48 Emphasis added.
49 See Haines, 'Vacancies in Heaven,' 153. Haines concludes that Anglo-Saxon texts generally depict 'the doctrine of replacement as a resettlement of the abandoned realms of heaven' (ibid.).

ðær eow næfre   fore nergende
leohtes leoma   ne lifes hyht
in godes rice   agiefen weorþeð,
for þam oferhygdum   þe eow in mod astag
þurh idel gylp   ealles to swiðe.
Wendun ge ond woldun,   wiþerhycgende,
þæt ge scyppende   sceoldan gelice
wesan in wuldre.   Eow þær wyrs gelomp,
ða eow se waldend   wraðe bisencte
in þæt swearte susl,   þær eow siððan wæs
ad inæled   attre geblonden,
þurh deopne dom   dream afyrred,
engla gemana.   Swa nu awa sceal
wesan wideferh,   þæt ge wærnysse
brynewylm hæbben,   nales bletsunga. (651b–72)

[Truly I am fairly filled in my inner soul with the light of faith and the love
of the Lord, fired in my heart for the better home, charged with light for
the most beloved eternal country where the homeland is, fair and delight-
ful in the glory of the Father, where neither the radiance of light before the
Saviour nor the hope of life in God's kingdom will ever be granted to you
because of the arrogance which excessively rose up in your spirit through
idle boasting. Set on opposition, you fancied and yearned that you should
be like the Creator in glory. It turned out worse for you there, when the
Ruler in his wrath plunged you into that dark torment where afterwards
flame was ignited for you, chased with poison, and where by solemn verdict the joy and the fraternity of angels were removed from you. It shall
ever and always be so, that you have the seething fire of damnation and no
blessings whatsoever.]

These lines conceptualize the promise of salvation as the promise of land
given in eternal and hereditary right (*ecan eard* and *eþellond*, line 656). The
first seven lines of this passage feature double alliteration with sustained
consonance on the 'l' sound – this pattern notably breaks at line 658 when
Guthlac turns his attention to the punishment of the rebel angels. This
shift underscores the contrast between Guthlac's salvation, figured as a
form of eternal possession, and the damnation of the fallen angels, which
is conversely figured as dispossession and deprivation. The displaced devils are denied a secure place in either the heavenly or the earthly domain.
They must suffer,

in helle hus,   þær eow is ham sceapen,
sweart sinnehte,   sacu butan ende,
grim gæstcwalu.   Þær ge gnornende
deað sceolon dreogan,   ond ic dreama wyn
agan mid englum   in þam uplican
rodera rice,   þær is ryht cyning,
help ond hælu   hæleþa cynne,
duguð ond drohtað.[50] (677–84a)

[in the house of hell where a home has been created for you, in dark and perpetual night, dispute without end, a grim killing of the soul. There you must suffer death as you mourn, and I shall have the delight of joy among the angels in that upper kingdom of the heavens, where the true king is, the help and salvation of mankind, and where there is camaraderie and community.]

This hellish *ham* represents the dark mirror of 'the better home' which Guthlac will find for himself in heaven (654b). Whereas the heavenly home is held in eternal right, the *helle hus* offers eternal darkness (*sweart sinnehte*) and never-ending dispute (*sacu butan ende*). While Guthlac enjoys perfect peace and community in the light of heaven, the fallen angels must suffer perpetual strife in endless darkness. Guthlac seems to make a decisive claim here – one which significantly goes unanswered by the demons – but his words actually represent just another salvo in a deadlocked argument over possession. The disputants push back and forth to no lasting effect. Guthlac stays put, firm in his resolve and in his faith, and the demons refuse to surrender their claim to the contested ground. Even though the poem clearly places Guthlac in the right, the dispute itself remains a stalemate.

This impasse is dramatically broken when St Bartholomew suddenly appears to arbitrate the dispute. Announcing that he is the judge ('se dema,' 703a) sent by God, Bartholomew quickly and unequivocally decides in favour of Guthlac: 'He sceal þy wonge wealdan, ne magon ge him þa wic forstondan' [He shall control the field, and you cannot defend the dwelling against him] (702). The last direct speech in the poem notably belongs to Bartholomew. Neither Guthlac nor the demons reply to his decision, directly or indirectly – the sentence of the lone

---

50 Every line in this passage features double alliteration.

judge is final and conclusive. Bartholomew's speech furthermore contains a small cluster of legal vocabulary which intensifies the poem's tenurial interests at this key moment. As *dema*, Bartholomew forbids the 'þeostra þegnas' [retainers of darkness] (696a) to defend (*forstondan*) their claim to the land any longer. The verb *forstandan* appears in several law-codes with the meaning 'to defend (someone *acc.*) at law, stand in someone's defense,'[51] and its appearance here adds a particular legal force to Bartholomew's decision. Bartholomew furthermore promises to visit 'þær se freond wunað / on þære socne' [where the friend will live in the *socn*] (715b–16a). *Socn* is a difficult word to translate here.[52] Roberts recommends 'visitation, persecution,' largely based upon the word's use in *Beowulf* 1777a.[53] Considering the scene of arbitration and its attendant cluster of legal vocabulary, however, the well-attested meaning of jurisdiction within a particular area seems more appropriate to the context.[54] As part of the common phrase *sacu and socn* (sake and soke) the word signifies a jurisdictional right to judicial fines and other profits of justice from those people resident in a region.[55] Stephen Baxter has summarized soke as follows:

> Soke rights evolved from early royal support systems: they are a relic of an age of 'extensive lordship', when the dominant mode of surplus extraction

51　*DOE*, s.v. 'forstandan (4b).' The word appears in Ine 62, II Æthelstan 1.5 and 10.1, VI Æthelstan 1.4 and 8.2, I Æthelred 4.2, and II Cnut 33.1a. The application of the verb to a physical location (*þa wic*) in *Guthlac A* line 702b is not entirely consistent with the use of the verb in the law-codes. BTs, s.v. 'forstandan,' cites *Guthlac A*, line 702, as one example for the sense 'to protect from (dat.)' (II.2a). Considering its proximity to *dema* and its appearance within a formal judgment in a property dispute, however, *forstondan* in line 702 clearly carries legal connotations.

52　Shook suggested in passing that *socn* in line 716a 'could imply a political or ecclesiastical territory' ('Burial Mound,' 4). See also BT, s.v. 'socn (VIII)'; BTs, s.v. 'socn'; BTa, s.v. 'socn'; Liebermann, *Gesetze*, 'socn,' s.v. 'Gerichtsbarkeit' (2:454–5); Roffe, 'From Thegnage to Barony'; and Baxter, *Earls of Mercia*, 210–11.

53　Roberts, *Guthlac Poems*, 154–5 and 218. The word appears in Hrothgar's 'sermon': 'Hwæt, me þæs on eþle edwenden cwom, / gyrn æfter gomene, seoþðan Grendel wearð, / ealdgewinna, ingenga min; / ic þære socne singales wæg / modceare micle' (*Klaeber's Beowulf*, 1774–8a at p. 60) [Lo, a reversal came to my homeland, suffering after joy, after Grendel was my invader, an ancient foe; I perpetually endured a great sorrow for that persecution]. *Beowulf* 1777a is the only appearance of the word as a simplex in a verse text other than *Guthlac A* 716a.

54　The meaning of 'a seeking' seems not to fit the context of the lines.

55　See Harmer, *Anglo-Saxon Writs*, 73–8.

was the collection of renders and dues from large land units, centred on royal or princely vills. Those who owed these renders 'sought' the lords of the central vill (*socn* has the primary meaning of 'seeking'); and those who owned the central vills enjoyed rights of soke over those who rendered to them. Kings gradually alienated these rights, and by the mid eleventh century it was possible for several landholders other than the king to possess soke rights.[56]

Other forms of soke might include rights to some of the traditional dues and services (such as seasonal labour or renders in kind) that had long been attached to the land. Line 716a thus suggests that that in addition to receiving land for habitation, Guthlac will also enjoy the fiscal and material benefits generated through possession. Moreover, the close proximity of *sacu* (678b) and *socn* (716a) in the poem sounds a clear legal note through repetition and contrast.[57] The strategic word pair echoes tenurial language at the very moment of arbitration and furthermore underscores the disparity between the constant strife which the demons must endure in hell and the eternal benefits which will be granted to Guthlac. Bartholomew's verdict provides Guthlac with proprietary rights over the land even as it forbids the demons from pursuing their counter-claim further.

The dispute is finally over. The prolonged quarrel which the disputants seemed unable to resolve between themselves could only come to a conclusive end through the intervention of a superior authority.[58] In many ways, this process represents an idealized settlement in which a single authority ends the dispute through a final settlement which erases the trace of competing claims. Just as the property dispute itself has been set in an abstract space, a single supernatural judge settles the case in visionary space, removing the case from historicity. Disputes in Anglo-Saxon England typically involved 'collective judgement in an atmosphere of public witness,'[59] but this aspect of communal deliberation is notably absent in the decision made before the Hell-Mouth in *Guthlac A*. As God's

---

56 Baxter, *Earls of Mercia*, 210. See also Sawyer, '1066–1086: A Tenurial Revolution?'
57 *Socn* appears only at line 716a and *sacu* only at 678b and 300b (as *sæce*).
58 Bartholomew's superior standing is also lexically evident in his description as *ofermæcga* (692b), a hapax legomenon meaning 'illustrious being.'
59 Davies and Fouracre, *Settlement of Disputes*, 216. Patrick Wormald observed that 'in nearly every text the judging, decreeing or settling verb is in the plural: the rhetoric of Anglo-Saxon process remained participatory and communal' ('Charters, Law and the Settlement of Disputes,' 305–6). For the role of support networks in settling feud and dispute in Anglo-Saxon England, see Hyams, *Rancor and Reconciliation*, 71–110, esp. 87–92.

sole representative, Bartholomew passes final judgment while the disputants remain silent. This fantasy of miraculous arbitration suppresses the
complications of lingering interests or the potential re-emergence of old
challenges. The subsequent description of Guthlac as *domeadig* (727a), or
'blessed by judgment,' is apt indeed.[60]

The demons bear Guthlac back 'to þam onwillan eorðan dæle' [to that
desired piece of earth] (728), silently conceding the territorial prize to the
saint. They significantly disappear from the poem at the very moment
Guthlac takes possession of the once-contested ground. Guthlac then
finds the desolate spot transformed into an ideal landscape miraculously
free from traces of past activity or competing interests. What had originally seemed a *locus horribilis*, an empty waste haunted by adversarial
spirits, is now a verdant *locus amoenus*.[61]

> Sigehreðig cwom
> bytla to þam beorge.   Hine bletsadon
> monge mægwlitas,   meaglum reordum,
> treofugla tuddor,   tacnum cyðdon
> eadges eftcyme.   Oft he him æte heold,
> þonne hy him hungrige   ymb hond flugon
> grædum gifre,   geoce gefegon.
> Swa þæt milde mod   wið moncynnes
> dreamum gedælde,   dryhtne þeowde,
> genom him to wildeorum wynne,   syþþan he þas woruld forhogde.
> Smolt wæs se sigewong   ond sele niwe,
> fæger fugla reord,   folde geblowen;
> geacas gear budon.   Guþlac moste
> eadig ond onmod   eardes brucan.
> Stod se grena wong   in godes wære;
> hæfde se heorde,   se þe of heofonum cwom,
> feondas afyrde.   Hwylc wæs fægerra
> willa geworden   in wera life,
> þara þe yldran   usse gemunde,
> oþþe we selfe   siþþan cuþen? (732b–51)

---

60 The *DOE* gives 'blessed with glory, illustrious' as a general definition for *domeadig* (*DOE*,
s.v. 'domeadig'), but in this particular usage the word clearly signifies in multiple ways.

61 For these landscape types see Howe, 'Creating Symbolic Landscapes'; and Curtius,
European Literature and the Latin Middle Ages, 183–202.

[Victorious, the builder came to the mound. Many species and kinds of tree-dwelling birds favoured him with strong voices and by these signals declared the return of the blessed man. Often he held food for them when they were hungry and flew about his hand, greedily eager, and they rejoiced in his help. So that gentle spirit separated himself from the joys of mankind and served the Lord; he found his happiness among the wild creatures after he had put aside this world. The triumphant field was peaceful and the dwelling new, the voice of the birds fair, the earth blossoming; cuckoos rang in the year. Guthlac, blessed and resolute, could enjoy the land. That green field stood under God's covenant; the keeper, the one who had come from heaven, had cast out the enemies. What wish more fair has come to pass in mankind's lifetime, among those which our elders remembered or we later knew ourselves?]

The site of conflict has been transformed. Once a *beorg*, a single location in a desolate landscape, it now assumes a multiplicity of place: it is a plain (*sige-wong* and *grena wong*), a new dwelling place (*sele niwe*), and land for living (*eard*).[62] Guthlac lives alone among the wild animals, untroubled by human challenges to his pastoral holding. This paradisiacal scene notably defies the poem's early statement that all earthly things diminish and decay in time:

Ealdað eorþan blæd   æþela gehwylcre
ond of wlite wendað   wæstma gecyndu;
bið seo siþre tid   sæda gehwylces
mætræ in mægne.   Forþon se mon ne þearf
to þisse worulde   wyrpe gehycgan. (43–7)

[The glory of the earth grows old in each of its noble things, and the nature of its bounties turns away from beauty; the later time of every seed is lesser in power. Therefore there is no need to hope for improvement in this world.]

In contrast to this bleak model of inevitable regression, Guthlac inhabits a renewed space of growth under God's protection (746b).[63] Instead of earthly

---

62 Jennifer Neville has argued that landscape in *Guthlac A* primarily functions as a demonstration of sanctity (*Representations of the Natural World in Old English Poetry*, 122–8). For a discussion of *Guthlac A* and Latin pastoral traditions, see Clarke, *Literary Landscapes*, 45–58.
63 Line 746 is distinguished by its cross alliteration: 'Stod se grena wong in godes wære.'

decay, the poem imagines a space of regeneration, one formed out of but finally exempt from dispute.[64]

This ideal landscape clearly prefigures the eternal homes which await the faithful in heaven. The poem accentuates this figuration by moving almost immediately to Guthlac's ascension to the heavenly kingdom, passing over the many intermediate events of the saint's life which are related in Felix.[65] This compression bolsters the deep association between land and salvation and underscores the transformative quality of the dispute and its settlement in Guthlac's favour. Just fifty lines after he first sets foot on the idyllic *wong*, Guthlac receives his permanent place in heaven:

Swa wæs Guðlaces   gæst gelæded
engla fæðmum   in uprodor,
fore onsyne   eces deman
læddon leoflice.   Him wæs lean geseald,
setl on swegle,   þær he symle mot
awo to ealdre   eardfæst wesan,
bliðe bidan. (781–7a)

[And so Guthlac's spirit was carried to heaven in the arms of angels. They led him lovingly into the presence of the eternal Judge. To him was given a gift, a seat in heaven, where he might always and forever be secure in land and dwell happily.]

With their keen attention to lasting security and eternal possession, these lines recall the *aeterna hereditas* promised in Latin diplomas. Indeed, *Guthlac A* shares with those documents a conflation of the tenurial and the sacred within a reward of property for service and loyalty. Guthlac receives a grant of land in the kingdom of heaven which fulfils the dream of eternal possession inherent in bookland, but which remains largely

---

64 Jones reads this scene as illustrating the monastic ideal of *stabilitas*: 'Here the poet makes explicit the truth that spiritual stability best proceeds from a foundation of physical or "local" stability' ('Envisioning the *Cenobium*,' 285). This ideal of a stability grounded in place accords well with the poem's pronounced tenurial interests.

65 The transition from Bartholomew's appearance at the hell-gate to Guthlac's ascension is immediate in the Vercelli redaction. See Zacher, *Preaching the Converted*, 262–3. The element of tenurial reward which appears so prominently in *Guthlac A* is largely absent from the homily's presentation of the saint.

untroubled by the unsettling potential of forfeiture. In this sense, the poem sanitizes the disquieting elements which typically circulate in tenurial discourse and which frequently emerge in those texts that appropriate or engage that discourse. Land tenure, with its attendant problems of dispute and dispossession, provides a positive medium in *Guthlac A* for modeling the struggle of faith and the transformative reward of salvation.

Guthlac A models sanctity and salvation largely through the proving ground of a single decisive dispute. This redemptive conflict, however, importantly occurs within an abstraction of place which frees it from the pressure of historical forces and context.[66] The poem employs its tenurial topos in a positive sense by removing dispute from the web of competing claims and possible reversals. *Guthlac A* in this way offers a vision of dispute which is insulated from the negotiations, compromises, and potential for renewed troubles which characterize the historical evidence from Anglo-Saxon England. The aggrieved in *Guthlac A* are the ultimate villains, the fallen angels who long ago forfeited any and all rights to possession of land or place. Through dispute the contested land is made new again, cleansed entirely of any legitimate trace of past human use or possession. The poem in this sense offers an idealized vision of productive dispute. At the same time, however, Guthlac's heavenly endowment is enabled partly through the displacement of the *ealdfeondas* from their old places both in heaven and on earth. Dispossession thus remains the negative condition of possession, the anterior and potential event which troubles affirmations of secure and lasting tenure.

Deor: Losing Place

While *Guthlac A* uses property dispute as an extended metaphor for spiritual struggle and salvation, another poem in the Exeter Book utilizes tenurial tropes and language in a more negative sense. *Deor* imagines the act of dispossession as a personal tragedy in which the loss of land represents the loss of social position and security. As in *Guthlac A*, land ownership provides a transformative experience, but in *Deor* that

---

66 While the poem does not seem tied to a particular time or place, several scholars have argued that the poem was most likely written for a monastic audience. See Hill, 'The Middle Way'; Conner, 'Source Studies, the Old English *Guthlac A* and the English Benedictine Reformation'; Nicholas, 'Monasticism and the Social Temptation in the Old English *Guthlac A*'; Jones, 'Envisioning the *Cenobium*'; and Butler, 'Glastonbury and the Early History of the Exeter Book,' 200–4.

transformation is figured not as salvation or the acquisition of an enduring home, but rather as deprivation and a sundering from community.
This book has considered the various ways in which Anglo-Saxon texts
address this awareness of potential loss in writing about land. If dispossession is the spectre that haunts tenurial discourse, how do texts exor-
cize that intrinsic threat? Old English poems like *Deor* which deal in an
antiquarian Germanic past can uniquely engage this troubling issue
through the poetic legendary. Because such texts are set 'elsewhere' they
can acknowledge negative conditions which are partially suppressed in
other tenurial texts situated in the present time and space of Anglo-
Saxon England. While some of these poems show individuals being rewarded for their accomplishments with gifts of land, others feature the
hard consequences of losing that entitlement. This is not to suggest that
such poems are concerned only with land issues, but rather that they
draw upon and participate in a discourse of property in order to achieve
a particular resonance and force of meaning. Within tenurial writing, the
idea of lasting possession is often troubled by the potential for loss and
the abiding threat of forfeiture. This negative element can emerge more
directly and intensely, I contend, in a literary space which speaks to the
cultural present but is safely displaced elsewhere in space and time. In
this fashion, *Deor* gives poetic expression to the problem of precarious
tenure through the antiquarian imaginary.

We encounter a number of cases in Old English poetry in which a king
or lord rewards a follower with a grant of property. The seven thousand
hides of land that Beowulf receives from Hygelac may be the most dramatic example of a landed endowment in heroic verse, but there are other
poems in which the grant of property prominently represents personal
distinction and good fortune. The catalogue poem *The Fortunes of Men*,
for example, mentions the goldsmith whose craft earns him a generous
endowment of land:

> Sumum wundorgiefe
> þurh goldsmiþe   gearwad weorþað;
> ful oft he gehyrdeð   ond gehyrsteð wel,
> brytencyninges beorn,   ond he him brad syleð
> lond to leane. He hit on lust þigeð.[67] (72b–6)

---

67 Krapp and Dobbie, *Exeter Book*, 156.

[Wondrous gifts are given to one for working in gold. Very often he fortifies and adorns the mighty king's coat of mail, and he gives him spacious lands as a reward. He accepts it with pleasure.]

The hapax legomenon *brytencyning* (75a) suggests a ruler with an expansive realm who is able to share his substantial resources with his dutiful followers.[68] This particular compound offers an idealized sense of territorial sovereignty and generosity; that idea of spacious land transfers in miniature to the *brad* estate granted to the appreciative goldsmith. These lines imagine a man doubly favoured, first by a God-given ability to work gold, and second by the reward of land which that craftsmanship inspires. In both cases the man receives a transformative boon from a superior power or patron: his artistic abilities separate him from the unfortunate cases listed in the first half of the poem;[69] and his holding in land allows him a degree of prosperity and prestige which might otherwise be unattainable. Within this catalogue of the blessed and unfortunate, the possession of land both distinguishes the prosperous life and marks the man favoured by God.

Widsith contains a similar example of a ruler rewarding an artistic retainer with land. At one point, the well-traveled poet expresses his gratitude for the land he has received from Eadgils, lord of the Myrgingas:

Ond ic wæs mid Eormanrice   ealle þrage,
þær me Gotena cyning   gode dohte;
se me beag forgeaf,   burgwarena fruma,
on þam siex hund wæs   smætes goldes,
gescyred sceatta   scillingrime;
þone ic Eadgilse   on æht sealde,
minum hleodryhtne,   þa ic to ham bicwom,
leofum to leane,   þæs þe he me lond forgeaf,
mines fæder eþel,   frea Myrginga.[70] (88–96)

---

68 See *DOE*, s.v. 'bryten.'
69 The poem provides a gruesome catalogue of the ill-fated: one is devoured by wolves; one dies in famine, another in war; one is blind, another lame; one falls from a tree; one is gutted in a drunken quarrel, and so on. After such a harrowing list, the life of a landed goldsmith seems fortunate indeed.
70 Krapp and Dobbie, *Exeter Book*, 152.

[And I was with Eormanric for a long time where the king of the Goths was good to me; the leader of city-dwellers gave me a ring in which there were six hundred coins of pure gold, reckoned by count of shillings; when I returned home I gave it into the possession of Eadgils, my lord and protector, as a gift to that dear man since he, the lord of the Myrgingas, had granted me land, my father's ancestral holding.]

The grant of land here merits a reciprocal gift from the beneficiary. The fact that the given property was *eþel* (ancestral land) enables continuity in possession within the kindred and thus makes the grant all the more precious. This confirmation of family land appears prominently within a legendary travelogue of the poet's many accomplishments and distinctions. The possession of property again provides a metonym for general prosperity, but in this case that distinction is amplified through the land's transmission from father to son. In both *The Fortunes of Men* and *Widsith*, the grant of property provides a determinative example of service or performance being rewarded by a lord. Both texts furthermore call attention to the gratitude of the beneficiary, a point of emphasis which accentuates the multiple values of holding land.

Unlike these poems, each of which celebrates the acquisition of land as a mark of personal distinction, *Deor* attends to the tragedy of dispossession and the loss of entitlement.[71] In the process, the poem dramatizes the precarious nature of all tenure as being subject to reversal and contingent upon the abiding favour of a higher authority. The poem famously consists of a series of allusive fragments drawn from Germanic legend, each one followed by a refrain, a rare device in Old English poetry; the final lines offer a short philosophical rumination on the dispensation of fortune, followed by the speaker's closing comment on his own condition.[72] Near the end of

---

71 *Deor* has traditionally been included among the Old English elegies along with *The Wanderer*, *The Seafarer*, *The Riming Poem*, *Resignation*, *The Husband's Message*, *The Wife's Lament*, *The Ruin*, and *Wulf and Eadwacer*. Anne L. Klinck offers a general definition for the genre: 'Old English elegy is a discourse arising from a powerful sense of absence, of separation from what is desired, expressed through characteristic words and themes, and shaping itself by echo and leitmotiv into a poem that moves from disquiet to some kind of acceptance' (*Old English Elegies*, 246). This definition assumes a common resolution in consolation, but such a movement is far from certain in *Deor*. For the elegiac group, see also Greenfield, 'Formulaic Expression of the Theme of "Exile."'

72 An initial capital letter marks each of the six sections in the manuscript and end punctuation appears after each refrain; the manuscript, however, does not mark the introduction of the first-person speaker at line 35 with a capital letter.

the poem, the self-identified poet laments the loss of his *landriht* after his lord shifts favour to another *scop* – within the poem's imagistic sequence of misfortune, this act of dispossession provides a culminating proof of the world's changeability. *Deor* has traditionally been read as a poem of consolation with implicit links to the Boethian tradition,[73] but *Deor*'s particular loss of land and place – the final misfortune in a violent catalogue of pain and oppression – evades the closure of consolation. The dispossessed speaker remains in stasis, fixed in a moment of in-between, and the poem's refrain ('that passed away, so may this') offers an ambivalent statement of indeterminacy just as much as it does a promise of recuperation.[74] By including the loss of land as the final element in an accumulative survey of worldly affliction, *Deor* gives direct expression to the anxiety of dispossession which haunts tenurial discourse.

The poem begins with images of suffering and loss and then moves to allusions to historical rulers. The first two fragments are both drawn from the story of the legendary Weland and his gruesome vengeance upon his captor and tormenter, King Niðhad. The first stanza shows Weland in misery, alone with his 'sorge and longaþ' [sorrow and longing] (3b) after he has been imprisoned by Niðhad.[75] In the Scandinavian tradition Weland takes

---

73 Kemp Malone, for example, argues that each narrative unit in the poem 'teaches the same lesson: bear misfortune patiently, for in the end one's troubles will pass' (*Deor*, 22). See also Whitbread, 'Pattern of Misfortune'; Boren, 'Design of the Old English *Deor*'; and Kiernan, '*Deor*: The Consolations of an Anglo-Saxon Boethius.' Joseph Harris has questioned this strain of interpretation: 'A critical consideration of the "fit" between the conventional interpretation and the "exempla" shows a certain circularity: without the conventional interpretation of the refrain few of the exempla – a term which begs several questions – would have suggested the happy ends demanded by the traditional reading of the poem' ('"Deor" and Its Refrain,' 41). For a similar view, see Fulk and Cain, *History of Old English Literature*, 216–17.

74 The refrain ('þæs ofereode þisses swa mæg') has generated a great deal of discussion, particularly in its use of the genitive. Malone proposed reading *þæs* and *þisses* as genitives of reference or respect (*Deor*, 23–4n7), while Bruce Mitchell has suggested that *þæs* and *þisses* in the poem are genitives of point of time from which, with the translation, 'It passed over from that; it can from this' (*Old English Syntax*, 1:588). The meaning of *mæg* has also occasioned differences of opinion. The word is traditionally defined as 'to be able,' but some have understood the word to have an optative or future sense with a greater force of possibility. Klinck, for example, argues that *mæg* in the refrain 'expresses something stronger than possibility; it indicates what is desired and expected' (*Old English Elegies*, 161). Malone defines *magan* as 'MAY, be able, be possible; by litotes, will' (*Deor*, 36). Both definitions obviously favour a particular interpretation of the poem. I understand *magan* to indicate potentiality without the promise of actuality.

75 All citations of *Deor* are from Krapp and Dobbie, *Exeter Book*, 178–9.

his revenge by killing Niðhad's young sons and raping his daughter, Beadohild. The second stanza dramatizes Beadohild's plight as she faces the shock of her brothers' murder and the discovery of her own pregnancy. The implicit connection between the first two fragments in conjunction with the refrain might suggest some narrative continuity, but the enigmatic third section seems to frustrate that promise. These lines describe 'seo sorglufu' [the sad love] (16a) between Mæðhild and Geat which robs them of all sleep. This allusion remains cryptic despite much investigation and speculation, but the given information clearly presents another situation of emotional pain. The refrain may suggest the possibility of better things to come, but the poem thus far speaks directly of loss and suffering. The element of consolation in the refrain remains distant and only implied.[76]

The fourth and fifth stanzas notably shift focus as the poem moves from allusive vignettes of individual suffering to depictions of infamous rulers from Germanic antiquity. Both of the figures featured in these sections notably appear in other Anglo-Saxon texts as cruel despots who oppress their people.[77] This rising presence of grim rulers and suffering subjects in the poem importantly prepares a suggestive environment for Deor's own loss of favour and position with his own lord.

The Theoderic from the fourth section has been variously identified as Theoderic the Ostrogoth or as a Frankish hero,[78] but the poem itself tells us very little about him aside from his longstanding power:

Ðeodric ahte   þritig wintra
Mæringa burg;   þæt wæs monegum cuþ.
Þæs ofereode,   þisses swa mæg! (18–20)

---

76 Daniel Donoghue has underscored the refrain's ambiguity: 'Þæs refers in a general way to the misfortune that each stanza alludes to, but the referent for þisses is ambiguous until the final stanza, when the voice of Deor locates "this" within his present desolation. It is not a hopeful or consolatory conclusion for Deor, because the crucial word in the stanza is the auxiliary mæg, which means that hard times can pass, not that they will' (Old English Literature, 53–5).

77 For a discussion of the poem's motif of cruel rulers, see Frankis, 'Some Conjectures.' Much of Frankis' analysis remains cogent regardless of whether or not we accept his particular reconstruction of the poem's back-story and its proposed link with the enigmatic Wulf and Eadwacer.

78 See ibid., 162–4; and Hill, Minor Heroic Poems, 19–20 and 124–5 (s.v. 'Þeodric' [1 and 2]). Theoderic the Ostrogoth ruled Italy from 489–526, during which time he infamously ordered the execution of Boethius. For the theory, now largely discounted, that the poem instead refers to Theoderic the Frank, see Malone, Deor, 9–13.

[Theodric held the city of Maeringas for thirty winters. That was known to many. That passed away, so may this!]

While these lines are sparse in content, other Anglo-Saxon texts present Theoderic the Ostrogoth as a tyrant and the murderer of Boethius and Pope John.[79] This idea of a cruel leader becomes more explicit in the next section as it describes those subjects who suffered under King Eormanric, a ruler of mixed repute in Anglo-Saxon texts.[80] In *Deor*, however, he is unequivocally a harsh king:

> We geascodan   Eormanrices
> wylfenne geþoht;   ahte wide folc
> Gotena rices.   Þæt wæs grim cyning.
> Sæt secg monig   sorgum gebunden,
> wean on wenan,   wyscte geneahhe
> þæt þæs cynerices   ofercumen wære.
> Þæs ofereode,   þisses swa mæg! (21–7)

[We have learned of Eormanric's wolfish mind; he held sway widely over the people of the kingdom of the Goths. That was a grim king. Many a man sat bound in sorrows, in expectation of trouble, and often wished that the kingdom might be overcome. That passed away, so may this!]

Because Theoderic and Eormanric were both known as tyrants in the Anglo-Saxon tradition, their consecutive appearance in *Deor* enables a new motif of cruel rulers within the poem.[81] In the Eormanric section, moreover, sorrow significantly manifests not in the figure of the ruler, but among

---

79 Frankis, 'Some Conjectures,' 162. The first chapter of *The Old English Boethius*, for example, describes Theoderic as 'se wælhreowa cyning' (Godden and Irvine, *The Old English Boethius*, 1:244) [the bloodthirsty king]. See also Godden and Irvine, *The Old English Boethius*, 2:251–7; and Godden, 'Anglo-Saxons and the Goths,' 62–8.

80 In *Widsith*, for example, Eormanric is described both as 'wraþes wærlogan' [cruel pledge-breaker] (9a) and as a generous benefactor (88–92). See also Wilson, *Lost Literature of Medieval England*, 3–6.

81 The attention to cruel rulers in stanzas four and five also retroactively accentuates the suffering which Weland experienced under King Niðhad in the first stanza. The legendary smith knew persecution (*wræces*, 1b) and misery (*earfoþa*, 2b), the poem tells us, after the king put him in 'supple sinew-bonds' (*swoncre seonobende*, 6a). The motif of grim kings thus emerges incrementally in the poem until it finds full expression in the figure of Eormanric.

those subordinates who suffer under his persecutions; the poem thus re-
directs attention to a specific type of misery which occurs within the context of lordship and its network of obligation and reward. Deor's own lord
may not appear as despot in the poem, but the eclipsed *scop* nonetheless
experiences deprivation through the actions of his *dryhten*.

Deor's particular situation, however, emerges only in the final lines
of the poem. The passage prior to his appearance departs from the
poem's established allusive method to offer a general reflection on
worldly fortune:

> Siteð sorgcearig,   sælum bidæled,
> on sefan sweorceð,   sylfum þinceð
> þæt sy endeleas   earfoða dæl.
> Mæg þonne geþencan,   þæt geond þas woruld
> witig dryhten   wendeþ geneahhe,
> eorle monegum   are gesceawað,
> wislicne blæd,   sumum weana dæl. (28–34)

> [One sits heavy with sorrow, deprived of happiness; he grows dark in spirit
> and thinks to himself that his share of troubles might be endless. He can then
> consider that throughout this world the wise lord often makes change; he
> shows favour to many a man, a certain success, and to some a share of woe.]

These lines suggest the possibility of recovery for the *sorgcearig* individual, but they certainly do not guarantee it. The statement that the *witig
dryhten* makes change within the world does not promise an improvement
of circumstance – it merely affirms fluctuation and variation among the
conditions of human life, all determined by distribution from a higher
power.[82] If these universalizing lines do offer consolation, it is one that also
demands the acceptance and endurance of hardship. The section furthermore ends with the one who receives 'a share of woe' (34b), thus prominently placing the negative condition in the final position of an appositive
sequence. The phrase *weana dæl* also assumes a transitive position between
the poem's early images of suffering and Deor's own specific misfortune,
the loss of place and land.

---

82 While the poetic appellation *dryhten* (32a) most directly connotes God in the passage
    above, it could also signify a secular lord, a meaning which would seem contextually
    fitting against the content of the previous stanzas.

Because of his delayed appearance in the poem, Deor's voice emerges contextually through the miscellany of Germanic legend which precedes the statement of his own condition. Renée R. Trilling has recently discussed this effect in relation to Walter Benjamin's theory of the constellation in which a critic perceives an array of relational patterns as meaningful from a particular vantage at a particular historical moment. In *Deor*, Trilling argues, 'The episodes are not narrative, but emotive; their meaning for Deor, as for the poem's readers, is not established by the time line of their stories, but by their placement in relation to other non-narrative, emotive episodes. As a result, events have meaning in *Deor* not because of their place in a linear progression from past to present, but because of their associative connections and relations to other events from other places on the chronological spectrum. The legendary examples do not lead to or point toward Deor's current situation, but they allow him to construe it as meaningful.'[83] Trilling's analysis of the formation of relational meaning in the poem offers productive insight into how all the material which comes before Deor's moment of self-identification incrementally and associatively prepares the way for the final presentation of the speaker's dispossession. The prior episodes invest his particular experience of loss with overdetermined tragic meaning as the poem's imagistic sequence of suffering individuals and cruel rulers coalesces in its concluding lines:

Þæt ic bi me sylfum   secgan wille,
þæt ic hwile wæs   Heodeninga scop,
dryhtne dyre.   Me wæs Deor noma.
Ahte ic fela wintra   folgað tilne,
holdne hlaford,   oþþæt Heorrenda nu,
leoðcræftig monn   londryht geþah,
þæt me eorla hleo   ær gesealde.
Þæs ofereode,   þisses swa mæg! (35–42)

[I want to say of myself that I was for a time the scop of the Heodeningas, dear to my lord. My name was Deor. For many winters I held a good position, a favourable lord, until now Heorrenda, a man skilled in song, has received the land-right that the protector of warriors before gave to me. That passed away, so may this!]

---

83 Trilling, *Aesthetics of Nostalgia*, 46.

Deor's honoured place among the Heodeningas comes to an abrupt end in an unforeseen reversal signaled by the *oððæt* of line 39b.[84] Deor has been replaced by another poet, the fabled Heorrenda, and subsequently lost both his lord's patronage and the *landriht* that went along with it.[85] The loss of land thus provides a closing crescendo to the poem's polyphonic dirge of worldly suffering. The *ahte* in line 38a evokes a possession now lost even as it ironically echoes the appearances of that same verb in the earlier lines on Theodric and Eormanric (18a, 22b). Deor too suffers under a tyrant – or at least that is how he perceives his experience – and the juxtaposition of his own disappointment with the reigns of great persecutors artfully amplifies the gravity of his loss of land and place.

Moreover, the closing revelation of Deor's dispossession recursively reconfigures the significance of the preceding gnomic lines and their commentary on the vicissitudes of worldly fortune (28–34). The statement that the 'wise lord' (32a) makes change in the world in retrospect seems to anticipate the reversal wrought by Deor's own *dryhten* (37a) when he redistributes the poet's position and land. Line 33 particularly assumes a new resonance in light of what follows: 'eorle monegum are gesceawað' (he shows favour to many a man). As we have seen, *ar* has a potential tenurial sense, but the word would seem generally to mean 'honour' in line 33b, especially when placed in apposition to *blæd* (glory) in the next halfline. The particular nature of Deor's plight, however, encourages us to reconsider the word's full connotative range. Deor has lost his *ar* in every sense of the word: he has been deprived of position, distinction, favour, and landed property.[86] This deprivation assumes additional associative meaning with what has come before in the poem: the loss of *landriht*

---

84 For *oððæt* as a foreboding poetic cue, see Lapidge, '*Beowulf* and Perception.'

85 The reference to the bard Heorrenda evokes the story of Hild and Heoden from Scandinavian tradition and the Middle High German *Kudrun*. In the *Skaldskaparmal*, the story ends in a battle between Heodon, son of Hjarrandi (OE Heorrenda), and Hogni, father of Hild, which will repeat itself endlessly until Ragnarok. Roberta Frank has memorably commented on the allusion's place in *Deor*: 'A story of suffering destined to last until the end of the world was an odd choice for a scop wanting to console himself with the thought that sorrow, like joy, is transitory, or a poet to assure his audience that, man being mortal, his miseries must pass' ('Germanic Legend in Old English Literature,' 100). A reference to ceaseless and cyclical struggle, however, would be apt enough for a scenario which speaks to cultural anxieties over the precarious possession of property and the abiding potential of dispute or forfeiture. See also Hill, *Minor Heroic Poems*, 108 (s.v. 'Hagena' [2]); and Sturluson, *Edda*, 122–4.

86 See the various senses of the word given by the *DOE*, s.v. 'ar.'

becomes a traumatic event to be considered alongside horrors of mutila-
tion, imprisonment, murder, rape, and tyranny. Dispossession thus assumes a powerful negative value as the poem's culminating manifestation
of worldly tragedy and injustice.

The compound *landriht* (40b) provides a powerful keyword for evoking this trauma of loss in *Deor*. The term, which appears in both poetic and
legal texts, carries both emotive and tenurial force; moreover, its distribution in extant texts indicates that the word was equally at home in both
vocabularies.[87] There is some generic variation in the word's sense and
connotation, but as we shall see, among all the extant usages *Deor* uniquely draws upon the word's full semantic range.

In other poetic texts, *landriht* has a clear sense of land collectively shared
among a people or kindred. In *Beowulf*, for example, the word appears
during Wiglaf's fierce rebuke to those retainers who deserted Beowulf
during his fight against the dragon:

Nu sceal sincþego ond swyrdgifu,
eall eðelwyn eowrum cynne,
lufen alicgean; londrihtes mot
þære mægburge monna æghwylc
idel hweorfan, syððan æðelingas
feorran gefricgean fleam eowerne,
domleasan dæd. Deað bið sella
eorla gehwylcum þonne edwitlif![88] (2884–91)

[Now all the joys of ancestral land shall come to an end for your people;
the getting of treasure, the giving of swords and desired things! Each man
of your kindred must go without the right to land after noblemen hear
from afar of your flight, a base deed. Death is better for any warrior than
a life of shame!]

These lines juxtapose the deprivation of *landriht* with separation from the
eðel, part of a low condition which Wiglaf suggests is worse than death
itself. *Landriht* here stands parallel to *eðelwyn* with both compounds

---

87 *Landriht* appears four times in the poetry (*Deor*, *Beowulf*, *Genesis A*, and *Exodus*) and
    four times in legal texts (*Rectitudines singularum personarum*, *Gerefa*, the law-code
    Episcopus, and S 582, a Wilton charter dated to 955). My findings are based on a search
    of the Dictionary of Old English Web Corpus on *landr** and *londr**.
88 *Klaeber's Beowulf*, 98.

together signifying the benefits of a collective existence on ancestral ground. The loss of land represents a social shaming and obliteration of status and security through separation. The failure of the cowardly retainers to honour their obligations to their lord also ironically echoes Wiglaf's own heroic moment when he steps forward to face the dragon with Beowulf:

> Gemunde ða ða are   þe he him ær forgeaf,
> wicstede weligne   Wægmundinga,
> folcrihta gehwylc,   swa his fæder ahte.[89] (2606–8)

[He remembered then the distinction which Beowulf had granted him before, the wealthy residence of the Waegmundings, all the customary rights which his father had held.]

These lines, like Wiglaf's speech to the deserters, are charged with the vocabulary of property. Lines 2606b–8 clarify the potential tenurial sense of *ar* (2606a) through apposition, while line 2608 indicates that Beowulf had confirmed upon Wiglaf the ancestral property and privileges held by his father.[90] Moreover, the verb *forgeaf* (2606b) commonly appears in charters where it means specifically 'to grant land, privileges, goods, etc. by bequest or charter.'[91] An Anglo-Saxon audience would have been attuned to such a cluster of connotations for landholding and inheritance. As the end of the poem strongly forecasts, however, the Geats will soon be overwhelmed by their enemies. *Eðelwyn* and *landriht* will come to an end for all the Geatish people, not just for those cowards who failed to protect their lord in the crucial moment. Because *landriht* is held collectively, its accumulative loss is equivalent to a collective death or erasure of an entire people.

   Genesis A and *Exodus* also accentuate the communal nature of *landriht*, but they attend to the process of formation and survival rather than dissolution and destruction. The word appears in *Genesis A* when Abraham and Lot decide to separate and seek out different territories in order to avoid conflict among their households. The land on which they are currently

---

89 Ibid., 89.
90 Jurasinski, *Ancient Privileges*, 73–4.
91 *DOE*, s.v. 'forgyfan (A.3.c).' While this is a common verb with a wide range of attested meanings (the *DOE* notes approximately 1600 occurrences), the cluster of tenurial vocabulary in lines 2606–8 would accentuate the verb's potential legal connotations.

living is insufficient for their numbers, and their neighbours, the Canaanites and Perizzites, Abraham tells Lot, are not eager to allow them more space:

> Ne willað rumor unc
> landriht heora;   forðon wit lædan sculon,
> teon of þisse stowe,   and unc staðolwangas
> rumor secan.[92] (1910b–13a)

[They do not wish for us to have more rights to their land; so the two of us must take enmity away from this place and seek out more spacious places to settle.]

In this passage *landriht* signifies an abiding claim to the use and habitation of communal land. The Canaanites and Perizzites do not wish to surrender part of their own ancestral domain to the newcomers and the Israelites choose to move on to new lands in order to preserve peace within the kindred. God's chosen people are again on the move, looking for the land God promised them. In his discussion of the Junius 11 poems, Nicholas Howe argues, 'The only sense of place within Junius 11 that endures beyond the changing rhythm of human history, and in fact makes the rhythm tolerable, rests on the covenant that God makes with Abraham.'[93] In *Exodus*, that redemptive promise of an enduring homeland is explicitly signified as *landriht*:

> Him wæs an fæder,
> leof leodfruma,   landriht geþah,
> frod on ferhðe,   freomagum leof.
> Cende cneowsibbe   cenra manna
> heahfædera sum,   halige þeode,
> Israela cyn,   onriht Godes.[94] (353b–8)

[For them there was one father, a beloved founder of the people; wise in spirit and beloved to his noble kinsmen, he received the right to land. One of the high-fathers, he brought forth a nation of bold men, a holy people, the tribe of Israel, directed by God.]

---

92 Krapp, *Junius Manuscript*, 58.
93 Howe, *Writing the Map of Anglo-Saxon England*, 206.
94 Lucas, *Exodus*, 122.

Landriht here compresses the divine covenant within a single word to represent the originary grant of ancestral land to a *halige þeode* (357b). In both biblical poems, the compound positively denotes the formation and endurance of community through land.

The sense of *landriht* in the legal texts differs significantly from poetic usage in several key ways: first, the word in a legal environment consistently indicates individual possession; second, it designates both the privileges and the obligations attendant upon landholding; and third, it generally signifies land held by book. *Landriht* appears in four miscellaneous texts of tenurial or legal character: *Rectitudines singularum personarum*, *Gerefa*, the law-code *Episcopus*, and a Wilton charter dated to 955. In the two tracts on estate management, the word signifies the obligations owed to a lord by the one who holds an estate.[95] In *Rectitudines* the word appears in the opening section on 'the thegn's law' (*ðegenlagu*), where it clearly means those services due to the king: 'Eac of manegum landum mare landriht arist to cyniges gebanne, swilce is deorhege to cyniges ham ꝺ scorp to friðscipe ꝺ sæweard ꝺ heafodweard ꝺ fyrdweard, ælmesfeoh ꝺ cyricsceat ꝺ mænige oðere mistlice ðingc'[96] (Also on many estates additional land duties might arise at the king's command, such as the deer hedge at the king's residence and fittings for a guard ship, and coast watch and personal protection and military watch, payment of alms and church dues, and many other various things). The thegn envisioned in *Rectitudines* clearly holds bookland: he enjoys the entitlement of *bocriht* and he owes the three common burdens associated with bookland.[97] Even with this superior form of tenure, however, the thegn must maintain certain obligations to the power that granted him the estate – specific duties remain attached to the land even after it has been alienated by the king.

A similar sense of *landriht* appears in the first sentence of *Gerefa*: 'Se scadwis gerefa sceal ægðær witan ge hlafordes landriht ge folces gerihtu, be

---

95 Unlike its modern English derivative, Old English *riht* signifies both privileges and obligations (see BT, s.v. 'riht [IV and V]'). Rosamond Faith has described Anglo-Saxon society generally as 'a network of entitlements and obligations' (personal correspondence), and *landriht* in the legal texts clearly illustrates this sense of a social relationship predicated on a system of benefits and responsibilities.

96 Liebermann, *Gesetze*, 1:444. Liebermann in this instance translates *landriht* as *Grundlast* (land burden).

97 'Ðegenlagu is, þæt he sy his bocrihtes wyrðe ꝺ þæt he ðreo ðinc of his lande do: fyrd-færeld ꝺ burhbote ꝺ brycgeweorc' (ibid.) [The thegn's law is that he be worthy of his book-right and that he perform three things for his land: military service, fortification maintenance, and bridge-work].

ðam ðe hit of ealddagum witan geræddan, ¬ ælcre tilðan timan, ðe to tune belimpð'[98] (The discriminating reeve must know both the lord's duties with the estate and the duties of the people according to how councillors decided it in the old days, as well as the time for all work related to the manor). *Landriht* here seems just as indicative of specific obligations as it does of privileges, especially if we consider the precedent of the word's use in *Rectitudines*.[99] The contrastive pair of 'hlafordes landriht' and 'folces gerihtu' furthermore suggests that *landriht* here applies to land held by book as it does in *Rectitudines*. Both texts attach *landriht* to the elite landowner who holds his or her property by royal diploma. Even with the many benefits and powers of bookland, however, the landowner remains beholden to a superior power which maintains some hold on the property.

A similar association between *bocland* and *landriht* appears in S 582.[100] This charter records one hundred hides that King Eadwig 'booked' (*gebokede*) to the nuns at Wilton in 955. A vernacular note added after the witness list stipulates that no one shall change the terms of the document unless they have received permission from the minster community 'mid rihtum landrihte ¬ leodrihte swa hit on lande stonde'[101] (in accordance with the proper obligations and customary law established for the land). The doublet of *landriht* and *leodriht* recalls the distinction between proprietary and customary rights made in *Gerefa*, suggesting again that *landriht* in legal texts typically represents those rights and duties attached to bookland.[102]

The sense of *landriht* in *Deor* conflates the word's signification in both poetry and law. Among the poetic texts, *Deor* uniquely uses *landriht* to designate a private holding of property. In the other poetic texts, the right to land is inseparable from the security of a collective people – without land there can be no ancestral identity or continuity. When Deor loses his *landriht* to a rival poet, he loses more than a place in his lord's hall. By grouping this

---

98 Ibid., 1:453.

99 See Goebel, *Felony and Misdemeanor*, 374n132. Goebel translates *landriht* as 'charges on the land.'

100 *BCS*, vol. 3, no. 917 at pp. 83–6.

101 Ibid., 3:86.

102 In the *Episcopus* text, *landriht* appears as part of the doublet 'ge burhriht ge landriht,' which in context seems to convey an inclusive sense of 'every law' (*æghwylc lahriht*), whether in town or country, regarding weights and measures (Whitelock, Brett and Brooke, *Councils and Synods*, 1:419 [ch. 6]). The editors translate 'ge burhriht ge landriht' as 'whether law of a borough or law of a country district.' This more generalized usage of *landriht* lacks the clear association with bookland evident in the other legal texts.

particular loss among the great tragedies and injustices of Germanic legend, the poem evokes a cultural sense of land as the necessary bedrock of security and survival. This poetic sense of the word charges Deor's individual loss with a particular emotive force. By designating *landriht* as an individual possession, however, the poem also draws upon the vocabulary of Anglo-Saxon law and its associations between *landriht* and *bocriht*. In this sense, *landriht* in *Deor* gestures to practices of documentation (and the idea of permanency which such writing promised) which would be entirely out of place within the poem's antiquarian imaginary. The word calls attention to what is absent, that is, the written guarantee of the royal diploma and its ideal of endurance, underwritten by a synthesis of divine and royal endorsement. The poetic and legal senses of *landriht* coexist within the poem in a productive tension as the term dramatizes the problem of precarious tenure and the theoretical value of the written instrument in securing possession over time.

The anxieties of dispossession which circulate in Anglo-Saxon tenurial discourse are entirely at home in *Deor*. Holding land remains a desirable but limited privilege, subject to a superior power and always vulnerable to challenge and loss. As the historical evidence from the period abundantly demonstrates, property in Anglo-Saxon England was never entirely secure from the depredations of the powerful or well-connected. The way in which a retainer once dear to his lord experienced the unanticipated reversal of political favour would have presented a familiar scenario to an Anglo-Saxon audience, regardless of how well-versed they may or may not have been in ancient Germanic lore.

Guthlac A and *Deor* each employ tenurial vocabulary and motifs at select moments in order to underscore particular ideological or philosophical ideas. And while neither poem directly features motifs of legal writing, each text engages or appropriates key issues attached to landholding and tenure in Anglo-Saxon England. *Guthlac A*, as we have seen, portrays property dispute as a transformative experience, a means to salvation, while *Deor* imagines the loss of land as the culminating reversal in its survey of worldly misfortune. These narrative ends speak to the cultural notion that the possession of land determines identity and status, whether it be through gain or loss. Each poem also frames the potential of loss as an intrinsic aspect of holding land, a steady element of threat within the rhetoric and procedures of property: Guthlac gains an earthly holding and a heavenly seat through the dispossession of the fallen angels; Deor loses his own place, his *landriht*, through the elevation of another poet. As possession changes hands, land is revealed as a mobile commodity, a ready unit of exchange. These two poems from the Exeter Book dramatize this potential-ly unsettling idea through different poetic legendaries, each one situated in a different heroic past but each still speaking to the desires and apprehen-sions of a tenth-century culture of property.

Finally, each of these texts faces another potentially troubling element of Anglo-Saxon land tenure: the decisive power of a higher authority in assigning and maintaining possession. In *Guthlac A*, a stalemate dispute is ended and possession assigned by an irrefutable agent of the divine sover-eign; in *Deor*, a retainer loses land and position through a sudden shift in his lord's favour. In both cases, possession and status turn on the deter-minative power of a single authority. Each text, then, accentuates the transformative power of property even as it acknowledges the double-edged potential for an issuing power to both give and remove that entitlement. Both poems accordingly teach that possession remains con-tingent on the enduring support of that higher authority, whether it be earthly or divine. In other words, ownership is a limited privilege liable to change, one in which the possessor always occupies a vulnerable position. In this way, *Guthlac A* and *Deor* each register the multivalent value of land as a possession which is at once eternal and impermanent, secure and un-reliable, a means to either salvation or exile. This effect is achieved through the resonance of contemporary tenurial language and practices within an-tiquarian settings, demonstrating once again the flexibility and generic range of land tenure as a discursive and conceptual field.

Conclusion: The Question of Limits

Land comprehends all things of a permanent, substantial nature, being a word of a very extensive signification.

— William Blackstone, *Commentaries on the Laws of England*

Proprietary rights in land are, we may say, projected upon the plane of time.

— Pollock and Maitland, *The History of English Law Before the Time of Edward I*

By the tenth century property had become for the Anglo-Saxons an issue of great economic, social, and political importance with a well-developed procedural and technical apparatus. The Anglo-Saxons actively used different modes of writing to record and control proprietary claims to land over time, but as we have seen the discourse of property was not limited to what we would today classify as legal documents. As land became property through the operations of textuality, it assumed a complex range of conceptual values which could inform other writings beyond the legal or practical. Land in writing consequently acquired a level of emotive force and abstract attachment which distinguished it from other forms of real property. Moreover, the energy of tenurial discourse in Anglo-Saxon England provided a locus for rhetorical intensification in both practical and imaginative writing. In the process, land assumed a multifaceted potentiality: it could be the ideal possession, eternal and always secure; an imperfect commodity tied to a decaying world; a means to security and social prestige; a site of contention and dispute; a powerful metaphor for salvation; an emblem of earthly vanity; grounds for affirming ideology and authority; a basis of social and political obligations; or a possession vulnerable to sudden and devastating loss. In short, land in writing could signify in multiple, even contradictory, ways.

This multivalent aspect of land in writing, I have argued, provided a productive influence within the literature of Anglo-Saxon England. The various challenges of managing possession and inheritance over time – particularly the problem of dispute and the possibility of loss – not only fostered formal innovation in legal writing, but also stimulated elevated styles of writing across a range of textual forms. This aesthetic mode in tenurial discourse appears in various forms and works toward various ends, but its widespread presence and flexibility testify to the practical importance of property in Anglo-Saxon England as well as to the symbolic capacity of landholding. Indeed, the confluence of land issues and rhetorical invention produced a rich discursive field for articulating and engaging a number of cultural concerns vital to the Anglo-Saxons: the imperative of salvation, the affirmation of political sovereignty, status and distinction, the anticipation of conflict and reversal, and problems of continuity. By putting land in writing, the Anglo-Saxons performed creative acts of textual and conceptual transformation. Land became more than a material asset or ground for habitation as it acquired through writing a weighty array of theoretical meanings and potentialities.

Within this matrix of meaning, several key issues have arisen over the course of this book. One recurrent concern in Anglo-Saxon writings on property involves the question of duration.[1] The unique permanency of land makes it something more than a thing, an object of ownership. In physical terms a tract of land always pre-exists its owner and will always survive his or her death. How can an impermanent being achieve and maintain lasting ownership of a permanent thing? In the long view of time, land always remains anterior, a found object which to some extent evades efforts to control and classify. Land will always outlast any mortal holder, thereby challenging tenurial ambitions of transmission and continuity over time. Human industry might imprint land with a network of physical and political signs which designate possession or determine limits of use – and which would consequently allow one to define and thus *know* land – but that system of signs remains an imposed invention which imagines but can never guarantee absolute and abiding possession.

---

1 Maitland memorably described the categories of duration imposed upon the possession of land as 'that wonderful calculus of estates' (Pollock and Maitland, *History of English Law*, 2:11).

The Anglo-Saxons were acutely aware of these proprietary challenges. A good deal of tenurial writing consequently insists on longstanding possession in a declarative mode even as it underwrites contradictions or qualifications to those terms and expectations. This phenomenon is most evident in the composite form of the royal diploma. These solemn documents invested property with an eternal value even as they assumed a defensive position against future challenges to possession. Diplomas amplified their authority through various means in order to combat or circumvent possible dispute: divine and royal sanction, rhetorical display, the singular and abiding status of the document itself, and the supplement of ceremonial ritual. The Latin diploma consequently became a talismanic text which not only gave material proof of possession, but also through its form and language signified both the idea of eternal possession and the promise of salvation. At the same time, the diploma's defensive function brought with it a sense of land as a temporal possession always at risk. This sense of risk was amplified further in tenth-century diplomas through ornamental or supplemental content which often called attention to the evidence of transience or alteration. These instrumental texts thus enable a theory of property in which the ideal of lasting possession carries the apprehension of potential loss.

This tension, which migrates and manifests across texts and genres, arises in part from an awareness of old claims and competing expectations which could produce property disputes in the future. Tenurial writing could at times preserve such disconcerting remnants within otherwise determinative claims about ownership and use. Because property carries traces of its past history, tenurial writing must always contend with the presence and pressure of that history. In this sense, the problems of dispute and loss act as a negative space within texts such as Latin diplomas or even the Anglo-Saxon Chronicle which are primarily devoted to the affirmation of lasting power and control. This element of felt competition over land emerges most clearly, perhaps, in those narrative charters which record stories of past dispute and controversy. These documents were written to provide evidence against competing claims to land, but their content can also inscribe evidence of discontinuity, forfeiture, or injustice which troubles claims to secure possession. Some charters, like S 1447, notably work to master these traces of disruption through artful prose and ordered narrative. In this sense, narrative charters meet the problem of dispute with strategic storytelling which retrospectively tames the dangerous contingencies and reversals of human activity. Things may once have been a mess, these texts affirm, but they have been made right through due process and proper documentation. This narrative function makes the history of land sensible, but it also inscribes the abiding presence of competing claims and underscores the potential for loss. In both the vernacular charter and the Latin diploma, then, moments of formal and rhetorical invention can accentuate worrying problems of dispute and duration and consequently call attention to tenurial or proprietary limitations.

A third issue prominent in tenurial discourse involves the maintenance of those rights and obligations which accompanied the possession of property in Anglo-Saxon England. As we have seen, landholding was situated in a hierarchical network which delivered to the possessor a set of privileges and benefits while also demanding the observance of certain tenurial and social responsibilities. All forms of possession carried these obligations. Failure to meet them could result in forfeiture, a condition which impressed property with an aspect of both liability and vulnerability. This sense of the burdens and duties attached to land assumed a solemn element of religious significance through metaphors of the obligations of faith and the rewards of salvation; these spiritual metaphors themselves drew freely from the vocabulary and practices of land tenure and property dispute, thereby achieving a synthesis of the earthly and divine similar to the conflation of royal and heavenly sanctions in the Latin diploma. In these figural environments landholding could prove a transformative enterprise which raised the dutiful tenant to new heights of privilege and security, a phenomenon which manifests quite clearly in the metaphor of the dutiful tenant from the preface to the Old English *Soliloquies*. The ideal of salvation concurrently took on tenurial aspects as it emulated the notion of elevated status which could be gained through the substantial ownership of property. Such conceits could work toward different pedagogical ends, however: tenurial metaphors might provide inspirational instruction in some texts, but in others they could easily model the heavy punishment of negligence and presumption (as in the parable of the angry landlord from the preface to the lawcode known as IV Edgar). The system of social status and obligations attached to landholding in Anglo-Saxon England thus became an integral part of tenurial discourse as a determinative force in the formation and maintenance of both possession and identity. Moreover, the subordination of the possessor to a higher power within a system of obligations further heightened the awareness that the privileges of possession could be revoked by that issuing authority. We can see this sense of vulnerability most acutely in a poem like *Deor*, which imagines the loss of land through the withdrawal of a lord's favour as a personal trauma equivalent to the renowned tragedies of Germanic legend. The transformative capacity of property which resided in the grantor could work toward productive or destructive ends. This double-edged potentiality instils an additional sense of limitation and prospective loss in tenurial discourse, which can trouble accompanying claims to security and longevity.

Each of these three focal issues – duration, dispute, and obligation – can emerge with particular force during moments of rhetorical embellishment or figural invention. In this fashion, an elevated style can amplify resonant content and prominently frame particular problems or ideals in writing about land. The various texts analysed in this book all demonstrate this phenomenon to some degree. The legal texts examined in the first two chapters of the book – the royal diploma and the narrative charter – contain pronounced instances of rhetorical self-consciousness and stylistic embellishment, aspects which we typically associate with the literary. Conversely, the several vernacular texts examined in the later chapters – many of which are considered literary – exhibit legal and tenurial elements within their specific vocabulary and situational content. Annals 900–46 of the Anglo-Saxon Chronicle, for example, can be read as a triumphal record of dynastic inheritance and territorial expansion which shares certain formal and syntactical techniques with contemporary Latin diplomas. Furthermore, this accumulative narrative is largely predicated on conflict, internal and external, and the resolution of contested claims to land and power. Likewise, a poem such as *Guthlac A* underscores the oppositional and transformative elements which can inhere in landholding – the saint gains a place (and salvation) through the testing crucible of dispute. These shared characteristics, concerns, and tropes of tenurial discourse challenge traditional distinctions between the legal and the literary, the practical and the aesthetic, and suggest a broad field of Anglo-Saxon literary activity which cuts across genre and language.

Consequently, this book has considered the widespread circulation and referential power of tenurial discourse in Anglo-Saxon texts. The very breadth and complexity of the subject, however, has meant that this book cannot be comprehensive in its survey. I have instead favoured texts which have been under-represented in the scholarship and also sought connections between genres which have traditionally remained separated by discipline.[2] Despite their volume of production and occasional moments of stylistic brilliance, Latin diplomas in particular have attracted limited

---

2 This decision of focus explains the book's limited attention to vernacular wills and law-codes, both of which have already received a good deal of attention in recent criticism.

interest in discussions of Anglo-Saxon literature.[3] Even historians have at times apologized for the dryness of the material: F.M. Stenton once observed, for example, that aside from those documents produced under Æthelstan, tenth-century charters 'form a monotonous series' which does not 'invite consecutive reading.'[4] Surveys of Anglo-Saxon literature have typically passed over diplomas entirely or afforded them only the most cursory discussion.[5] Such omissions and evasions are unfortunate in that they limit our understanding of Anglo-Saxon literary production. This book has accordingly given Latin diplomas a more prominent place in its analysis of textual culture, for these documents have much to offer beyond strata of historical data. Instead of reading diplomas only as 'transparent texts which can assert objective truth independent of the subjective act that intended the document and of the operations of language within it,' for example, Brigitte Bedos-Rezak has advocated a mode of criticism which considers 'the specific process of meaning production implied by the discursive and existential mode of that [documentary] source and permits the retrieval both of the ideological and evidential status of the text, and of the ideological and social standards from the past.'[6] I have minded this critical imperative by attending to the ways in which the language, form, and function of Anglo-Saxon diplomas play a vital role in forming and broadcasting cultural ideas about land in writing. This is not to suggest that Latin diplomas are the dominant force in shaping tenurial discourse, but rather that they deserve and reward serious attention as active participants in that discursive field.

As we have seen, Latin diplomas gathered multiple tokens of power within a single text: the sanction of God, the rhetoric of eternity, the voice of the king, the witness of the secular and ecclesiastical worthies gathered

3 Some notable exceptions include Lapidge, 'Hermeneutic Style'; Lapidge, 'Schools, Learning and Literature in Tenth-Century England'; Johnson, 'Fall of Lucifer'; Bremmer, 'Apocalyptic Expectations in Anglo-Saxon Charters'; and Foot, 'Reading Anglo-Saxon Charters.'

4 Stenton, *Latin Charters*, 66–7.

5 For examples see Greenfield and Calder, *New Critical History*, 111–13; Fulk and Cain, *History of Old English Literature*, 148–9; and Donoghue, *Old English Literature*, 1–5. Carole Hough's essay in Blackwell's *A Companion to Anglo-Saxon Literature* offers more generous coverage – devoting about five of its fifteen pages to diplomas – but it largely subordinates diplomas to considerations of Anglo-Saxon law-codes and case law ('Legal and Documentary Writings'). All these literary surveys primarily assign diplomas a supplemental or anecdotal value.

6 Bedos-Rezak, 'Diplomatic Sources and Medieval Documentary Practices,' 333 and 334.

in assembly around the king, and the longevity of writing within a solemn document. This display of power-in-writing created land-as-property and delivered it into human possession. The potent mix of symbolic and practical value in Latin diplomas, along with their frequency of use throughout the Anglo-Saxon period, goes some way in explaining the capacity of these documents to inform other writing about land. Additionally, the ranging signification in diplomatic content – such as the collaboration of secular and divine endorsements, the pull between the temporal and the eternal, and the jostling senses of abiding possession and imminent dispute – enables a productive conceptual field for framing weighty issues such as personal salvation or political power. The Anglo-Saxon Chronicle annals 900–46AB, for example, approximate certain formal features which were also cultivated in contemporary diplomas: the standardization of the vernacular boundary clause and the inclusion of distinctly stylized content as ideological supplement. The activities of West Saxon leaders as they reinscribe the bounds of *anweald* over time, in combination with the introduction of verse which prominently celebrates territorial victories within a prose environment, distinguishes the proprietary interest in this group of annals, albeit on the level of the dynastic realm. In addition to these diplomatic analogues in the Chronicle, we have also seen how the figure of the diploma itself has been utilized in exhortatory writing in innovative ways. The Vercelli X homily, for example, imagines salvation as a documentary act, actualized in and through the *frumgewrit* (i.e., the original charter), even as it presents the proprietary assurances of bookland as a man-made fiction; in the process, the homily plays across the positive and negative aspects of tenurial discourse, filtered through the idea of the Latin diploma as a written guarantee of possession. The prestigious form and content of the diploma, along with its practical and evidentiary value, then, could inform the textual conceptualization of land in various and productive ways.

This book has concerned itself with the ways in which property and land tenure become objects of writing in texts produced or circulated in tenth-century England. It has been interested not only in individual texts or genres, but also in the formation of aggregate textuality, in questions of how and to what end a particular issue or topic acquires collective mass across various forms of writing. The book has also considered how individual texts resonate, acquire meaning, or even generate dissonance within such a textual network of interest. Tenurial discourse was a widespread, flexible, and conceptually rich field which circulated across language and genre and which provided a ready medium for engaging an impressive array of intellectual, spiritual, and political issues. In short, land-as-property generated an active topos in Anglo-Saxon literature which has remained largely unrecognized. More than a legal or proprietary system, land tenure as both social practice and discursive field occupied a vital place in the Anglo-Saxon cultural imaginary.

Bibliography

Primary Sources

Ælfric. *Ælfric's Lives of Saints*. Edited by Walter W. Skeat. 2 vols. EETS, o.s., 76, 82, 94, 114. Oxford, 1881–1900.

Aldhelm. *Aldhelmi Opera*. Edited by Rudolf Ehwald. MGH, Auctores antiquissimi, 15. Berlin: Weidmann, 1919.

– *The Poetic Works*. Translated by Michael Lapidge and James Rosier. Cambridge: D.S. Brewer, 1985.

– *The Prose Works*. Translated by Michael Lapidge and Michael Herren. Cambridge: D.S. Brewer, 1979.

Arngart, O., ed. *The Proverbs of Alfred*. 2 vols. Skrifter utgivna av Kungl. Humanistiska Vetenskapssamfundet i Lund 32. Lund: C.W.K. Gleerup, 1942–55.

Baker, Peter S., ed. *MS F*. Vol. 8 of *The Anglo-Saxon Chronicle: A Collaborative Edition*. Cambridge: D.S. Brewer, 2000.

Bately, Janet M., ed. *MS A*. Vol. 3 of *The Anglo-Saxon Chronicle: A Collaborative Edition*. Cambridge: D.S. Brewer, 1986.

Bede. *De Natura Rerum*. In *Bedae Venerabilis Opera, Part I: Opera Didascalica*. Edited by Ch.W. Jones, 174–234. CCSL 123A. Turnhout: Brepols, 1975.

– *In Lucae Evangelium Expositio*. *Bedae Venerabilis Opera, Part II, No. 3: Opera Exegetica*. Edited by D. Hurst. CCSL 120. Turnhout: Brepols, 1960.

– *Libri II De Arte Metrica et De Schematibus et Tropis: The Art of Poetry and Rhetoric*. Edited and translated by Calvin B. Kendall. Bibliotheca Germanica: Series Nova 2. Saarbrücken: AQ-Verlag, 1991.

Birch, Walter de Gray, ed. *Cartularium Saxonicum: A Collection of Charters Relating to Anglo-Saxon History*. 3 vols. London, 1885–93.

Blake, E.O., ed. *Liber Eliensis*. Camden Third Series 92. London: Offices of the Royal Historical Society, 1962.

Brooks, N.P., and S.E. Kelly, eds. *Charters of Christ Church, Canterbury*. Anglo-Saxon Charters 15–17. Oxford: Oxford University Press, forthcoming.

Byrhtferth of Ramsey. *The Lives of St Oswald and St Ecgwine*. Edited and translated by Michael Lapidge. OMT. Oxford: Clarendon Press, 2009.

Campbell, Alistair, ed. *The Battle of Brunanburh*. London: W. Heinemann, 1938.

– ed. *Charters of Rochester*. Anglo-Saxon Charters 1. London: Oxford University Press, 1973.

Carnicelli, Thomas A., ed. *King Alfred's Version of St. Augustine's* Soliloquies. Cambridge, MA: Harvard University Press, 1969.

Colgrave, Bertram, ed. *Two Lives of Saint Cuthbert: A Life by an Anonymous Monk of Lindisfarne and Bede's Prose Life*. Cambridge: Cambridge University Press, 1940.

Cubbin, G.P., ed. *MS D*. Vol. 6 of *The Anglo-Saxon Chronicle: A Collaborative Edition*. Cambridge: D.S. Brewer, 1996.

Dobbie, Elliott Van Kirk, ed. *The Anglo-Saxon Minor Poems*. ASPR 6. New York: Columbia University Press, 1942.

Douglas, David C., and George W. Greenaway, eds. *English Historical Documents 1042–1189*. English Historical Documents 2. 2nd ed. London: Eyre Methuen, 1981.

Dumville, David, and Simon Keynes, eds. *The Anglo-Saxon Chronicle: A Collaborative Edition*. 9 vols. Cambridge: D.S. Brewer, 1983–.

Earle, John. *A Hand-book to the Land-Charters and Other Saxonic Documents*. Oxford, 1888.

Felix. *Felix's Life of Saint Guthlac*. Edited by Bertram Colgrave. Cambridge: Cambridge University Press, 1956.

Fischer, B., I. Gribomont, H.F.D. Sparks, W. Thiele, Robert Weber, and Roger Gryson, eds. *Biblia sacra iuxta Vulgatam versionem*. 5th ed. Stuttgart: Deutsche Bibelgesellschaft, 2007.

Förster, Max, ed. *Zur Geschichte des Reliquienkultus in Altengland*. Munich: Verlag der Bayerischen Akademie der Wissenschaften, 1943.

Fulk, R.D., Robert E. Bjork, and John D. Niles, eds. *Klaeber's Beowulf*. 4th ed. Toronto: University of Toronto Press, 2008.

Godden, Malcolm, and Susan Irvine, eds. *The Old English Boethius: An Edition of the Old English Versions of Boethius's* De Consolatione Philosophiae. 2 vols. Oxford: Oxford University Press, 2009.

Gonser, Paul, ed. *Das angelsächsische Prosa-Leben des hl. Guthlac*. Anglistische Forschungen 27. Heidelberg: C. Winter, 1909.

Gregory the Great. *Homiliae in Evangelia*. Edited by Raymond Étaix. CCSL 141. Turnhout: Brepols, 1999.

Harmer, F.E., ed. and trans. *Anglo-Saxon Writs*. Manchester: Manchester University Press, 1952.

– ed. and trans. *Select English Historical Documents of the Ninth and Tenth Centuries*. Cambridge: Cambridge University Press, 1914.

Hart, C.R. *The Early Charters of Northern England and the North Midlands*. Bristol: Leicester University Press, 1975.

Hill, Joyce, ed. *Old English Minor Heroic Poems*. Durham Medieval and Renaissance Texts 2. 3rd ed. Co-published by the Centre for Medieval and Renaissance Studies, Durham University. Toronto: Pontifical Institute of Mediaeval Studies, 2009.

Irvine, Susan, ed. *MS E*. Vol. 7 of *The Anglo-Saxon Chronicle: A Collaborative Edition*. Cambridge: D.S. Brewer, 2004.

John of Worcester. *The Chronicle of John of Worcester*, Vol. 2: *The Annals from 450 to 1066*. Edited by R.R. Darlington and P. McGurk and translated by Jennifer Bray and P. McGurk. OMT. Oxford: Clarendon Press, 1995.

Kelly, S.E., ed. *Charters of Abingdon Abbey*. 2 vols. Anglo-Saxon Charters 7 and 8. Oxford: Oxford University Press, 2000–1.

– ed. *Charters of Bath and Wells*. Anglo-Saxon Charters 13. Oxford: Oxford University Press, 2007.

– ed. *Charters of Malmesbury Abbey*. Anglo-Saxon Charters 11. Oxford: Oxford University Press, 2005.

– ed. *Charters of Peterborough Abbey*. Anglo-Saxon Charters 14. Oxford: Oxford University Press, 2009.

– ed. *Charters of Selsey*. Anglo-Saxon Charters 6. Oxford: Oxford University Press, 1998.

– ed. *Charters of Shaftesbury Abbey*. Anglo-Saxon Charters 5. Oxford: Oxford University Press, 1996.

– ed. *Charters of St Augustine's Abbey, Canterbury and Minster-in-Thanet*. Anglo-Saxon Charters 4. Oxford: Oxford University Press, 1995.

Keynes, Simon, and Michael Lapidge, eds. and trans. *Alfred the Great: Asser's Life of King Alfred and Other Contemporary Sources*. London and New York: Penguin Books, 1983.

Klinck, Anne L., ed. *The Old English Elegies: A Critical Edition and Genre Study*. Montreal and Kingston: McGill-Queen's University Press, 1992.

Krapp, George Phillip, ed. *The Junius Manuscript*. ASPR 1. New York: Columbia University Press, 1931.

Krapp, George Phillip, and Elliott Van Kirk Dobbie, eds. *The Anglo-Saxon Poetic Records*. 6 vols. New York: Columbia University Press, 1931–53.

– eds. *The Exeter Book*. ASPR 3. New York: Columbia University Press, 1936.

Lapidge, Michael, ed. *The Cult of St Swithun*. Winchester Studies 4.2. The Anglo-Saxon Minsters of Winchester. Oxford: Clarendon Press, 2003.

Liebermann, Felix, ed. *Die Gesetze der Angelsachsen*. 3 vols. Halle: Max Niemeyer, 1903–16. Reprint, Aalen: Scienta, 1960.

Lucas, Peter J., ed. *Exodus*. Rev. ed. Exeter: University of Exeter Press, 1994.

Mac Airt, Séan, and Gearóid Mac Niocaill, eds. *The Annals of Ulster (to A.D. 1131)*. Part 1, Text and Translation. Dublin: Institute for Advanced Studies, 1983.

Malone, Kemp, ed. *Deor*. 4th ed. Methuen's Old English Library. New York: Appleton-Century-Crofts, 1966.

Marsden, Richard, ed. *The* Old English Heptateuch *and Ælfric's* Libellus de Veteri Testamento et Novo. Vol. 1 of EETS, o.s., 330. Oxford: Oxford University Press, 2008.

Miller, Sean, ed. *Charters of the New Minster, Winchester*. Anglo-Saxon Charters 9. Oxford: Oxford University Press, 2001.

O'Brien O'Keeffe, Katherine, ed. *MS C*. Vol. 5 of *The Anglo-Saxon Chronicle: A Collaborative Edition*. Cambridge: D.S. Brewer: 2001.

O'Donovan, M.A., ed. *Charters of Sherborne*. Anglo-Saxon Charters 3. Oxford: Oxford University Press, 1988.

O'Neill, Patrick P., ed. *King Alfred's Old English Prose Translation of the First Fifty Psalms*. Cambridge, MA: Medieval Academy of America, 2001.

Plummer, Charles, ed. *Two of the Saxon Chronicles Parallel*. 2 vols. Oxford, 1892–9.

Roberts, Jane, ed. *The Guthlac Poems of the Exeter Book*. Oxford: Clarendon Press, 1979.

Robertson, A.J., ed. and trans. *Anglo-Saxon Charters*. Cambridge: Cambridge University Press, 1956.

– ed. and trans. *The Laws of the Kings of England from Edmund to Henry I*. Cambridge: Cambridge University Press, 1925.

Sanders, W.B. *Facsimiles of Anglo-Saxon Manuscripts*. 3 vols. Southampton, 1878–84.

Sawyer, P.H. *Anglo-Saxon Charters: An Annotated List and Bibliography*. Royal Historical Society Guides and Handbooks 8. London: Royal Historical Society, 1968.

– ed. *Charters of Burton Abbey*. Anglo-Saxon Charters 2. Oxford: Oxford University Press, 1979.

Scragg, D.G., ed. *The Vercelli Homilies and Related Texts*. EETS, o.s., 300. Oxford: Oxford University Press, 1992.

Stubbs, William, ed. *Memorials of Saint Dunstan, Archbishop of Canterbury*. Rolls Series 63. London, 1874.

Sturluson, Snorri. *Edda*. Translated and edited by Anthony Faulkes. London: Everyman, 1987.

Swanton, Michael, trans. and ed. *The Anglo-Saxon Chronicle*. New York: Routledge, 1998.

Sweet, Henry, ed. *King Alfred's West-Saxon Version of Gregory's Pastoral Care*. 2 vols. EETS, o.s., 45, 50. London, 1871–2.

Tapp, W.H. *The Sunbury Charter*. Sunbury-on-Thames: W.H. Tapp, 1951.

Taylor, Simon, ed. *MS B*. Vol. 4 of *The Anglo-Saxon Chronicle: A Collaborative Edition*. Cambridge: D.S. Brewer, 1983.

Thorpe, Benjamin, ed. *Diplomatarium Anglicum Ævi Saxonici*. London, 1865.

Whitelock, Dorothy, ed. and trans. *Anglo-Saxon Wills*. Cambridge Studies in English Legal History. Cambridge: Cambridge University Press, 1930.

– ed. *English Historical Documents c. 500–1042*. English Historical Documents 1. 2nd ed. London: Eyre Methuen, 1979.

Whitelock, Dorothy, M. Brett, and C.N.L. Brooke, eds. *Councils and Synods with Other Documents Relating to the English Church, I, A.D. 871–1204*. 2 vols. Oxford: Clarendon Press, 1981.

William of Malmesbury. *Gesta Regum Anglorum: The History of the English Kings*. Edited and translated by R.A.B. Mynors, R.M. Thomson, and M. Winterbottom. 2 vols. OMT. Oxford: Clarendon Press, 1998–9.

Wulfstan. *The Homilies of Wulfstan*. Edited by Dorothy Bethurum. Oxford: Clarendon Press, 1957.

– *Sammlung der ihm zugeschriebenen Homilien nebst Untersuchungen über ihre Echtheit*. Edited by Arthur Napier. Berlin, 1883.

Wulfstan of Winchester. *The Life of St Æthelwold*. Edited and translated by Michael Lapidge and Michael Winterbottom. OMT. Oxford: Clarendon Press, 1991.

Secondary Sources

Abels, Richard. 'Bookland and Fyrd Service in Late Saxon England.' *ANS 7* (1985): 1–25.

– 'Heriot.' In Lapidge et al., *Blackwell Encyclopaedia of Anglo-Saxon England*, 235–6.

– *Lordship and Military Obligation in Anglo-Saxon England*. Berkeley: University of California Press, 1988.

Abrams, Lesley. 'Edward the Elder's Danelaw.' In Higham and Hill, *Edward the Elder*, 128–43.

Andrews, Charles McLean. *The Old English Manor: A Study in English Economic History*. Baltimore, 1892.

Auerbach, Erich. *Mimesis: The Representation of Reality in Western Literature*. Translated by Willard R. Trask. Princeton, NJ: Princeton University Press, 1953. First published 1946 in Berne, Switzerland by A. Francke Ltd. Co.

Bailey, Maggie. 'Ælfwynn, Second Lady of the Mercians.' In Higham and Hill, *Edward the Elder*, 112–27.

Barlow, Frank. *Edward the Confessor*. Yale English Monarch Series. 3rd ed. New Haven, CT: Yale University Press, 1997. First edition 1970 by Eyre Methuen Ltd.

– *The Feudal Kingdom of England 1042–1216*. 5th ed. London and New York: Longman, 1999.

Barrow, Julia, and Andrew Wareham, eds. *Myth, Rulership, Church and Charters: Essays in Honour of Nicholas Brooks*. Aldershot, UK, and Burlington, VT: Ashgate, 2008.

Baxter, Stephen. 'Archbishop Wulfstan and the Administration of God's Property.' In Townend, *Wulfstan, Archbishop of York*, 161–205.

– *The Earls of Mercia: Lordship and Power in Late Anglo-Saxon England*. Oxford: Oxford University Press, 2007.

Baxter, Stephen, Catherine Karkov, Janet L. Nelson, and David Pelteret, eds. *Early Medieval Studies in Memory of Patrick Wormald*. Farnham, UK, and Burlington, VT: Ashgate, 2009.

Becker, Wolfgang. 'The Latin Manuscript Sources of the Old English Translations of the Sermon *Remedia peccatorum*.' *MÆ* 45 (1976): 145–52.

– 'The Manuscript Source of Ælfric's Catholic Homily II 7 – a Supplementary Note.' *MÆ* 48 (1979): 105–6.

Bedos-Rezak, Brigitte. 'Diplomatic Sources and Medieval Documentary Practices: An Essay in Interpretive Methodology.' In *The Past and Future of Medieval Studies*, edited by John Van Engen, 313–43. Notre Dame, IN: University of Notre Dame Press, 1994.

Bergin, Thomas F., and Paul G. Haskell. *Preface to Estates in Land and Future Interests*. 2nd ed. Mineola, NY: Foundation Press, 1984.

Bethurum, Dorothy. 'Episcopal Magnificence in the Eleventh Century.' In *Studies in Old English Literature in Honor of Arthur G. Brodeur*, edited by Stanley B. Greenfield, 162–70. Eugene: University of Oregon Books, 1963.

Biggs, Frederick M. 'Edgar's Path to the Throne.' In Scragg, *Edgar, King of the English*, 124–39.

Blackstone, William. *Commentaries on the Laws of England*. 4 vols. Oxford, 1765–9.

Blair, John. *The Church in Anglo-Saxon Society*. Oxford: Oxford University Press, 2005.

Blanton, Virginia, and Helene Scheck, eds. *Intertexts: Studies in Anglo-Saxon Culture Presented to Paul E. Szarmach*. Tempe, AZ: Arizona Center for Medieval and Renaissance Studies and Brepols, 2008.

Boren, James L. 'The Design of the Old English *Deor*.' In *Anglo-Saxon Poetry: Essays in Appreciation for John C. McGalliard*, edited by Lewis E. Nicholson and Dolores Warwick Frese, 264–76. Notre Dame, IN: University of Notre Dame Press, 1975.

Bosworth, Joseph, and T. Northcote Toller. *An Anglo-Saxon Dictionary*. Oxford, 1898.

Bowman, Jeffrey A. *Shifting Landmarks: Property, Proof, and Dispute in Catalonia around the Year 1000*. Ithaca and London: Cornell University Press, 2004.

Boyle, Leonard E. 'Diplomatics.' In *Medieval Studies: An Introduction*, edited by James M. Powell, 82–113. 2nd ed. Syracuse, NY: Syracuse University Press, 1992.

Brand, Paul. '*In perpetuum*: The Rhetoric and Reality of Attempts to Control the Future in the English Medieval Common Law.' In *Medieval Futures: Attitudes to the Future in the Middle Ages*, edited by J.A. Burrow and Ian P. Wei, 101–13. Woodbridge, UK, and Rochester, NY: Boydell Press, 2000.

Bredehoft, Thomas A. *Textual Histories: Readings in the* Anglo-Saxon Chronicle. Toronto: University of Toronto Press, 2001.

Bremmer, Rolf H., Jr. 'The Final Countdown: Apocalyptic Expectations in Anglo-Saxon Charters.' In *Time and Eternity: The Medieval Discourse*, edited by Gerhard Jaritz and Gerson Moreno-Riaño, 501–14. Turnhout: Brepols, 2003.

Brett, Caroline. 'A Breton Pilgrim in England in the Reign of King Æthelstan.' In *France and the British Isles in the Middle Ages and Renaissance*, edited by Gillian Jondorf and D.N. Dumville, 43–70. Woodbridge, UK, and Rochester, NY: Boydell Press, 1991.

Brooks, Nicholas. 'Anglo-Saxon Charters: The Work of the Last Twenty Years.' *ASE* 3 (1974): 211–31. Reprinted as 'Anglo-Saxon Charters: Recent Work,' with a new 'Postscript: Anglo-Saxon Charters, 1973–1998' in his *Anglo-Saxon Myths: State and Church 400–1066*, 181–215. London and Rio Grande: Hambledon Press, 2000.

– 'Arms, Status and Warfare in Late-Saxon England.' In *Ethelred the Unready: Papers from the Millenary Conference*, edited by David Hill, 81–103. BAR, British Series 59. Oxford: British Archaeological Reports, 1978.

– 'The Development of Military Obligations in Eighth- and Ninth-Century England.' In *England Before the Conquest: Studies in Primary Sources Presented to Dorothy Whitelock*, edited by Peter Clemoes and Kathleen Hughes, 69–84. Cambridge: Cambridge University Press, 1971.

– *The Early History of the Church of Canterbury: Christ Church from 597 to 1066*. London and New York: Leicester University Press, 1984.

– 'The Fonthill Letter, Ealdorman Ordlaf and Anglo-Saxon Law in Practice.' In Baxter et al., *Early Medieval Studies in Memory of Patrick Wormald*, 301–17.

– 'Why is the *Anglo-Saxon Chronicle* about Kings?' *ASE* 39 (2011): 43–70.

Brown, Michelle P., and Carol A. Farr, eds. *Mercia: An Anglo-Saxon Kingdom in Europe*. Studies in the Early History of Europe. London and New York: Leicester University Press, 2001.

Brown, Warren. 'Charters as Weapons. On the Role Played by Early Medieval Dispute Records in the Disputes They Record.' *JMH* 28 (2002): 227–48.

– *Unjust Seizure: Conflict, Interest, and Authority in an Early Medieval Society*. Ithaca and London: Cornell University Press, 2001.

Bruckner, Albert. 'Zur Diplomatik der älteren angelsächsischen Urkunde.' *Archivalische Zeitschrift* 61 (1965): 11–45.

Brunner, Heinrich. *Zur Rechtsgeschichte der römischen und germanischen Urkunde*. Berlin, 1880.

Bullough, D.A. 'The Educational Tradition in England from Alfred to Ælfric: Teaching *Utriusque Linguae.' La scuola nell'occidente latino dell'alto medioevo*. Settimane di studio del Centro italiano di studi sull'alto medioevo 19 (1972): 453–94. Reprinted in his *Carolingian Renewal: Sources and Heritage*, 297–334. Manchester and New York: Manchester University Press, 1991.

Butler, Robert M. 'Glastonbury and the Early History of the Exeter Book.' In *Old English Literature in its Manuscript Context*, edited by Joyce Tally Lionarons, 173–215. Medieval European Studies 5. Morgantown: West Virginia University Press, 2004.

Campbell, Alistair. *An Anglo-Saxon Dictionary, Enlarged Addenda and Corrigenda to the Supplement by T. Northcote Toller*. Oxford: Clarendon Press, 1972.

– *Old English Grammar*. Oxford: Clarendon Press, 1959.

Campbell, James. 'Some Agents and Agencies of the Late Anglo-Saxon State.' In *Domesday Studies: Papers Read at the Novocentenary Conference of the Royal Historical Society and the Institute of British Geographers, Winchester, 1986*, edited by J.C. Holt, 201–18. Woodbridge, UK, and Wolfeboro, NH: Boydell Press, 1987.

– 'What is Not Known about the Reign of Edward the Elder.' In Higham and Hill, *Edward the Elder*, 12–24.

Chadwick, H. Munro. *Studies on Anglo-Saxon Institutions*. Cambridge: Cambridge University Press, 1905.

Chaplais, Pierre. 'The Anglo-Saxon Chancery: From the Diploma to the Writ.' *Journal of the Society of Archivists* 3 (1966): 160–76. Reprinted in Ranger, *Prisca Munimenta*, 43–62.

– 'The Origin and Authenticity of the Royal Anglo-Saxon Diploma.' *Journal of the Society of Archivists* 3 (1965): 48–61. Reprinted in Ranger, *Prisca Munimenta*, 28–42.

– 'The Royal Anglo-Saxon "Chancery" of the Tenth Century Revisited.' In *Studies in Medieval History Presented to R.H.C. Davis*, edited by H. Mayr-Harting and R.I. Moore, 41–51. London: Hambledon Press, 1985.

– 'Some Early Anglo-Saxon Diplomas on Single Sheets: Originals or Copies?' *Journal of the Society of Archivists* 3 (1968): 315–36. Reprinted in Ranger, *Prisca Munimenta*, 63–87.

– 'Who Introduced Charters into England? The Case for Augustine.' *Journal of the Society of Archivists* 3.10 (1969): 526–42. Reprinted in Ranger, *Prisca Munimenta*, 88–107.

Charles-Edwards, T.M. 'Kinship, Status and the Origins of the Hide.' *Past and Present* 56 (1972): 3–33.

Clark, Stephanie. 'A More Permanent Homeland: Land Tenure in *Guthlac A*.' *ASE* 40 (2012), forthcoming.

Clarke, Catherine A.M. *Literary Landscapes and the Idea of England, 700–1400.* Cambridge: D.S. Brewer, 2006.

Clunies Ross, Margaret. 'Land-Taking and Text-Making in Medieval Iceland.' In *Text and Territory: Geographical Imagination in the European Middle Ages*, edited by Sylvia Tomasch and Sealy Gilles, 159–84. Philadelphia: University of Pennsylvania Press, 1998.

Cohen, Jeffrey J. *Medieval Identity Machines.* Medieval Cultures 35. Minneapolis: University of Minnesota Press, 2003.

Colgrave, Bertram. 'The Earliest Saints' Lives Written in England.' *PBA* 44 (1958): 35–60.

Conner, Patrick W. *Anglo-Saxon Exeter: A Tenth Century Cultural History.* Studies in Anglo-Saxon History 4. Woodbridge, UK, and Rochester, NY: Boydell Press, 1993.

– 'Source Studies, the Old English *Guthlac A* and the English Benedictine Reformation.' *Revue Bénédictine* 103 (1993): 380–413.

Crick, Julia. 'Church, Land and Local Nobility in Early Ninth-Century Kent: The Case of Ealdorman Oswulf.' *Historical Research* 61 (1988): 251–69.

– 'Women, Posthumous Benefaction, and Family Strategy in Pre-Conquest England.' *The Journal of British Studies* 38 (1999): 399–422.

Cross, James E. 'A *Sermo de Misericordia* in Old English Prose.' *Anglia* 108 (1990): 429–40.

– '*Ubi Sunt* Passages in Old English – Sources and Relationships.' *Årsbok, Vetenskaps-Societeten i Lund* (1956): 25–44.

Cubitt, Catherine. '"As the Lawbook Teaches": Reeves, Lawbooks and Urban Life in the Anonymous Old English Legend of the Seven Sleepers.' *EHR* 124 (2009): 1021–49.

Curtius, Ernst Robert. *European Literature and the Latin Middle Ages.* Translated by Willard R. Trask. Princeton, NJ: Princeton University Press, 1990. First published in 1953 by Bollingen Foundation, Inc.

Davidson, Michael R. 'The (Non)submission of the Northern Kings in 920.'
  In Higham and Hill, *Edward the Elder*, 200–11.
Davies, Wendy, and Paul Fouracre, eds. *The Settlement of Disputes in Early
  Medieval Europe.* Cambridge: Cambridge University Press, 1986.
Davis, R.H.C. 'Alfred the Great: Propaganda and Truth.' *History* 56 (1971): 169–82.
Dempsey, George T. 'Legal Terminology in Anglo-Saxon England: The *Trimoda
  Necessitas* Charter.' *Speculum* 57 (1982): 843–9.
Di Sciacca, Claudia. *Finding the Right Words: Isidore's* Synonyma *in Anglo-
  Saxon England.* Toronto: University of Toronto Press, 2008.
Dictionary of Medieval Latin from British Sources. Edited by R.E. Latham.
  London: Oxford University Press for the British Academy, 1975–.
Dictionary of Old English: A to G online. Edited by Angus Cameron, Ashley
  Crandell Amos, Antonette diPaolo Healey, and Joan Holland. Toronto:
  Dictionary of Old English Project, 2007. http://tapor.library.utoronto.ca/doe/
  dict/index.html.
Dictionary of Old English Web Corpus. Edited by Antonette diPaolo Healey,
  with John Price Wilkin and Xin Xiang. Toronto: Dictionary of Old English
  Project, 2009. http://tapor.library.utoronto.ca/doecorpus/.
Donoghue, Daniel. *Old English Literature: A Short Introduction.* Malden, MA,
  and Oxford, UK: Blackwell, 2004.
Drögereit, Richard. 'Gab es eine angelsächsische Königskanzlei?' *Archiv für
  Urkundenforschung* 13 (1935): 335–436.
Drout, Michael D.C. *How Tradition Works: A Meme-Based Cultural Poetics
  of the Anglo-Saxon Tenth Century.* Medieval and Renaissance Texts and Studies
  306. Tempe, AZ: Arizona Center for Medieval and Renaissance Studies, 2006.
Dumville, David N. 'The Ætheling: A Study in Anglo-Saxon Constitutional
  History.' *ASE* 8 (1979): 1–33.
– 'The Anglo-Saxon Chronicle and the Origins of English Square Minuscule
  Script.' In his *Wessex and England*, 55–139.
– 'Between Alfred the Great and Edgar the Peacemaker: Æthelstan, First King
  of England.' In his *Wessex and England*, 141–71.
– 'English Square Minuscule Script: The Background and Earliest Phases.' *ASE*
  16 (1987): 147–79.
– 'English Square Minuscule Script: The Mid-Century Phases.' *ASE* 23 (1994):
  133–64.
– *Wessex and England from Alfred to Edgar: Six Essays on Political, Cultural,
  and Ecclesiastical Revival.* Studies in Anglo-Saxon History 3. Woodbridge,
  UK, and Rochester, NY: Boydell Press, 1992.
Edwards, Heather. *The Charters of the Early West Saxon Kingdom.* BAR, British
  Series 198. Oxford: British Archaeological Reports, 1988.

Ekwall, Eilert. *The Concise Oxford Dictionary of English Place-Names*. 4th ed. Oxford: Clarendon Press, 1960.

– *Studies on English Place- and Personal Names*. Lund: C.W.K. Gleerup, 1931.

Erskine, R.W.H., and Ann Williams, eds. *The Story of Domesday Book*. Chichester: Phillimore & Co. Ltd., 2003. First published in 1987 by Alecto Historical Editions as *Domesday Book Studies*.

Faith, Rosamond. *The English Peasantry and the Growth of Lordship*. Studies in the Early History of Britain. London: Leicester University Press, 1997.

– 'Peasant Families and Inheritance Customs in Medieval England.' *The Agricultural History Review* 14 (1966): 77–95.

Fell, Christine. 'Perceptions of Transience.' In Godden and Lapidge, *The Cambridge Companion to Old English Literature*, 172–89.

Finberg, H.P.R. 'Anglo-Saxon England to 1042.' In *The Agrarian History of England and Wales I.ii, A.D. 43–1042*, edited by H.P.R Finberg, 385–525. Cambridge: Cambridge University Press, 1972.

Fisher, D.J.V. 'The Anti-Monastic Reaction in the Reign of Edward the Marty.' *Cambridge Historical Journal* 10 (1950–2): 254–70.

Flight, Colin. 'Four Vernacular Texts from the Pre-Conquest Archive of Rochester Cathedral.' *Archaeologia Cantiana* 115 (1995): 121–53.

Fontes Anglo-Saxonici Project, ed. *Fontes Anglo-Saxonici: A Register of Written Sources Used by Anglo-Saxon Authors*. http://fontes.english.ox.ac.uk.

Foot, Sarah. *Æthelstan: The First King of England*. Yale English Monarch Series. New Haven and London: Yale University Press, 2011.

– 'Finding the Meaning of Form: Narrative in Annals and Chronicles.' In *Writing Medieval History*, edited by Nancy Partner, 88–108. London: H. Arnold, 2005.

– 'Reading Anglo-Saxon Charters: Memory, Record, or Story?' In *Narrative and History in the Early Medieval West*, edited by Elizabeth M. Tyler and Ross Balzaretti, 39–65. Turnhout: Brepols, 2006.

– 'Where English Becomes British: Rethinking Contexts for *Brunanburh*.' In Barrow and Wareham, *Myth, Rulership, Church and Charters*, 127–44.

Fouracre, Paul. '"Placita" and the Settlement of Disputes in Later Merovingian Francia.' In Davies and Fouracre, *The Settlement of Disputes*, 23–43.

Frank, Roberta. 'Did Anglo-Saxon Audiences Have a Skaldic Tooth?' *Scandinavian Studies* 59 (1987): 338–55.

– 'Germanic Legend in Old English Literature.' In Godden and Lapidge, *The Cambridge Companion to Old English Literature*, 88–106.

Frankis, P.J. '*Deor* and *Wulf and Eadwacer*: Some Conjectures.' *MÆ* 31 (1962): 161–75.

Fulk, R.D., and Christopher M. Cain. *A History of Old English Literature*. Malden, MA, and Oxford, UK: Blackwell, 2003.

Gameson, Richard. 'The Origin of the Exeter Book of Old English Poetry.' *ASE* 25 (1996): 135–85.

Ganz, David. "The Ideology of Sharing: Apostolic Community and Ecclesiastical Property in the Early Middle Ages.' In *Property and Power in the Early Middle Ages*, edited by Wendy Davies and Paul Fouracre, 17–30. Cambridge: Cambridge University Press, 1995.

Ganz, David, and Walter Goffart. 'Charters Earlier than 800 from French Collections.' *Speculum* 65 (1990): 906–32.

Gatch, Milton McC. 'King Alfred's Version of Augustine's *Soliloquia*: Some Suggestions on its Rational and Unity.' In Szarmach, *Studies in Earlier Old English Prose*, 17–45.

Geary, Patrick J. 'Land, Language and Memory in Europe 700–1100.' *TRHS*, 6th series, 9 (1999): 169–84.

Gelling, Margaret, and Ann Cole. *The Landscape of Place-Names*. Stamford: Shaun Tyas, 2000.

Gerould, Gordan Hall. 'The Old English Poems on St. Guthlac and their Latin Source.' *Modern Language Notes* 32 (1917): 77–89.

Gneuss, Helmut. *Handlist of Anglo-Saxon Manuscripts: A List of Manuscripts and Manuscript Fragments Written or Owned in England up to 1100*. Medieval and Renaissance Texts and Studies 241. Tempe, AZ: Arizona Center for Medieval and Renaissance Studies, 2001.

– 'The Study of Language in Anglo-Saxon England.' In *Textual and Material Culture in Anglo-Saxon England: Thomas Northcote Toller and the Toller Memorial Lectures*, edited by Donald Scragg, 75–105. Rochester, NY: D.S. Brewer, 2003.

Godden, Malcolm. 'The Alfredian Project and its Aftermath: Rethinking the Literary History of the Ninth and Tenth Centuries.' *PBA* 162 (2009): 93–122.

– 'The Anglo-Saxons and the Goths: Rewriting the Sack of Rome.' *ASE* 31 (2002): 47–68.

– 'Did King Alfred Write Anything?' *MÆ* 76 (2007): 1–23.

– 'Literary Language.' In *The Beginnings to 1066*, edited by Richard M. Hogg, 490–535. Vol. 1 of *The Cambridge History of the English Language*. Cambridge: Cambridge University Press, 1992.

Godden, Malcolm, and Michael Lapidge, eds. *The Cambridge Companion to Old English Literature*. Cambridge: Cambridge University Press, 1986.

Goebel, Julius, Jr. *Felony and Misdemeanor: A Study in the History of Criminal Law*. New York: Commonwealth Fund, 1937. Reprint, Philadelphia: University of Pennsylvania Press, 1976.

Gray, Kevin, and Susan Francis Gray. *Elements of Land Law*. 5th ed. Oxford: Oxford University Press, 2009.

Greenfield, Stanley B. 'The Formulaic Expression of the Theme of "Exile" in Anglo-Saxon Poetry.' *Speculum* 30 (1955): 200–6.

Greenfield, Stanley B., and Daniel G. Calder. *A New Critical History of Old English Literature*. New York and London: New York University Press, 1986.

Gretsch, Mechthild. *The Intellectual Foundations of the English Benedictine Reform*. CSASE 25. Cambridge: Cambridge University Press, 1999.

Grinsell, L.V. 'Barrows in the Anglo-Saxon Land Charters.' *Antiquaries Journal* 71 (1991): 46–63.

Haines, Dorothy. 'Courtroom Drama and the Homiletic Monologues of *The Vercelli Book*.' In *Verbal Encounters: Anglo-Saxon and Old Norse Studies for Roberta Frank*, edited by Antonina Harbus and Russell Poole, 105–23. Toronto: University of Toronto Press, 2005.

– 'Vacancies in Heaven: The Doctrine of Replacement and *Genesis A*.' *N&Q*, n.s., 44 (1997): 150–4.

Harbus, Antonina. 'Metaphors of Authority in Alfred's Prefaces.' *Neophilologus* 91 (2007): 717–27.

Hargreaves, A.D. *An Introduction to the Principles of Land Law*. 4th ed. London: Sweet & Maxwell, 1963.

Harris, Joseph. '"Deor" and Its Refrain: Preliminaries to an Interpretation.' *Traditio* 43 (1987): 23–53.

Hart, Cyril. 'The B Text of the *Anglo-Saxon Chronicle*.' *JMH* 8 (1982): 241–99.

Harvey, Barbara F. 'The Life of the Manor.' In Erskine and Williams, *Story of Domesday Book*, 54–9.

Harvey, P.D.A. 'Rectitudines Singularum Personarum and Gerefa.' *EHR* 108 (1993): 1–22.

Harvey, Sally. 'Domesday England.' In *The Agrarian History of England and Wales II: 1042–1350*, edited by John Thirsk, 45–136. Cambridge: Cambridge University Press, 1988.

– 'Evidence for Settlement Study: Domesday Book.' In *Medieval Settlement: Continuity and Change*, edited by P.H. Sawyer, 195–9. London: Edward Arnold, 1976.

Heslop, T.A. 'English Seals from the Mid Ninth Century to 1100.' *Journal of the British Archaeological Association* 133 (1980): 1–16.

Heuchan, Valerie. 'God's Co-Workers and Powerful Tools: A Study of the Sources of Alfred's Building Metaphor in his Old English Translation of Augustine's *Soliloquies*.' *N&Q*, n.s., 54 (2007): 1–11.

Higham, N.J., and D.H. Hill, eds. *Edward the Elder, 899–924*. London and New York: Routledge, 2001.

Hill, David. *An Atlas of Anglo-Saxon England*. Toronto: University of Toronto Press, 1981.

Hill, Thomas D. 'The Middle Way: *Idel-Wuldor* and *Egesa* in the Old English *Guthlac A*.' *RES* 30 (1979): 182–7.

Honoré, A.M. 'Ownership.' In *Oxford Essays in Jurisprudence: A Collaborative Work*, edited by A.G. Guest, 107–47. London: Oxford University Press, 1961.

Hooke, Della. *The Landscape of Anglo-Saxon England*. London: Leicester University Press, 1998.

– *Trees in Anglo-Saxon England: Literature, Lore and Landscape*. Woodbridge, UK, and Rochester, NY: Boydell Press, 2010.

Hough, Carole. 'Legal and Documentary Writings.' In *A Companion to Anglo-Saxon Literature*, edited by Phillip Pulsiano and Elaine Treharne, 170–87. Oxford, UK, and Malden, MA: Blackwell, 2001.

Howe, John. 'Creating Symbolic Landscapes: Medieval Development of Sacred Space.' In Howe and Wolfe, *Inventing Medieval Landscapes*, 208–23.

Howe, John, and Michael Wolfe, eds. *Inventing Medieval Landscapes: Senses of Place in Western Europe*. Gainesville: University Press of Florida, 2002.

Howe, Nicholas. 'The Landscape of Anglo-Saxon England: Inherited, Invented, Imagined.' In Howe and Wolfe, *Inventing Medieval Landscapes*, 91–112.

– 'Looking for Home in Anglo-Saxon England.' In *Home and Homelessness in the Medieval and Renaissance World*, edited by Nicholas Howe, 143–63. Notre Dame, IN: University of Notre Dame Press, 2004.

– *Migration and Mythmaking in Anglo-Saxon England*. New Haven and London: Yale University Press, 1989. Reprint, Notre Dame, IN: University of Notre Dame Press, 2001.

– *Writing the Map of Anglo-Saxon England: Essays in Cultural Geography*. New Haven and London: Yale University Press, 2008.

Hyams, Paul R. 'The Charter as a Source for the Early Common Law.' *Journal of Legal History* 12 (1991): 173–89.

– *Rancor and Reconciliation in Medieval England*. Ithaca and London: Cornell University Press, 2003.

Insley, Charles. 'Charters and Episcopal Scriptoria in the Anglo-Saxon South-West.' *Early Medieval Europe* 7 (1998): 173–97.

– 'Where Did All the Charters Go? Anglo-Saxon Charters and the New Politics of the Eleventh Century.' *ANS* 24 (2002): 109–27.

Irvine, Susan. 'Old English Prose: King Alfred and His Books.' In Beowulf & Other Stories: A New Introduction to Old English, Old Icelandic and Anglo-Norman Literatures, edited by Richard North and Joe Allard, 246–71. Harlow: Pearson Longman, 2007.

Jayakumar, Shashi. 'Eadwig and Edgar: Politics, Propaganda, Faction.' In Scragg, *Edgar, King of the English*, 83–103.

– 'Reform and Retribution: The "Anti-Monastic Reaction" in the Reign of Edward the Martyr.' In Baxter et al., *Early Medieval Studies in Memory of Patrick Wormald*, 337–52.

John, Eric. *Land Tenure in Early England: A Discussion of Some Problems*. Studies in Early English History 1. Leicester: Leicester University Press, 1960.

– *Orbis Britanniae and Other Studies*. Studies in Early English History 4. Leicester: Leicester University Press, 1966.

Johnson, David F. 'The Fall of Lucifer in *Genesis A* and Two Anglo-Latin Royal Charters.' *JEGP* 97 (1998): 500–21.

– 'Spiritual Combat and the Land of Canaan in *Guthlac A*.' In Blanton and Scheck, *Intertexts: Studies in Anglo-Saxon Culture*, 307–17.

Jolliffe, J.E.A. 'English Book-Right.' *EHR* 50 (1935): 1–21.

Jones, Christopher. 'Envisioning the *Cenobium* in the Old English *Guthlac A*.' *MS* 57 (1995): 259–91.

– Review of *The Old English Boethius: An Edition of the Old English Versions of Boethius's* De Consolatione Philosophiae, by Malcolm Godden and Susan Irvine. *Speculum* 86 (2011): 200–4.

Jones, G.R.J. 'Nucleal Settlement and its Tenurial Relationships: Some Morphological Implications.' In *Villages, Fields and Frontiers: Studies in European Rural Settlement in the Medieval and Early Modern Periods*, edited by B.K. Roberts and R.E. Glasscock, 153–70. BAR, International Series 185. Oxford: British Archaeological Reports, 1983.

Jorgensen, Alice, ed. *Reading the Anglo-Saxon Chronicle: Language, Literature, History*. Studies in the Early Middle Ages 23. Turnhout: Brepols, 2010.

Jurasinski, Stefan. *Ancient Privileges:* Beowulf, *Law, and the Making of Germanic Antiquity*. Medieval European Studies 6. Morgantown: West Virginia University Press, 2006.

Kelly, Susan. 'Anglo-Saxon Lay Society and the Written Word.' In McKitterick, *Uses of Literacy in Early Mediaeval Europe*, 36–62.

Kemble, J.M. 'Anglo-Saxon Document Relating to Lands at Send and Sunbury, in Middlesex, in the Time of Eadgar and the Writ of Cnut on the Accession of Æthelnoth to the See of Canterbury, A.D. 1020.' *Archaeological Journal* 14 (1857): 58–62.

Kennedy, A.G. 'Disputes about *Bocland*: The Forum for their Adjudication.' *ASE* 14 (1985): 175–95.

– 'Law and Litigation in the *Libellus Æthelwoldi episcopi*.' *ASE* 24 (1995): 131–83.

Ker, N.R. *Catalogue of Manuscripts Containing Anglo-Saxon*. Oxford: Clarendon Press, 1957.

Keynes, Simon. 'Anglo-Saxon Charters: Lost and Found.' In Barrow and
    Wareham, *Myth, Rulership, Church and Charters*, 45–66.
– 'A Conspectus of the Charters of King Edgar, 957–75.' In Scragg, *Edgar, King
    of the English*, 60–80.
– 'Crime and Punishment in the Reign of King Æthelred the Unready.' In Wood
    and Lund, *People and Places in Northern Europe*, 67–81.
– *The Diplomas of King Æthelred 'the Unready' 978–1016: A Study in Their Use
    as Historical Evidence*. Cambridge: Cambridge University Press, 1980.
– 'The "Dunstan B" Charters.' *ASE* 23 (1994): 165–93.
– 'Edgar, *rex admirabilis*.' In Scragg, *Edgar, King of the English*, 3–58.
– 'Edward, King of the Anglo-Saxons.' In Higham and Hill, *Edward the Elder*,
    40–66.
– 'England, 700–900.' In *The New Cambridge Medieval History, Vol. 2:
    c.700–c.900*, edited by Rosamond McKitterick, 18–42. Cambridge: Cambridge
    University Press, 1995.
– 'The Fonthill Letter.' In *Words, Texts, and Manuscripts: Studies in Anglo-Saxon
    Culture Presented to Helmet Gneuss on the Occasion of his Sixty-Fifth Birth-
    day*, edited by Michael Korhammer, 53–97. Cambridge: D.S. Brewer, 1992.
– 'King Alfred and the Mercians.' In *Kings, Currency and Alliances: History and
    Coinage of Southern England in the Ninth Century*, edited by Mark A.S.
    Blackburn and David N. Dumville, 1–45. Studies in Anglo-Saxon History 9.
    Woodbridge, UK, and Rochester, NY: Boydell Press, 1998.
– 'King Athelstan's Books.' In *Learning and Literature in Anglo-Saxon England:
    Studies Presented to Peter Clemoes on the Occasion of his Sixty-Fifth Birthday*,
    edited by Michael Lapidge and Helmut Gneuss, 143–201. Cambridge:
    Cambridge University Press, 1985.
– 'Mercia and Wessex in the Ninth Century.' In Brown and Farr, *Mercia: An
    Anglo-Saxon Kingdom in Europe*, 310–28.
– 'The Power of the Written Word: Alfredian England 871–899.' In Reuter,
    Alfred the Great, 175–97.
– 'Regenbald the Chancellor (*sic*).' *ANS* 10 (1988): 185–222.
– 'Re-Reading King Æthelred the Unready.' In *Writing Medieval Biography
    750–1250: Essays in Honour of Professor Frank Barlow*, edited by David Bates,
    Julia Crick, and Sarah Hamilton, 77–97. Woodbridge, UK: Boydell Press, 2006.
– 'Royal Government and the Written Word in Late Anglo-Saxon England.' In
    McKitterick, *Uses of Literacy in Early Mediaeval Europe*, 226–57.
– 'The West Saxon Charters of King Æthelwulf and His Sons.' *EHR* 109
    (1994): 1109–49.
Kiernan, Kevin S. '*Deor*: The Consolations of an Anglo-Saxon Boethius.'
    Neuphilologische Mitteilungen 79 (1978): 333–40.

King, Vanessa. 'St Oswald's Tenants.' In *St Oswald of Worcester: Life and Influence*, edited by Nicholas Brooks and Catherine Cubitt, 100–16. London and New York: Leicester University Press, 1996.

Knappe, Gabriele. 'Classical Rhetoric in Anglo-Saxon England.' *ASE* 27 (1998): 5–29.

Korhammer, P.M. 'The Origin of the Bosworth Psalter.' *ASE* 2 (1973): 173–87.

Kretzschmar, William A., Jr. 'Adaptation and *Anweald* in the Old English Orosius.' *ASE* 16 (1987): 127–45.

Krier, James E. *Property*. 17th ed. Chicago: Thomson West, 2006.

Kurtz, Benjamin P. 'From St. Antony to St. Guthlac: A Study in Biography.' *University of California Publications in Modern Philology* 12 (1926): 103–46.

Lapidge, Michael. *Anglo-Latin Literature 900–1066*. London and Rio Grande: Hambledon Press, 1993.

– 'B. and the *Vita S. Dunstani*.' In *St Dunstan: His Life, Times and Cult*, edited by Nigel Ramsay, Margaret Sparks, and Tim Tatton-Brown, 247–59. Woodbridge, UK, and Rochester, NY: Boydell Press, 1992. Reprinted in his *Anglo-Latin Literature 900–1066*, 279–91.

– '*Beowulf* and Perception.' *PBA* 111 (2001): 61–97.

– 'The Hermeneutic Style in Tenth-Century Anglo-Latin Literature.' *ASE* 4 (1975): 67–111. Reprinted in his *Anglo-Latin Literature 900–1066*, 105–49.

– 'Israel the Grammarian in Anglo-Saxon England.' In *From Athens to Chartres, Neoplatonism and Medieval Thought: Studies in Honour of Edouard Jeauneau*, edited by Haijo Jan Westra, 97–114. Leiden and New York: Brill, 1992. Reprinted in his *Anglo-Latin Literature 900–1066*, 87–104.

– 'Old English Compounds: A Latin Perspective.' In Blanton and Scheck, *Intertexts: Studies in Anglo-Saxon Culture*, 17–32.

– 'Schools, Learning and Literature in Tenth-Century England.' *Settimane di studio del Centro italiano di studi sull'alto medioevo* 38 (1991): 951–98. Reprinted in his *Anglo-Latin Literature 900–1066*, 1–48.

– 'Some Latin Poems as Evidence for the Reign of Athelstan.' *ASE* 9 (1981): 61–98. Reprinted in *Anglo-Latin Literature 900–1066*, 49–86.

Lapidge, Michael, John Blair, Simon Keynes, and Donald Scragg, eds. *The Blackwell Encyclopaedia of Anglo-Saxon England*. Malden, MA, and Oxford, UK: Blackwell, 1999.

Lavelle, Ryan. 'Geographies of Power in the Anglo-Saxon Chronicle: The Royal Estates of Anglo-Saxon Wessex.' In Jorgensen, *Reading the Anglo-Saxon Chronicle*, 187–219.

Lees, Clare A., and Gillian R. Overing. *Double Agents: Women and Clerical Culture in Anglo-Saxon England*. Philadelphia: University of Pennsylvania Press, 2001.

Lennard, Reginald. *Rural England, 1086–1135: A Study of Social and Agrarian Conditions*. Oxford: Clarendon Press, 1959.

Levison, Wilhelm. *England and the Continent in the Eighth Century*. Oxford: Clarendon Press, 1946.

Levy, Ernst. *West Roman Vulgar Law: The Law of Property*. Philadelphia: American Philosophical Society, 1951.

Leyser, Karl. 'Ritual, Ceremony and Gesture: Ottonian Germany.' In his *Communications and Power in Medieval Europe: The Carolingian and Ottonian Centuries*, edited by Timothy Reuter, 189–213. London and Rio Grande: Hambledon Press, 1994.

Liebermann, Felix. 'Ueber ostenglische Geschichtsquellen des 12., 13., 14. Jahrhunderts, besonders den falschen Ingulf.' *Neues Archiv der Gesellschaft für ältere deutsche Geschichtskunde* 18 (1892): 225–67.

Lionarons, Joyce Tally. 'Napier Homily L: Wulfstan's Eschatology at the Close of his Career.' In Townend, *Wulfstan, Archbishop of York*, 413–28.

Livingston, Michael, ed. *The Battle of Brunanburh: A Casebook*. Exeter: University of Exeter Press, 2011.

Love, R.C. 'The Sources of Vita S. Guthlaci (L.E.2.1).' 1997. *Fontes Anglo-Saxonici*.

Lowe, E.A. *English Uncial*. Oxford: Clarendon Press, 1960.

Lowe, Kathryn A. 'The Development of the Anglo-Saxon Boundary Clause.' *Nomina* 21 (1998): 63–100.

– 'The Nature and Effect of the Anglo-Saxon Vernacular Will.' *Journal of Legal History* 19 (1998): 23–61.

Loyn, H.R. 'Gesiths and Thegns in Anglo-Saxon England from the Seventh to the Tenth Century.' *EHR* 70 (1955): 529–49.

– *The Governance of Anglo-Saxon England 500–1087*. London: Edward Arnold, 1984.

– 'The Hundred in England in the Tenth and Early Eleventh Centuries.' In *British Government and Administration: Studies Presented to S.B. Chrimes*, edited by H. Hearder and H.R. Lyon, 1–15. Cardiff: University of Wales Press, 1974.

Loyn, H.R., and J. Insley. 'Folkland.' In *Reallexikon der germanischen Altertumskunde*, edited by Johannes Hoops, 9:311–13. 35 vols. Berlin and New York: W. Gruyter, 1995.

Lund, Niels. 'King Edgar and the Danelaw.' *Mediaeval Scandinavia* 9 (1976): 181–95.

Maitland, Frederic W. *Domesday Book and Beyond: Three Essays in the Early History of England*. Cambridge, 1897.

McKitterick, Rosamond. *The Carolingians and the Written Word*. Cambridge: Cambridge University Press, 1989.

– ed. *The Uses of Literacy in Early Mediaeval Europe*. Cambridge: Cambridge University Press, 1990.

Michelet, Fabienne L. *Creation, Migration, and Conquest: Imaginary Geography and Sense of Space in Old English Literature*. Oxford: Oxford University Press, 2006.

Mitchell, Bruce. *Old English Syntax*. 2 vols. Oxford: Clarendon Press, 1985.

Nelson, Janet L. 'Reconstructing a Royal Family: Reflections on Alfred, from Asser, Chapter 2.' In Wood and Lund, *People and Places in Northern Europe*, 47–66.

Neville, Jennifer. *Representations of the Natural World in Old English Poetry*. CSASE 27. Cambridge: Cambridge University Press, 1999.

Nicholas, George E. 'Monasticism and the Social Temptation in the Old English *Guthlac A*.' *American Benedictine Review* 46 (1995): 444–58.

Niles, John D. 'Skaldic Technique in *Brunanburh*.' *Scandinavian Studies* 59 (1987): 356–66.

O'Brien O'Keeffe, Katherine. 'Guthlac's Crossings.' *Quaestio: Selected Proceedings of the Cambridge Colloquium in Anglo-Saxon, Norse and Celtic* 2 (2001): 1–26.

Oosthuizen, Susan. 'Sokemen and Freemen: Tenure, Status and Landscape Conservatism in Eleventh-Century Cambridgeshire.' In *Anglo-Saxons: Studies Presented to Cyril Roy Hart*, edited by Simon Keynes and Alfred P. Smyth, 186–207. Dublin: Four Courts Press, 2006.

Pelteret, David A.E. 'An Anonymous Historian of Edward the Elder's Reign.' In Baxter et al., *Early Medieval Studies in Memory of Patrick Wormald*, 319–36.

– *Slavery in Early Mediaeval England: From the Reign of Alfred until the Twelfth Century*. Studies in Anglo-Saxon History 7. Woodbridge, UK: Boydell Press 1995.

Pollock, Frederick. 'Anglo-Saxon Law.' *EHR* 8 (1893): 239–71.

Pollock, Frederick, and Frederic W. Maitland. *The History of English Law Before the Time of Edward I*. 2nd ed. 2 vols. Cambridge, 1898.

Potter, Simeon. 'King Alfred's Last Preface.' In *Philologica: The Malone Anniversary Studies*, edited by Thomas A. Kirby and Henry Bosley Woolf, 25–30. Baltimore: Johns Hopkins Press, 1949.

Powell, Timothy E. 'The "Three Orders" of Society in Anglo-Saxon England.' *ASE* 23 (1994): 103–32.

Prescott, Andrew. 'The Developing State: Manuscripts.' In *The Making of England: Anglo-Saxon Art and Culture, AD 600–900*, edited by Leslie Webster and Janet Backhouse, 39–47. Toronto: University of Toronto Press, 1991.

Prosopography of Anglo-Saxon England. http://www.pase.ac.uk/. Accessed June 2011.

Rabin, Andrew. 'Anglo-Saxon Women Before the Law: A Student Edition of Five Old English Lawsuits.' *Old English Newsletter* 41, no. 3 (2008): 33–56.

- 'Female Advocacy and Royal Protection in Tenth-Century England: The Legal Career of Queen Ælfthryth.' *Speculum* 84 (2009): 261–88.
- 'Old English *Forespeca* and the Role of the Advocate in Anglo-Saxon Law.' *MS* 69 (2007): 223–54.
- 'Testimony and Authority in Old English Law: Writing the Subject in the "Fonthill Letter."' In *Law and Sovereignty in the Middle Ages and the Renaissance*, edited by Robert S. Sturges, 153–71. Turnhout: Brepols, 2011.

Rabuck, Mark William. 'The Imagined Boundary: Borders and Frontiers in Anglo-Saxon England.' PhD diss., Yale University, 1995.

Ranger, Felicity, ed. *Prisca Munimenta: Studies in Archival and Administrative History Presented to A.E.J. Hollaender.* London: University of London Press, 1973.

Reed, Michael. 'Anglo-Saxon Charter Boundaries.' In *Discovering Past Landscapes*, edited by Michael Reed, 261–306. London: Croom Helm, 1984.
- 'Buckinghamshire Anglo-Saxon Charter Boundaries.' In Margaret Gelling, *The Early Charters of the Thames Valley*, 168–87. Bristol: Leicester University Press, 1979.

Reichardt, Paul F. '*Guthlac A* and the Landscape of Spiritual Perfection.' *Neophilologus* 58 (1974): 331–8.

Reuter, Timothy, ed. *Alfred the Great: Papers from the Eleventh-Century Centenary Conferences.* Studies in Early Medieval Britain 3. Aldershot, UK, and Burlington, VT: Ashgate, 2003.

Reynolds, Andrew. *Anglo-Saxon Deviant Burial Customs.* Medieval History and Archaeology. New York and Oxford: Oxford University Press, 2009.
- *Later Anglo-Saxon England: Life & Landscape.* Stroud: Tempus, 1999.

Reynolds, Susan. 'Bookland, Folkland and Fiefs.' *ANS* 14 (1992): 211–27.
- *Fiefs and Vassals: The Medieval Evidence Reinterpreted.* Oxford: Oxford University Press, 1994.

Rio, Alice. *Legal Practice and the Written Word in the Early Middle Ages: Frankish Formulae, c. 500–1000.* Cambridge: Cambridge University Press, 2009.

Roberts, Jane. '*Guthlac A*: Sources and Source Hunting.' In *Medieval English Studies Presented to George Kane*, edited by Edward Donald Kennedy, Ronald Waldron, and Joseph S. Wittig, 1–18. Wolfeboro, NH: D.S. Brewer, 1988.
- 'An Inventory of Early Guthlac Materials.' *MS* 32 (1970): 193–233.

Robinson, J. Armitage. *The Times of Saint Dunstan.* Oxford: Clarendon Press, 1923.

Roffe, David. 'From Thegnage to Barony: Sake and Soke, Title, and Tenants-in-Chief.' *ANS* 12 (1990): 157–76.

Rumble, Alexander R. 'Old English *Boc-land* as an Anglo-Saxon Estate-Name.' *Leeds Studies in English* 18 (1987): 219–29.

Sawyer, Peter. '1066–1086: A Tenurial Revolution?' In *Domesday Book: A Reassessment*, edited by Peter Sawyer, 71–85. London: Edward Arnold, 1985.

Scharer, Anton. *Die angelsächsische Königsurkunde im 7. und 8. Jahrhundert.* Vienna: H. Böhlaus, 1982.

Schwyter, J.R. *Old English Legal Language: The Lexical Field of Theft.* North-Western European Language Evolution. Supplement, vol. 15. Gylling: Odense University Press, 1996.

Scragg, Donald, ed. *Edgar, King of the English 959–975: New Interpretations.* Publications of the Manchester Centre for Anglo-Saxon Studies 8. Woodbridge, UK, and Rochester, NY: Boydell Press, 2008.

– 'A Reading of *Brunanburh*.' In *Unlocking the Wordhord: Anglo-Saxon Studies in Memory of Edward B. Irving, Jr.*, edited by Mark C. Amodio and Katherine O'Brien O'Keeffe, 109–22. Toronto: University of Toronto Press, 2003.

Seebohm, Frederic. *The English Village Community.* 4th ed. London, 1896.

Semple, Sarah. 'A Fear of the Past: The Place of the Prehistoric Burial Mound in the Ideology of Middle and Later Anglo-Saxon England.' *World Archaeology* 30 (1998): 109–26.

Sheehan, Michael M. *The Will in Medieval England: From the Conversion of the Anglo-Saxons to the End of the Thirteenth Century.* Studies and Texts 6. Toronto: Pontifical Institute of Mediaeval Studies, 1963.

Sheppard, Alice. *Families of the King: Writing Identity in the* Anglo-Saxon Chronicle. Toronto: University of Toronto Press, 2004.

Shook, Laurence K. 'The Burial Mound in *Guthlac A*.' *MP* 58 (1960): 1–10.

Siewers, Alfred K. 'Landscapes of Conversion: Guthlac's Mound and Grendel's Mere as Expressions of Anglo-Saxon Nation-Building.' *Viator* 34 (2003): 1–39.

Sisam, Kenneth. 'The Exeter Book.' In his *Studies in the History of Old English Literature*, 97–108. Oxford: Clarendon Press, 1953.

Smith, A.H. *English Place-Name Elements.* English Place-Name Society, nos. 25 and 26. 2 vols. Cambridge: Cambridge University Press, 1956.

Smith, Scott Thompson. 'Of Kings and Cattle Thieves: The Rhetorical Work of the Fonthill Letter.' *JEGP* 106 (2007): 447–67.

Smyth, Alfred P. *Scandinavian York and Dublin: The History and Archaeology of Two Related Viking Kingdoms.* 2 vols. Dublin: Templekieran Press, 1975-9. Reprint, Dublin: Irish Academic Press, 1987.

Stafford, Pauline. '"The Annals of Æthelflæd": Annals, History and Politics in Early Tenth-Century England.' In Barrow and Wareham, *Myth, Rulership, Church and Charters*, 101–16.

– *The East Midlands in the Early Middle Ages.* Leicester: Leicester University Press, 1985.

- 'Political Ideas in Late Tenth-Century England: Charters as Evidence.' In *Law, Laity, and Solidarities: Essays in Honour of Susan Reynolds*, edited by Pauline Stafford, Janet L. Nelson, and Jane Martindale, 68–82. Manchester: Manchester University Press, 2001.
- 'Political Women in Mercia, Eighth to Early Tenth Centuries.' In Brown and Farr, *Mercia: An Anglo-Saxon Kingdom in Europe*, 35–49.
- 'Succession and Inheritance: A Gendered Perspective on Alfred's Family History.' In Reuter, *Alfred the Great*, 251–64.
- *Unification and Conquest: A Political and Social History of England in the Tenth and Eleventh Centuries*. London: Edward Arnold, 1989.
Steen, Janie. *Verse and Virtuosity: The Adaptation of Latin Rhetoric in Old English Poetry*. Toronto: University of Toronto Press, 2008.
Steiner, Emily. *Documentary Culture and the Making of Medieval English Literature*. Cambridge: Cambridge University Press, 2003.
Stenton, F.M. *Anglo-Saxon England*. 3rd ed. Oxford: Oxford University Press, 1971.
- *The Latin Charters of the Anglo-Saxon Period*. Oxford: Clarendon Press, 1955.
- *Types of Manorial Structure in the Northern Danelaw*. Oxford Studies in Social and Legal History 2. Oxford: Clarendon Press, 1910.
Stevenson, W.H. 'The Anglo-Saxon Chancery.' http://www.kemble.asnc.cam.ac.uk/sites/default/files/files/Stevenson%202011.pdf. Accessed May 2012.
Stodnick, Jacqueline. 'Sentence to Story: Reading the Anglo-Saxon Chronicle as Formulary.' In Jorgensen, *Reading the Anglo-Saxon Chronicle*, 91–111.
- 'What (and Where) is the *Anglo-Saxon Chronicle* About?: Spatial History.' *Bulletin of the John Rylands University Library of Manchester* 86 (2004): 87–104.
Strohm, Paul. *Hochon's Arrow: The Social Imagination of Fourteenth-Century Texts*. Princeton, NJ: Princeton University Press, 1992.
Szarmach, Paul E. 'Æðelflæd of Mercia: *Mise en page*.' In *Words and Works: Studies in Medieval English Language and Literature in Honour of Fred C. Robinson*, edited by Peter S. Baker and Nicholas Howe, 105–26. Toronto: University of Toronto Press, 1998.
- 'A Return to Cotton Tiberius A. III, art 24, and Isidore's *Synonyma*.' In *Text and Gloss: Studies in Insular Learning and Literature Presented to Joseph Donovan Pheifer*, edited by Helen Conrad O'Briain, Anne Marie D'Arcy, and John Scattergood, 166–81. Dublin: Four Courts Press, 1999.
- ed. *Studies in Earlier Old English Prose*. Albany: State University of New York Press, 1986.
- 'The Vercelli Homilies: Style & Structure.' In *The Old English Homily & Its Backgrounds*, edited by Paul E. Szarmach and Bernard F. Huppé, 241–67. Albany: State University of New York Press, 1978.

- 'The Vercelli Prose and Anglo-Saxon Literary History.' In *New Readings in the Vercelli Book*, edited by Samantha Zacher and Andy Orchard, 12–40. Toronto: University of Toronto Press, 2009.

Thompson, Susan D. *Anglo-Saxon Royal Diplomas: A Palaeography*. Publications of the Manchester Centre for Anglo-Saxon Studies 6. Woodbridge, UK, and Rochester, NY: Boydell Press, 2006.

Thormann, Janet. 'The *Anglo-Saxon Chronicle* Poems and the Making of the English Nation.' In *Anglo-Saxonism and the Construction of Social Identity*, edited by Allen J. Frantzen and John D. Niles, 60–85. Gainesville: University Press of Florida, 1997.

Tinti, Francesca. *Sustaining Belief: The Church of Worcester from c.870 to c.1100*. Studies in Early Medieval Britain 5. Farnham, UK, and Burlington, VT: Ashgate, 2010.

Toller, T. Northcote. *An Anglo-Saxon Dictionary, Supplement*. Oxford: Clarendon Press, 1921.

Tollerton, Linda. *Wills and Will-Making in Anglo-Saxon England*. University of York: York Medieval Press, 2011.

Townend, Matthew. 'Pre-Cnut Praise-Poetry in Viking Age England.' *RES* 51 (2000): 349–70.

- ed. *Wulfstan, Archbishop of York: The Proceedings of the Second Alcuin Conference*. Studies in the Early Middle Ages 10. Turnhout: Brepols, 2004.

Trilling, Renée R. *The Aesthetics of Nostalgia: Historical Representation in Old English Verse*. Toronto: University of Toronto Press, 2009.

Verhulst, Adriaan. *The Carolingian Economy*. Cambridge: Cambridge University Press, 2002.

Vinogradoff, Paul. 'Folkland.' *EHR* 8 (1893): 1–17.

- *The Growth of the Manor*. 2nd rev. ed. London: George Allen & Unwin Ltd., 1911.

Wainwright, F.T. 'Æthelflæd, Lady of the Mercians.' In *The Anglo-Saxons: Studies in Some Aspects of their History and Culture Presented to Bruce Dickins*, edited by Peter Clemoes, 53–69. London: Bowes and Bowes, 1959.

- 'The Chronology of the "Mercian Register."' *EHR* 60 (1945): 385–92.

Wallace-Hadrill, J.M. 'The Franks and the English in the Ninth Century: Some Common Historical Interests.' *History* 35 (1950): 202–18. Reprinted in his *Early Medieval History*, 201–16. Oxford: Blackwell, 1975.

Wareham, Andrew. 'The Transformation of Kinship and the Family in Late Anglo-Saxon England.' *Early Medieval Europe* 10 (2001): 375–99.

Waterhouse, Ruth. 'Tone in Alfred's Version of Augustine's *Soliloquies*.' In Szarmach, *Studies in Earlier Old English Prose*, 47–85.

Webber, Teresa. *Scribes and Scholars at Salisbury Cathedral, c. 1075–c. 1125.* Oxford: Clarendon Press, 1992.

Wentersdorf, Karl P. '*Guthlac A*: The Battle for the *Beorg.*' *Neophilologus* 62 (1978): 135–42.

Whitbread, Leslie. 'The Pattern of Misfortune in *Deor* and Other Old English Poems.' *Neophilologus* 54 (1970): 167–83.

White, Hayden. 'The Value of Narrativity in the Representation of Reality.' *Critical Inquiry* 7 (1980): 5–27.

White, Stephen D. '"*Pactum ... Legem Vincit et Amor Judicium*": The Settlement of Disputes by Compromise in Eleventh-Century Western France.' *American Journal of Legal History* 22 (1978): 281–308.

Whitelock, Dorothy. *The Beginnings of English Society.* Pelican History of England 2. Harmondsworth: Penguin Books, 1952.

– 'Wulfstan *Cantor* and Anglo-Saxon Law.' In *Nordica et Anglica: Studies in Honor of Stefán Einarsson,* edited by Allan H. Orrick, 83–92. The Hague: Mouton, 1968.

Wilcox, Jonathan. 'Variant Texts of an Old English Homily: Vercelli X and Stylistic Readers.' In *The Preservation and Transmission of Anglo-Saxon Culture: Selected Papers from the 1991 Meeting of the International Society of Anglo-Saxonists,* edited by Paul E. Szarmach and Joel T. Rosenthal, 335–51. Studies in Medieval Culture 40. Kalamazoo: Medieval Institute Publications, 1997.

Williams, Ann. 'A Bell-house and a Burh-geat: Lordly Residences in England before the Norman Conquest.' In *Medieval Knighthood IV: Papers from the Fifth Strawberry Hill Conference 1990,* edited by Christopher Harper-Bill and Ruth Harvey, 221–40. Woodbridge, UK, and Rochester, NY: Boydell Press, 1992.

– 'How Land was Held Before and After the Norman Conquest.' In Erskine and Williams, *Story of Domesday Book,* 50–3.

– 'Land Tenure.' In Lapidge et al., *The Blackwell Encyclopaedia of Anglo-Saxon England,* 277–8.

– '*Princeps Merciorum gentis*: The Family, Career and Connections of Ælfhere, Ealdorman of Mercia, 956–83.' *ASE* 10 (1982): 143–72.

Williams, Howard. 'Monuments and the Past in Early Anglo-Saxon England.' *World Archaeology* 30 (1998): 90–108.

Wilson, R.M. *The Lost Literature of Medieval England.* 2nd ed. London: Methuen, 1970.

Winterbottom, Michael. 'Aldhelm's Prose Style and its Origins.' *ASE* 6 (1977): 39–76.

Wood, Ian, and Niels Lund, eds. *People and Places in Northern Europe 500–1600: Essays in Honour of Peter Hayes Sawyer.* Woodbridge, UK, and Rochester, NY: Boydell Press, 1991.

Wood, Susan. *The Proprietary Church in the Medieval West*. Oxford: Oxford University Press, 2006.

Wormald, Patrick. 'Bede and the Conversion of England: The Charter Evidence.' Jarrow Lecture, 1984. Reprinted in his *Times of Bede*, 135–66.

– 'Charters, Law and the Settlement of Disputes in Anglo-Saxon England.' In Davies and Fouracre, *The Settlement of Disputes*, 149–68. Reprinted in his *Legal Culture in the Early Medieval West*, 289–311.

– 'A Handlist of Anglo-Saxon Lawsuits.' *ASE* 17 (1988): 247–81. Reprinted in his *Legal Culture in the Early Medieval West*, 253–87.

– *Legal Culture in the Early Medieval West: Law as Text, Image and Experience*. London and Rio Grande: Hambledon Press, 1999.

– '*Lex Scripta* and *Verbum Regis*: Legislation and Germanic Kingship, from Euric to Cnut.' In *Early Medieval Kingship*, edited by P.H. Sawyer and I.N. Wood, 105–38. Leeds: Leeds University Press, 1977. Reprinted in his *Legal Culture in the Early Medieval West*, 1–43.

– *The Making of English Law: King Alfred to the Twelfth Century, Vol. 1: Legislation and Its Limits*. Oxford: Blackwell, 1999.

– '*On þá wæpnedhealfe*: Kingship and Royal Property from Æthelwulf to Edward the Elder.' In Higham and Hill, *Edward the Elder*, 264–79.

– '*Quadripartitus*.' In *Law and Government in Medieval England and Normandy: Essays in Honour of Sir James Holt*, edited by George Garnett and John Hudson, 111–47. Cambridge: Cambridge University Press, 1994. Reprinted in his *Legal Culture in the Early Medieval West*, 81–114.

– *The Times of Bede: Studies in Early English Christian Society and its Historian*. Edited by Stephen Baxter. Malden, MA, and Oxford, UK: Blackwell, 2006.

Yorke, Barbara. 'Æthelwold and the Politics of the Tenth Century.' In *Bishop Æthelwold: His Career and Influence*, edited by Barbara Yorke, 65–88. Woodbridge, UK: Boydell Press, 1988.

Zacher, Samantha. 'Multilingualism at the Court of King Æthelstan: Latin Praise Poetry and *The Battle of Brunanburh*.' In *Conceptualizing Multilingualism in England, c.800–c.1250*, edited by Elizabeth M. Tyler, 77-103. Studies in the Early Middle Ages 27. Turnhout: Brepols, 2011.

– *Preaching the Converted: The Style and Rhetoric of the Vercelli Book Homilies*. Toronto: Toronto University Press, 2009.

Index of Charters Cited

General Index

Abels, Richard, 13–14
ablative absolutes, 44
aduentus Saxonum, 183n122, 184
Ælfgifu, 96, 96n83, 98n89
Ælfheah (ealdorman), 81, 88, 89, 90, 101–2
Ælfhere (ealdorman), 102
Ælfric (archbishop of Canterbury), 77, 97n87
Ælfric of Eynsham, 86–7n59, 110
Ælfstan (bishop), 57, 57n125
Ælfweard (son of Edward the Elder), 172, 172n86, 173
Ælfwynn (daughter of Æthelred and Æthelflæd), 171–2, 171n79, 172n80
Ælle (Ælfwine) (bishop), 38n58
Æthelberht (king) (son of King Æthelwulf of Wessex), 32–3
Æthelflæd (Lady of the Mercians), 157, 161, 165, 167–72, 167–8n65, 171n77
Æthelred (ealdorman of Mercia), 161, 171, 171n77
Æthelred (king of the Mercians) (r. 674/5–704), 32, 33
Æthelred II (king) (r. 978–1016): charters of, 50–62, 50n104, 62n134, 74; and despoliation of St Andrews,

57nn125, 127; notions of kingship in charters of, 23–4; restoration of lands by, 139n126; and Snodland dispute (S 1456), 76–8
– law-codes: I Æthelred 4.2, 208n51; V Æthelred 28, 13n39
Æthelstan (ealdorman), 80, 80n40, 82–6, 87, 101
Æthelstan (king): and Anglo-Saxon Chronicle, 157, 173, 174, 175, 180–5; in *The Battle of Brunanburh*, 181–5; and bookland, 176; charters issued by, 30n30, 37–46, 166n60; confirmation of kingship, 172; and developments in Latin diplomas, 25n11, 176, 178n105; donation list (Exeter), 127, 127–8n85, 128; gift of gospel book by, 154–5, 175; Latin works during reign, 175; and royal titles in diplomas, 25n11, 30n30, 39, 43, 178–9; and style of diplomas, 177–80; succession of, 180–1n114. *See also* 'Æthelstan A'
– law-codes: Æthelstan 1.5 and 10.1, 208n51; IV Æthelstan 1.4 and 8.2, 208n51
'Æthelstan A': about, 37–8; charters attributed to, 38, 38n59; identity of,

Toronto Anglo-Saxon Series

General Editor
ANDY ORCHARD

Editorial Board
ROBERTA FRANK
THOMAS N. HALL
ANTONETTE DIPAOLO HEALEY
MICHAEL LAPIDGE
KATHERINE O'BRIEN O'KEEFFE